Be Brave, Be Strong

A Journey Across the Great Divide

By Jill Homer

Edited by Diana Miller

Arctic Glass Press is a collaboration of independent authors dedicated to exploration, enjoyment and adventure in the outdoors.

www.arcticglasspress.com

2240 Homestead Court, No. 307,
Los Altos, California, 94024

© 2011 by Jill Homer
All rights reserved
First edition, 2011
No part of this book may be reproduced in any form, or by any electronic, mechanical, or other means, without permission in writing from the publisher.
Distributed in the United States by Arctic Glass Press,
www.arcticglasspress.com
Manufactured in the United States

Editor: Diana Miller
Cover Design: Jill Homer
Interior Design: Jill Homer
Photographers: Jill Homer, John Nobile, and Jed Homer

Cover, top: Jill Homer collects herself after crashing her mountain bike in the Marin Headlands, California. Self portrait by Jill Homer.
Cover, bottom: The "last tree in a hundred miles" stands in Great Divide Basin near Atlantic City, Wyoming. Photo by Jill Homer.
Adjacent page: Jill Homer pushes her bike through avalanche debris on Red Meadow Pass in Montana. Photo by John Nobile.
Contents page: Jill Homer and John Nobile line up at the start of the Tour Divide in Banff, Alberta. Photo by Keith Brodsky.

ISBN 978-1-257-65858-9

This is a work of narrative nonfiction. Dialogue and events herein have been recounted to the best of the author's memory.

For Beat, my next adventure

Contents

Chapter One
Disaster on the Iditarod   9

Chapter Two
Picking Up the Pieces   25

Chapter Three
Nearing an End   34

Chapter Four
Being Led to the Flood   47

Chapter Five
Marin   58

Chapter Six
The Kokopelli Trail   71

Chapter Seven
Indecision   89

Chapter Eight
Banff   99

Chapter Nine
Into the Great Divide   108

Chapter Ten
The First Border   122

Chapter Eleven
Raising Montana   142

Chapter Twelve
Savage Side   157

Chapter Thirteen
Beyond Idaho   175

Chapter Fourteen
Heart of Wyoming   187

Chapter Fifteen
The Great Divide Basin   199

Chapter Sixteen
Kindness   213

Chapter Seventeen
Turning Right   227

Chapter Eighteen
Untouchable   241

Chapter Nineteen
Stunner Pass   254

Chapter Twenty
After the Storm   268

Chapter Twenty One
The High Desert   281

Chapter Twenty Two
Independence Day   297

Chapter Twenty Three
The Gila   309

Chapter Twenty Four
Lonely Highway   322

Riding the Spine of the Rocky Mountains

Each year on the second Friday in June, several dozen mountain bikers from around the world set out to challenge speed records on the world's longest off-pavement cycling route, the Great Divide Mountain Bike Route. Scouted and mapped by Adventure Cycling Association in 1998, the unmarked route features gravel roads, dirt tracks and jeep trails that follow the contours of the Continental Divide.

The Great Divide Mountain Bike Route begins in Banff, Alberta, and travels 2,740 miles through the Canadian provinces of Alberta and British Columbia, and the states of Montana, Idaho, Wyoming, Colorado, and New Mexico. By the time cyclists reach the Mexican border, they will have climbed nearly 200,000 feet over some of the highest and most remote passes in the Rocky Mountains.

Endurance legend John Stamstad became the first to set a speed record on the Great Divide, blitzing the route in eighteen days and five hours in 1998. In 2004, a handful of mountain bikers collaborated to challenge that time, organizing a self-supported race on the route beginning at the Montana border. Mike Curiak established a new record at sixteen days. Since then, Great Divide racing has steadily grown and evolved. However, it maintains the same minimalist format: No entry fee, no course markings and no support. For many distance mountain bikers, completing the Great Divide Mountain Bike Route as fast as possible has become the ultimate challenge.

The following is the story of one woman's journey to do just that.

Map courtesy of http://eatsleepridegreatdivide.com.

Chapter One
Disaster on the Iditarod

Page 9: Sean Grady rides his bicycle across the Susitna Valley during the 2009 Iditarod Trail Invitational.

Page 10: A cyclist rounds a sign pointing the direction to Nome on the Iditarod Trail.

Somewhere on a blank slate of tundra, where the shadows of nameless mountains devour the snow, I tried to bury the pieces of myself that I longed to leave behind — the pieces that were careless, the shards that were weak, and the remnants that were terrified of the unknown. Beneath crushing cold and fatigue, they cracked like glass in my cupped mittens. Low-angle sunlight reflected moments from an impossibly distant past — my existence beyond this frozen swamp, before this odyssey that left me both shattered and enigmatically whole. As a ground blizzard raged around my ankles, the wind scattered the pieces like so much glitter. I watched glimmering reflections of myself swirl through the snow until they were invisible, and then gone. I felt like I had crossed an irrevocable divide — one I would likely never approach again.

One year passed. The winter sun glared hard and heatless when I lined up for the Iditarod Trail Invitational a second time. Forty-five runners, skiers and cyclists crowded the starting line for an adventure race across the frozen wilderness. My boyfriend Geoff, a runner, stood next to me, though my bicycle created a barrier between us. A small crowd of spectators gathered around the race start, which was little more than a single banner stretched over the edge of a frozen lake. Anxiety crackled in the cold air. We looked like specks on the tongue of Alaska's backcountry, staring down its cavernous throat. With only minutes remaining before the start, I contemplated the overwhelming task of pushing deep into its frigid heart.

I felt like a skydiver in an uncontrolled free fall, watching the wilderness close in around me. I took short, quick breaths. One for each of the 350 miles in front of me. Seconds languished on clouds of breath. Geoff coughed and cleared his throat. A gurgling sound rose from his lungs, broadcasting a deepening infection.

"This is going to suck," he said.

"Are you feeling any better?" I asked, not taking my eyes off the powder-swept lake.

"No," he said. "I feel even worse than yesterday." He coughed again. I struggled to feel sympathy for him. It was a terrible thing, the fact Geoff was sick, but overarching instinct told me that traversing 350 miles of Alaska wilderness during the winter was a bigger battle than either of us should have had the capacity to fight, healthy or not. And yet, I had finished the race before. It took every ounce of energy from my emaciated body, but I had finished it one year earlier. For reasons I couldn't quite explain, even to myself, I needed to believe I could do it again. And because we were partners in life, I needed to believe Geoff could do the same.

An informal "go" rang out and we launched over the starting line. I rolled my bicycle onto the lake and bogged down almost immediately. Geoff jogged past as I wrestled the bike through the loose snow.

"I'll see you at Yentna," I said. "Good luck." Geoff nodded and continued ahead.

I watched him fade into the crowd of skiers and runners as I struggled with the other anchor-weighted cyclists. "I forgot to hug him goodbye," I thought, with selfish disappointment that he hadn't bothered to hug me either. Justifiable pre-race anxiety had strained our final interaction before the start. But there was something more, too — something more ominous, a thinly veiled sadness, as though we both suspected certain doom.

I crossed a frozen lake and labored up the first hill, finally mounting my bike as the snowmobile trail became more packed at the top. I wove around runners and skiers. I passed Geoff, running steady with his sled attached to a harness, about a mile down the trail. "With this cruddy trail, you're going to pass me again," I said.

"Maybe," he replied. I slowed my pedaling and thought about saying goodbye, just in case I didn't see him again, but no words came to my lips.

The last non-cyclist I passed was Pete Basinger, a multi-year veteran and record-holder for the 350-mile race to McGrath. The human-powered race on the Iditarod Trail had reshaped itself frequently over the years, but Pete remained a constant, lining up for the adventurous if obscure event with his bicycle. He always finished, and usually won. In 2009, he decided to try something different. I approached him as he chopped up a small incline on a pair of skis, his first venture into the medium.

Pete was the athlete I credited with sparking my otherwise inexplicable desire to enter a race that involves riding a bicycle over 350 miles of snow during winter in Alaska. Pete's endeavors had a way of inspiring passion, simply because he consistently refused to give up even as situations became so difficult and ridiculous that they defied all logic and sensibility. Then he would return to race the Iditarod again, even though the race did nothing to garner success or even notoriety. A tiny circle of endurance athletes revered him, but to everyone else, he was nobody. As Pete toiled year after year through unrewarded suffering and solitude, his silence spoke volumes about a deeper meaning behind the race. I listened to his terse reports. I looked at his stark, mostly colorless photographs. Through both, I sensed a power and beauty that I could scarcely comprehend. I wanted so badly to understand.

In 2008, I signed up for the race. Then I finished it. My six days on the Iditarod Trail had been the most eye-opening and intense experience of my entire life. Amid my body's slow-motion collapse at the finishing point, I convinced myself I had reached my goal — a deeper understanding of beauty and strength that I could reference for the rest of my life. And yet there I was, just one year later, riding a bicycle into the Alaska wilderness again.

"Thanks for working on my bike, Pete," I said as I passed. "It's running awesome."

"Thanks," he said. "Can I borrow it?"

I laughed. "Skiing is rough, huh?"

"It's OK," he said. "I just can't get a good glide."

"It has to beat pushing a bike," I said. "I doubt this trail will hold up for much longer."

"Good luck," Pete called out as I pedaled farther ahead. I smiled and hoped I'd see him again. In the low sunlight of mid-afternoon, spruce trees cast long shadows over the clean, new snow. Alder branches glistened with hoarfrost, forming a white wall along the straight and narrow trail. The undulating surface of the snow created a sensation of rolling waves. Pedaling a bicycle felt like paddling a canoe on a stormy lake. I caught up to a group of five cyclists riding in a line. The last cyclist in the peloton was a woman, Catherine Shenk, a rookie from Colorado. I pedaled behind her and made small talk, asking where she was from, what other races she had entered and what kind of time she hoped to make. She was, after all, my competition.

"I don't know," she said. "I've always wanted to ride in Alaska, ever since I heard about this race. I just want to finish the thing."

"That's certainly the goal," I said.

We entered an open swamp where a blast of unobstructed and shockingly cold wind spurred us to silence. Against an ice-blue sky, we caught our first glimpse of the Alaska Range, with the hulking white mass of Denali piercing the horizon.

"This place is incredible, just … " Catherine said as the wind stole her words.

"Isn't it?" I answered.

As we rode across the swamp, the trail became more drifted with snow until it was no longer distinguishable from the untrammeled surface. Our bicycle wheels no longer rolled through the deep powder, and we had to probe the snow with our feet, searching for the packed trail. Our group, which for an hour had worked so well together, proved to be mismatched while pushing our bikes. The cyclists at the front of our pack languished and often stopped to rest in the middle of the trail. I walked around them, looking back one last time just as the evening sun cast orange light on their faces. "See you soon," I said to Catherine.

The trail veered back into the woods. I was able to get back on my bike for a slow-motion ride through the soft snow. Ski tracks were etched like brush strokes into the powder, and after a mile I caught up to their graceful calligrapher, skier Cory Smith.

Cory, from what little I knew about him, was a former world-class Nordic skier who had since retired to raise a family. He had no aspirations to greatness in a race like the Iditarod Trail Invitational, only adventure, but he seemed to be holding a solid lead over everyone but the fast cyclists. I pedaled harder to catch Cory, but he remained a few strides ahead of me. Eventually we reached a long slough, where the trail became wind-drifted again. I hopped off my bike and commenced pushing, watching with envy as Cory glided over the choppy snow. The gap between us grew quickly, and his graceful figure faded around a bend.

Nearly a half hour later, I rounded the bend and emerged on the open expanse of Flathorn Lake. It was there I crossed that vague line between day and night, drawn by the orange glow on the southwestern horizon as a purple shadow advanced from the east. I turned my head away from its ominous cloak of darkness, focusing instead on the iridescent pink edges of Mount Susitna. The wind felt stronger and colder on the lake, without even the meager protection of spruce trees to hold it back. I squinted into the wind-driven snow until the sunlight faded to nothing more than narrow strokes of crimson paint on black canvas. The inevitable prospect of night made me nervous. I had traveled only twenty-five miles with an unknown number to go before I slept. Pulling on my mittens, I rifled through my pocket until I found my thermometer. The temperature was several degrees below zero already, and dropping fast.

I trudged through wind-driven powder and fed myself M&Ms that I had stowed inside my handlebar covers. In the fading light, I couldn't distinguish the official trail from a maze of snowmobile tracks slashed across the surface of the lake. I flipped on my headlight, but its white glare only made things worse. Granules of snow pummeled my face like a frigid sand blast.

"Please stay," I said to the slivers of red light, the last hint of color in an increasingly bleak landscape. It answered only with the roar of wind, and squeaks from my footsteps on the deep-frozen snow.

How I came to take my last innocent step, I can't be sure. I've relived the scene in my mind a thousand times, with no clear conclusion about what exactly took place. I remember seeing the footprints of other racers, swept with drifted snow. Their bikes' tire tracks were almost obliterated even though our separation could still be measured in minutes. I remember following those fading footprints, the only way I could discern the trail from a seemingly bottomless basin of powdered sugar.

Then the bottom fell out, literally. I lifted my boot from the snow and set it down on nothing. My leg swiftly dropped into a gut-sinking void, pulling my body and bike down a shallow trench. My right foot had punched through a thin layer of ice and plunged into the lake. I wrenched my body sideways but my mitten-covered fingers still clung to the overturned bike, as though it had the ability to save me somehow. My right leg sank all the way to my upper thigh as frigid water gushed into my boot, which dangled freely over what I later determined had to be the icy depths of the lake bottom. My left leg, which twisted painfully but managed to stay planted on solid ice, sprung up as I let go of the bike and plunged my hands into the snow. I clawed up the shallow embankment, pulling my right leg out of the pressure crack through which I had broken.

My bike still lay atop a sliver of thin ice. The handlebars had punched through the surface, and slushy water surrounded the entire front end. I dropped to my stomach and slowly inched down the trench until I could wrap my fingers around the ice-coated rear wheel. With what felt like a fully exhaustive burst of strength, I wrestled the bike out of the water. The right handlebar cover was completely soaked. A white layer of ice coated my sleeping bag cover and frame bag. I reached into the handlebar cover to rescue my bag of M&Ms, but they were already gone — sinking, most likely, to the bottom of Flathorn Lake.

Hot adrenaline seared my veins as I knelt down to assess my own damage. A veneer of flaky ice formed around my pant legs, and larger chunks clung to my boot and gaiters. I shook my foot and heard water sloshing inside the boot. I tugged at the Velcro on the gaiters, but they had already frozen shut. Subzero air needled into my wet clothes, driving a powerful cold, along with its accompanying fear and hopelessness, directly to my core. This was the kind of mistake that ends races. This was the kind of mistake that ends lives. But it couldn't happen here, I told myself — not on Flathorn Lake. Not so close to civilization and the beginning of my Iditarod adventure.

I stood up and looked toward the tree-sheltered shoreline, which was still about a mile across the lake. If I could just make it to there, just to extract myself out of the deadly wind, then I could deal with my wet foot. I could build a fire, put on my down booties and crawl into my sleeping bag. I didn't know what my most rational option was. All I felt capable of understanding was a primal sort of fear, driven by the wind to an intolerable intensity, and I had to escape it.

I continued marching down the lake with my headlamp beam fixed on the fading footprints. Water sloshed around inside my boot, but the liquid didn't feel cold. In fact, the water felt like it had already warmed up to the same temperature as my foot. I wiggled my toes. "Maybe my insulated boot is allowing my body to heat the water," I thought. "Maybe the temperature has reached equilibrium. Maybe it's not so bad."

About forty-five minutes passed before I reached a cluster of spruce trees at the end of the lake. By then, a solid barrier of ice had wrapped around my entire lower leg. I stopped in a sheltered spot, took off my frozen-stiff mittens, and clawed at the ice on my gaiters. It was at least a centimeter thick, as solid as an ice cube, and it refused to budge. If I couldn't take my gaiters off, then I couldn't take my boots off, and if I couldn't take my boots off, then I had no hope of extracting the water that was still sloshing around my foot. And even if I did, what then? I still had wet socks and a wet lining inside the boot, so even spare socks wouldn't stay dry for long. I could crawl into my sleeping bag, but that would only put the situation on hold until I some kind of help came along. I could build a fire, but didn't like the idea of stopping forward motion for an extended period of time. The temperature was plummeting with the deepening night, taking with it my capacity for patience. The wind was so cold, and the water in my boot felt so warm.

"If I just leave the water in there, maybe it will keep my foot warm, like a chemical warmer," I told myself. "I can monitor this. I'll just wiggle my toes, and as soon as I can't wiggle them anymore, I'll stop and build a fire."

I put my mittens back on and continued to beat at my ice-coated leg just as another cyclist, Sean Salach, walked up. His beard was crusted in ice and his nose was a dark shade of red.

"Um, are you okay?" he asked.

"I'm great," I said. "I'm just stopping for a little break."

His eyes betrayed skepticism. "Really?"

I sighed. Sean wasn't in any position to help me, but it seemed pointless to lie to him.

"I went through the ice," I said. "Back there on Flathorn. I soaked my whole leg."

"Oh, that was you," he said. "I saw the hole. What are you going to do?"

I told him my toe-wiggling plan. "I want to make it to Yentna Station," I said. "Then I'll assess."

I grabbed my bike and started walking with him toward a wind-swept clearing known as the Dismal Swamp. "I lost my gear bag," he admitted to me. "It bounced off my bike or something. All of my spare clothing and a sleeping pad."

"What are you going to do?" I asked.

"I'm hoping someone grabs it," he said.

We trudged through the knee-deep powder and let the shame of our rookie mistakes swirl around the void of conversation. Through the howling wind, I heard what sounded like the hum of a mosquito. As it grew louder, a yellow headlight approached. A snowmobiler pulled up beside us and shut off his engine.

"You two okay?" he yelled.

The little voice of reason in my head screamed "No! No! Tell him no! Take a ride!"

"We're great," I said. I looked over at Sean. His face was expressionless.

"And you know where you're going?" the snowmobiler asked.

"Yes," I said. "We're headed to Yentna Station tonight."

"Still a ways from here," the snowmobiler said. "Do you know where to connect up with the Yentna River?"

"Yes," I said. Sean nodded.

"OK then," the snowmobiler said. "You two take care."

I turned to watch his red taillights disappear into the shadows and wondered if I had just made a mistake. Without exchanging another word, Sean and I kept walking. We crossed into another cluster of trees where the trail was firmer. I sat on my bike and started pedaling. Sean, who had skinnier tires than I did and not as much flotation, was still walking. I stopped and turned to him. "Sorry," I said. "I really have to hurry as fast as I can." And with that, I pedaled away, into the shadow-drenched night, alone.

I descended onto the Susitna River in a state of peace, my body released from anxiety by single-minded purpose. The pedals turned in smooth circles; the tires crunched over the uneven snow. I could ride over the loose surface, but the trail was still soft enough that movement was difficult and slow. Sweat trickled from beneath my hat and froze midstream on my cheeks. I felt hot, not cold. I wiggled my toes and marveled at the furnace of warmth my body was capable of maintaining amid subzero wind. Water sloshed around in my boot. The air temperature pushed into negative double digits, which felt significantly colder in the driving wind, and still it could not touch me.

Every ten minutes or so, I would jump off my bike and run down the trail for a minute or two to crank up the body furnace even more. As I ran, I noticed a headlamp bobbing several hundred yards ahead of me. I assumed because I was getting off the bike and running in intervals, I would not catch up any other racers, but soon I realized the person's light was not moving. I caught up to the dark-eyed grimace of Billy Kotzich, another Iditarod cyclist who was aiming to ride 1,100 miles to Nome.

"Do you have a bike pump I could borrow?" he said in a hoarse voice. "Mine won't work. I kept letting air out of my tires and I think I let too much out. I don't want to ride with the tires this low."

I breathed out, irritated. I did not want to stop, but I had to help him. How could anyone start out a 1,100-mile race and not be absolutely sure something as simple as an air pump worked? The rookie mistakes were stacking up, although I wasn't about to admit my mistake to Billy. He pumped at an achingly slow pace. I shivered as the roaring wind sucked heat out of my body like a vacuum. I checked my thermometer. The temperature had dropped to nearly twenty below zero. For the first time that night, I could not feel my right foot. I started jumping up and down.

"You cold?" Billy asked.

"Yeah," I said. "I really should get moving."

"Okay," he said. "I think I have enough air to get to Yentna. Hopefully I can fix my pump there."

He got on his bike and we rode together for a hundred yards, but I quickly started to outpace him.

"Can't keep this pace up," Billy yelled out to me. "I have to keep steady if I'm going all the way to Nome."

"I gotta make some heat," I called back. Still annoyed, with a right foot that had lost all sensation during the break, I couldn't envision Billy or Sean, both lacking crucial equipment, making it much beyond Yentna. I, on the other hand, felt amazing — fast and fresh and strong despite the cold. If only I could warm up my foot. As soon as I was well out of range of Billy's headlamp, I hopped off the bike and started running again. The cold wind stung my nostrils like a shot of menthol vapor. It scoured my lungs and pricked my nerves in a way that made me feel more alive than I had felt in a long time. The night sky glittered in a gown of stars. I ran faster, until my blood ran hot and my right foot started to tingle. I jumped back on the bike and wiggled my toes, hoping for quick passage to Yentna Station.

It took me five more hours to travel twenty-five miles along the soft river trail, although it felt like minutes. I was joyful, awestruck by the intensity of the open landscape, and amazed at how simple it was to be warm and alive and pedaling a bicycle into the heart of a frozen wilderness. I'm not sure how many times I stepped off the bike to run during the last twenty-five miles. The abstract notion of time and miles, along with a survivalist sense of urgency, were all swallowed by the simple pleasure of being.

Yentna Station appeared as a tiny, flickering gold light amid the twisting black spruce trees that lined the wide river. I felt strong enough to consider continuing down the trail that night, without rest. I just needed to change my socks, dry my vapor barrier as much as I could, and acquire some sort of plastic bag for my wet boot.

I stepped into the small log structure just after 2 a.m. A handful of racers snoozed in the front room, lit only by red flames flickering inside a wood stove. A dim light glowed in the next room. I assumed the race official was waiting in there. But no one stirred; only the popping fire interrupted a reverent silence. I sat next to the stove and yanked at my ice-crusted gaiter. It was still too frozen to unlatch, so I sat and watched the flames until the ice around the buckle melted, then ripped at the Velcro until it let go in a shower of ice flakes. I pulled up my pant leg and began to work on the boot. The laces were frozen as well. I clawed at them with my fingernails until I had worked enough of the ice away to undo those. With great effort, I pulled away the tongue of the boots and tried to yank out my foot. Nothing happened. I chipped more ice away from the laces, loosened them some more, and tried again. Nothing. I stood up, pressed my hands on the top of the boot, and pulled with all the strength my leg could muster. Still my foot wouldn't budge. I plopped down on the wood floor, breathing hard.

My foot was stuck inside my boot.

With a sinking sense of dread, I realized my foot was probably frozen inside my boot. As I shook my foot, it made no sound. There was no water to slosh around. The force I was fighting was in all likelihood a solid block of ice.

I lifted my leg and propped the boot directly on top of the stove. That the hard plastic might melt seemed a minor concern. I glanced toward the lit room. No one moved. Perhaps even the checker was taking a nap. Good. I wasn't ready to explain why I was lying on the cold floor, roasting one of my feet on the stove top. Hot blood pounded in my head, like a fever, and I thought I might pass out. But I stayed awake, listening to the clock in the kitchen tick away seconds as painfully slow as any I had ever known.

I fought with my boot several more times. Finally, about thirty minutes after I first entered the building, I managed to wrestle a ghost-white appendage out of my socks, which were still frozen to the inside of the boot. Despite finally achieving its freedom, my foot felt strangely detached from my body. I pulled it close to my face. All five of my toes were the color of chalk, but if I tried to wriggle them, they still moved. "A little frost nip," I thought. "It could be worse." I pulled on my down booties and walked into the lit room to check in.

The checker set me up in a sleeping spot right next to the stove, the same section of floor where I had spent the previous thirty minutes trying to thaw my boot. I didn't tell him I had actually arrived a half hour earlier. I ate a hastily prepared meal of tomato soup and a grilled cheese sandwich, and then crawled into my sleeping bag. I pressed my still-cold toes into the pit of my left knee, and drifted to a thin, troubled sleep.

About three hours later, at 5:30 a.m., Geoff sauntered in the door. He was the next person to arrive after me, Billy, and Sean. Even on foot, he had managed to make it to Yentna Station a mere three hours after I did. He was ahead of about half the field, who were still somewhere behind the first checkpoint — likely sleeping in bivy sacks in the brutal cold. At that point, the temperature outside was twenty-five below. Geoff coughed loudly. The sound woke me up.

"Hey," I said as I peeked out of my bag. "How are you feeling?"

"I feel horrible," Geoff said, and coughed again. "How about you?"

I looked around. Everyone was still sleeping. "Um, not great," I said. "I stepped in some overflow on Flathorn Lake. I think I might have frostbite."

"What? Really? Let me see."

I got out of my bag and pulled off my down bootie. My toes had taken on a slate gray color, but they weren't black.

"Those don't look too bad," Geoff said. "Do they hurt?"

"Actually, they don't hurt at all."

Just then, a group of three cyclists clomped down the stairs. They were preparing to go back out into the frigid morning. I felt awake and strangely energetic, but uncertain enough about my toes that I wasn't prepared to leave quite yet. Geoff and I decided to take their place in the room upstairs. I dragged my sleeping bag up the rickety staircase to a small room that already had one other occupant. Moonlight streamed in a tiny window through tattered curtains, revealing the spare furnishings of a single full-size mattress, a thin brown quilt, and a single wooden chair. The room was at least eighty-five degrees, a dry sauna directly above the wood stove. Geoff lay down next to the man fast asleep on the mattress. I spread out my sleeping bag in the narrow space between the foot of the mattress and the wooden wall. "I'll just wait here until morning," I decided. "Geoff and I can head out together."

For the next hour, I listened to Geoff cough and moan in the suffocating room. I felt restless but otherwise normal. Then, almost imperceptibly at first, a sharp sensation began to poke my right foot. It started as a hot tingle but quickly grew to a crescendo of unhinged pain more intense than anything I had ever felt. The pain held my foot in a searing blaze I could do nothing to extinguish. I simply writhed and bit my knuckles and leaked hot, silent tears on my sleeping bag as Geoff continued to cough through the first stages of pneumonia. I could scarcely comprehend what was happening; I had no concept of what it meant to thaw frozen flesh still attached to a living creature. For the next two hours, there was no race, no frostbite, no bicycle, and no grand Alaska wilderness; there was nothing but sickness and pain. I envisioned a Civil War triage tent in a hot southern battlefield, where patients strapped to beds screamed in a chorus of agony. The imagery would have been humorous if it weren't close to reality.

Slowly, the white fire began to flicker and fade. My mind felt numb after twelve hard hours of cycling in the cold wind, the adrenaline-charged lake mishap, and the intense pain of thawing my frozen toes. Despite a stubborn desire to stay in the race, my stronger instincts simply bowed in resignation, as if to say, "You're done." All at once, I felt peace and dread. I knew that if my pain was any gauge of the physical damage I had done, I was in big trouble.

I lay back down and waited for daylight to reach the room. By then, it was well after 8 a.m. Geoff seemed to be awake but didn't show any interest in speaking or getting out of bed. The man next to him was still snoozing. I sat up and pulled off my bootie. As I suspected, bulging purple and yellow blisters had formed around my toenails, and the tips of my toes were turning black. Even then, I held onto a fading hope. I pulled my bootie back on and tried to stand. Pain shot up my leg as soon as I put my weight on my foot, and I had to lean on my left leg quickly to keep from toppling over.

"You going back out?" Geoff wheezed.

"No," I said. "I'm just going downstairs. I need to tell the checker about my situation."

The race official's name was Rich Crane; he was a longtime volunteer on the Iditarod Trail, often helping out with the dogsled race, and I assumed he would naturally be an expert on frostbite. I explained what happened, pulled off my boot, and showed him my toes.

"I have seen worse," he said. "But those are definitely damaged. I can't promise you'll keep them if you go back out there, especially now that they're warm. Can you walk?"

"Kind of," I said. The truth was, I had hobbled so badly just to walk down the stairs that I was surprised I didn't fall. Even my ability to put pressure on bike pedals without intense pain was doubtful, and that was assuming I wouldn't have to do any more walking — something the soft, unpredictable Iditarod Trail usually demanded in large amounts. And still, I held on to that tiny hope. I had put everything into that race. All of my money, all of my time, and all of my focus for an entire winter were single-mindedly funneled toward the Iditarod Trail Invitational. To turn my back on the race was more than just a defeat; it was an admission that my year up to that point was a complete waste of time. And for something as stupid as dipping my foot in a lake? I couldn't accept it. I just couldn't.

Rich could tell I was mulling options I did not have. "In the end, it's your decision," he said. "But I wouldn't recommend it."

At that moment, Tim Hewitt, a longtime and incredibly successful veteran of the 1,100-mile foot race to Nome, turned around from the table where he had overheard Rich and me talking. He stood up and walked toward us. His white hair stuck out in spikes like a frozen crown. His face was wrinkled and wizened; the hardships of four walks to Nome were etched in his frown. He looked at me with a piercing gaze. I inhaled deeply and held my breath, as though I were waiting for the words of a prophet about to hand down a revelation.

"You know you can't go back out there," he said. His eyes were filled with flecks of empathy and sadness. "You know you can't."

I nodded and didn't even try to hold back the hot tears now flooding my eyes. Everything Tim said was right, and Tim was one who would know. It was over. He understood that truth, and as one of a tiny group of athletes who had put all of his heart and effort into this tiny, obscure race in a remote part of Alaska, he understood exactly what that meant.

"I know," I said.

Sunlight streamed into the room as I sidled up against the window. Flakes of frost peeled off the pane and an outdoor thermometer registered twelve below. The air outside was so clear that the snow-swept surface of the Yentna River shimmered. In a distance too close to bear, white peaks of the Alaska Range pierced an indigo sky. After months of preparation I could nearly touch those mountains, and yet I had never felt so far away.

I pressed my forehead against the cold glass, hoping to numb the pain-seared blood that still coursed through my veins. Every capillary tingled, reverberations of the thawing process. The only parts of my body that I couldn't feel were my toes. I looked down at the alien digits, nearly consumed by purple skin and pus-colored blisters. I tried to wiggle them and they only quivered, like moldy slabs of meat that had been left out of the freezer too long. They no longer felt like part of me. Imposters. Parasites. If I could only work up the courage to limp into the kitchen, I could carve them off with a butcher's knife and free the parts of me that still ached to continue the journey. But pain and fear kept me pressed against a window in the cramped building, consumed with a helpless sort of yearning.

Behind me, a pair of boots stomped down the rickety staircase. I turned see the pale face of George Azarias, a rookie cyclist who had rolled in late that morning. He wore a thin black hat and a gaze that seemed perpetually focused far into the distance. I pulled my bootie over my disfigured foot. "Headed back out?" I asked.

"Aye," he said in a slow Australian drawl that betrayed the depth of his fatigue.

I mustered a weak smile. "I'm really jealous," I said. "I wish I could go with you, but I have to fly out from here."

He smiled back. "I heard. Sorry about that foot. But we go on, don't we? We go on. You'll be back next year, then?"

I shook my head. "Probably not. I'm not sure what comes next, but next February seems a long way off."

"I suppose," he said, and laughed. "Right now, McGrath seems a long way off."

I looked out at the narrow trail stamped into an expanse of snow and wondered what made me want it so badly. "It's closer than you'd think," I said.

George exited out the side door, letting a rush of invigoratingly frigid morning air into the room. I attempted to stand up. Pain erupted from my foot and I collapsed back into the chair. A dark oily spot appeared on the tip of my wool sock — a broken blister. I stared in disbelief as it spread, wondering which truth was more ridiculous — the fact that something so trivial could disrupt a monumental adventure, or the fact that something so serious could arise from a trivial bike ride. My foot just rested on the wood floor, lifeless and leaking. I was beginning to see that the line where my body ended and my experiences began was no clearer than the horizon in a blizzard, and no more permanent than a footprint in a storm.

Chapter Two
Picking Up the Pieces

Page 25: Jill Homer's shadow stretches over the snow-covered ice during a walk with crutches on Mendenhall Lake.
Page 26: A mountain bike rests against Mendenhall Glacier.

"Hey Jill, can I see you in my office?"

"Sure, Charles," I said to the voice on the speakerphone. "I'll be right in."

I grabbed my crutches and leaned against my desk as I stood up. My right foot was wrapped in white gauze. Over that, I wore an oversized, brightly colored sock that my mom had mailed from Utah in an effort to lift my spirits. The gift was strangely effective, as though loud pink stripes really could erase the oozing decay surrounding my toes.

It was March 11, nine days after Geoff and I boarded a small ski plane outside Yentna Station and lifted off the white ice toward our decidedly grayer lives in Juneau. I had always thought it would be a blast to ride a bush plane over Alaska wilderness, but the flight out of Yentna was partially humiliating and partially agonizing. After I decided to scratch from the Iditarod Trail Invitational, Geoff admitted he wasn't likely to recover his stamina since he could hardly breathe through all the gunk in his lungs, and dropped out as well. We split the expensive air taxi flight with a Spanish woman who was concerned that the frigid wind had possibly damaged her eyes. We were three quitters who, most reasonable people would agree, had good reasons to leave; still, a thick shame wafted through the small cabin of the plane. Geoff and the Spanish woman sat in the back seat in silence while I leaned against the passenger-side door, half wishing for a hinge to pop open and forever release me from my uncertain future. The snaking Yentna River sparkled in suspended animation below us, and the clear air revealed row upon row of mountains in a far distance. It was beautiful, but all I could do was stare at my bandaged right foot and wonder what the hell I had done. Normal people don't have to be evacuated from the Alaska bush with frostbite on their feet. Normal people don't risk everything for an amateur bicycle race.

That afternoon, I spent more than six hours inside an emergency room in Palmer. A whole team of Alaskan doctors, who I assumed treated cold injuries as often as California doctors see sunburn, hemmed and hawed about what to do with my frostbitten toes. Surgery on the spot was discussed, followed by recommendations for a specialist in Anchorage. Finally, the Palmer doctors just drained my blisters, wrapped my foot in gauze, handed me a pair of crutches, and told me to change my dressings twice a day and consult a doctor in Juneau.

"There's still a chance you'll lose the tip of your big toe," one Palmer doctor told me before I left, "but we can take a wait-and-see approach."

Back in Juneau, I sought the second opinion of a podiatrist. Although she had recently relocated from California, and previously only dealt with seared flesh in the form of actual burns, the doctor told me I was going to be fine.

"I used to work at the burn unit in Santa Monica," she said. "I've seen flesh black to the bone. You're not going to lose anything, at least not if you're careful. What you have is just going to take a while to heal."

"How long?" I asked.

"I don't know," she said. "You definitely have some pretty deep damage. Possibly eight weeks or ten, hard to say. Your body will decide that."

I leaned back on the paper-wrapped bed, adding the time in my head. "Will I be able to ride a bicycle before then?"

"I don't know," she said. "I don't think you should start putting weight on your foot any time soon. If you want to exercise, you could try weight machines, upper body stuff."

"But what about my legs?" I asked. "I want my legs to stay in shape."

She laughed. "Be patient! These are your toes we're talking about. You only get ten of them." She turned to grab more gauze out of a cabinet on the other side of the room.

"Yeah, but do you need all ten of them?" I said under my breath. I couldn't wait ten weeks to start riding my bike again. That would put my frostbite recovery well into the middle of May, less than a month before I planned to launch what promised to be the largest single undertaking of my entire life: a 2,740-mile mountain bike race down the spine of the Rocky Mountains called the Tour Divide. The race loosely followed the Continental Divide from Banff, Alberta, to the southern border of New Mexico, along a series of logging paths, gravel roads, and trails that ceaselessly ascended and descended North America's largest mountain range.

I had become fixated on this race a year before, when Geoff attempted it but had to drop out in Kremmling, Colorado, with what he called "total body failure." Geoff was already an accomplished ultra-runner, regularly winning one-hundred-mile foot races in record times. But he still insisted that mountain biking the Great Divide was the hardest physical challenge he had ever attempted. For reasons that seemed just as inexplicable to me as my draw to cold-weather adventures like the Iditarod Trail Invitational, Geoff's assertions of the Great Divide's difficulty made me want it even more. It seemed like the ultimate mountain biking adventure, the kind of thing that rewarded mule-like labor and stubbornness, which were my only two athletic talents.

I understood I would have to commit 100 percent of my energy to the goal, with complete devotion. In January, I announced my intentions to quit my job as an editor at a daily newspaper, the Juneau Empire, in April and travel to the Lower 48 to train extensively in regions with heat and high elevation. Even before we left for the Iditarod race, Geoff and I started sorting out our things and preparing to move away from Juneau. I had already given up so much for the simple dream of riding the Divide; I couldn't stomach the thought of giving up everything for a few blackened toes. But I wasn't about to share this inclination with my doctor.

When my boss Charles called me into his office, he also knew the status of my health and my ability to ride a bicycle all day long for three weeks straight was still very much in question. It was mid-March, the Divide race was a mere three months away, and I was on crutches. As long as I clutched them, I couldn't offer a believable defense of my ambitions: To embark on the longest mountain bike race in the world in less than ninety days.

"Please, sit down," Charles said as he directed me toward the chairs in front of his desk. Charles was the new managing editor of the Juneau Empire. He had taken the job just a few weeks after the former editor stepped down, citing unmanageable stress and the questionable health of the business, which, like many other daily newspapers across the United States, was undergoing large budget cutbacks and layoffs. In the Juneau Empire's small newsroom of twelve reporters and editors, I had seen three of my own co-workers escorted out the door, never to be replaced, and their absence made all of our lives and workloads much more difficult.

The teetering work environment generated an underlying motive for my Divide dream — an excuse to extricate myself from my increasingly stressful job. I already had one foot out the door when Charles took over the editor position just a few weeks before my Iditarod race. It was early February and I was set to leave Juneau for good. Charles begged me to stay for two more months, to help smooth over what was already becoming a rough transition for him.

I had been reluctant. I was tired of budget cuts, tired of layoffs, and tired of the downward slide in the quality of my own work. And, if I was honest with myself, I was becoming tired of Juneau. The Southeast Alaska city is disconnected from the North American road system and has one of the wettest climates in the United States. Juneau is an isolated town of 30,000 wedged between the rugged Coast Range and the sea. It's a good place to be adventurous, but too isolated and remote to facilitate the life of an adventurer. I had always wanted to dabble in the life of a career adventurer, even if only for a few months. And while I did enjoy newspaper work, I was pretty sure most adventurers did not spend sixty hours a week sitting at a desk beneath buzzing florescent lights, designing newspaper pages on a computer screen.

But Charles had a way of getting what he wanted. He was a thirty-year-old Iraq War veteran from Kentucky, a large man with military-short hair, an intimidating scowl, and a disarming smile. He had worked his way to the top of the ranks at such a young age with a cocktail of old-fashioned persistence, charisma and workaholism. With a few simple words of flattery and a sprinkling of grand promises, he had managed to coerce me into staying on for two extra months after the Iditarod. He hinted that further negotiations might net me a new job title complete with a fifty-percent pay raise. I sensed another one of those negotiations heading my way.

I propped my crutches against his office chair and plopped down with my cheerful pink-striped sock extended in the aisle. Charles gestured toward my foot and got right to the point. "So how does this affect your plans to leave in April?" he asked.

"What do you mean?" I asked.

"I mean, you're not going to be able to do the bike race anymore, right? Not like that."

"I don't know," I said. "June is still three months away. I'm not ready to give up on it yet."

"Right," Charles chuckled slightly. "But you're on crutches."

I smiled at Charles. I admired his bluntness. No one else had the nerve to tell me that the Great Divide was a stupid dream, and I was a stupid person to throw away a job for it when the economy was tanking, the entire newspaper industry was struggling, and my foot was still leaking yellow puss. Charles turned around and pulled an overstuffed binder out from under a stack of papers. He handed it to me.

"Look inside," Charles said. "Those are all resumes, people who have applied for your job. I have more than fifty of them." He grabbed another binder and handed it to me. "These are resumes for the reporter job. The entry-level reporter job. I have even more of those. There are a lot of journalists out there looking for work. The newspaper business isn't getting any better." He leaned back in his chair, looking supremely satisfied. "I can almost guarantee you that once you leave here, you are not going have an easy time finding another job."

I smiled. "But I don't want another job. At least not for a while."

A look of confusion flashed across his face. He had worked hard all his life, and had always been rewarded for hard work. The harder he worked, the more he was rewarded, until it was difficult for him to understand why anybody would turn down an opportunity to slave away for sixty hours a week in front of a flickering computer screen.

"But you don't really think you're going to ride a bicycle like that?" he said. "How long did you say your race was? A thousand miles?"

"More than twenty-five hundred," I said. "And I'm certainly going to try. I've already pretty much planned it out. Geoff and I have a cabin in Utah reserved and everything. I'm going to train for the Great Divide, and he's going to train for Western States and a few other ultramarathons. Anyway, all of the time I've spent training for the Iditarod while working long hours here has been horrible on my relationship. Geoff's more excited about this sabbatical than I am. If I back out now, I'm pretty sure he'll leave me forever."

"But I'm offering you a promotion," Charles said. "A raise. A big raise. Surely Geoff can get behind that."

"Geoff cares about money even less than I do," I said. "And you've already seen how big of a motivator money is for me. I live in a two-bedroom condo with two roommates and drive a 1996 Geo Prism."

"But you have a nice bike," Charles offered.

"I think you'd be surprised how basic my bike is when you compare it to other people who take cycling as seriously as I do."

"Well, you don't make a bad salary now. What do you spend your money on?" he asked.

"I save my money and buy myself time," I said, "which is all I'm asking for now. I'm leaving in April. I've made up my mind. Frostbite doesn't change things."

Charles leaned back in his chair with a concerned look on his face. I smiled serenely. It felt good to be wanted, and at the same time have my resolve tested so I could prove to myself that riding the Great Divide really was the path I wanted to choose. Charles smiled back, because he liked this game. He recognized me as a rare hard sell, and if he could knead my desires to shape his way of thinking, then he'd win this battle of wits. Charles was used to winning.

"I'd hoped it wouldn't come to this," he said, "but what would you say if I said you could take the time off to do your race?"

"What?" I asked. "What do you mean?"

"I mean, go race the Great Divide. Take a long vacation. Take a month or two if you need it. Unpaid, of course. We'll call it a furlough. Then, when you're done, come back here and take the new job. It's a big promotion. You'll finally have enough money to buy a nice bike. I mean, really, what do I need to say to get you to stay? When does the race start?"

"On the twelfth of June," I said, drawing out the last syllable suspiciously.

"Good," Charles said. "How long do you think it will take?"

"Three weeks at least," I said. "Maybe a month."

31

"Okay," he said. "Then the first of July. Can you be back by then? My family is coming up here for the Fourth of July. If you can be back by July first, you can take a furlough and keep your job."

I ran my teeth over my bottom lip. The Great Divide was going to be the hardest thing I had ever attempted. The last thing I needed was a timeline, especially a timeline that held me to a finishing time that was significantly faster than the current women's record. At the same time, I was being offered the best of both worlds — the Great Divide and job security. I might even be able to maintain my company health insurance plan while I was gone. But what were my chances of finishing in twenty days? On the other hand, what were my chances of even finishing? Unless I could figure out a way to train with a foot that was still too injured to even push pedals, what were my chances of even starting? I might be able to promise that I could be back by the first of July. And even if I couldn't keep that promise, what was Charles going to do — call me in New Mexico and demand I come back? I could always say no. I'd be no worse off than if I had quit in the first place. Still, what would Geoff say? He'd been pressuring me to move away from Juneau since we moved there from Homer two and a half years previously. Geoff might say no. I'd still be no worse off than I was.

"I don't know," I said slowly. "I'd still need to leave on April twentieth. We have all these plans we made. And I need to train. I can't train here. I have to go somewhere where I can ride my bicycle in the desert heat and high mountain elevation."

"Hmm," Charles said. "That's only about two months of leave. That's not so bad. It won't be easy but I'm used to doing four jobs at once. I can handle one more for two months." When the Great Divide Race was really all over, I thought, it'd be closer to three months. I didn't state that fact out loud.

"And there's travel time," I said. "If I actually make it all the way to New Mexico, it's a long way back to here."

"Take a plane," Charles said. "You can rest when you're here."

"It's tempting," I said. "Really tempting."

"And if the race doesn't work out," he said as he gestured at my sock-covered foot, "you can always come back early."

"Tell you what," I said. "Let me talk to Geoff about it."

Charles grinned victoriously. "Tell Geoff it's an offer he can't refuse. It's the best offer I've ever given. I can't give you any more."

"I realize that," I said. "It's very generous. I'll let you know in a few days."

I stood up, grabbed my crutches, and limped out of Charles' office. The whole building seemed to hover ominously over me as I slowly made my way back to my own office. I felt as though I had cracked open a door I believed led to freedom, only to discover an identical room on the other side. In rows beside me, my coworkers sat their cubicles, clicking away at keyboards. They seemed oblivious to the bright winter sunlight that was pouring in the room. I was pretty sure this wasn't what I wanted, and yet, who was I to give up the few things everyone wanted — money, security, and respect? Charles played a dangerous game, one whose rules made everything that mattered to me seem trivial, and vice versa. It was a dangerous game because I suspected he was right.

I walked outside and started my car. I had only an hour for a dinner break before I had to be back at work. Should I tell Geoff now, or wait? I pressed my sock foot tenderly on the gas pedal and lifted the clutch. The sky was dark blue, and beams of orange sunlight stretched out beyond the mountains of Douglas Island, my home. A shimmering channel of seawater encircled the island like a gown. Juneau wasn't such a bad place to be stuck, if you had to be stuck somewhere.

I realized that I was already feeling homesick for Juneau. I had gotten outside so little in the past week — only enough to drive to and from work and my doctor's office. It was such a different lifestyle than the one I had practiced before the race, when I'd ride my bike for hours in the worst subzero winds and blowing snow. Now spring was on its way and I spent all my time reclined, staring at computer screens or sleeping. My mind, so accustomed to its daily dose of endorphins, couldn't adjust to the sedentary life, and depression was starting to creep around the edges of my demeanor. Geoff started to notice it shortly after we returned from the Iditarod, and asked me what I thought about leaving in March instead of April.

Now not only was I nixing any chance of an early departure, I was considering keeping a job that had demanded increasingly longer hours since Charles took over. All the time I spent locked to my desk certainly wasn't going to diminish just because I was planning to leave for three months. And while I was gone for three months, all the demands of that job were going to fall directly on Charles. It was a strange win-win situation, because it was also lose-lose. I could keep my job and lose my idealism, or I could lose my job and keep my dreams. Still, it seemed like now, no matter what I chose, I could hold on to the dream of the Great Divide. And if I could believe in the Great Divide, I reasoned, maybe I could believe in anything.

Chapter Three
Nearing an End

Page 34 and 35: Looking out across Stephens Passage during a snow bike ride on Douglas Island in Juneau.
Page 36: A street ends at the Mendenhall Wetlands in Juneau.

Standing atop a snow-swept mountain with a bicycle, where bleached clouds swirl above and indigo seawater glitters below, is just one of a thousand moments when it's impossible not to fall in love with Alaska.

    I had become deeply attached to these moments, which often took place in the first hours after long spans of dreary weather finally opened up and I serendipitously found myself at a perfect point between light and shadow, washed in the warm glow of the low northern sun and surrounded by far-reaching wilderness. I was beginning to wonder if I could live without these moments, even if I had more light in my life, more bike trails, less rain.

    It was April 14, and Geoff and I planned to leave Juneau in one week. Just one more week, and we would board a ferry that would return the two of us, my car, and our two bikes to the North American road system, where we would be free to wander as far south as we desired. We had tentatively planned a road trip down the coast to San Francisco, where Geoff would race and I would sightsee, before heading east to my home state, Utah, to take up residence in a single-room cabin in the high desert near Capitol Reef National Park. There, we planned to live simply, train extensively, and enjoy a lifestyle in which little existed beyond the two of us and our passions.

But it wasn't Alaska. Although he accepted my boss's ultimatum to take a couple months off and then come back to Juneau, Geoff admitted he still wasn't certain he wanted to return. The damp isolation had a way of closing in, dropping curtains of gray over everything from our jobs to our relationship. I told him I wanted to give the prospect of staying in Juneau the summer to settle — we didn't have to make any decisions right away. I suspected Juneau had pulled in Geoff more than he realized, and after a summer away, he would ache for the North in the same way I knew I would. He would remember that there was more to Alaska than latitude, lore, and lack of services. He would realize that the strength we both found in our three and a half years as Alaskans didn't come from within — it came from everywhere around us. He would feel the love that I had found. It wasn't the extremes I loved about the land, but the constants. The brightest moments always came after the darkest storms, and because I knew this, I could fully embrace both.

It was Geoff's thirty-third birthday. He asked me to accompany him to the local ski area to take photographs of him running in the snow, which he planned to send to the shoe company Montrail, a new major sponsor with whom he had just signed. Geoff's and my forays into ultra-running and endurance biking both coincided with our move to Alaska. But while my biking endeavors became increasingly more abstract, Geoff became more successful as a runner. He dabbled in mountain biking — culminating in his scratch in the 2008 Great Divide Race — but he was seemingly unstoppable on his feet. He had yet to lose a hundred-mile race, and held course records on a number of shorter distance runs as well.

In fact, the only thing he had ever failed at as a runner was the Iditarod Trail Invitational, but since no one paid attention to a race like that, Geoff was starting to gain recognition and corporate sponsors were taking notice. Geoff had several races lined up during the summer, and I was sure he was about to have his big breakthrough. I looked forward to being a part of that, because it felt important in a way my races never could. Geoff's races were about winning, not surviving, and there was something more meaningful about ending an adventure not only standing, but standing on top. I knew I would never be the person at the top. But I didn't mind the role of the smiling, supportive girlfriend in the background.

"Light's really flat today," I said as we made our way up the slope. "Lucky you wore the orange shoes — that's going to be about the only thing that shows up in all this gray."

"Yeah, I just need a few shots of the shoes," Geoff said.

I set down my bike and scanned the overcast sky for the tiniest break in the clouds. Nothing. Gray sky, gray snow. I bent down and loosened my shoelaces. I wasn't used to wearing shoes on both feet. I had only started putting a shoe on my right foot a few days earlier. The hard leather pinched my still-tender toes, which remained ultra-sensitive to pressure and cold in the aftermath of frostbite. I wore a sock, sandal, and bootie on my foot for six weeks following my dip in Flathorn Lake. After about four weeks, I started using that setup to tentatively pedal my bicycle down the road. My legs were weak, my muscles were shrunken, and my toes were sore, but it felt good just to turn the cranks once again. Geoff's birthday was my first time out with my snow bike since the Iditarod. I knelt atop a thin layer of ice crust that was swiftly disintegrating beneath spring's warmth. Everything about the simple act of being outside, with a bicycle, wearing shoes, felt both novel and familiar at the same time.

"Okay, now run toward me," I called out to Geoff, who had jogged a few hundred feet up the hill.

He loped down the hill and I fired off the camera, steadying my hands as much as possible to coax the point-and-shoot to recognize motion in the low light. Geoff turned around and made a few more passes before announcing, "That's good."

"I'm not sure if any of these are very crisp," I said. "It's hard to tell."

"As long as the shoes are in focus, they should be good," Geoff said. "I need to get going if I'm going to fit in a run before work. Do you want me to take you home?"

"No," I said. "I feel like taking my bike up the hill. I'll just ride home."

Geoff nodded and continued down the hill at a near sprint. I climbed on my bike and cranked hard up the slope. The ice crust crackled beneath my wheels. Beyond the mountain ridge, the slate sky was beginning to break apart; strips of sunlight glowed through the cracks. Sweat streamed from beneath my helmet, but my bare fingers felt icy. The air bit like winter but smelled sweet like spring — a perfect limbo between the two seasons.

As I neared the top of the mountain, the clouds continued disintegrating until the sky was a patchwork of deep blue and billowing white. The air was warm and I left my gloves off as I turned to begin my well-earned descent. All around me, the lingering veneer of winter was bathed in golden light. I released the brakes and launched the bike down the ski hill, swerving wildly at first. I pushed my butt behind the saddle and leaned into the handlebars until the front wheel straightened. Chunks of icy snow hit me from behind as momentum carried the bike away. I laughed out loud because I hadn't felt anything like it in months — just me, my bike, and the guiltless ease of gravity. I tore down the mountain, holding back nothing, taking in great gulps of oxygen as spruce trees and steel lift towers streamed past. Exhilaration pumped through my heart and emerged as love — the warm sentiment for the past, the beauty of the present, and the promise of the future. I was riding my bike again. I was going home to celebrate Geoff's birthday. I was heading south to pursue my dreams. I had the promise of job security waiting for me in this beautiful place. It seemed like there was nothing that could stop me, nothing.

Six days passed. It was April 20, two days before we were set to leave on the ferry. Tiny green buds were emerging from alder branches and my hours at work were piling up like the last rotten leaves of fall. My boss wasn't about to let me leave town with a single piece of paper left in the inbox, so I logged twelve- and fourteen-hour days even as my trip to-do list grew longer and more neglected. My car was still filled with boxes that needed to go to the storage unit, boxes that needed to go to friends' houses, and boxes that needed to go to the dump. I could no longer remember which was which. As the hours closed in I had no time to ride my bike, but I tried not to stress about it. I still had nearly two months before the race. The time to train would come.

Geoff had managed to clear out most of our room when I returned home late on a cool Monday night. The bed was one of the last pieces of furniture remaining, scheduled to go out the next day with a stranger who responded to an online ad. Geoff's gear lay alone in neat piles next to the bed — a small duffle of clothing, a thin sleeping bag, and a large duffle full of running shoes. On my side of the room, belongings were still strewn everywhere — fleece jackets and chamois-padded tights, bicycle tires, and books that had yet to find a home. Geoff lay in bed with a single lamp shining on the pages of the magazine he was reading. I took off my shoes and pants and crawled between the crisp sheets still wearing my work shirt.

"How was work?" he asked.

"Ugh," I said. "My boss has taken the rest of the week off, for one last vacation before he has to do my job for three months. He has me fielding all of the calls from crazies, wrangling the reporters, trying to type a one-page job description of everything I do at the Empire. Two more days of this. I'm not sure I can make it."

Geoff nodded but continued reading. "How was your day?" I asked.

"Good," he said. He had wrapped up his last day of work the day before. "I did a lot of packing. I went for a run."

"I can't wait to get out for a bike ride," I said. "I think I might be able to cram a few hours in when we stop over in Whitehorse."

Geoff set his magazine on the floor. He reached for the light. "Are you going to bed now?" he asked.

"Yeah," I said. "I'm exhausted."

The room went dark and I settled into the sheets. There was a strange chill to the air. I let my body shiver gently and took deep breaths, drifting into the wavering limbo between alertness and oblivion. Several minutes passed while I floated through that gray space before Geoff spoke up again.

"You still awake?"

"Yeah," I mumbled.

Geoff hesitated as he took several deep breaths, each time nearly releasing words that couldn't quite leak out. I waited. "There's something I should tell you before we take off Wednesday," he said quickly.

A streak of cold pierced my heart like a thin needle. There was fear in his voice, and the simple words themselves signaled danger.

"What is it?" I asked quietly.

Nearly a minute passed in more silence. Geoff breathed deeply. Every second, every labored breath, fueled a rising chorus of fear. The delay was unbearable. A thick, gurgling anger rose up from my gut. I wanted to roll over and grab his shoulders, shake him and scream at him to spit it out. I wasn't sure I even cared what he said. He could tell me he had frequent thoughts about murdering me in my sleep, and that admission would not have been worse than his gulping silence. Geoff and I had been together more than eight years, and he had never made any confession to me. Nor did I ever suspect he should have one to make. What awaited me was a confession, and I knew from the coldness in the air that it was not going to be a happy one.

"It's just — that," he finally said slowly. "It's just that I'm not sure I can do this anymore."

The words born of sharp ice hit me like dead wood, blunt and meaningless but powerful in their unfocused pain. "What the hell are you talking about?" I said, doing nothing to mask my anger. "Do what anymore?"

More gulping silence. At the second when I was reeling with thoughts about strangling the words out of him, he said, "This — oh, this is really hard for me to say. You and I. This. I don't think this is what I want anymore."

The wood block of words hit me directly between the eyes. My mind flailed at them like a paper shredder, ambitious but fully inadequate to digest the whole weight of their meaning. In our eight years together, for all the times it had passed through both of our minds, Geoff and I had never talked openly about splitting up. It had come to the point where I didn't even consider the end of the relationship to be a real possibility. Sure, we never married, but that was just a formality, more of a sign of our apathy to tradition and dedication to our own independence than a lack of commitment. Geoff and I had been partners since long before I considered a bicycle as anything more than a lousy form of cheap transportation. We had crossed the continent several times, both under our own power on those lousy forms of transportation, and in the very same half-rusted red Geo Prism that sat in our driveway, waiting to board a ferry in forty-eight hours. We exhausted our youth together. We camped and backpacked together. We climbed mountains together. We learned to ride bicycles long distances together. We made the giant leap to Alaska together. We discovered the world together.

"So is that what you're saying?" I said loudly, with no regard for our roommate in the next room. "Are you telling me you want to break up?"

Geoff answered with more impenetrable, unbearable silence.

"I think you need to tell me what exactly you want," I yelled.

"I'm — I'm not sure what I want," Geoff said. "I'm scared."

"Why?" I gasped, groping for coherent thoughts to piece together as my mind stampeded through a near-decade worth of seemingly happy history. "Why are you telling me this? Now? Geoff, we're supposed to be on a ferry in two days!"

"That's why I needed to tell you now," Geoff stammered. "I need to make sure you still want to go."

"What do you mean, still go? Still go south? Still go to Teasdale?"

"Yeah," Geoff said hesitantly.

"Why?" I gulped, now fighting back hot tears. "Why would I still want to go if you're breaking up with me? That doesn't make any sense. Either you want to be with me, or you don't."

"I don't know what I want," Geoff squeaked.

"Oh, that's so pathetic," I yelled. I scoured my flood of thoughts for something with more substance, something to relate both my disbelief at his words and hope that our plans and lives could somehow remain the same, but found nothing beyond brute anger. I leapt out of bed and stormed toward the bathroom.

"Come back," Geoff said quietly. "Please come back."

"I'll be back," I said. "I can't be in here right now."

I slid down the backside of the bathroom door and crumpled on the cold tile floor, my head spinning through an unbearable reel of sunshine-soaked memories like children's cartoons in a torture chamber. Geoff and I were grilling cheese sandwiches atop a red-checkered tablecloth on a June afternoon in Maine. Geoff was imitating E.T. saying "phone home" as we paddled down the Dirty Devil River in his canoe. Geoff was stroking my hair in the empty kitchen of our brand-new cabin in Homer. Geoff was running triumphantly toward me as he shattered the course record at the HURT 100 ultramarathon in Hawaii. The memories pounded hot blood through my throbbing skull. Why? Why would Geoff want to throw all of it away?

I spent several minutes releasing the happy memories through a muffled series of sobs, and then charged back into the bedroom with renewed rage.

"Why are you doing this? Why now? Is there someone else?" I asked with a steady voice.

"Well," he said, drawing out the syllable.

"Just tell me," I spat.

"Lately, I've started to form a really strong connection, with, with Misty," he stammered.

I wracked my throbbing memories. I could barely recall who Misty was. But it slowly came to me. Geoff's short-haired, twenty-one-year-old coworker. The chick he went to weird parties with and had bonfires with, yeah, that was her, along with her hippy friends, who I could never hang out with because I was always working nights. Misty was cute but she was young — what else? I couldn't even picture it. On the surface, she seemed to have little in common with a thirty-three-year-old cook and distance runner. I wanted to say, "You've got to be joking," but the words hung on trembling lips. For eight years I had built up Geoff in my mind as someone who valued substance above all else, and the words he was saying to me sounded superficial, and strange.

"It's just that she and I have been hanging out a lot lately, and we've formed a really strong connection. It really just started to hit us this past week, how we felt about each other. I mean, I know she's young. It's not that I even think it can work between us. It's just that being with her has helped me see that there's something ... missing, in what you and I have."

I looked at him mutinously, an expression he could not see in the dark room. Over our basement-level bed, the lights of the parking lot flickered between the railings of a fence, like shadows in a prison cell. I studied the dim reflection and realized that I would remember that image, forever, and everything about that memory would be wrapped in hate.

"What exactly are you looking for?" I asked. "We've been together eight years. The honeymoon doesn't last forever, you know."

"I know," he said. "But there should be something stronger there, something deeper. I'm not sure we have that anymore. Maybe we could, but I don't know."

"What are you saying? Do you want to keep trying or not?"

"I mean, I still think we should go on this trip, go to the cabin," Geoff said. "Maybe we'll find it. I don't know."

"What about Misty?"

"It's not about her," Geoff said. "She's just someone that helped me to better see who I am."

I looked into his eyes; they reflected a sort of hollow exhaustion. I wanted to tell Geoff that I didn't know who he was. I wanted to scream that I couldn't be sure even he really knew who he was. But before the words could leave my lips, I realized with a calming tremor that his explanation did have rings of truth. Geoff and I lived in the same house in Juneau, but we went to our separate jobs and did our separate runs and bike rides and hung out with our different friends and co-workers. For so long, too long, we had floated on memories and routine. There was little else to salvage. Geoff and I hadn't been close in a long time. But people don't just give up eight years like that, not like that, with hollow words in rooms lit like prison cells. I tried to form the words to tell him that people don't just throw away a decade of investment in a relationship on fleeting whims. But I was again silenced by cold realization — people do that all the time.

"So," Geoff's voice cracked. "Will you still go to Utah with me?"

My mind resumed racing. I wanted to get Geoff on the ferry with me so I could kick him out of my car in the middle of northern British Columbia. I wanted to turn on the lights and stare into his eyes so he could see all the happy memories that raced through my mind, exactly the way I saw them. I couldn't believe the words he was saying, and yet I couldn't discern how to read between the lines. If he wanted to get with some twenty-one-year-old woman, why not just get on with it? Stringing me along was so much worse than a clean break, and I would be a fool to allow it.

As I groped for understanding, there was nothing to cling to. And yet, the Great Divide loomed like a soft shadow over all the chaos. I might still have an opportunity to salvage a life-changing experience from this trash heap of a relationship. I could not have it if I did not board that ferry to drive south. Through the night's confusion, the Divide seemed like the only solid image I could still hold. I had never wanted something and not wanted it so intensely at the same time.

"I need time to think about it," I said.

"There's not much time," Geoff said.

"I know that," I said, my voice approaching a yell again. "Don't think I don't know that."

"Okay," Geoff said, and let the horrible, prison-cell-lit silence soak in again. "But I think we should go."

"I don't know," I said. I let the silence fester, staring hatefully at the striped windowpane until Geoff's breathing became heavy. Then I stood up, pulled my pants back on, and rushed out into the chilled early morning. It felt bitterly cold for April. Everything about the quiet darkness, the chilled air and the specific date seemed so calculated, so significant. Both of my other significant breakups in life had been set in motion on April twentieth.

The second, when I was nineteen, started when my college boyfriend of six months told me he had just been accepted to the Peace Corps for a two-year tour in El Salvador. He wrote me love letters for six more months before letting longer periods of silence launch the end of our long-distance relationship. And when I was sixteen, after lying to my parents and rushing off to Park City to stand in line for Tori Amos concert tickets, a boy held my hand and told me he'd call in that quiet, hollow voice that even the most naive teenagers understand means the boy's never going to call. Big flakes of snow fell on the spring grass as the boy drove away for the last time. Every end started on April twentieth. The date was significant to me. This was a significant end.

I slumped into my Geo Prism and fired up the engine. My newly tuned mountain bike perched on the roof rack. I felt an urge to go for a ride. But as soon as I thought of it, all my hate focused on that bike, and I wanted it to disappear and not consume my life any more. I drove north — to where, I didn't know. I needed to go somewhere. I needed to talk to someone. My whole family in Utah was asleep. It was after 5 a.m. in that state. My good friends in Utah hadn't heard from me in months. My friends in Juneau had babies, they had jobs, they had sleeping husbands, and they didn't have any real time for a sobbing, naive, pathetic, newly single friend like me. I could not let co-workers know about the level of turbulence that had just kicked up in my personal life; my boss might take that as a signal that I wasn't going to leave. I had no real close friends after three years in town. Geoff had been nearly everything to me there.

I pulled up to Geoff's and my storage unit, punched in the code, fought back tears as I blindly scrolled the right combination in the padlock, closed the door behind me, crumpled in the cave-like darkness and sobbed. All around me loomed the unseen mass of Geoff's and my worldly possessions — our battered furniture, our worn clothing, our homemade shelves, and my now-little-used snow bike. It was all crap and all meaningless, just filling space in a dark and hollow room. Tears plummeted into the empty space, because there was nothing for me in Alaska, nothing.

Chapter Four
Being Led to the Flood

Pages 47: Jill Homer looks out across the Yukon River Valley during a training ride in Whitehorse, Yukon.

Page 48: A dam of broken ice clogs the Telkwa River, flooding the town of Smithers, British Columbia.

The first hints of sunrise cut scarlet gashes in the sky where Geoff and I sat in my parked car, locked in silence. An Alaska Marine Highway ferry cast a morning shadow over a line of cars, in which we were last. I nibbled on a cinnamon cookie and looked blankly across the calm waters of Auke Bay. This would be the last I would see of Juneau for a while. Perhaps forever.

I thought Geoff and I should be talking, but the words hadn't yet come. A hollow lump of malaise had churned inside my gut for so many hours that it was self-perpetuating now. My cookie tasted like sand and I felt little but fatigue and boredom. I had just spent the past forty-eight hours staring apathetically at my office computer, carelessly stuffing random belongings in my car, and crying in the bathroom. Nothing seemed to have a purpose or a place. I was boarding that ferry because when life is most turbulent, often the only thing we can hold onto is our routine. My routine dictated that I head south. No matter what I wanted or needed, the only plan I had penciled into my calendar was change.

Geoff on I followed the procession onto the boat and wordlessly walked upstairs, taking our usual seat in the ferry's dining room.

"Do you want breakfast?" Geoff finally asked.

"I just had a cookie," I said.

"That's not breakfast," Geoff said.

"It's breakfast to me," I said with a scowl. Geoff had always been the cook in our relationship. I was the kind of inept food preparer who could ruin a bowl of cereal. If Geoff and I stopped living together, we both knew I was facing a long descent into junk food and Subway sandwiches. I wanted him to feel bad about that. I wanted him to feel bad about anything. But the peaceful look on his face revealed the freedom he was feeling at having finally come clean. I resented his tranquility more than I resented his leaving me.

Geoff stood up, walked away and returned several minutes later with a tray of eggs and bacon. I leaned over as he started to eat.

"Geoff, I've been thinking about our situation," I said. "If we're going to do this, I guess we have to agree that we're going to try to make this work as friends."

He paused with a fork in his mouth. "Is that really what you want?"

"I don't know," I said. "I can't really picture what that would even be like, but it's worth a try. At least, it will beat spending two months living in tight spaces and not talking to each other."

He nodded. "I think it will be good. I think we can still have a fun summer."

I feigned a weak smile. Fun didn't really fit into the equation for me. Keeping our comfortable status quo alive long enough for me to start the Great Divide — that was a factor. Trying to help Geoff see that he was making a big mistake — that may have added variable or two. I certainly didn't want to just be another friend of his, but I realized the decision wasn't up to me. My only choices were hope or hopelessness, and two days into our separate-but-together separation, I still longed for the path of hope.

The ferry bobbed north and we moved to the solarium, where Geoff fell asleep on a lawn chair. I managed to unknowingly take the nearest spot to the boat's designated ashtray, and inhaled large quantities of secondhand smoke while I shuffled through what seemed like an unusually high percentage of sad songs on my mP3 player. The sand-flavored cookie churned in my stomach. I couldn't tell what was more nauseating — the situation or my reaction. I had never been so angry with anyone in my life, and there I was, handing him everything he wanted with a smile on my face.

The sky remained unusually clear when we departed the ferry in Skagway and continued north in my small red Geo. Geoff drove and I ignored a call from my mother, knowing full well that my cell phone wasn't going to work the entire time I was in Canada. She knew vaguely about the breakup situation, but I wasn't ready to explain the current plan, the asinine plan that had Geoff and I still driving south together and stopping to see all the friends we had planned to see before moving together into a cabin in southern Utah. My parents would tell me I was being naive and making a bad choice. And they would be right.

That evening in Whitehorse, I went for my first bike ride in nearly a week. Geoff announced he was going for a run and planned to go to bed early, so I didn't expect to see him again that day. Our friends pointed me in the direction of the only viable mountain bike route in town, a plowed dirt road that snaked up a snow-covered mountain. The sun hung in the sky late into the evening as I began the climb, slowly turning the pedals in the booties I specifically brought to protect my frostbite-sensitive toes. The night chill settled in even as the sun clung to the horizon. I had forgotten my gloves, but I did not care. The cold wind breathed air into the stagnant pit in my gut, and the fatigue of the climb sucked up two days worth of malaise and pain.

I had told my friends I would be gone for just ninety minutes. I had a dim headlamp with me, but no other lights to cut into the encompassing darkness. I had no spare coat or hat to block out the deepening cold. But physical safety had become unimportant to me, and discomfort helped dull my emotional anguish. With every pedal stroke, my gray and hollow world faded back a little bit more, replaced by soothing endorphins and gritty determination. The road became steeper, and big rocks from winter slides littered the muddy surface. Sweat poured over my lips in the same way so many tears had, but instead of defeat, these salty streams tasted like triumph. The lights of Whitehorse glittered behind me. I pedaled harder. The unlit void of the sparsely developed North spread out in front of me.

The peak of the mountain loomed, hidden behind six-foot-high walls of old snow, sliced away to make room for maintenance vehicles. But in its deserted state, the snow walls seemed to be a fortress of solitude built only for me.

A red light blinked from some sort of communication tower at the top. Whitehorse appeared as a shimmering island in a sea of night, but the last rosy streaks of sunset still clung to the western horizon. I breathed erratically. That eight-mile climb had taken a lot out of me. I thought with a flicker of comedic terror that in less than two months, I'd be asking my body to work just as hard for ten to fifteen times as long, every single day.

It seemed impossible in the dim fatigue of the April night, but this also didn't mean much to me. My suspicion about my inability to ride the Divide was a vague theory, a fear of failure, nothing more. My reality, what mattered, was that I had ridden to the top of this one mountain, this nondescript Yukon mountain with a cell phone tower on top, and this single act proved that I could still embrace a world beyond the hollow, gray one that awaited me below. My refusal to quit a job that I believed was holding me back, my failure to make my relationship work, my isolation in Juneau, and my resignation to spend the summer with a man who did not love me — I did not have to let these things define me. I was still a cyclist, and I still had the physical power to seek new places where I could leave my mistakes behind.

But I was still uncertain as to what exactly did define me as Geoff and I left Whitehorse and turned onto the Alaska Highway. In the southern Yukon, there are only two roads, and only one fork. We veered right on the Cassier Highway, largely deserted and lined with five-foot-deep walls of snow. A sign read "South to Alaska: 664 kilometers to Hyder." I thought about the southern tip of the Alaskan panhandle and shuddered at the realization of how far we had yet to descend. After two days of ferry travel and driving, we were still at the same latitude as Juneau, slowly picking away at the miles through an impenetrable silence. Winter lingered. It showed no signs of ending.

In Dease Lake, British Columbia, I slept in the second bed in a dark room of an otherwise unoccupied hotel. I set my alarm for 6 a.m., hoping to log a three-hour training ride before our scheduled 9 a.m. departure. The temperature was still well below freezing in the early morning. Geoff didn't even stir as I applied my warm clothing layers: Tights, jersey, fleece pullover, light raincoat, gloves, wool socks and a hat. It didn't seem like enough, but it was all I had. My pared-down possessions had been chosen with heat and distance in mind. Slow, uncomfortable progress through the last remnants of winter had never been factored into my training plan.

The morning was gray and coated in thick frost as I wheeled my bike across the empty parking lot. I pedaled south down the Cassier, because it made more sense than riding north. South was new territory. That was where I wanted to go. Small spruce trees and alders lined the road, their branches permanently twisted by hard winds and harder winters. The cold air bit at the skin on my neck and face as I pedaled; I had no means to ward it off.

I passed a sign that said: "Arctic Ocean/Pacific Ocean Divide, 889 meters." I smiled. It was my first continental divide crossing, in a season where my only remaining ambition was to pass through a fair number more of those. I pedaled hard, trying to outrun the creeping chill and net some distance in what seemed like an unreasonably short period of time. Surprisingly, after the divide, the road continued to climb. I breathed heavy and dripped sweat, and focused on a narrowing tunnel of fatigue. I didn't even notice the wall of snow growing higher and the alders and spruce growing smaller, until there was nothing left but twigs and a rolling, snow-covered meadow. I had climbed high. My clothing was drenched in sweat. And I was becoming deeply cold.

I removed my thin gloves and held my raw hands to my mouth, trying to breathe some life into my fingers. Shivers were rising up from my core and I shook my shoulders and hips to push them back. The long, wind-chilled descent promised to be painful, and I briefly considered running the whole way back. I didn't have time. I pulled my gloves back on, jumped on my bike, released the brakes, and braced myself.

The cold tore through my body like a full-blast stereo with a broken volume button. There was nothing I could do but face the undulating waves of frigid shock with a steel-faced grimace as every single cell in my body writhed and screamed. Torture comes to mind, but torture isn't the right word, because torture implies a state of extreme discomfort that isn't your fault. This bike ride was my fault. The cold wind chill was my fault. It passed through my watering eyes and throbbing fingers and toes with serene indifference.

I returned to the hotel already past the point of shivering, my limbs half-frozen in place as I hobbled stiffly toward the room. The door was locked. I rapped my blue knuckles against the door, but nobody answered. I kicked the door with the dead weight inside my shoe, but I already knew that Geoff had either gone out for a run or he deliberately wasn't going to answer. Whichever scenario it was, I did not care. I zombie-walked toward the lobby and placed my useless fingers against the coffee pot, hoping they would thaw enough that I could pour a cup. I needed hot liquid. I needed warmth. I needed love. And I really didn't have anything. I had my bike. Only the bike.

When Geoff returned from his run twenty minutes later, I was slumped on the floor of the lobby, red hands clasped around a Styrofoam cup, returning from hypothermia just enough to at least be shivering again.

"Cold today!" Geoff exclaimed too cheerfully.

"You could have left the key outside the door," I grumbled. "It's not like there's anyone else at this hotel. It's still winter up here."

"You got back early," he said. "Anyway, does it kill you to wait out here?"

The days churned through the resulting silence. We rolled south. The walls of snow along the road grew shorter until winter disappeared beneath the brown grass clumps of early spring. Spruce trees grew taller and more varied. I sat in the passenger's seat and watched the pavement curve and climb over the mountainous terrain. We passed darkened trinket shops and restaurants still closed for the season. Oncoming traffic was infrequent; vehicles traveling our direction nonexistent. The road was as cold and empty as the space between Geoff and me. My emotions felt muted and barren, like the landscape, clinging to the vague if inevitable promise of spring.

"So how do you want to work out the Great Divide?" Geoff said, breaking an extended silence. His face was still locked solemnly on the road.

"What do you mean?"

"I mean, I'm not going to be able to go with you to Montana. What do want to do with your car? Or do you think you'll fly?"

"Wait a minute — now you're not even going to drive me to Montana?" I hadn't yet visualized when Geoff and I would actually make the physical split. But I envisioned him taking me at least as far as the race start.

"Well, it kinda cuts into my plans with Western States," Geoff said. "I just figured you'd work out something else."

"But our plan ..."

"I know," Geoff said. "But it's really not convenient for me."

I pressed my back against the seat, fuming. It was becoming more obvious that, to Geoff, I had become little more than a person with a car and the ability to split gas money. When he no longer needed a ride, he no longer needed me. But I still believed I needed Geoff's help to prepare for the Divide race. I wasn't sure I had enough passion or drive left over to do it on my own.

"To be honest," I said through clenched teeth, "I'm not really sure what I'm going to do about the Divide. Since this all went down I've lost a lot of my interest in that stupid race; I really have. What's the point? What's the point of any of it?"

Geoff turned to face me for what felt like the first time in days. "Really? You're thinking about not doing the GDR?"

"Well, you know as much as anyone, the Divide's really something you can't even begin unless you're willing to give it everything you have, physically and mentally. There's no way you can keep yourself in it without having it be the one thing you want so badly. I definitely don't want it that badly. I don't know what I want, but I do know that spending three weeks riding a bicycle by myself in the middle of nowhere does not sound appealing right now."

"What do you think you'll do?"

"I don't know," I said. "Maybe instead of going with you to Teasdale, I'll just head up to Salt Lake and visit my family for a while, and then go back to Juneau. The sooner I get back to my job, the better, really."

"Really? That's what you want to do?"

"I told you. I don't know what I want."

"And all that leave you took at your job, you're just going to give up?"

"Somehow I don't feel like I'm the one giving up," I growled. "I think even you'd agree that the Divide is pretty frivolous compared to our situation. Why should I focus on that when I have to figure out what the hell I'm going to do with my life?"

"But why the rush?"

"Why wait?"

Geoff shook his head and stared forward. It occurred to me then that Geoff and I weren't actually going to be spending any amount of time living in a cabin in the Utah desert. He never had any real intention of that happening. I guess I was the only one who clung to this vacuous dream, although I couldn't think of many places I'd be less likely to endure. No, Geoff and I were going to split apart as soon as the car could no longer take us where we both needed to go.

We made it to Smithers, British Columbia, and drove to the doorstep of the home of Geoff's friends, Kelly and Adrienne. I had never before met the couple, and had already grown weary of the "smile and pretend everything's fine" routine I had tried to project since the initial split. At least amid the heavy tension inside the car, Geoff and I didn't have to wear suffocating masks. But the alternative — trying to explain eight years worth of rejection rolled up in a really long drive — seemed impossible. Kelly and Adrienne only knew us as a couple. Geoff and I suited up to go out for our separate pre-dinner run and ride, and they laughed about our matching base layers. I returned from the bike ride to a table heaping with lentils and rice and three people laughing over near-empty glasses of wine. Life was so normal in Smithers, and I hated it.

Darkness seemed to descend more quickly in the southern latitudes. When I mentioned this to Kelly, she laughed, because in her mind, we were still in the "far" north. When the bottles of wine were drained, Geoff announced he was going to bed. I sat up and chatted with Kelly and Adrienne until the phone rang at 11:30 p.m. Adrienne answered the call. His voice quickly turned low and serious. "Uh huh. Hmmm. Where. Are you sure? On the river? Oh no. Hmmm. Well, I'll check it out. Let me know if they need any help."

Adrienne hung up the phone and Kelly and I stared at him, wide-eyed. "An ice dam backed up across the river," he said grimly. "It's coming up quick."

"On the flats?" Kelly asked. Adrienne nodded.

"Where is that?" I asked.

"About a block from here," Kelly said.

As Geoff continued sleeping, we pulled on warm coats and gloves and strode out into the night. Flashing lights spun through the darkness and sirens wailed. "The neighbor told us they're rescuing people from trees," Adrienne said. "The water's coming up that fast."

I shivered in the cold stillness. "Do you think we should all evacuate?"

I said.

"She said the cops will come knock on the door if we have to go," Adrienne said. "In the meantime, we should probably think about grabbing our valuables."

"I already have the emergency kit in the car," Kelly said. "We just have to grab the cat and the computer. Nothing else really matters."

I thought about my car sitting in the driveway with my whole life inside of it. My bicycle rested on the roof rack. If the river would rise high enough to engulf the car and carry it away, it would release me from this whole twisted situation, I wouldn't have to keep up the charade anymore. I would be free.

We walked down the street. Three doors down from Kelly and Adrienne's house, we saw boiling black water rushing across the neighbor's long gravel driveway. It filled the deep embankment below the street like a canal. We walked another block until we could see a roiling tributary of the actual river, and beside it were mobile homes nearly submerged in water. The windows and street lamps were eerily dark, the rushing water frighteningly loud.

"We should go back," Kelly said, sounding nervous for the first time. "This is coming up really fast."

Back at the house, Kelly and Adrienne started collecting belongings. I woke Geoff up and told him what was going on.

"Did they receive an evacuation order?" he asked groggily.

"No, not yet," I answered.

"It's probably fine," he said. "The cops would be here by now if they thought the water was going to reach this level."

"I don't know," I said. "Just look out the window. There are fire trucks and cop cars everywhere. They're probably too busy rescuing people to do door-to-door evacuations."

"So what are you saying? Are you saying you want to leave now?"

"No," I said. "I just thought you should be aware, that's all."

Kelly knocked on the door. "Just talked to one of the police," he said. "They've blocked off the road into the neighborhood, but he said the flood has tapered and they don't think anybody on this side of the river will be affected. I'll wait up to make sure, but it doesn't seem like the flood is going to hit us."

"That's a relief," I said. I felt a sting of guilty disappointment, too. If the river didn't interrupt our anguishing march south, then it would have to continue as planned. I felt a strong urge to cut off the trip right there, but if the river didn't make that decision for me, I was going to have to make it myself. I resigned myself to the long and continued descent to the Lower 48, because I knew I wasn't strong enough to stop.

Chapter Five
Marin

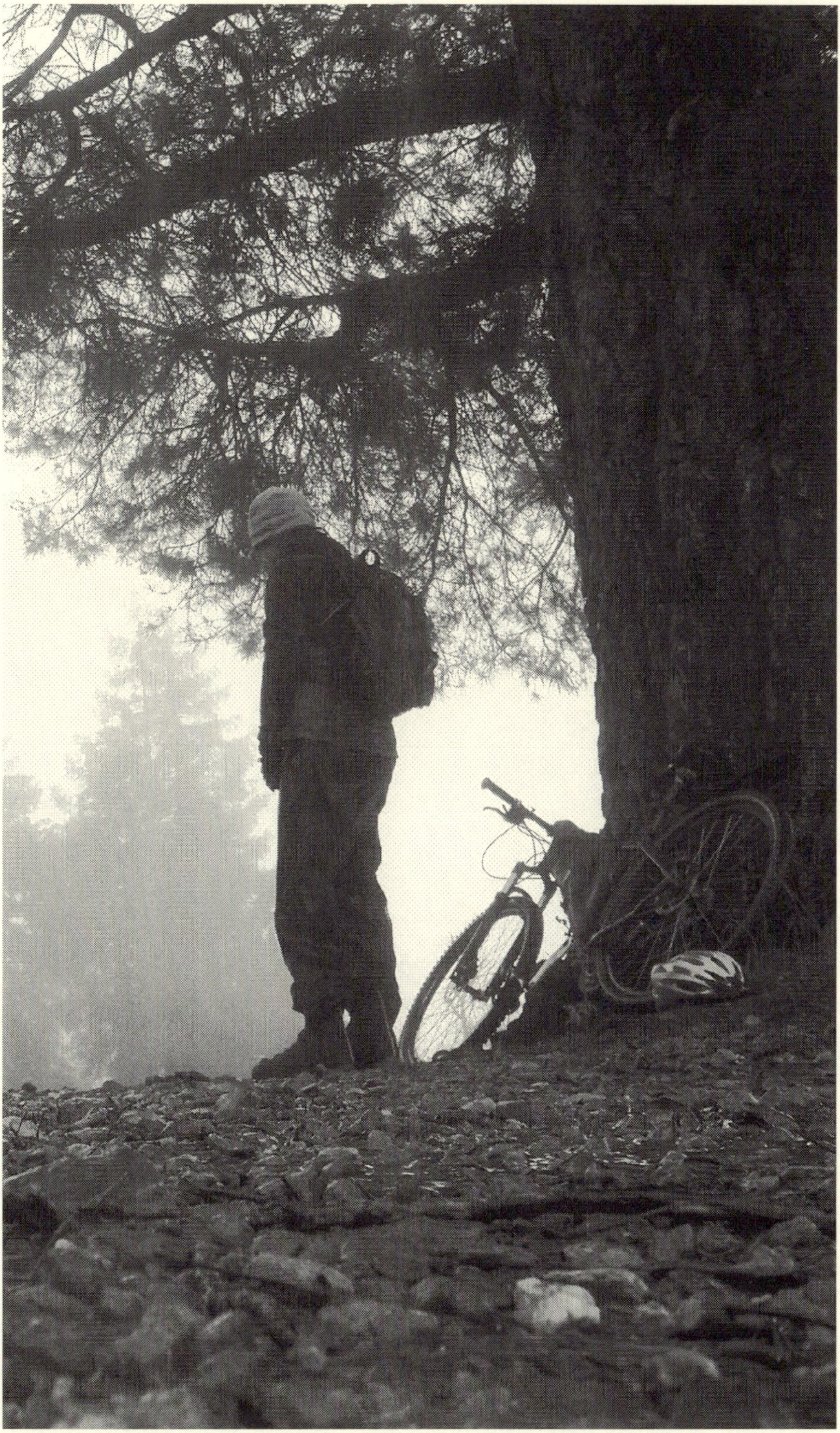

Page 58 and 59: Jill Homer collects herself following a mountain bike crash in the Marin Headlands north of San Francisco.
Page 60: Fog shrouds redwood trees in Golden Gate Park.

Wisps of low clouds clung to the cables of the Bay Bridge when we entered San Francisco. The sea air was thick with salty sweetness despite the gas fumes from the traffic streaming beside us. I was homesick for everywhere else, with the fog painting a blurry image of my coastal Alaska home, and the traffic echoing the sounds of my sprawling suburban origins. The city beyond was just another stop in an opaque future, masked behind a curtain of gray.

I was ready to be anywhere else. The 3,000-mile drive left me numb to my own weariness, but I still felt the unease of movement without clear purpose. The periods of silence between Geoff and me only grew longer the farther we drove south. We spent a carefree day in Vancouver, avoiding direct contact with each other as we caught up with old friends. We spent two nights with a mutual friend in Portland. I spent as long as I could each day piloting my bike along the fog-shrouded streets of the city. The last night, I lost my temper with Geoff when he wandered back inside the house at 1 a.m. after spending more than an hour on the phone with Misty.

"How can you continue to build a relationship with her right in front of me?" I cried. "Even if you don't love me anymore, even if I'm nothing more to you than a friend, or even just a chauffeur, I'm still here! Do you have any idea how that makes me feel?"

"This is hard for me, too" he yelled back. "I can't just ignore everything else that's going on."

"I can't believe you dragged me down here," I fumed. "That was such an incredibly selfish thing to do. You think you can have it all, and the amazing thing is you seem to get it."

The next day we pressed through the thick silence into northern California. I took out my anger and hurt on a small mountain, mashing the pedals up a sandy road as I climbed from 2,000 feet to 6,000 feet into what at the time was noticeable altitude. Mount Shasta shimmered in the far distance like a mirage. I returned to the hotel calmer and more grounded and crawled into bed. Geoff wrapped his arms around me and softly kissed my neck. "This still feels so right," he whispered. Tears streamed down my cheeks because what he said was true, and it was the cruelest thing he had said yet.

The next day, I threaded a few more strands of hope around my fraying nerves. Geoff still gravitated toward me on some level. What if I could make him see that maybe that could be enough? It seemed pathetic to yearn for a partnership where love was only attached to one side, but people did that every day. So many marriages were based on partnership, and people didn't give up on those because, as much as it pains romantics to admit it, partnership and survival are the basis for love. Geoff still needed me, somehow, and for that reason alone it was impossible for me to cling to the anger I felt toward him indefinitely.

But we had to push any threads of progress under the table again once we arrived at our friends' house in San Francisco. My pain, and our breakup, went back in the closet. Paul and Monika lived at the edge of a ritzy neighborhood in the heart of the city. Their semi-glamorous urban lifestyle was intoxicating, and I started spending most of my time with them, visiting Alcatraz, touring the Mission, walking the pier, eating Ethiopian food, and sipping coffee at a sidewalk café. The more I spent fully immersed in the San Francisco tourist routine, the more Geoff withdrew into his cell phone and its hateful connection with Misty. He rarely went out with us, and when he did, he was quiet and distant. I was losing him fast.

I reacted by spending even more time away on my bike. When Paul and Monika were at work, I trolled the city streets without a plan or a destination, making turn after turn until I was hopelessly lost. I weaved the empty corridors of big industrial areas and tore through the clatter and screams of run-down neighborhoods. I raced behind streetcars and darted in front of buses. I stumbled into the Golden Gate Bridge and crossed it in fog so thick I could hardly see the bridge towers ten feet in front of me. Usually I didn't even want to find my way back, but I always did.

The day before his race, Geoff finally spoke to me directly.

"Would you be okay with taking down the tent after the race starts?" Geoff said. "I think it would be best if I could just sleep as long as possible beforehand."

I nodded. In our three days in the city, I had almost forgotten that the reason we had even come to San Francisco was so Geoff could run the Miwok 100, a one-hundred-kilometer foot race through the steep hills of the Marin Headlands. I had promised months before that I would provide support for him during the race, and reminders of that duty only cropped up occasionally after we broke up. Now it was here and I just wanted to head out alone on my bike, to get lost yet again in a wilderness of pavement and noise. But if I abandoned Geoff now, that truly would be the end. I clutched my strained threads of hope as I got in the car with him to drive to the race start.

Since my blow-up in Portland, we hadn't talked directly about our cabin in Teasdale, Utah. As far as I was concerned, that option was still on the table even if both of us were silently acknowledging that was never going to happen. An actual open disavowal of the plan had yet to be voiced by either of us. And even as I loathed Geoff's brutal honesty and even crueler emotional distance, I still wasn't willing to let him go, not yet. I vowed to help make the Miwok 100K his best race ever. Maybe if he saw my devotion, he might think about me differently.

We crossed the Golden Gate Bridge into the thick, sustaining fog. For the area's proximity to the city, the Marin Headlands are startlingly remote, a series of steep grass hills rising as high as 2,000 feet above the sea. The rolling landscape is webbed with fire roads and singletrack trails, but with the exception of a few small towns at sea level, it's mostly clear of human-built structures. For early May, the weather was dismal — forty degrees and raining with a stiff, gusting wind. With some difficulty, we set up our as-yet-unused, new car camping tent at the campground closest to the race start. Given the state of the weather, I wasn't surprised we were the only ones there.

While Geoff organized his race gear, I sat in the tent and warmed up leftover pasta for a late-night second dinner. As he ate, he detailed exactly what gear he wanted at exact checkpoints, the time range he expected to reach those checkpoints in, and what kind of schedule I would need to keep in order to drive my car around and reach them in time.

"How do you want me to get you the stuff?" I asked.

"Just hand it to me," he said.

"So, you want me to stand at the checkpoint with stuff in my hand and wait for you for an indefinite amount of time?" I asked.

"Um, yeah," he said, as though that part of my support duties made perfect sense. Hard rain was pelting on the tent. It was as near freezing as San Francisco ever gets. I envisioned an entire next day standing out in the cold dampness, waiting for the five seconds he needed me to hand him a bundle of race crap.

He pointed to a single checkpoint and said, "I won't need you between these miles — just at this checkpoint both times I come through. There will probably be, I don't know, about four hours between them. You can either wait there, head back to town for a couple hours, go for a bike ride, whatever you want to do. Just be there in four hours or less."

"Okay," I nodded. I had to devote an entire day, but his requests didn't seem that complicated. Maybe it wouldn't be so bad.

Geoff's cell phone alarm went off at 4:45 a.m. We rolled out of bed and he pulled on his shorts and shirt, and rain gear over that. "I'm going to hand all this stuff to you just before the race starts," he said. "But I'd rather not freeze, so if you could stick with me right up until the race actually starts, that would be great."

"Oh yeah," I said. "I want to see the start."

"Then come back here and take down the tent," Geoff said. "You might have to hurry, because I'll probably be at the first checkpoint within an hour."

The rain had diminished to an icy drizzle by the time we reached the race start. Hundreds of people milled around in the morning darkness. Shorts-clad racers did jumping jacks to stay warm. Large men bundled in down coats kissed their runner wives. I stood as a placeholder in the long line for the men's bathroom while Geoff collected his number and registration packet, then handed him a banana and a couple packets of Gu. I followed him with one hundred or so other runners to the starting line. As the race director counted down from ten, Geoff quickly stripped off his rain gear and shoved it in my arms.

"See you in an hour," he said tersely. "Remember it's the vest this time, then the stuff in the drop bag the next time."

"Um, good luck," I mumbled, but he was already sprinting into a rush of headlamps as they bounded into the foggy morning.

Daylight broke, bringing with it a thick shroud of blue fog. I stood at the first checkpoint with Geoff's hydration vest in my arms, and included a dry bag full of warm clothing because it was still in the low forties and raining, and I expected him to be soaked and cold. After about fifteen minutes, he bounded down the hill in first position and grabbed the vest out of my arms, not even breaking his stride as he discarded his used Gu packets and water bottles in a trail of debris.

"You cold?" I called out.

"I'm fine," he yelled back, and continued running past the checkpoint station as a pack of five other runners followed close on his heels.

The next checkpoint was a long way around. I stopped for coffee and inched my car up the switchbacks on the narrow, shrouded road. The fog was still thick enough to prevent me from even seeing road signs ten feet away, and I was terrified that I was going to plunge off a cliff, one thousand feet into the sea. That was, if I was even on the west side of the headlands. I wasn't sure any more. I reached the checkpoint, grabbed the latest bundle and stood outside, chatting with other forlorn-looking race wives who clutched running gear and shivered in the cold rain. I waited nearly a half hour before Geoff blasted through, showering me with more discarded items and yelling that he needed the vest refilled with water and drink mix for his next time through that same checkpoint.

"Still four hours?" I called out.

"Yeah, probably," he yelled back.

I crawled back into my car and started the ignition to warm up. I started to pull on my own athletic gear — thick polar fleece leggings and jacket beneath heavy-duty rain gear. I figured I could get in about three hours of riding before I had to be back to attend to Geoff's needs. It was a horrible day for a ride — all discomfort and no views — but I figured I had been fairly lazy in San Francisco and I could use the training miles.

As I strapped on my helmet and moved to open the door, I noticed Geoff's cell phone wedged in the side pocket. I eyed it with intrigue and revulsion, both for what I knew was in that phone and for what I was badly tempted to do. I felt a tinge of shame, masked by my growing well of blind jealousy. I found my hand reaching for it with the guilty thrill of a child reaching into a cookie jar. I flipped it open and started shuffling through the text messages. Geoff had deleted his incoming messages, but his outbox was full of more than fifty, all directed to Misty.

"I miss u so bad."

"Really wish u were here."

"Lots of driving, not fun. Cant wait to c u in idaho."

Blood drained away from my face and rushed into my brain. As much as already knew exactly what I was going to find, it was so much more difficult to see it in bold, black print. Before, in our silences, I could allow myself to read signals the way I wanted to read them. The signals displayed on Geoff's cell phone left no mixed messages. And what did he mean about

Idaho? Then I remembered. There was another race near the end of May in Idaho. He had told me that he was marginally interested in running it. Now I could see that not only was he actually planning on running it, but also was planning to meet Misty there. This clarified that Geoff had no intention of spending a month in Teasdale with me or driving to the start of the Great Divide race. This explained why the timing of my race had been so inconvenient for him. From this perspective, we were a dead relationship on wheels. He probably couldn't wait to slough off the baggage and start his new life.

All the brave acceptance of reality I had mustered during the past two weeks could no longer cut through my devastation. Geoff and I really were over. He had already moved on. I knew where that left me — standing alone in the foggy rain, clutching the debris of our spent relationship. And I had followed Geoff along three thousand miles of lonely road just to land in this spot. I had embraced him when he reached out to me and I had taken down his campsite in the morning and I had held his stuff in the cold as he sprinted past without even looking me in the eye.

Tears returned to my eyes and I fought them back. I flung open the car door and pulled my bike down from the roof rack. I threw my leg over the saddle and stormed across the parking lot. A race official waved me down. "No bikes on the trail!" he yelled. I regarded him with a deadly glare. "Fuck you," I seethed. "I'm going to the fire road, not the trail. At least let me out of the parking lot before you yell at me." It was possibly the first time in my life I had openly cursed at a stranger. I felt no remorse.

I mashed the pedals up the muddy fire road. The fog quickly swallowed the parking lot scene, muffling the hum of generators and chatting race volunteers. Within seconds I thought I could hear the lapping of waves on the shoreline, but it could have just been the flow of fog so thick that was close to liquid. Anyway, the ocean was probably more than fifteen hundred feet below. But I fixated on the ocean sounds as my heart pounded like a pressure cooker. I pedaled with every ounce of strength in my legs, and still a strengthening hate boiled inside my core.

I fought to keep my heart rate near maximum capacity, in a place of dull darkness where thoughts only register in muffles and screams. Cloudy emotional pain could not enter this cave of intense but pure physical suffering. My vision began to blur. I didn't know if it was fatigue or tears or the fog. It only made me pedal harder. The fire road rounded a sharp corner and began to drop steeply. The soft silhouettes of trees and brush blended into blurry shadows as I gained velocity. The road dipped into an opaque gray void. I hoped it would pull me all the way to the sea. I didn't care if I was gone for three hours or three days. Geoff didn't need me — not in life, and not in this race.

Although I couldn't see the odometer amid the blur, I would later discover that it topped out at thirty-three miles per hour. That's how fast I was likely moving when the front wheel skidded across a mostly buried metal pipe that cut diagonally across the width of the fire road. It was the same color as the dirt, coated with rain, and I didn't see it until that last heart-stopping second when I noticed my front wheel connecting with slick steel. The wheel skidded down the length of the pipe and launched skyward like a snowboarder dismounting a rail. Then, as though the back wheel were an edge suddenly caught in a groove, the bike went from thirty-three miles per hour to a dead stop in a fraction of a second, slamming me into the gravel with a deafening thud. My right arm hit first, followed by my face. My rain pants and fleece tore as I skidded down the fire road for more than ten feet before coming to a stop. My bike landed a good distance from my body, twisted sideways with the wheels still spinning in a suddenly still air.

I lay paralyzed with shock for several seconds. As my eyes blinked involuntarily against the pelting rain, I held my hand to my helmet and slowly pulled myself to my knees. My right arm throbbed with sharp streaks of pain. I could see blood seeping from a hole ripped in the arm of my jacket. I was too scared of what I might find to roll up the sleeve and look any closer. I stood up and staggered toward my bike. The pain in my arm rushed to my head and forced me to kneel back down on the gravel again. I was convinced my arm was fractured. There could be no other explanation for such blunt and intense pain.

Amid the electric streaks of pain rose a new sort of agony. It was distant at first, a quiet hum in the back of my mind. But like a long-falling nuclear bomb finally connecting with the ground, it exploded in a cacophony of emotion so overwhelming, and a darkness so complete, that I heard nothing, saw nothing, knew nothing but pain. The pain was almost merciful in its totality, long festering beneath a hard shell only to finally be detonated by the fuse of a bike crash. My possibly broken arm, the road rash on my face and legs ... these things were just fleeting, unimportant, consumed by an abstract mushroom cloud of despair. It was the pain of loss, and like a nuclear explosion, it swallowed everything.

Still on my knees, I shuffled off the road and slunk beneath the low branches of a bush. I lay on my side and pulled my knees to my chin. There was nothing I could do but absorb the fallout. I clutched the arm I still believed to be broken and sobbed. My tears had no trigger or destination. They were just darkness settling, like ashes to a scorched Earth. Geoff didn't love me. Possibly, he never loved me. Possibly, I wasn't capable of being loved. But either way, I was alone in a dark, cold world, and I had no one I could rely on except for myself. The tragedy was that I wasn't reliable. I was a broken person.

Long minutes trickled away as I sobbed beneath the bush. Slowly I started to return to self-awareness. I wiped away thick streams of snot with my good arm. The throbbing in my left arm had diminished slightly and I had started to doubt that the injury was as severe as I initially thought. My bike was still strewn across the middle of the road. Someone else might come along and see it lying there, and try to help me. Or maybe no one would come along. I didn't really care either way. They could let me lay here a few minutes longer.

As soon as my sobs finally dissipated, I listened for the ocean. I could no longer hear the imaginary waves. My body remained in the fetal position and I wondered if I would ever find the courage or strength to crawl out from under that bush. Footsteps approached. I slithered out from under the branches and shuffled on my knees back to the road. A group of three cyclists were walking their bikes up the steep gravel. I had tossed my helmet aside earlier, and the bike was still in its original twisted position.

"You OK?" one cyclist asked me as he approached me.

"Yeah, I'll be fine," I said hoarsely. I was sure my eyes were bloodshot, and my skin blotchy and red. "I crashed my bike on that pipe over there. I'm still trying to collect myself but I don't think I'm injured."

"You need us to send back help?" he asked.

"No," I said. "I was just at Pantoll about twenty minutes ago. It can't be a long ride back to there."

"I think it's about six miles, probably mostly uphill," he said. "You sure you're okay?"

"Yeah," I said. "Just give me a second. I'll be right behind you guys."

They left me alone and I slowly rolled up the sleeve of my injured arm. Long cuts sliced into my skin, and surrounding them was a large bruise already turning a dark shade of purple, but I couldn't see any signs of a fracture. As I grabbed my overturned bike, the streaks of pain immediately returned. I righted the bike with my good arm and tried to grab the handlebars again, but even gripping the bars hurt my left arm more than I could stand. There was no way could I ride terrain like this, uphill, one-handed, and risk falling again on my injured arm. I resigned myself to the fact I would likely have to walk six miles back to the parking lot.

For the next two hours, rain fell hard, fog swirled around, my arm throbbed, and I filled the remaining space with self-loathing. How could I have been so stupid? So blind? What made me think I could ever ride a mountain bike? What made me think I could make this disaster of a trip work? When I finally reached the parking lot, I was drenched to the skin, and shivering so uncontrollably that every movement returned pain to my bruised arm. As I wheeled the bike to my car, I saw Geoff approaching from the race tents. In my single-minded march through the rain, I had genuinely forgotten why I was even out there in the first place. Seeing Geoff made me realize I was probably late for my race duties. He was going to be pissed that I missed his run-through. I didn't really care. For once he could be angry at me. Anger would be a welcome relief from his cruel indifference. But as he got closer, I saw his skin was pale, his eyes bloodshot and his face twisted into a miserable scowl. That wasn't the face of anger — it was the face of disappointment.

"I'm sorry," I mumbled feebly. "Sorry I missed you. I went out for a ride and I crashed my bike. Bike's fine but my arm's screwed up. I've been walking for six miles."

"Doesn't matter," Geoff said. "My race is over."

I propped the bike against my car and clutched my arm. I wanted him to notice that I was really hurt, but he wasn't even looking directly at me. He was glancing back at the race tents, probably watching for someone else to come through. "What happened?" I asked.

"I don't know," he exhaled loudly. "I really have no idea. Things were going great. I was running well. I was feeling strong, holding first place, and then my stomach turned on me. I threw up like five times out on the trail. I couldn't keep any food down. I'd try to eat something and I'd throw up again. And I just felt worse and worse and weaker and weaker. I came to that last checkpoint and I knew I was done. I caught a ride back to here, so I'm early anyway."

"You just tossed it in like that?" I asked. "Weren't you still in first place?"

"I maybe could've walked to the finish. But I wasn't going to place in the top three, not even in the top ten at that point. The only reason to run this race was to get in the top three so I could get into Western States, and it wasn't going to happen."

"So what do you want to do now?" I asked.

"Now, I just want to sit in the car and warm up. Then I want to change my clothes. Then we can go home."

"And then?" I started to ask, but he was no longer listening to me. He took the keys I had just fished out of my pocket from my outstretched hand and ducked into the car to start the engine. I watched him through the window. Even through streaks of rain I could see the frustration etched in his face. I had the strong feeling that this would be the last time I would ever see Geoff through old eyes, because no matter how many times I saw him after this point, he would never look the same. This was the real break up, the final moment of truth. The one thing both of us needed more than anything in the world was someone to comfort us in our pain, and that was the one thing we couldn't give each other.

Chapter Six
The Kokopelli Trail

Page 71: Jill Homer's Surly Karate Monkey, loaded for overnight camping, stands on the Kokopelli Trail near Fruita, Colorado.
Page 72: The thin ribbon of the White Rim Trail stretches across a wide desert plateau in Canyonlands National Park, Utah.

Beyond a fortress of sandstone pinnacles, sunbeams stabbed through dark clouds. "God light," my grandmother used to call sunbeams, because they projected peace even as the sky threatened storms.

I turned down the volume on the car stereo and listened for thunder. Interstate 70 cut a razor-straight line through the desert, which was further divided by gold steaks of light and sweeping shadows. Through the open window I could smell subtle hints of sage, and tar.

It had been a week since I left Geoff in San Francisco and drove in a single, angst-ridden, twelve-hour Interstate marathon to my parents' house in Salt Lake City. I walked through the front door in tears, leaking more resignation and disappointment than anger. My mom and dad greeted me compassionately but quietly wondered what my next step would be. Surely not the Great Divide thing? And although I acknowledged that there were hundreds of more important things I could be doing, I had no idea what they were, and for now I intended to stay the course.

"First," I said, "I need to see if I even have a long trip in me."

I spent my first few days at home browsing my Utah maps. I stared blankly at the curving lines and red streaks that represented mountains and trails, failing to make any real sense of the abstraction. Since I couldn't concentrate long enough to even determine simple mileage breakdowns, I decided planning my own route was out of the question. I settled on a three-day connection of two well-worn mountain bike routes in the desert, the 140-mile Kokopelli Trail linking Fruita, Colorado, and Moab, Utah, followed by the 100-mile White Rim loop in Canyonlands National Park. The beauty of the Kokopelli Trail was that it was marked with reflective trail signs, so I didn't even need to pay attention to a map. I could just mindlessly follow the markers to my destination.

The established nature of the route made my parents feel more at ease about me striking out alone, but it made me feel complacent. I packed up my bike bags with the bare essentials as I saw them — one change of clothing, light rain gear, a down sleeping bag rated to thirty-two degrees, a light air mattress, a bivy sack, tools, medicine, granola bars, sunflower seeds, chocolate, a sixteen-ounce plastic jar of peanut butter, and a six-liter bladder full of water.

The desert drive to Fruita was unspeakably lonely. I had driven back from San Francisco with my friend, Jen, in the passenger's seat, and had spent most of the following days with family and friends, taking only the occasional break from companionship to go for a training ride. This was the first time since I left Alaska that I had been completely alone.

I arrived at the Kokopelli trailhead well after dark. With the car still idling, I flicked off the headlights and let my eyes focus on the ominous silhouettes of sandstone cliffs, eerily backlit by the moon. Trickling down my throat was that same layer of vague doom that always seemed to build before I started anything big. I took my bike down from the roof rack and started putting the pieces together. I figured I could get a few miles behind me and sleep near the trail before the hot sun came up. I tested the shifters and lubed the chain, then tested the brakes. As I spun the front wheel, it made a disheartening "clink, clink, clink" sound. I grabbed the rim and ran my hand along the spokes until I connected with the loose one. It was nearly broken off.

"Damn it!" I yelled, and stood up, pacing around my car. Why didn't I check over my bike before I left Salt Lake? I certainly couldn't start a three-hundred-mile mountain bike tour with a broken spoke. That was only asking for wheel failure and the possibility of becoming stranded in the middle of the desert. But it seemed just as idiotic to admit defeat right there. If I didn't even start my first overnight test run, I might as well scrap the entire Great Divide right there.

As I mulled my options, I remembered my friend, Dave, telling me about a bike shop he had worked at in Fruita, about five miles down the road. Despite my resolve to start early and spend as little money as possible, I decided to rent a hotel room in Fruita and visit the bike shop in the morning. The thought of actually interacting with humans before I hit the long and lonely trail made me feel more at ease.

The next morning, the bike mechanic in Fruita had me in and out the door in less than ten minutes, gripping a freshly trued wheel as I walked into the blazing sunlight. The temperature neared 85, more heat than I had been exposed to in nearly a year, and promised to become hotter. I drove back to the trailhead and reconfigured my bike. Between sleeping in at the hotel, breakfast, and the bike shop, it was already nearly 11 a.m. I had hoped to start twelve hours earlier, but I didn't fret about the late start. I could still ride the route in three days, no problem. It was only 240 miles plus a thirty-mile road connector.

I had everything mounted on my bicycle, my car locked, and my butt on the saddle, seconds away from launching into the sweltering desert, when my cell phone rang.

"Hey Jill. Do you have a minute to talk?" Geoff asked.

"I guess," I said. "I'm in Fruita right now. I'm about to go for a bike tour on the Kokopelli Trail."

"That's cool," Geoff said. "That's a fun ride. I think you're really going to enjoy it. I'm still visiting my family in New York. But I wanted to call to talk about our stuff."

"What stuff?"

"Everything in your car," Geoff said. "What we're going to do with it — I'm going to need some of that stuff when I go back to Juneau."

"Well, you're either going to have to wait or come here and deal with it," I said. "Because I'm not going back to Juneau until July, at least, if at all."

"I'm flying back to Salt Lake tomorrow," Geoff said. "For a little while. But since I'm not getting into Western States, I'm probably not going to stay down there long."

"That's fine," I said. "You can stop by my parents' house. I left a lot of stuff there. The rest is in my car, which is going to be parked for the next few days at the Kokopelli trailhead outside of Fruita."

"Good," Geoff said. "I was talking to Jen about taking a trip to Moab. Maybe we can swing out there and grab stuff out of your car."

"Actually, if you're going to do that, maybe you could just drive my car to Moab," I said. "I'm going to need it in town when I'm done."

"That could work," Geoff said. He paused, and I let the silence ferment. It was the first time Geoff and I had spoken since San Francisco, and I didn't quite feel comfortable yet dealing with him directly, even if it was only through formalities and logistics. There was still so much anger and hurt flapping out in the open. But the truth was, we were still connected in more tangible ways, ways that involved camping gear and clothing, and the quicker we could break those strained ties, the more likely we'd grow more comfortable with the distance.

"Well, I'll leave the key on top of the front wheel," I said. "If my car's in Moab when I get there, great. If not, just leave a message on my phone letting me know you couldn't pick it up and I'll hitchhike."

"Okay," Geoff said. "Either way, I think we'll be able to help you get back. When do you think you'll be done?"

"Um, Thursday," I said. "Three days from now. Hopefully. I'm getting a much later start today than I wanted to, so I guess we'll see."

"You're starting right now?" Geoff asked. "At noon?"

"I had bike trouble," I said. "Broken spoke. It's fixed now."

"Hmm," Geoff said.

"Yeah," I said. The fermented silence returned. I inhaled and exhaled long and slow, until I started to feel dizzy. Then Geoff said, "I am sorry. I'm sorry for everything."

"Well, I'm sorry, too," I said and breathed out. "There's probably more we need to figure out. But maybe later. I'm standing in direct sunlight. I'm roasting, and I really have to go."

"Okay. Talk to you later."

"Bye." I turned the phone completely off and stuffed it in my pocket. My bike seat felt warm even though I had spent the last ten minutes simply standing next to it. The noon sun bleached the sky white, and washed out the surrounding sandstone cliffs to a sickly pale orange. I placed my last foot on the pedal and started rolling down the gravel road. The road narrowed to a singletrack trail, turned east and started following a sandstone bench several dozen feet above the Colorado River.

The trail skirted the edge of the cliff, rolling over jagged boulders and plunging into sandy basins. One bad error would mean a quick trip to chocolate-covered river far below, and the exposure rattled me. I wasn't really a desert mountain biker, I was more of a snow rider — soft surfaces and softer falls. Desert trails meant hard rock and cactus and plunges off cliffs, and I was timid, out of practice and loaded with twenty-five extra pounds of weight. I hit a few rocks too far to one side and tipped. I pedaled slower. I ran up against a wall of boulders so I got off my bike and walked. I was two miles into the 140-mile Kokopelli Trail, and already struggling.

Singletrack closed in on my muddled mind, until my thoughts were nothing more than a tunnel filled with rocks and sand. I squinted away from the hard sun and focused solely on the washed-out trail. All of my capacity for hope was directed at maintaining my connection to to that thin thread of dirt. There was no future beyond the next obstacle, no pain beyond the muscle burn and searing heat. I forgot that there was a Geoff, or a Juneau Empire, or even an Alaska. The desert filled the newly emptied space with hard apathy and sweat-drenched suffering.

It took me nearly three hours to cover the first fourteen miles. If I really wanted to complete my ride in three days, I was going to have to ride at least seventy miles the first day, and it was already 3 p.m. I sucked on the hose of my water bladder as warm liquid sloshed around in my empty stomach. I tried to stuff down sunflower seeds but they tasted like sawdust, so I went for the chocolate, which was gooey and hot. The trail veered down a slope so steep that I had to balance my bike on my shoulder as I picked my way down a rocky outcropping. At the bottom, I crossed a trickling creek that, according to the small sheet of cues I had printed out, would be the last on-route water I'd see before I crossed the Colorado River at mile seventy. As the rust-colored stream gurgled by, I weighed the prospect of filtering water. The cues also mentioned that the creek was tainted with mining runoff, and could be contaminated with toxic metals. In Fruita, I had filled my large MSR bladder with six liters of water, enough to last two solid days in Alaska. The heavy weight pulling on my shoulders made it difficult to anticipate a water emergency in the first seventy miles.

The trail out of the creek gorge was just as steep, a strenuous climb under the full weight of my bike and gear that left my head spinning and my lungs gasping for hot, dry air. I glanced up the gorge and saw a distant sliver of Interstate 70. Trucks streamed effortlessly east and west, mere minutes from the place I left three hours earlier. I put the bike down and leaned into the sparse shade of the rocks. It wouldn't be too hard to just follow the stream up the gorge, climb onto the freeway bridge, and hitch a ride. I'd probably be back to Fruita in an hour. I couldn't think of any good reason why I should keep riding my bike in the desert. I certainly wasn't very good at it. It wasn't comfortable, or fun, or even purposeful. It was lonely, hot, and hard. And yet, my tired mind wouldn't let me accept the ease of quitting. My mind understood that deeper needs trumped temporary pain. That quitting the Kokopelli Trail probably meant quitting everything.

The trail turned in the opposite direction of the freeway and continued toward the Colorado River, now a distant line through the large, rolling plateau. The open desert seemed to swallow all sound. The shadows of towering buttes slowly devoured the sunlight. An ochre sunset stretched over the horizon, deepening to orange and then red. The summer evening descended the way it would in Alaska, yawning lazily across the sky as though darkness was reluctant to return. I pedaled south toward the growing darkness on an unbroken line of gravel. Velocity came effortlessly as the road dropped toward the river and the heat of the day finally released its suffocating grip. The sudden ease of movement reminded me that I should never quit short of a goal because things are always bound to get better — that is, of course, before they inevitably get worse.

I arrived at the Dewey footbridge across the Colorado River just before midnight, having pedaled for nearly twelve unstopping hours to cover seventy miles. On the first day alone, the Kokopelli Trail had crossed every level of difficulty, from technical rock to smooth gravel to sand so deep that my legs wobbled as I fought to push my bike forward. Streaks of dried salt clung to my face and arms. I had sucked the last drops of my water from my six-liter bladder more than an hour before, and I was already feeling desperately thirsty, though not painfully so. I dropped to my knees in a basin of gelatinous quicksand lining the riverbank and stretched the water filter hose into the cocoa-colored water. I grunted as I pumped the filter, straining to extract precious ounces of water from a prison of silt. I stuck the release hose directly into my mouth and let the slightly bitter water gush down my throat. I had known the enveloping comfort of warmth after deep cold before, but never before had I experienced the intense relief of water after deep thirst. If life had a taste, the muddy water of the Colorado River reflected it perfectly — cool and refreshing, infused with little bits of the world.

I pedaled another two miles up the road and laid out my bivy sack and sleeping bag beneath a juniper tree. The clarity of the nearly full moon revealed a startling pattern of craters and mountains. It was a cartoon moon, a moon out of a children's book, full of features and laughing. The sky was half white with stars, blazing from the deepest corners of the universe. I pulled a jar of peanut butter from my frame bag and dug two fingers in, relishing its smooth sweetness garnished with the salty flavor of my skin. I excavated nearly half the jar, and confirmed with satisfaction my consumption of a thousand calories. I ate dried cherries and a handful of pumpkin seeds for dessert and lay down with my face to the glittering sky, supremely satisfied with my solitude, my slowness, and the stark simplicity of life on a bike.

The sun woke me up at 7 a.m. The morning sky was still tinted with streaks of pink and purple, but dawn was rapidly disintegrating at a rate inversely proportional to the meandering twilight the night before. The air was sharp and cool. I felt slightly hung over, probably from spending many of the final hours of my ride dehydrated. I had no coffee to combat the feeling, only a few pieces of chocolate, which were dry and chalky from melting all day and nearly freezing all night. My peanut butter also bore no resemblance to the delicacy I had consumed the night before, but instead stuck tastelessly in my throat like a lump of caulk. I packed up my bike and flung my lead-weighted legs over the saddle, knowing the Colorado River crossing had been the low point on the trail, and there was no way out of my current situation except to climb.

But I could not have anticipated the climb that lay in front of me. It was straight up, several thousand vertical feet of grinding gravel and slipping in the sand. I cranked with all the energy peanut butter and a full night of sleep could give me, and still I struggled for four miles per hour, and then three. I slumped off the bike and walked, with the 8 a.m. sunlight already hot and bright enough to pierce exposed skin. The trail crested in a new climate zone, a place where pinion trees grew. A deer streaked across the road, looked back with what I swore was a bemused smile, and bounded down the road in the direction I was heading. It disappeared beneath a horizon line that looked like the edge of a waterfall. I squinted in disbelief because as far as I could see, that was still the road. As I approached it, the other side of the canyon came into view, so close it seemed almost possible to jump the gap. But the road instead plummeted into a narrow chasm down a series of dramatic switchbacks. I couldn't even tell where exactly the road went after the first bend, fifty feet in front of me. But the fifty feet I could see were the most disheartening of all — broken steps carved out of chunky slickrock, smeared with sand and studded with large boulders.

I throttled the brakes as I dropped over the first step, inching my way down a minefield of rocks and sand. I bashed my knee against a larger rock and swore loudly, cursing the four-wheel-drive maniacs who built this nightmare of a road. I also cursed myself for never, in all of my gusto to become an endurance cyclist, actually learning to ride a mountain bike. The bike screeched and halted and lunged over the hard drops, then screeched and halted again. I couldn't finesse my way over the boulders like an experienced technical rider, so I would simply ferry awkwardly around them, locking the brakes and piloting the bike through a semi-controlled crash. Downward progress was slower and more physically taxing than climbing. I was quickly running out of steam.

At the bottom of the canyon, the trail started rolling again, climbing and dropping steeply over smaller drainages. My progress was excruciatingly slow. By noon, nearly five hours after I had pulled myself out of my sleeping bag, I had covered twenty-three miles. I pushed my bike to the top of what felt like a near-vertical sandstone wall and rode the brakes to a shady spot at the bottom. I slathered more sunscreen on my skin and checked my water bladder. It was less than half full. I had chugged more than three liters of water in five hours, and there were no known reliable water sources before Moab, forty miles away. Less than five miles down the rugged jeep track, I was supposed to cross a paved road at a place called Onion Creek. I didn't know whether Onion Creek was actually a creek, if it was an alkaline creek, or if it was simply a name for another barren strip of desert. I did know I would need to get water there before continuing on to Moab. If I couldn't, riding all the way to Moab was out of the question. I would have to follow that road until I either found water or found my way out.

I sat dejected beneath the tree, stewing about the massive failure that my first big mountain bike trip was becoming, when I head a woman's voice say, "Jill? Is that you down there?"

I stood up and saw two figures walking around a cluster of trees. They were the first humans I had seen since just a few miles after I left Fruita, twenty-four hours before. I squinted until I recognized them — my friend Jen and her boyfriend, Mike.

"Jen!" I said in a voice that was startlingly hoarse. "What are you doing out here?"

"Mike and I came down here to go camping. Geoff said we might see you around here. He said you were on the Kokopelli Trail."

"Geoff's with you?" I asked.

"He's out for a run right now," Jen said. "Mike and I drove down here to look for Cottonwood Canyon, but this road is kind of sketchy for my truck. We thought we'd hike and check it out. What's the road look like beyond here?"

"It gets worse," I said. "A lot worse."

"Oh," Jen said. "That sucks. And how are you doing? You looked kind of tired under that tree."

"I'm running out of water," I said as I juggled my backpack. "Do you have any I could borrow?"

"Oh yeah, we have a lot," Jen said. She directed me to a jug in the back of her truck. I topped off my bladder, took a few large gulps and topped it off again. "Better?" Jen asked.

"Man, I'm having a hard time with all of this," I said. "I'm not used to how hot and dry it is, and this trail has been really tough so far. I'm starting to wonder if I should just call it good here."

"Well, if you want, Geoff's got your car just a few miles down the road. You could get it back if you want. He can ride home with us."

"Thanks," I said. "And thanks for the water. I'll probably see you guys again in Moab."

I shouldered my guiltily acquired water. This ride was becoming less self-supported and more difficult than I wanted it to be, and quitting at this point would have been easy. At the same time, I had no real reason to quit. As in physics, motion sought to prevail. I pedaled because pedaling was the most natural course of action.

I emerged into an open valley and joined the wide gravel road. My car was parked at a junction of another four-wheel-drive track. I intersected Geoff running just a few miles beyond that. He smiled as he approached. His sweat-drenched T-shirt hugged his thin body, and his quads bulged below his shorts. I felt a rush of attraction followed by loathing, and through this wide range of emotions washed a confusing sense of relief. I didn't know how to feel about Geoff. Our break in San Francisco had been anything but clean, and now he was here muddying it up even more. But the truth was, I needed to see him here. I needed to believe I wasn't completely alone.

"I thought we might see you here," he panted as he stopped next to me. "But then I assumed we missed you. I thought you'd be beyond here by now."

"This is going pretty slow for me," I said. "I can't believe you rode the Kokopelli Trail in a day last year. This thing is hard!"

"Eighteen hours," he corrected me. "But yeah, that Yellowjacket section is the most technical part you'll have to ride through."

"And it's all climbing from here," I lamented. "I know. I checked the elevation profiles."

"It's not so bad," Geoff said. He looked at his watch. "I bet you'll be to Moab before sunset."

"Maybe," I said. "But tomorrow I was going to ride the White Rim. That's thirty miles past Moab. I really wanted to do that paved part tonight so I could focus on the century tomorrow."

"Tell you what," Geoff said. "I'll meet you at the end of the trail. We'll camp there, and then tomorrow I'll take you to the White Rim trailhead."

"What about Jen and Mike?"

"They already have a site reserved, so they'll probably stay here," Geoff said. "But it's not a big deal. I have your car. I can meet back up with them tomorrow."

I bit my bottom lip. If I agreed to meet Geoff in Moab, at least that would mean not quitting at that spot. I had already blown my self-support rule, so catching a thirty-mile shuttle ride on the pavement wasn't a huge deal, and was probably the only thing that would make this whole ride even possible. Finally, agreeing to his plan would mean spending one more night with Geoff. As we both stood apart in the hot desert sun, drenched in sweat, the thought of making some kind of peace with each other seemed more important than any athletic goal.

We set up a meeting space and parted. I continued up the road, another backbreaking climb that seemed to flow easier than the first of the day. The gravel was still loose, the grade still steep, but my mind was more at ease with the pain — more resigned, maybe. I climbed to nearly 9,000 feet, where I could look toward the La Sal Mountain Range and see snow, although those cool distances couldn't provide real relief from the midday sun. Sandstone mesas and layered canyons rippled toward infinity, studded with green brush and broken only by the curving stroke of the Colorado River, so far below it almost looked blue.

I plummeted down the next canyon and climbed to yet another pine-choked plateau. My GPS unit registered nearly 12,000 feet of climbing over the course of seventy miles that day, nearly as much vertical space as Mount

Everest climbers cover between base camp and the highest summit in the world. The sun dipped behind the canyon-rippled horizon in yet another sweeping light display of crimson and gold. I had ten more miles to ride into Moab, nearly a vertical mile below me. It seemed like an excess of elevation to lose in that short of a distance, and I knew that worst of the day's riding could still be in front of me. I expected a white-knuckle rock garden. Instead, I found a steep but smooth gravel road plunging through the forest. The red glow of sunset lit the pinion trees on fire, brighter than the brightest sandstone cliff beside them. I coasted effortlessly as my odometer rose to nearly thirty miles per hour. Tears streamed from my eyes and joy poured through my veins. It was the simplest kind of joy, born of raw freedom, blocked from interpersonal clashes and washed with well-earned fatigue. It was joy free of analysis, free of consequence and free of guilt. It was the joy of being, the joy that all animals know, and the joy that self-aware humans only seem to find while propped up against the boundaries of fear and turmoil.

Cool purple twilight descended as the jagged canyon swallowed me whole. The ambient temperature climbed even as daylight disappeared. I coasted into the dull beam of my headlamp until I saw orange light dancing on the canyon wall. I approached a flickering campfire and found Geoff sitting on the picnic table beside it. He stood up and waved at me.

"I was just about thinking of going to look for you," he said. "I thought you'd be here a couple of hours ago."

"I thought I made good time," I said. "I told you it was going to be slow."

He opened a cooler on the table and pulled out a bottle of Diet Pepsi and a container of grocery store sushi. He handed them to me before I had even let go of my bike.

"I got these for you," he said. "I'll heat up some pasta for dinner, too, but I thought you might want a snack to eat before."

I clutched the appetizer that was nutritionally questionable but otherwise my most favorite comfort food in the world. I expressed enthusiastic gratitude, but inwardly I felt suspicious about possible ulterior motives for Geoff's kindness. It felt like a shallow peace offering, the kind you might make to a neighbor after accidentally burning their house down. "Sorry I ruined your life … brownie?"

"How was the ride?" Geoff asked as he fired up the propane stove.

"Fantastically beautiful," I said. "And hard. Did you realize there are

19,000 feet of climbing in those 140 miles? That's what my GPS says."

"That makes sense," Geoff said. "It was pretty tough when I rode it. But at least you had two days to finish."

"Yeah," I said. "Even if I pieced it together without sleep, that would still be … what, like twenty-four or twenty-five hours of continuous riding. Glad I didn't decide to race this thing. I'm actually pretty terrible at technical desert riding. How come you never warned me about that?"

Geoff shrugged. "I guess I didn't really get a chance. But you're going to encounter a lot more rough roads on the Divide, so you might as well get used to it."

"I'm still uncertain about the Divide," I said. "Now more than ever."

"You'll be great at it," Geoff said. "I know you will."

He smiled disarmingly, and I took a long swig of the Diet Pepsi. The cold carbonation burned as it tumbled down my throat. My head still throbbed from dehydration. My heart still raced from two long days of effort. I knew I needed sleep soon if I stood any chance of riding a full desert century the next day, but I also knew I didn't have a good chance of achieving sleep, wired and exhausted as I simultaneously was. I gobbled up my dinner, refilled my water bladder, drank the entire bottle of Pepsi and two quarts of Gatorade, and lay down in the tent next to Geoff.

I looked up at the tall nylon ceiling, flapping in the night breeze. It was only my second night in the large tent, the one we purchased together to serve as our home away from home over the long summer. That was in late March, well into our trip planning. Did Geoff know then that he was going to break up with me?

I listened to my restless heart pound as the silence swirled. After what seemed like hours Geoff asked me if I was "okay with things."

"Yeah," I said. "I don't have much of a choice, at this point."

"Good," Geoff said. "Because you still mean a lot to me. I want things to be good between us."

I felt strong affection for Geoff, and I tried to fight it. The words that passed between us were going to be mostly meaningless at this point, because they wouldn't do much more than assuage his guilt and massage my ego. I was too tired to argue, too resigned to question. I just wanted to sleep beside him for one more night and pretend the big tent still had room for both of us, in a world where two people really could find complete fulfillment in partnership and didn't have to troll the lonely desert in search of something more. Everything Geoff said only confirmed this delusion wasn't true, but after two days of solitude, there was something soothing about simply listening to the sound of his voice. We talked until 2 a.m., about running and Juneau, about the Great Divide and the blank slate of the future, until my heart slowed down and I drifted in and out of consciousness. Geoff said good night and I dropped immediately into a hard, dreamless sleep.

The next morning, Geoff dropped me off at the top of the White Rim, a wide plateau that covered the heights of a region known as Island in the Sky. I dropped down the steep, rocky gravel road and pedaled hard along the rolling sandstone shelf that rose more than a thousand feet from the Colorado River. Towering pinnacles cast long shadows over the red sand, which was dotted with salt brush and yellow sprigs of rice grass. I felt significantly stronger than I had on either the first or second morning of the trip, the result of a couple gallons of liquid and a successful straddle over my typical day-two hump. My theory about long-distance cycling was that it only took two days to get over the worst of the mental and physical fatigue, and then pedaling became second nature for an indefinite number of days after that. I could only hope that my theory was true.

Still, on day three of my desert tour, miles had never come more easily. The hard sun throbbed in a cloudless sky and temperatures climbed into the eighties, and then low nineties. But I was surrounded in the cool breeze of my own swift movement. Sweat streamed down my skin. The day seemed like it had hardly begun when I reached mile fifty. The trail made a series of slow climbs that culminated in a pinnacle-cresting monster of a climb called Murphy's Hogback. I dismounted my bike and walked up — no need to kill myself — and greeted a group of vehicle-supported, multi-day touring cyclists at the top. Despite that fact that it was mid-May and this was one of the more popular distance rides near Moab, the group was only the second I had seen all day. Six or seven mountain bikers crowded around the bed of a white truck as the driver sat next to a clear five-gallon jug of water and doled out refilled bottles. The jug looked nearly empty — only a thin layer of liquid sloshed around the bottom as he poured — and I didn't see any other provisions in the back of the truck. Maybe they had another vehicle further down or a nearby camp. Most cyclists take two or three days to ride the White Rim, with vehicle support, and they camp along the way. But as I passed the group, they regarded me indifferently, their eyes glazed with fatigue and their faces coated in white salt. I wondered if they were truly that low on water, but they had that truck, which could certainly head up the canyon and fetch more for them. I didn't have anything I could offer them, so it didn't feel right asking them if they had any to spare.

I said hello and goodbye and dropped down the Hogback, toward another open, shadeless plateau. It was just after 1 p.m., and I was proud of the time I was making — fifty-three miles in four hours. At this rate, I'd complete the loop before dark. I had been slightly concerned that six liters of water wasn't going to be enough, but confident enough in my supply and sure enough about the limited water on the route that I left my filter with Geoff. Which is why I was beyond shocked when hollow slurping sound rang through my water tube, indicating there was nothing left in the bladder.

I stopped and opened up my pack, removing the shriveled red bladder from its pocket with a sinking feeling of dread. What happened? Did it spring a leak? I would have felt the water running down my back. Did I really burn through six liters of liquid in fifty miles? What about the next fifty? I knew the trail dropped down to the Green River eventually, but that was at least twenty miles away. And everything before that was just open, barren plateau, where even puddles of urine only wet the sand for a few short minutes before disappearing.

Sweat evaporated from my skin as I stood in the sun. I felt dizzy. Far below, the Colorado River churned toward its nearby confluence with the Green. As a bird flies, the greatest river in the West was less than two miles away. But the sheer cliffs dividing the river from the plateau made it seem as far away as Alaska.

I pedaled a few more miles, feeling increasingly more distressed. Dark blotches began to cloud my vision, and a thick, salty film formed around my lips. I stopped frequently to try to assess whether or not I was about to pass out, but I genuinely could not tell. I had no knowledge of desert thirst. I had been an Alaska cyclist for too long, too concerned with warding off hypothermia to pay attention to dehydration. But I did know that my strength was flagging, that I felt weaker and more helpless than I had during my mental collapse on the foggy hills of the Marin Headlands, and that I was still a daunting distance from the only thing I truly needed — water.

I stopped near a shallow rock outcropping and crouched beside the hot sandstone. In the afternoon sun it provided just a strip of shade, not even large enough to reach my legs or tall enough to cover my head. It was the only shade for miles. Everything else was barren, open and blazing beneath waves of heat-condensed air. I tried to force down some gummy bears and pumpkin seeds, hoping that the sugar and electrolytes would somehow bring me back to balance. I wondered if I should crouch in this spot until nightfall, and seek out the river when the relentless sun had faded. But shade was nearly nonexistent, and I knew that spending more hours in the hot sun would only hurt my chances.

For the first time in the trip, I felt truly scared. I was in completely unknown territory, a place where heat kills much more swiftly than extreme cold. The heat wasn't too extreme — my thermometer indicated 94 degrees — but it was more than I had experienced in well over a year, and I was in direct sunlight, atop pale, heat-reflecting sand, without water. I knew the details didn't really matter. My only choice was to continue moving. I might meet another group of touring cyclists along the way, or campers willing to share with me. I might not. But, either way, I had to find water.

The trail dropped slowly off the plateau, so gradually that I still felt like I was pedaling uphill. The smooth surface of the Green River snaked below, taunting me with obsessions about ice-cold quarts of Gatorade and Coke-flavored Slurpees. After nearly three hours of increasingly slower mileage readings on my odometer, I reached the Green River basin, still out of sight of water. I continued along the road, wondering if I should leave the bike and walk directly toward the river. But the late afternoon sun had dipped low enough to be hidden behind the massive canyon walls, and in the shade I felt a renewed sense of confidence.

The road eventually butted up against the river, which was still below a steep embankment. The loose, sandy slope seemed slightly dangerous; the frothing river looked like dirty dishwater that hadn't been drained for days. I was desperate, but that was disgusting. I pulled out the complimentary map given to me by Canyonlands rangers and saw that there was a primitive campground not more than three miles away. Perhaps someone there would be able to give me clean water. And, if not, the road was never more than a short distance from the river.

A mile later, the sandy road began to climb again. My throat had withered beyond simply being dry to a hard, almost solid mass that made it difficult to swallow my own saliva, of which I didn't have much left. The effort of climbing made my vision go dark, but I reasoned that it could only be a short hump because the road, as the nearly featureless map indicated, was supposed to follow the river.

But the route continued to climb. I pedaled until I swooned, actually slumping sideways on my bike and jerking my body in the other direction just in time to stop myself from toppling over. I laughed because I was too tired to feel fear, but I was conscientious enough to realize that I was in bad shape. I slid off the bike and staggered up the road, taking slow, curving steps like a drunk driver trying to walk a straight line. My personal policeman was the bad decision I had made to ride away from the river without collecting water, my drunkenness the dehydration that had worked its way into my blood.

I topped out on a narrow ledge five-hundred feet above the river, and saw with overwhelming relief that the road dropped quickly back to the dark brown line that mocked me far below. Although I felt too drunk to ride, I couldn't help but coast as quickly as gravity would carry me to the bottom. I pushed my bike through a tangle of tamarisk, propped it against a cottonwood tree over a small clearing, and started stripping off all my clothing. The Green River was known to be polluted with a number of parasites. I didn't want to become too eager while I waited for my iodine tablets to kick in, so I planned to soak my body in the cool water for the entire half hour I was supposed to wait. I was certain I couldn't ride another meter until I had liquid in my cells, so waiting seemed to be my only option. I walked naked to the silt-choked shoreline, where I sank to my knees in quicksand. I grabbed a tamarisk branch and yanked myself out, only to sink in even deeper with my other leg. The chocolate-colored water lapped alongside me, and I could see no way to drop into it without becoming treacherously stuck in mud. Defeated, I crawled back onto the more solid, sandy part of the bank, gripped a tamarisk branch to support my outstretched body, and reached my bladder as far as I could into the putrid water. I collected three liters, dropped in my iodine tablets in and continued down the bank, looking for a solid entrance.

That's when the mosquitoes found me. At first, I just felt pinpricks on my bare butt, and then the stinging sensation moved up my back. As I looked behind me, I noticed a large cluster of black insects latched onto my shoulders. I yelped and tore into the tamarisk, unconcerned about the sharp branches scratching my skin as I slapped at my back. I sprinted back to my bike and pulled on my shorts and jersey, grabbed my toxic bug repellent, and sprayed every square inch of exposed skin, which was at that point coated in either the foul quicksand of the river bank or a gritty film of sand and sweat. I had never felt so disgusting or dirty, and I wanted nothing more than to jump in the river and swim upstream as long as I could, maybe until I reached the road junction or even the town of Green River, more than a hundred miles away. Even if both were impossible, I never wanted to leave the river. But there was no way to even enter it.

I pushed through the tamarisk to retrieve my bladder, grabbed my bike, and continued toward a raft-launching point called Mineral Bottom. A steep series of switchbacks carved into the side of a thousand-foot-high canyon wall. As I climbed, I stopped often to look at my watch. It seemed like seconds were moving as minutes, and minutes as hours.

When a half hour finally passed, I stopped beside the narrow ledge of the road and sucked greedily at my bladder. A thick, silty liquid filled my throat — cool and bitter and more than slightly foul. I gagged, took a deep breath, and sucked at the bladder again. The water was sickening but I needed it. Despite my revulsion, coolness began to return to my light head, and I felt more grounded than I had since early afternoon.

I reached the plateau and continued the long, infuriatingly gradual climb to the paved road, where Geoff had promised to meet me at a nearby campground. Clouds obscured the horizon, and a muted sunset slipped somewhat imperceptibly into twilight. I continued to force muddy water down my throat. The grit coated my teeth and I couldn't stomach the thought of eating. My energy was flagging fast and I felt a strong urge to roll out my bivy on the slickrock and sleep, but I knew that if I did, Geoff would come looking for me. And, anyway, the one thing I could think of that sounded more appealing than sleep was a shower, and I certainly wasn't going to find one of those on this desert Island in the Sky.

Soon I was simply following the yellow orb of my headlamp, a small oasis of light in a sea of night. The sky had become overcast. There were no stars, no distant town lights, just seemingly infinite black space that my headlamp did little to diminish. Logic dictated that the road had to go somewhere eventually, but I continued to pedal for what felt like hours, going nowhere.

And yet, despite my fatigue and hunger and the horrific state of my hygiene, the farther I pedaled into the darkness, the more I felt connected with the space outside my body. Some philosophers have speculated that if you could peer inside of the particles that make up an atom, you would find small particles surrounded by empty space, and if you looked inside of those particles, you would find even smaller particles surrounded by yet more empty space, on and on into infinity. Therefore, the world and everything in it was nothing more than infinitely smaller particles of energy and empty space. Substance was an illusion, a construct of perception from a vast distance. That theory had never made more sense to me than it did that night. The hardness of the world had stripped my needs down the barest of essentials. I emerged in the darkness with understanding that, for all of the convention we inject to fill the remaining space, those throbbing particles of energy really are all we have, and all we are.

Chapter Seven
Indecision

Page 89: A narrow trail threads through the Stansbury Mountains of northwestern Utah.

Page 90: The Pipeline Trail cuts a sharp line in the mountainside above Millcreek Canyon in Salt Lake City.

The next three weeks slid away beneath the edge of sharp focus. After his trip to Moab, Geoff promptly left Utah for Alaska. Before we parted ways, he asked me whether I still planned to ride the Great Divide.

"Not likely," I told him, meaning it. "But I'm going to milk my time off for all it's worth."

And for the next three weeks, everything went into my bicycle — my time, my energy, my attention, my occasional bursts of joy, and my creeping angst. All of it siphoned from my body, flowing through the rotating pedals and filling the hollow steel frame until my bike was full of character and I was little more than a fatigued shell, albeit fit and vaguely content. As long as I could ride my bicycle, I didn't have to approach the gaping void of my uncertain future. And as long as I had the Great Divide — or at least the cover of Great Divide race training — I had no reason to leave my bicycle.

My routine was as focused as it was frivolous. I woke up in the morning, often late. I had breakfast alone in the spacious kitchen of my childhood home long after my mom, dad, and youngest sister had left for a day of real-world activities. I put on a jersey and shorts and went to the garage to sit next to my bicycle for a half hour or so, lubing the chain, fiddling with the brake pads, thumbing through Zinn and the Art of Mountain Bike Maintenance, and kidding myself into believing I was effectively learning trailside bike repair skills. Then I opened the garage door into the rich brightness of late morning in Salt Lake City in May. It was generally eighty or ninety degrees, prompting grumblings about the heat. I switched on my GPS; the elevation registered as 4,500 feet, prompting grumblings about the altitude. Then I sweat and struggled on my way up to 9,000 feet in Little Cottonwood Canyon. Some days I rode farther north to hit up singletrack in Millcreek Canyon. Sometimes I sought technical terrain on the maze of trails in Corner Canyon. Other days, I rode south to American Fork Canyon or west to the Oquirrh Mountains.

Everywhere was directly connected to the fresh-cut grass and rumbling traffic of the suburban Salt Lake Valley. But in my wanderings, I discovered surprising pockets of deep solitude that I never knew in twenty-five years of living just a short tangent from these wild places. There was Oquirrh Summit, reached by a steep gravel road that had been wash-boarded into teeth-chattering obscurity. It looked out over the gaping wound of the open-pit Kennecott Copper Mine, a stair-cut blight with no bottom and no soul. I found a rim trail in the Stansbury Mountains, dropping into canyons so lost, so quiet, that they seemed to wend back in time. Just a few miles south of my parents' home was Tibble Fork, a narrow canyon still clogged with snow in late May, where a hidden stream roared beneath the white crust. I became acutely aware that I was a small person in a big, mostly empty world. It made me wonder what it would be like to spend more than three weeks immersed in these lonely places by myself. Alone.

In the evenings, I returned home to tap out the logistics of a Divide ride. I had gear to buy, gear to test, transportation to plan. But there was also the matter of picking an event. In the summer of 2009, there were two organized races on the Great Divide Mountain Bike Route that followed the exact same course. Both applied a similar list of rules that demanded absolute route adherence and self-support. But that is where their similarities effectively ended.

The Great Divide Race was to start on June 19 at the border of Montana and Canada. There was no direct organization, no compiled start list, and no specific information on the Web site. It simply asked that participants show up at a certain time, in a particular place, and ride their bikes on the Great Divide Mountain Bike Route all the way to Mexico. On the way there, Great Divide Race (GDR) participants were strongly discouraged from riding with other racers, broadcasting their position to the outside world, or seeking visitation by friends and family, lest they be tempted to wander down a slippery slope of support that would detract from the solo, self-supported nature of the event. The race rules forbid cell phone use and mandated strict time cut-offs along the course.

The Tour Divide was to start in Banff, Alberta, about 270 miles north of the Great Divide Race start, on June 12. It had a well-publicized start list that was already numbering in the high thirties, and included two women. The race had a friendly, welcoming Web site that offered novice encouragement and advice. It allowed cell phone use and had no time cut-offs. Unlike the secrecy-cloaked Great Divide Race, the Tour Divide offered live online tracking and commentary.

Several of my endurance cycling acquaintances were already signed up for the Tour Divide. The advantages of that race were an opportunity for camaraderie, the earlier start date, the presence of friends, and the lack of time limits. And of course there was the cell phone rule. I hated to admit it to myself, but solitude scared me more than any other aspect of the Great Divide, and the idea of even a single, unreliable, mostly useless connection with the outside world was greatly comforting.

There was also the fact that Great Divide Race had been Geoff's race. He wrote off the Tour Divide as a softer — if longer — version of the original and had less respect for it. This made me want to enter the Tour Divide even more. It made me feel petty to admit it to myself, but I really needed something I could make my own. As the events trickled closer, I concluded the Tour Divide was the better race for me.

But whether to ride the Divide at all was the only decision that really mattered. I continued to invest heavily in the race. I studied maps. I purchased gear. I put in long days of training. But the more defined my leg muscles became, the more my conviction seemed to blur. Two weeks before the race start, I decided to conduct one last overnight test. I would go somewhere cold, high, and fairly remote. I would bring everything I planned to use in the race, and nothing more. I would ride long and late, camp, wake up early, and ride long and late again. And, most importantly, I would embrace my solitude, cycling into the deeper depressions of my thoughts that promised to haunt me on the long tour.

As I pored over my dog-eared and sun-faded book of Utah maps, my eyes kept stopping on the Uinta Mountains. The Uintas are Utah's highest mountain range, largely cloaked in wilderness areas, but there were a fair number of jeep roads and four-wheeler trails snaking around the Mirror Lake Highway. If there wasn't too much snow, I could climb as high as 11,000 feet. I decided on an overnight tour of about 200 to 250 miles on pavement and dirt, camping at high elevation.

I started my ride in the town of Heber much later than I planned. By the time I combed through the grocery store for candy, peanut butter, dried cherries, and a cheap pair of sunglasses, it was after noon. I veered onto the busy highway and pedaled into a light headwind. Traffic ebbed as the highway passed through increasingly smaller mountain towns.

The temperature dropped as the elevation increased. The cool air was a relief at first, but then slowly, almost imperceptibly, it crossed my discomfort threshold. As I climbed beside tall stands of pine trees, the weather started to deteriorate. Misting rain turned to harder rain, and then to sleet. I stopped to put on more layers and returned to grinding the pedals. I watched the elevation reading climb on my GPS — 8,004 feet ... 8,007 feet ... 8,012 feet. Pretty soon the sleet turned to large flakes of wind-driven snow. Although I prefer snow to cold rain, I eyed the accumulating dust with nervousness. My Divide gear amounted to a water-resistant but certainly not waterproof bivy sack, a thin air mattress and single down sleeping bag with a comfort rating of thirty-two degrees. It was likely already approaching that temperature, at four in the afternoon. If I climbed up to 11,000 feet and rode trails at the cusp of timberline, what kind of weather was I going to camp in? Snowing and twenty degrees? I wasn't properly equipped, and I had already passed the point where the road was still closed to vehicles, so I wasn't likely to see anybody else.

But, with the goal of education pulling me forward, I tried to push those doubts out of my mind. The snow tapered off as I climbed into the low clouds. Through the gray mist, I could see piles of last season's snow rising like a wall next to the road. Fresh gouges had been carved in the ice on the shoulder, indicating a snowplow had been through recently, even though the road was still closed. I wondered how far the snowplow had cleared the road, and how high I'd be able to climb.

Soon the clouds began to clear and I could see the snow-blanketed peaks of the high Uintas looming around me. My GPS indicated I was nearing 10,000 feet elevation. The roadside snow wall was nearly as high as my helmet, but the pavement remained mostly clear. The cold didn't seem any more intense than it had an hour before, but it also didn't feel any warmer.

I passed idle machinery, and then the icy road ended in a five-foot high wall of snow.

I had suspected that I would run into impassable snow before I reached my destination, and yet, once I was there, I remained steadfastly determined to keep moving forward without stopping. I lifted my bike onto the top of the snow wall and scrambled up to it. The surface of the crust was surprisingly solid for the last day of May, and it seemed strong enough support my wheels. I mounted the bike and pedaled as the tires dug into the snow. The cranks turned like they were clogged with rubber cement, but the bike lurched forward. I was in my lowest gear, pedaling as hard as my legs could push, and my forward motion registered about three or four miles per hour. The tire track I left behind was five inches deep, but I was pedaling. That fact alone made me feel satisfied with my progress. Although I understood the summit was ultimately out of my reach, I made the decision to continue that direction as far as my maxed-out legs would allow.

That distance turned out to be about five-hundred yards. I let my bike tip over into the snow as I coughed up the cold air and pressed my fingers to my neck, gauging a heart rate that was approaching 190. The elevation was 10,500 feet, as good as the sub-stratosphere for a person who had lived too long at sea level. I wheezed and gasped and smiled, because not once in that six-hour climb did I think about feeling lonely or frustrated. I felt tired, cold, and sometimes even scared — but those feelings were preferable to the disconnection and uncertainty I often wrestled with as I tossed in my warm bed at night. The climb had reduced me to simple needs, childlike wonder, and instinctual decisions. It was a difficult but undeniably pleasant way to live.

I struggled to push my bike back toward the pavement as I sank to my thighs in the snow. "This must look crazy," I thought, "Pushing a bike through unplowed snow in a random spot on the Mirror Lake Highway." Then again, all one has to do is shift their perspective to realize most actions can be viewed as crazy. It's crazy, I thought, that people spend their lives in pursuit of complications such as love and wealth when they could enjoy a simple life of moving and existing — possibly the true path to happiness.

Once I reached pavement again, I put on every last layer of clothing I had stored in my gear bags, then rocketed down the long, frigid descent. My self-adjusted brakes squealed horribly every time I squeezed the brake levers, so I let the bike fly free, much too fast to look down at my odometer, too fast to block my tears or wipe away what was becoming a steady stream of snot, too fast to even look around at the ever-blurring scenery as it changed from stark white and black, to misty gray, to the pale greens of early spring. I descended back to about 8,000 feet, and because it was still early in the day, veered off a side road I had picked out on my map and began the climb anew. What the map called a four-wheel-drive road was little more than parallel tracks through the mud, strewn with huge boulders and dotted down the center with spruce saplings that were already a couple of years old.

I worked on the technical climb for two more hours, until the sun slipped below the horizon and I returned to snowline. My toes, which had been throbbing under the pressure of my shoes for most of the day, suddenly released an electric shock of pain. I yelled out, hopped off my bike, took of my shoe and looked for damage. The toes looked normal. But as soon as the shoe went back on, the pain came back.

I repeated the steps with no improvement. My formerly frostbitten toes had remained extra sensitive to both cold and pressure, but this sensation mimicked the prickly pains of thawing all over again. I wondered briefly if I had possibly refrozen my toes, but they felt warm to the touch. The skin was soft and pink. I pressed hard on my big toe. Blood quickly flushed back into the capillaries after I released my thumb, a sure sign of circulation.

The only reason for the pain that I could surmise was my shoes. Shortly after I returned from Moab, I had acquired a proper pair of clipless bike pedals and matching shoes, because every known cycling expert and friend told me pedal connection and properly fitting shoes were crucial for long days of riding. Otherwise, they said, I risked knee injury, technical mistakes, or worst of all, lost power. I had been riding with my new shoes and pedals for three weeks with few problems, but my rides had never been longer than five or six hours. Even during those rides, I would start to feel uncomfortable pressure on my toes toward the end. This ride was approaching eight hours. A long day in the saddle had caused my feet to swell, resulting in unworkable discomfort in my sensitive, frostbite-damaged toes. It was a disheartening development.

I was still in the wilderness, however, and had no choice but to continue wearing the shoes and cope as well as I could. It was harder than I thought it would be. As I worked my way down the slow descent, I often had to stop and pull off the oppressive piece of plastic and leather just for a few seconds of relief. Walking around particularly large obstacles caused even more pain, and by the time I reached road level, I felt close to crippled, limping noticeably and swearing loudly every time I had to clip back into the pedal.

I had hoped to ride into the darkness for at least an hour or two, but the pain in my toes made every pedal stroke close to unbearable. Even a direct ride back to Heber was too daunting to think about, so I limped back up the jeep road a short distance and rolled out my bivy sack in a small clearing next to the abandoned road. I took off my shoes and collected firewood around camp wearing only my socks, not really caring if they got muddy and wet. I built a roaring kindling fire and huddled over it as a layer of frost started to form on my bivy sack and bike. Fifty-foot-tall spruce trees nearly blocked out the sky, but a narrow opening revealed a spectacular wash of stars.

The earlier storm had cleared. I remembered that I was camped in bear country, and I reluctantly put my shoes back to walk a few hundred feet up the road, where I ate a quiet, cold dinner of tuna fish, spoonfuls of peanut butter and Corn Nuts. Loneliness crept forward, but I couldn't be bothered with it. I had below-freezing temperatures to contend with, not to mention fatigue and bears, and a three-month-old case of frostbite that was proving to be a surprisingly difficult problem.

The next morning dawned with new warmth from the sun, rousing me from deep sleep. I blinked blankly at the treetops for several seconds before I remembered where I was. The frost on my gear had already melted to round droplets of water. I shook off my bivy sack and packed up quickly before eating my dried cherry and peanut butter breakfast over the snow-white remains of my campfire.

When there were no other chores to complete, I slipped my shoes back on. The pain in my toes wasn't quite as pronounced, but was definitely still there. It wasn't enough to demand a survival ride into Heber, so I proceeded with the day's plan. I traced several rocky jeep roads to their snow lines before turning around and traveling a few more miles down the main road. It was another long day on the pedals, and by the time I approached Heber, my toes were throbbing under the weight of more than two hundred miles of distance and 12,000 feet of climbing in a tour spanning less than thirty hours.

Most everything about the trip went well. My lungs handled the high elevation without too much protest, and my sleeping gear warded off the low temperatures without any discomfort. I had put in two back-to-back Divide-esque days without feeling too much fatigue. The food I ate gave me good energy and didn't cause gastrointestinal distress. My knees felt strong and my back and butt felt normal. I had even avoided the creeping loneliness that concerned me the most. But I had a new, surprisingly pressing concern — my frostbitten toes. Were they really unable to handle long days of pedaling? Toes seemed a silly thing to fret about, but I knew the level of pain I had experienced the night before was guaranteed to push me out of the Divide race in a matter of days. I couldn't believe that my ultimately useless toes might fail me out of yet another big adventure.

I spent that night in Heber at the house of a college friend, Anna, who was also a mutual friend of Geoff's. I hadn't said anything to her about our breakup, because I just wasn't ready to deal with disbelief and pity from our longtime friends. I wasn't sure if Geoff had said anything to her, but if he had, she mercifully did not bring it up. We sat down for a late-night snack of graham crackers and peanut butter — I didn't tell her I was becoming tired of peanut butter — and talked about my ride. I told her about the snow, the rocky jeep trails, and my great kindling fire. I didn't talk about my toes.

"So you feel pretty good right now?" Anna asked.

"Oh yeah," I said. "The ride went really well."

"And you think you're ready for your race?"

"Yeah," I said. "I mean, as much as I can be. Something like the Great Divide is so big and so long, I don't think anyone is every truly ready for it."

Anna's mouth curled into a slow, somewhat sad smile that caught me off guard. Anna was an experienced mountaineer, skier and cyclist, with more tenacity and talent than I would ever possess. But she also was the kind of person who was unfailingly positive about everything. You could tell her you planned to jump off of the Empire State Building with a hang glider you made out of coat hangers and toilet paper, and she would ask you where you planned to land. I didn't really expect any of my friends who had any understanding of the magnitude of the race to actually believe I could do it, but if anyone was going to enthusiastically pretend they did believe it, Anna would. But instead, she just nodded. "So you're really going to try it?"

I leaned forward and gave Anna a solemn look. "I know that this race is going to be prohibitively hard," I said. "And you know me. I mean, all the camping and hiking and riding we've done together in the past, you know me. I never really aspired to do anything extreme. For someone like me, this race is likely impossibly hard."

Anna's eyes widened into an understanding gaze. "But that's okay," I continued. "The fact that something's impossible has never been a good reason not to try."

And I realized, perhaps for the first time all summer, that it was true.

Chapter Eight
Banff

Page 99: Leslie Gerein walks beneath a beehive rock formation in Banff National Park, Canada.
Page 100: Leslie Gerein looks out over Lake Louise.

There are few better ways to manifest the finality of a decision than changing one's appearance. The day after I returned from Heber, I woke up in the morning and instead of setting out on my bike in yet another directionless tangent, I drove to a salon.

"Cut it about to here," I said to the stylist as I slid two fingers between strands of hair just below my ears. Nearly a foot of hair fell below my imaginary chop line, as long as it had ever been. I had been pleased with my hair in my old life, but as I slowly made the mental transition to life on a bike, my mind shifted from vanity and desire to need and simplicity, and my hair became just another excess. I only needed it long enough to pull it back in an elastic band, but short enough to stave off dreadlocks if I went a few days or a week without taking a shower. As the stylist snipped away large chunks of blond and light-brown strands, I felt no emotion. I didn't need my hair; therefore, it wasn't part of me, and I felt no loss.

I walked from the salon across the hot pavement of a strip mall to a shoe store. Amid stacks of running shoes, I located an inexpensive pair, size nine and a half — one size too large for me. I tried them on, found them to be sufficiently roomy for my sore toes, and purchased them.

I walked over to a pharmacy to pick up a pill case for some of my more crucial riding aids: allergy medication, antacids, ibuprofen (or as endurance athletes like to call it, "Vitamin I"), and a powerful prescription sleeping medication, Ambien. In the past, intense physical efforts often left me unable to sleep at night. My heart, which never seemed to get the memo that the long day had finally ended, continued to pound in my chest as my muscles processed a hefty dose of lactic acid and adrenaline. I never understood athletes who said they could easily collapse into a deep sleep after hard exercise. My experience had always been the opposite — the more physically exhausted I was, the harder it was for me to sleep. I realized that sleep was crucial to enduring the long days in the saddle on the Divide, so I turned to the powerful if dubious help of medication. After I secured my drug supply, I drove to a bike shop.

"Do you have platform pedals?" I asked the clerk.

"Excuse me?" the clerk looked almost suspicious.

"Platform pedals," I said. "You know, flats."

"Um, we do," he said. He took me to the very back corner of the store, away from the area where a wide selection of clipless pedals were displayed, and pointed to a single pair of cheap-looking pedals hanging from a wall.

"These are all we have," he said.

I looked at the price — cheaper than I had even expected — and frowned. "Really? These are it?"

"That's it," he said. "If you're thinking about becoming more serious about riding, you should really think about going clipless. You'll have a lot more control; a lot more power. You'll be more comfortable. If you want, you can try on some shoes and I'll give you a demonstration."

I smiled at the clerk. What could I possibly tell him? That I actually wasn't the clueless novice he took me for? That I had been using top-of-the line clipless pedals and shoes for more than a month of heavy riding already? That riding clipless meant I wasn't in control and wasn't comfortable, and that's why I was there, purchasing a cheap pair of plastic pedals that I could use with my cheap running shoes as I prepared to compete in the longest mountain bike race in the world? How do you explain that?

"No, these are all I need for today," I said as I handed the clerk the eighteen dollars in cash. I couldn't shake my discomfort with the fact that I was spending a mere eighteen dollars for an extremely important part that

I hoped would hold up to 2,700 miles of hard riding. I wondered if I was actually making a huge mistake. But it was too late. I had already cut my hair.

The transition from uncertainty to commitment certainly wasn't clean. A week before the race, I still had no real plan about how I was going to travel to Banff. I looked into plane tickets to Calgary and studied the viability of riding to Banff from there, but I felt dubious. How likely was I to actually get on that plane? Or find my way out of the city? How much could I trust myself to clear all those obstacles without clamping onto the nearest excuse to pack it all in and go home? I had a feeling that just getting to the starting line might turn out to be my biggest challenge in the race, and I was not too proud to ask for help.

I contacted a fellow racer and Internet acquaintance in Denver and asked him if I could hitch a ride to Canada. The ulterior motive was not just simple transportation, but a silent request for the moral support I was craving so badly. The company of someone else who intended to embark on this journey would keep my mind focused, and the companionship would help distract me from the tugging doubts I still wrestled when I lay awake at night.

Chris Plesko enthusiastically welcomed me on the two-day drive north. I packed my bike and all of my gear in a single box. That box held what was, to me, the barest essentials of modern living in the Rocky Mountains in the summer: a steel-framed bicycle with a good front shock; a cushy seat and ergonomic handlebar grips for long-distance comfort; a down sleeping bag rated to thirty-two degrees; a thin air mattress to cushion against the cold ground; a water-resistant bivy sack to ward off wind and rain; a comfortable pair of large shoes that would fit the several layers of socks I hoped would cushion against frostbite cold and pain; two bicycle jerseys; two pairs of running shorts; four pairs of socks; two pairs of underwear; two sports bras; arm and leg warmers; a thin polar fleece pullover; a waterproof nylon jacket and pants; fleece hat; thin balaclava; padded bike gloves; warm fleece gloves; a helmet; one headlamp; a strong headlight; a camera; small bike repair tools; extra batteries; a satellite locator beacon; a GPS unit; an mp3 player; two water bladders; one water bottle; a water filter; iodine tablets; sunglasses; various pain and allergy medications; and bear mace for defense against predators of both the animal and human kind.

I questioned the necessity of all of it as I hoisted my bike box across the Denver airport. The arm-burning weight forced me to take short, swift steps for fifty feet or so before dropping the heavy box to catch my breath. I came to a single flight of stairs and struggled mightily, lifting the box with great bursts of effort a few steps, resting, and then powering up again. At the top of the stairs, my hair was drenched in sweat and my heart was racing near its maximum capacity. It was just one flight of stairs, located at the end of one small airport terminal. How was I possibly going to power this stuff across the long spine of the continent?

Chris and his wife, Marni, welcomed me like an old friend. Chris's bike, a sleek white singlespeed, was dialed in to the smallest details. It glistened with brand new parts as it hung from the bike stand where he had just spent several hours freshly tuning it after just a few short rides. He handed me a spreadsheet of his own gear list — everything extensively tested, accounted for and accurately weighed. I glanced over it despite a revulsion that made me feel like a kid who had just gotten a D on a spelling test only to have a friend wave his A paper in her face. Chris' gear list resembled mine, at a base level. But there was a scientific certainty to his items, listed in precise terms and weighed down to fractions of an ounce.

"You weigh your chapstick?" I cried out. "Your chapstick?"

"Don't worry, Chris is just crazy," Marni said.

Chris laughed. "I like to know what I'm dealing with," he said. "Why? How much does your stuff weigh?"

"I don't have the slightest clue," I said. "I don't think I even want to know. I can tell you it weighs a lot more than yours."

"That's okay," said Chris, who had put so much time and thought into his gear that he was convinced he had reached the perfect balance between being light enough to move fast and having enough supplies to keep him going. "As long as you're comfortable. That's what's important if you want to finish."

"I probably have too much stuff," I said. "But, I don't know. Even if you're really fast, sixteen or seventeen days is still a long time to only have access to one pair of bike shorts."

"I'm shipping a fresh pair to myself in Salida," Chris said, referring to a town in Colorado that was a little more than halfway through the race. "It's going to be oh-so-sweet when I get there and put them on."

I laughed. "I guess the little things are worth fighting for. You'll remember those when you're stuck up on a mountain pass in a thunderstorm. They'll be great motivation. "If I only make it those last two hundred miles to Salida tonight, I can change my shorts!'"

Everybody laughed, and I was glad to be in the company of people who understood the depth of the journey ahead and were still willing to laugh about the absurdity of it. Even though every second I spent observing Chris and his meticulous preparations gave me more reasons for uncertainty, they also gave me a sense that I wasn't completely crazy, that something of this magnitude could actually be done by real people.

The drive north passed in a blur of gas station stops and open prairie. Chris and I scanned the snow line on the Front Range to the west. It reached all the way down to the foothills, with white-frosted trees that indicated recent snowfall.

"It's pretty low," I said. "Don't you think some of the passes are still snowed in?"

"I think the snow's all above 8,000 feet," Chris said. "Most of the route in Canada and Montana is lower than that, and by the time we get this far south, maybe it will be gone."

"That's a lot to melt in a week," I said. The high peaks were covered in a solid layer of white. I tried to comfort my unease by telling myself that I had pushed my bike through a lot of snow in Alaska. But even the soft snow I had dealt with in Alaska bottomed out after a few inches on a packed trail. In the untraveled sections of the Rockies, during the melt of summer, I envisioned sinking up to my neck in slush. The urge to call it quits nibbled at the edges of my thoughts, and I tried to ignore it.

We drove through Calgary without stopping and turned west toward a jagged wall of mountains. The Canadian Rockies loomed as though carved out of solid rock, chiseled to rugged beauty by the slow erosion of an unknowable amount of time. White and blue glaciers tumbled off the peaks into vertical waterfalls that cascaded into the green valley below. A herd of elk grazed in a field of purple flowers along the highway. After crossing nearly a thousand miles of prairie, the backdrop seemed too dramatic to be fully real — like a stage set in an old Technicolor movie.

"This place is unreal," I said after we drove through the gate of Banff National Park. "Seriously, it's like someone took a bunch of postcards and designed a mountain theme park."

"It is incredible," Chris said. "And wait until you see Banff. It's such a cool town."

Shortly after I had made travel arrangements with the Pleskos, a woman in Banff contacted me to tell me she knew about my race plans through my blog, and wondered if I needed a place to stay in town. Leslie and her husband, Keith, were both outdoor fanatics who had sculpted their lives in such a way that they could live in the small national park center, work the minimal amount of time needed to support themselves, and spend the rest of their time traveling and playing in the mountains.

Within minutes of my arrival, Keith whisked me away in his car. We wended up steep switchbacks to a hillside where I could see all of Banff. Small buildings clustered around the roaring whitewater of the Bow River, itself wedged in a narrow canyon between towering peaks. Keith talked vividly about ski touring in the winter, mountain running in the summer, riding bikes on deliciously technical trail, and, when the day started to wane, returning to the quaint town to enjoy a five-star dinner or exotic sushi afforded by the many tourism-centered luxury restaurants in town.

"And it's all regulated and maintained by the national park, so nothing about this is ever going to change," Keith said. "It's paradise in a bubble."

"I don't want to leave this place," I said. "Maybe we can make a trade. You can ride the Divide, and I'll take your lifestyle."

Keith laughed. "I'm jealous of you!" he said. "Leslie told me all about the Great Divide. It sounds like a grand adventure. I've traveled throughout this region and I can tell you that you're going to see a lot of beautiful country."

With the exception of packing up and making last-minute adjustments, I avoided my bike for the next two days. I hiked to the top of a peak on a trail that started in Keith and Leslie's back yard. I joined Chris and Marni for a soak in a natural hot spring. The night before the Tour Divide was set to start, Leslie and I traveled to Lake Louise, a deep turquoise body of water surrounded by glaciated slopes. We climbed a corduroy tower of a mountain and sat far above Lake Louise's sparkling water at sunset. I felt a deep sort of warmth, something more like happiness than anything I had felt since Geoff and I left Juneau in a cloud of cold finality. I didn't know if it was the beauty of Banff, the friendliness of people who had so recently been strangers, or the fact that I had finally made a solid decision to ride the Divide. But the reasons didn't seem to really matter. I felt happy.

"Feeling nervous about tomorrow?" Leslie asked as we hiked back around Lake Louise. The sun had already slipped behind the Continental Divide. I looked at my watch; there were less than twelve hours remaining until the race start.

"Of course," I said. "But at the same time, I feel this relief, because I'm here, and I know I'm going to try it, and now I just have to do it."

"That's right," Leslie said. "Git 'er one."

The Tour Divide organizers held a barbecue that night to allow all the racers a chance to get to know each other before we started spreading out over 2,700 miles of open road. I showed up on Leslie's beach cruiser, wearing a cotton hoodie and jeans, and trying to look as nonchalant as possible. Of course, few people at the barbecue picked me out as one of the racers, except for those who had stumbled across my blog. A couple other racers showed up in full kit with their loaded bikes. They leaned against the outskirts of the park pavilion, appearing both intensely focused and somewhat miserable. If I was honest with myself, I felt the way they looked — knotted up with anticipation that was on the verge of exploding into a full-blown panic attack. But I wanted to be the kind of person who finished 2,700-mile races like the Tour Divide all the time like it was no big deal, so I put on my act. I nibbled on half of a hamburger as though I was watching my calories instead of carbo-loading for the biggest race of my life. I laughed about the craziness of endurance athletes with the other racers' wives and girlfriends before admitting that I was actually one of those crazies. I met one of the two other women in the race. Cricket was a middle-aged mother from North Carolina. She looked even less like an endurance athlete than I did, small and slightly pudgy, but she projected an air of confidence that told me she had done her homework.

The morning of the race dawned several shades of perfect. The air was completely calm. Temperatures were in the high fifties, promising to rise to the seventies later that day. There wasn't a cloud in the sky. I hugged Keith and Leslie, mounted the loaded bike that would become my entire life for the next few weeks, and coasted down the hill to the pre-race meeting.

Racers gathered in front of a hostel in downtown Banff. The crowd buzzed with an energy that was much more palpable than the subdued nervousness that consumed the previous night's barbecue. Non-racers dashed in and out of a nearby building, handing off bottles of water and Power Bars. Dozens of loaded bicycles were propped against fences, laid on the sidewalk and held by racers in matching jerseys and shorts. I wore one of two outfits I had chosen for the next few weeks — a green polka-dotted jersey that had a black grease stain under one of the arms, and a pair of bike shorts I had worn during my first cross-country bicycle tour back in 2003. My only conceit was a pair of socks that I had received with my race packet before my first endurance event, the 2006 Susitna 100. They had already nearly disintegrated, but I decided I would lay them to rest somewhere on the Great Divide.

"Hey, are you Jill?" a man near the outskirts of the crowd said as he approached me. I smiled and nodded. "Hi, I'm John," he said.

John Nobile was the winner of the 2008 Great Divide Race and the current record-holder on the border-to-border course. He frequently rode with Geoff in the early part of the 2008 race while Geoff was doing well, and then surged ahead when Geoff faltered. The following spring, after I broadcast my Divide aspirations online, John contacted me to discuss logistics. He took me under his expert wing and gave me advice, which mostly included meticulous calculations and specific training regimes that were only moderately useful to a flighty person such as me. But I embraced his mentorship because he was the champion. The pre-race meeting was the first time I had an opportunity to shake his hand.

Before we could even get a few sentences in, a reporter sidled up to us and stuck a microphone in our face. He queried John about his unusual bike, which was custom designed with a fiberglass faring in the front and an aerodynamic trunk welded to the frame. John talked about his efforts to be as aerodynamic as possible, from his custom-made bike to his clothes, his aerodynamic wheels, his semi-slick tires, his clipless shoes and his shaved legs. "Everything I do is to go fast," John said.

Then the reporter turned to me. "What do you think of reports about snow on the first pass on Montana?" he asked.

"I heard that, too," I said. "Maybe it's there and maybe it's not. You know, snow. The secret is to hit it up early in the morning and then you can ride on top of it. But yeah, maybe you have to walk for five miles, postholing in the snow, going really slow for a while, but it's really not the end of the world."

And that was the truth of it. I could worry and fret all I wanted about the future, but when it came down to it, I had no choice but to put my head down and push onward. After the reporter left, I realized I didn't have my bear spray in my pack. "Shoot!" I said. "I forgot my weapon!" I left John and sprinted back up the hill. I breathlessly burst into my friends' house, where Leslie already had the bear spray in her hands when I reached the living room.

"Thanks," I panted, gave her one more hug, and sprinted back down the hill just as the racers were rolling out from the starting line. No grand send-off, no shotgun start, just cheers from the small crowd and a stream of cyclists moving wordlessly into the wilderness.

"By grace go I into the Great Divide," I whispered to myself as I followed them down the trail.

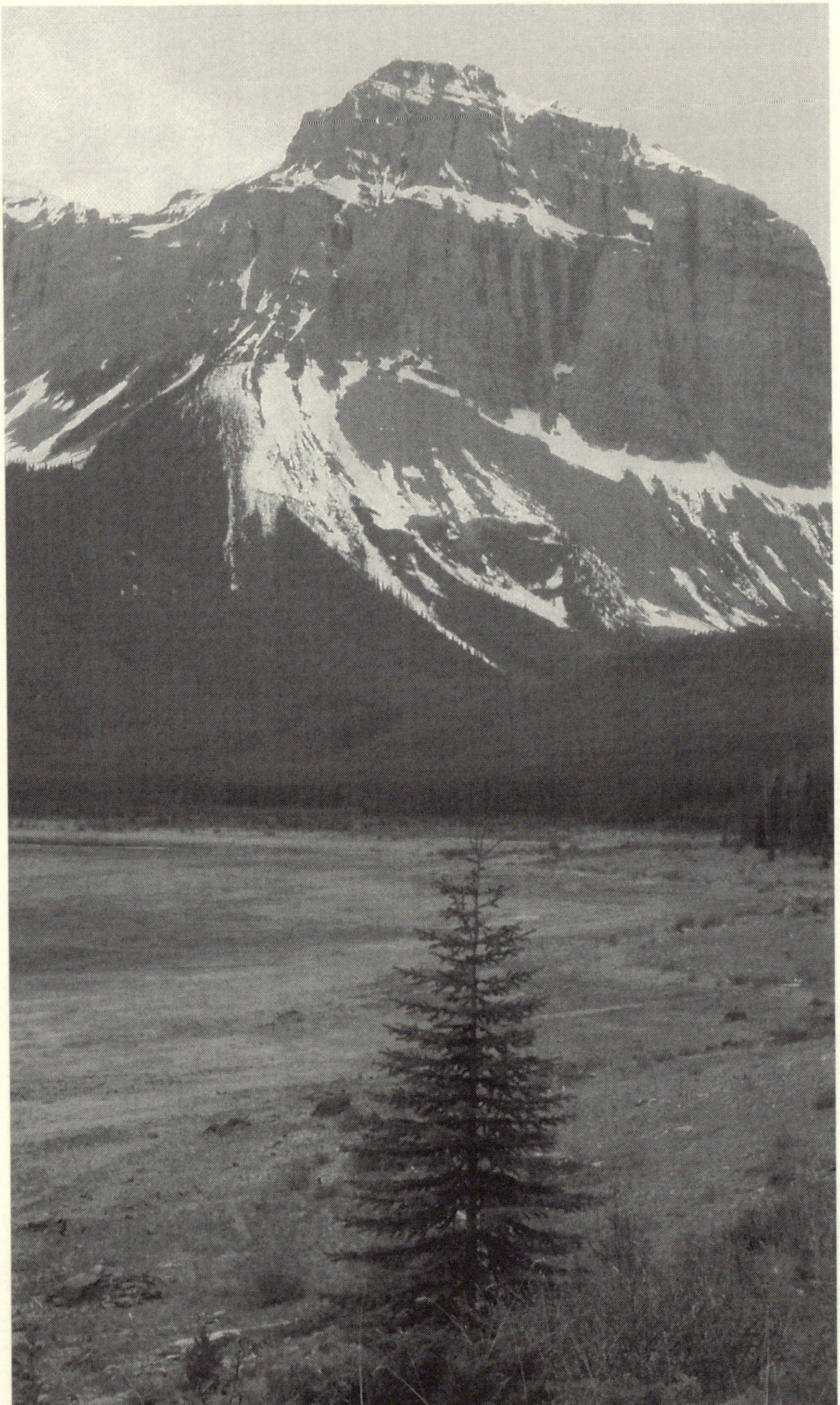

Chapter Nine
Into the Great Divide

Page 108 and 109: Jeff Kerby rides the Great Divide Mountain Bike Route in British Columbia.
Page 110: Two Tour Divide racers pedal on the Spray River Trail in Banff National Park.

It didn't look like the first mile of a grueling 2,700-mile mountain bike race. The freeze-dried leaves of the previous autumn still littered the trail, soft and disarming. Sunlight filtered through hemlock branches and mottled the ground with abstract shadows. Bicycles sporting all manner of bags and panniers and tarp-wrapped bundles streamed past a small group of tourists who had probably just been out for a morning stroll. They cheered in German and snapped a photo of me as I rode by.

Stress pumped through my blood like jet fuel and I pedaled a hard pace that I wouldn't be able to sustain for twenty-seven miles, let alone a hundred times that. I caught up to several small clusters of cyclists, gasped a quick hello, and surged forward. After one mile, the group of forty-two racers had already significantly spread out, and eventually I found myself somewhere in the mid-pack.

My throbbing lungs forced me to settle into an easier rhythm just as I caught up to two older men: an Italian who did not speak English, and a professor named Steve. The professor was a bald, powerfully built man in his mid to late-forties. The Italian drafted silently behind our new group of three as Steve and I talked through basic introductions: Name, place of origin, and bike set-up. Steve taught creative writing at a small college and lived with his wife in Iowa. He talked quickly, but I gathered that he had children and had ridden the Tour Divide before, but didn't finish. He said he planned to "take it easier" this time around, and "enjoy the view."

As I tried to describe my gear choices, I noticed Steve had a camera mounted to his handlebars. He said he intended to film his entire ride, which he would use later as the basis for performance pieces at his college.

"I use the footage mostly for inspiration," he told me. "I generally do monologues, no costumes or sets. I prefer to set up the scene myself."

I wondered what inspiration Steve could possibly extract from hundreds of hours of gravel, mud, grass and trees, and then smiled at my delayed self-recognition as a person seeking enlightenment in the same mundane scenario. "So what kinds of images are you hoping to capture?" I asked.

"Oh, everything," he said. "I have the camera angled up so I can talk into it. I'm going to tell it how I'm feeling, what I'm thinking about, things like that."

"I guess it would be nice just to have someone to talk to," I joked.

Steve shot back one of those squinty smiles that artist types tend to use when dealing with uncreative people who will never understand the true nature of their art. "And what brings you to the Tour Divide?" he asked me. "You said you were a journalist?"

"An editor, mostly, but yeah. I'm on leave from my job for a few months. I love bike touring and mountains, and the Tour Divide sounded fun. So I'm just here on vacation."

"This is your idea of a fun vacation?"

"Yeah, it is," I said. "Since I'm out here by myself, I needed something challenging to keep me going, but not so extreme that I'd be struggling every second of the day."

"No husband or partner?"

"Not anymore," I said. "Recently freed."

"Ah," Steve said. He looked ahead and asked no more questions; it seemed that was the end of his curiosity about my own story.

His indifference stung a little, because from what I could discern, Steve and I had a lot in common. We were riding those dusty miles for similar reasons. At its base level, a race like the Tour Divide attracts three kinds of people: Endurance athletes with strong resumes, fast legs, and aspirations for wins and records; wanderers with cheap, heavy bikes, an undying appetite for adventure and an ability to live on dirt; and introspective types similar to Steve and me, who look at the wholesale impossibility of the Tour Divide and hope, quite vainly, that we can cut the challenge into workable parts and then condense the experience into something artful and enlightening.

The interesting thing about these three groups of people is that the athletes and wanderers were the ones who approached the race honestly, with their intentions out in the open and their movements a simple, natural expression of who they are. As dreamers, Steve's and my place in the race was much more dubious. We had no solid goals or destinations, besides the simple act of just being there and a vague hope of eventually finishing. Our journey awaited in the rugged landscape of our minds.

The Italian surged ahead and Steve fell behind as the trail narrowed to rough singletrack at the edge of Banff National Park. Trees crowded in, so tall and thick that I didn't notice clumps of afternoon clouds starting to blot out the sunlight. I gripped the handlebars and narrowed my focus to the simple movements of a mountain biker: solid steering, strategic cadence, leaning into turns and avoiding trees. Singletrack has a way of forcing even the most unapologetic dreamers to leave the shadowy worlds of their minds and think only in the simple absolutes of the present: swerve around that stump; hop over those downed trees; steer hard right; jerk hard left; pedal harder, up, harder, up, harder, almost there; hard stroke, gasp for breath; rumble down. Singletrack, though sparse on the Great Divide Mountain Bike Route, was a fast embodiment of the kind of outside inspiration for which Steve and I were looking. In places of comfort, everything people do is a result of everything they've been through. Perspectives are colored and blurred by past experiences. But on tight, narrow trail, a moment is simply a moment, and a movement simply a movement. There is no room for vague indecision. The movement is either right or wrong. Either you swerve around a tree, or slam into it. Everything you did before that moment simply does not matter.

After about two hours of tight focus, the trail found its way out of the forest and entered an open river valley, still walled by the sharp purple peaks of the Canadian Rockies. I climbed a steep bluff and caught up to a group of three men sprawled out on the grass in the shade. A large man with bushy facial hair stood up and said, "Uh oh, guys, the women are catching up to us. We better get cranking or we're going to lose this race."

The two skinnier guys laughed heartily. Despite the fact I was already subdued by the effort of the afternoon and slightly offended, I couldn't help but crack a smile. The total distance of the Great Divide Mountain Bike Route was actually closer to 2,770 miles, and we had pedaled fifty. Sweat drenched our jerseys and foreheads, and we still had more than 2,700 miles in front of us. There wasn't even a race yet to lose, but we couldn't help but size each other up as competitors while laughing at our innate tendency to do so.

I followed the men for several miles through another tight section of singletrack, but couldn't keep up after a long stretch littered with fallen trees. I was riding solo again. It was the first day of the race and the forty-two racers were never again going to be any closer together. I didn't know how far in front of me the leaders were, nor did I have any clue how many people were behind me. I suspected I was in the back-center of the pack. But with the exception of my first short encounters, I mostly felt alone amid expansive valleys and granite pinnacles. I began to wonder what the race would feel like when people really spread out.

The afternoon clouds brought frequent showers. Still, the heat of the morning remained and I felt no need to pull a jacket over my short-sleeved jersey. The rain fell in gentle drops. Bursts of sun occasionally cut through the gray ceiling, illuminating the mist-shrouded pines in a virtual forest fire of golden light. Soon the occasional slices of light in the sky turned pink, and then red, and then the world almost imperceptibly fell into the purple shades of evening. I climbed and descended, then climbed and descended again, along a seemingly endless procession of drainages. For hours of effort, I was never fully maxed out, but I never felt completely comfortable, either. Still, the physical strain succeeded in carving away at my race anxiety, until I felt a subdued sort of peace.

I reached Elkford, British Columbia, at about 9 p.m., just as the mountain landscape began to dip into darkness. My maps indicated that I had traveled 110 miles that day. Lightning streaked across the sky and thunder rumbled closer as I pulled up to a campground on the outskirts of the tiny town. Across the street, a motel sign flickered with enviable warmth. I watched it greedily, debating the propriety of an $8 campsite versus a roach motel when it was still early in the race and I was relatively fresh and well-fed. Another bolt of lightning streaked over my head and rain began to fall hard.

"This is stupid," I grumbled to myself. "The only things that matter to me right now are rest and energy, and I certainly have enough money to obtain both." I crossed the street.

The bar attached to the motel pounded with the obnoxious vibrations of a cover band. The singer howled bad Van Halen tunes made worse by pounding volume from a cheap amplifier. I propped my bike against the window and walked inside.

"So, another biker," the woman at the desk chuckled. "I'm almost full with you people tonight."

"Really?" I asked. "There are quite a few others here?" I had expected most of the riders to go on to Sparwood, which was thirty miles down the route.

"I'd say at least twenty," she said. "So you'll be wanting a room, then?"

"Yes," I said. I didn't ask her how much it cost.

She drew up a ticket for $109 and I winced. "How late is that band going to be playing?" I asked.

"Probably until 2 a.m., maybe 3," she said. "We have ear plugs if you'd like."

Full eardrum removal wasn't going to be enough to block out that noise.

The walls were literally shaking. But thunder continued to rumble outside. I didn't want to bivy in the rain and I certainly didn't have the energy for thirty more hard miles, especially after I had let the prospect of sleep enter my consciousness. Bikers can't be choosers.

Upstairs, I stripped off my sweaty clothes and threw them in the bottom of the bathtub before I stepped beneath the shower head. As hot water stung my rain-numbed skin, I squatted down and scrubbed each article of clothing with a bar of soap. Then I turned the depleted remnants of the soap on my own grungy body. After twenty minutes of joyless washerwoman cleaning, I hung my wet bike clothes all over the room. I sat on the floor, stark naked, too unmotivated to pull my spare set of clothing out of my bike bags. I plunged granola bars into a jar of peanut butter and flipped through six channels until I found the local access weather report. I squinted at the little icons of thunderstorm clouds dangling over every day in the next week while trying convert Celsius temperatures in my head. Four degrees? What did that mean? It was above freezing, but wasn't that still pretty cold? Rain pelted the window and I felt grateful to be naked in the dry heat of a $109 roach room, even if walls did rattle with the terrible noise of some backwoods British Columbian band.

It was after midnight when I finally crawled into bed after burning up more than an hour typing a few e-mails on a tiny little handheld device and working up an iPod playlist for the next day. These were hardly smart activities for a racer, in a race in which every minute not spent eating, sleeping or pedaling was considered waste of time. Still, I felt proud of myself and decided my first day had been a success. I had overcome the personal challenge of starting the race and committed to going the distance. I also felt a tinge of pride just to be part of the Tour Divide, the ultimate mountain biking challenge. Sure, finishing the Divide was still close to impossible. And, yeah, I was still alone. But for a few blissful minutes before exhaustion overtook the roar of Friday night revelry, those realities did not seem relevant. I was there, on the Great Divide. In its own way, the hardest battle had already been won.

The morning of day two dawned as beautiful as the first. I managed to pry myself out of the stiff bed at about 6:30 a.m., well after the sun came up but still early enough to be considered respectable for a Divide racer. The hard rock motel was eerily quiet as I pulled away and pedaled through the streets of Elkford, searching for the route out of town. The maps weren't completely clear and I was too confused to even ask for directions. Was I on the north side of town or the south? Did the route head straight out of town or did it follow the highway? Was I even in Elkford? Suddenly even that detail wasn't clear.

I was lost for nearly a half hour, making wider circles around the motel until I finally stopped at a gas station and showed the attendant my map. She laughed and pointed to a gravel road across the street.

"That's the mining road," she said. "Besides the highway, it's the only road out of town."

I scrunched my nose and tried to suppress a grimace. It seemed obvious to her, but to a foreign cyclist, even the most inconsequential suburban streets look like they might go somewhere, and it takes a very long time to rule out every dead end in town. I sighed. This was going to be a long, frequently confusing race. Oh well. I had wasted nearly an hour but I was finally on the right track. I crossed the street and began climbing back into the mountains.

After I passed the belching smokestacks of the mine, the rutted gravel road dipped into a narrow canyon and wound playfully back to the highway that I had spent all morning bypassing on the primitive, and therefore preferable, forest road. That's the one big catch of the Great Divide Mountain Bike Route — it never takes the easy way. It takes the most scenic, most challenging, most remote ways, but never the easy way. And the one main stipulation of the race rules was that each racer must follow the marked route with an engineer's exactness. In some ways, it was nice to have free agency taken away from us, because it removed the doubt and guesswork that often accompany route-finding on bike tours. But in other ways, especially as the days wore on, it often seemed ridiculous to climb many thousands of feet over and down three difficult passes on flooded, rock-strewn roads, just to get around the perfectly good pavement of a smooth, flat highway.

Even though I did relish the rugged riding and scenery of the mountains, I was also grateful to return to the relatively mindless flow of the pavement. I felt like free bird flying into Sparwood, spinning an easy twenty miles per hour while accompanied by tunes on my iPod. I wondered if the time I spent compiling a rocking playlist really had been wasted, as it seemed to ease the burden substantially. I made it to town by 10:30 a.m. despite being lost in Elkford until 8. I stocked up on supplies at a small market and rolled deeper into town to choose a location for my first celebratory meal. The choices of eating establishments in Sparwood included an A&W hamburger stand and — an A&W hamburger stand. I frowned. I'm not a big fan of greasy fast food and would have preferred a Subway or the heaven-sent unlikelihood of a sushi bar, but bikers can't be choosers.

I tried to stuff down a heavy meal of a grilled chicken sandwich, onion rings, and root beer as I pored over the cue sheet for the next section of the route. While I ate, another Tour Divide rider walked into the restaurant.

"How are you doing?" he asked.

"Good," I said. "I spent the night in Elkford. Feeling pretty good right now."

"What do you think about that?" he asked, pointing to the cue sheet I had been browsing.

I frowned. I was not happy about the cue sheet, a wrench that the race organizers had thrown at us the night before the race started. It detailed the directions for an experimental section of the route that was not on the maps. On the sheet, the route was given only in cues about where to make turns, with none of the elevation profiles, detailed course illustrations and trail details that the official maps offered. The race organizers were essentially making guinea pigs out of the 2009 racers by foisting this untested, uncharted section of trail on us the night before the race. I understood that the Tour Divide was supposed to be an adventure race, but still. I had a hard enough time finding my way out of Elkford. I didn't want a silly cue sheet to become my undoing.

"It's pretty vague," I said grumpily. "I'm just hoping I don't get lost."

"The cues seem okay," he said. "I'm just wondering about the climbing and stuff."

"Either way," I said, "I will be a happy girl once we cross the border."

"Are you going to cross it tonight?" he asked.

"We'll see," I said. "These cues don't even say how far it is. For all I know, it could be 200 miles away still."

Outside of Sparwood, the official maps indicated the route turned left toward southern British Columbia, but the cue sheet directed me to turn right. I grumbled out loud and squinted to scan for bike tracks through the dust on the pavement. The cue sheets directed me to turn on another mine road, which deteriorated into a gravel forest road, which deteriorated further into a rocky double track and finally veered onto a streambed swollen with

117

spring runoff. I bounced over the boulders until I hit a deep rut and had to drop both feet into the cold water. I yelped and swung my leg over the bar, rushing to the shoreline, but it was too late. My feet were soaked.

The road finally veered away from the stream and began climbing steeply. I spotted more bike tracks pressed deep into the mud. All around, red pines towered over the road. The rolling mountains evoked memories of my grandparents' property in Northern Utah, where as children my sisters and I crawled through a stream to access a redrock cave. The scenery was breathtaking but I was still too annoyed to enjoy it. While I accepted that I was in a race and therefore had to go where the race went, I still resented being told what to do.

The cue sheet was not even remotely helpful in guiding me through its own unrealistic demands. It told me to "gain" a pass and failed to mention that said pass gained 2,000 feet on some of the worst road I had yet encountered on a bicycle — a deeply rutted gravel track that made it difficult to establish any kind of traction or flow. It told me to turn right in 2.9 miles, and five miles went by without any hint of a crossroad. Had it not been for the myriad bicycle tracks curving through the mud at the next right turn, I might have just exploded with frustration and turned back toward Sparwood. I couldn't fathom how the race leaders found the route.

Steve caught up to me on a section of the route called Cabin Creek Pass that seemed to have neither cabins nor a creek. But the road was quite steep, so it was definitely a pass. He only grunted softly when I said hello but instead of passing me, he sidled up behind my rear wheel. He seemed even more disinterested in talking to me than he had the day before, but I decided his terse replies to my questions could simply be fatigue. After all, the day's endless climbs had left my head swimming. Why would Steve be any different?

"Did you stay in Elkford last night?" I asked.

"We did," he said. "Me and Jeff Kerby and, ah, another man. I forget his name. We got in about eleven or so. It was raining pretty hard. We went into the hotel but there was all that awful noise. I couldn't spend another minute in there, so we sacked out beneath the canopy at the bank next door."

"Did you stay dry?" I asked.

"Not really," Steve said in a defeated tone. "I hardly got a lick of sleep. And Kerby snored. I just can't wait to get to Eureka. I'm going to sleep hard tonight."

"Think you'll make it to Eureka tonight?" I asked. Eureka was in Montana, about ten miles south of the United States border. Our cue sheets indicated we only had one more pass after Cabin Creek, but who really knew? There could be several, and they could all be over 6,000 feet high on roads that were nothing more than active streambeds. I had already resigned myself to the idea that I was going to get to Eureka when the cue sheet was good and ready to let me get there, and no sooner.

"I'd better," Steve said. "I have to make it there tonight. And so I will."

I admired Steve's resolve, but I pitied his inflexibility. Steve stuck to my wheel but maintained his silence. As we climbed, I slowly surged ahead until Steve was out of sight. Several thousand feet down the rocky pass, I rejoined a fairly civilized looking stretch of pavement, only to turn onto an even more rugged road that veered right off the cue sheet's rudimentary photocopied map. It climbed and dropped into a half dozen 200- to 500-feet-deep drainages in a section that didn't even indicate elevation change. After a dozen miles and another couple thousand feet of unrewarded climbing, I reached the most dreaded section of all — the primitive singletrack connector trail that linked two remote logging roads. Even the race director, who swore that all other directions on the cue sheet were crystal clear, admitted that this section was hard to find.

I approached the bridge that the directions warned I should not cross because it meant I had gone too far. I stopped and scanned the woods but saw nothing that appeared to be a trail. I did see a small tent pitched next to the road. The sun was settling but I figured there was at least another hour of usable twilight, and I wanted to continue moving. As I wheeled my bike past the tent, a woman's voice called out, "Who's there?"

"It's Jill with the Tour Divide," I said. "Are you Cricket?"

"Yes," she said.

"And is this the right way, the connector trail?" I asked.

"I think it's right over there, right behind me," she said. "I figured I'd camp here and try to cross it with someone in the morning."

"You think it's going to be that bad?"

"No," she said. "I've just gone far enough today. I'm happy here."

"Well, I think I'm going to cross while there's still a little daylight," I said. "Maybe shoot for the border tonight, but probably not. I'm just going to get some water in that stream over there and head out. I'm kind of a sleeper-inner, so I'm sure I'll see you in the morning."

"Well, let me know if you decide to camp here," Cricket said in a way that told me she didn't really want my company. I wondered if all of these racers I was meeting were as repelled by my presence as they seemed, or if that was just an insecurity born of my own imagination. Either way, I wasn't quite ready to stop for the night.

"I think I'll go on," I said. "But thanks."

Even in the brightest part of twilight, with Cricket's assurances that this was the right spot, I had a difficult time picking out the trail entrance from the meadow where she was camped. I doubted if I would have ever found it had her tent not been pitched right in front of it. The so-called "singletrack" barely made an indentation in the grass and moss. A thin ribbon was tied to a tree several feet away from the initial clearing, and only faint footprints on the dewy ground indicated any real passage at all. Obviously, everyone had walked their bikes through this section of "trail." I switched on my headlamp and picked out more footprints with bike tracks nearby.

In the deep forest, twilight turned quickly to darkness. Within the narrow beam of my headlamp, I pieced my way along the trammeled grass as it wove through the trees near a gurgling stream. Then, almost as imperceptibly as it started, the connector dead-ended in a virtually vertical bluff. I shined my headlight in a large circle, looking for some way around it, but all bike tracks indicated that the route went straight up.

The grade was at least sixty degrees. The cue sheet called it a "hike-a-bike" but it was in fact a virtual wall — a wall built of slippery mud with chocolate-colored water cascading down the face. I grunted, hoisted the bike a few inches forward and planted my right shoe in the gooey cliff. I took a few more steps before I lost traction and slid all the way back to the bottom. I swore and threw my bike on its side, lodging the handlebars in the mud and using it as an anchor to leverage my body up the first crumbling step. After several "ax" plants, I was drenched in sweat and nowhere near the top of the bluff. The climb was so difficult that I had to tap deep into what I call my "snow bike mode," a rather defeated state of mind I reserve for only the most ridiculous slog conditions, in which I tell myself that I'm merely living out some kind of bad dream, and to not be so uptight about it because I'll probably wake up soon.

For the next twenty minutes, I picked my way up 300 vertical feet by throwing my bike down, taking a couple of sliding steps, wedging one foot deep into the mud, picking my bike up and throwing it down again. By the time I reached the top of the bluff, I was exhausted. I staggered out of the forest into a large clear-cut area. The sky had become pitch dark, shrouded with clouds that blocked the stars. Within the faint beam of my headlamp, all I could see were piles of downed trees. There was no road or trail anywhere in sight.

I swore again, probably for the eightieth time in the past half hour, and began lifting my bike over the seemingly endless minefield of logs. The road had to be around here somewhere, but what if I didn't find it tonight? How far was I going to wander through this fallen-tree obstacle course before I finally just gave up and waited for daylight? I still had my GPS turned on, but the unit didn't have any embedded maps for Canada, and was therefore only good at showing me where I had been. The splintered remains of trees lay like bones on a battlefield, revealing nothing.

After fifteen minutes, I was on the verge of collapsing on a log in a shower of tears when I noticed a strip of gravel on the edge of my headlamp beam. As I approached it, the gravel grew wider until I was standing on a road. I clicked on my GPS to check my progress. It had been an hour and fifteen minutes since I left Cricket's tent. GPS indicated I had traveled less than a mile.

I swore for the eighty-seventh and final time, and set the bike down on a narrow patch of moss only a few feet from the road. It seemed unlikely that anyone would drive to a dead-end road in the middle of a clear-cut, so I wasn't worried about being run over by a car. I pulled out my bivy sack and laid it out next to my bike, which held all of my food, and then plopped down a few feet away in the middle of the road to eat a chocolate bar and a package of tuna for dinner. I tried to be careful with my crumbs because I was in the middle of the most concentrated bear country on the entire route, but I figured if I were a grizzly bear, I wouldn't want to live anywhere near this graveyard for murdered trees. It wasn't really safe, but I couldn't be bothered with technicalities. After finishing my sparse meal, I curled up with my bear spray propped next to my head and quickly drifted into the unconcerned sleep usually reserved for the dead.

Chapter Ten
The First Border

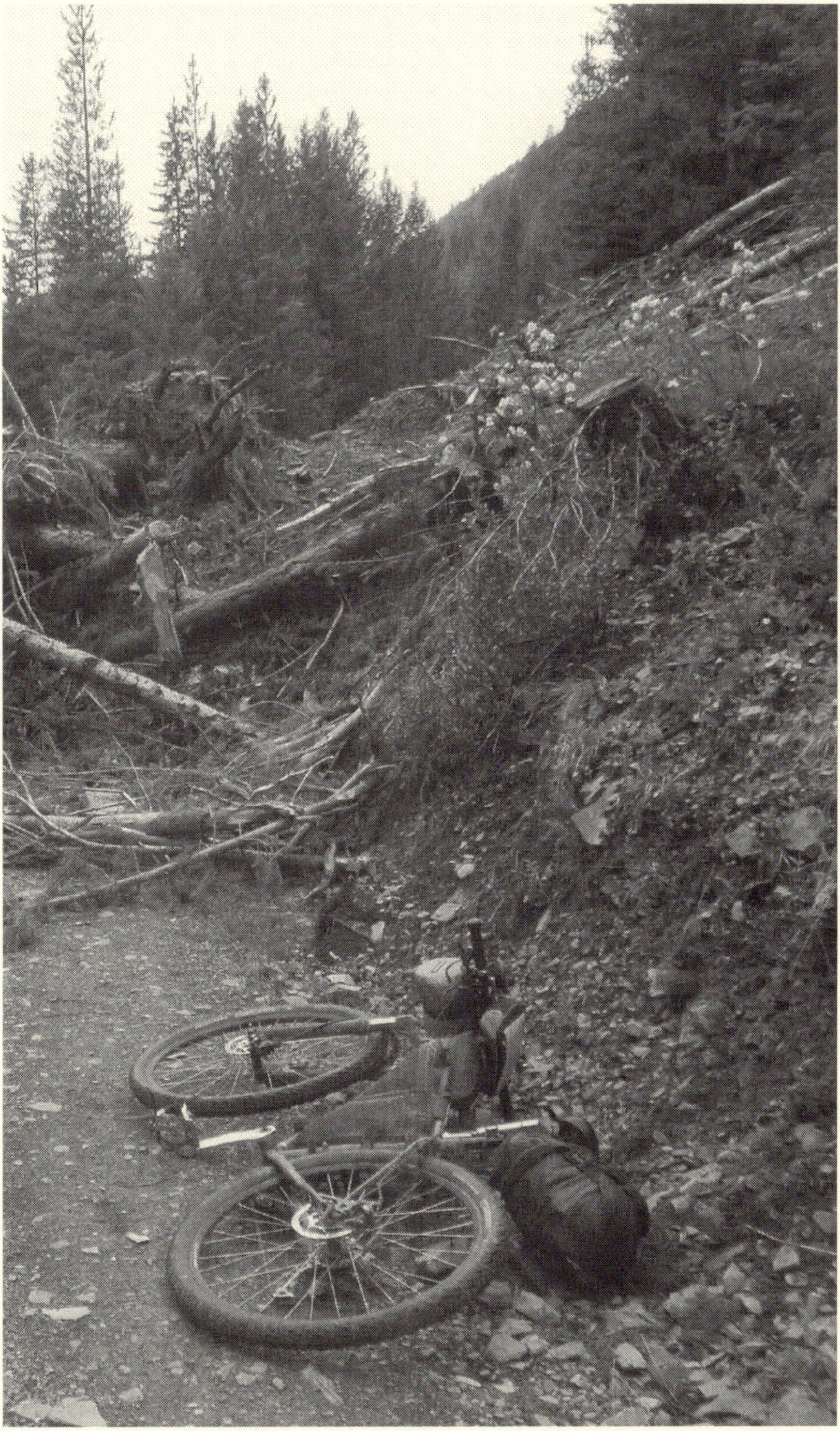

Page 122 and 123: An avalanche blocks passage on a pass in southern British Columbia.

Page 124: Jill Homer ponders the unclear directions on her cue sheet while negotiating a "trail" in the Flathead River Valley.

The soft jingle of a bear bell rang through the timber graveyard. I stirred in my sleeping bag cocoon and pressed one eye and cheek into the brisk morning air. The sun had already risen over the mountains that straddled British Columbia and Montana.

As the sound of the bell moved closer, I wrestled out of my sleeping bag. The morning chill gripped my bare legs as I kicked away the bivy sack and stood up in my socks. Cricket pulled up beside me.

"Good morning!" she said with a cheerful smile. "Wow, that was a mean piece of trail, wasn't it?"

"That's an understatement. How long did it take you to get through the connector?" I asked.

She looked at her watch. "Oh, I broke camp about forty-five minutes ago."

"It took me an hour fifteen in the dark," I said. "I got lost coming out of the forest and wandered around in the clear-cut for a while."

"Yeah, the trail through that logging area isn't even clear in the daylight," she said. "I just headed downhill until I saw the road. And here I am."

"So," I said. "Today, America!"

"I can't wait to cross the border," Cricket said.

"The cue sheet made it seem like there's one more pass," I said, "but it doesn't seem like it'll be a very big one."

Cricket laughed. "We'll see!" I suspected she had as much respect for the cue sheet as I did. She continued down the road as I pulled on more clothing and packed up my bike. My watch said it was 7 a.m., which meant I had slept continuously for seven hours. That seemed a good and bad thing, because while it was good to capture full nights of sleep in order to finish the race, I still felt surprisingly exhausted for a person standing at the bright end of a good night's sleep.

Twenty minutes after Cricket had passed, I mounted my bicycle and followed her faint track in the dirt. To the south, mountains loomed like an impenetrable fortress as I pedaled due west, paralleling the Montana state line that was, according to my GPS, less than six miles away in a direct shot.

The road grade steepened. After an hour of slow pedaling, I approached a fortress of debris, more than thirty feet high, piled across the entire width of the road and the steep gully below. I stopped and gaped at the towering remnants of a large avalanche — a tangle of trees, twisted branches, boulders and snow. Did other bikers really climb over this thing? I didn't see Cricket anywhere, so she must have surmounted the obstacle as well.

I propped my bike against the snow wall and scrambled to the top, balancing precariously on broken limbs and half-exposed tree trunks. I picked my way along the summit of the avalanche pile until I found what looked like a track made by others, then scrambled down to retrieve my bike. I lifted it inch by inch over the downed trees, digging the wheels into the hard-packed snow like an ice ax while I climbed up the mound. Clumps of pine branches slapped me in the face as I worked through the tangle. The painfully slow effort to cross a hundred feet of road felt as tiring as the entire first hour of the day.

On the other side of the avalanche debris, the rutted climb resumed. Switchbacks continued wrapping around the steep slope until patches of snow lined the road, and then stretched across it. My GPS indicated I was nearing 6,500 feet elevation, which meant I had climbed nearly 3,000 feet since that morning and was nearing the highest point on the route through Canada. The cue sheet said nothing about all of this seemingly important information. Its off-center black type seemed to laugh at me as the road turned due north, away from my home country that was so close I could almost reach out and touch it.

I crested a broad summit and looked out over fenced farmland tracts far below in the valley. I launched into the descent, zipping past fences, rotating sprinklers, and dull-eyed horses. Air screamed past my ears as my fingers hovered over the brakes, resisting the urge to slow the free acceleration. I cornered tight switchbacks and grinned into the frigid wind until my teeth hurt, but the pain of the morning melted away. It was my first taste of the Great Divide Mountain Bike Route's saving grace — for all of its unceasing elevation gain, there is a descent for every climb. And with every descent, there is an opportunity to escape sore joints, tight muscles, and sweat-streaked fatigue, in a vacuum of effortless joy.

I crossed onto the paved highway that only minutes before had appeared as a tiny ribbon rippling through a wide valley. The border was finally less than ten direct miles away. Filled with anticipation and adrenaline, I sprinted the entire way there. At the crossing, the border guard stamped my passport and asked me if I was "one of those bikers going to Mexico."

"I sure hope so," I said. "That's the plan."

He handed me his business card with my own name scrawled across the back. "If you make it, give this to the guy in Antelope Wells. He's my buddy. We do this every year with you all. We collect business cards from bikers."

I smiled. "Fun," I said. "I'll try to remember once I get there."

In crossing the border, I was finally released from the tyranny of the cue sheet and found myself back on the well-worn, well-mapped path of the Great Divide Mountain Bike Route. I switched on my GPS to the friendly black track that I had downloaded to help guide me through the endless twists and turns of unmarked forest roads and trails. The route joined the narrow pavement of a farming road and continued due south into the glaring sunlight of late morning. Within what felt like a few free-rolling minutes, I was in Eureka, settling down to lunch at the only fast-food restaurant in town — to my joy, a Subway.

I told the guy behind the counter to load my sandwich with vegetables and bought a salad on the side, knowing that fresh food was going to become increasingly rare as I travelled farther into cowboy country. I sat down with my huge meal to study what was becoming the only reading material I had any interest in — my maps — when another cyclist sauntered in the door and plopped down in the seat across from me. He appeared rested and clean but had a dejected look on his face.

"I saw your bike out front," the man said. "Awesome that you made it here. You seem to be doing really well."

"I'm feeling okay," I said. "Just taking it slow, trying to get a feel for it all. At least I made it out of Canada."

"I'm lucky I even made it out of Canada," he said. "I hit that last pass yesterday afternoon in a thunderstorm. I thought I was going get here a lot faster than I did, so I descended as fast as I could. It was raining hard. I was so cold I couldn't even move my arms. Now I think I have a cold and my knee is jacked up. I can't pedal hard without pain. I stayed here last night. Then I headed back to Roosville this morning, to start over at the border and see if it got any better, but I still have no power. I think my race is over."

"That sucks," I said. I studied him closely, trying to figure out who he was. He had cropped dark hair, a thin build, Lycra shorts stretched over his muscled legs and a logo-splashed cycling jersey augmented by black arm warmers and a rather useless looking performance vest. In short, he looked like every other male cyclist in the Tour Divide. I regarded him with a crooked smile, braced for the social awkwardness of admitting I had no idea who he was, even though he seemed to know me well enough to recognize my bike outside the restaurant.

"So, um," I said. "Did you see any of the leaders come through?"

"Of course," he said. "I was with them until my knee went out."

"So what do you think — do any of them have a shot at the record?"

"I hope not!" he said.

"Really?" I asked. "What about John? How's he doing?"

A look of confusion shot across his face. "John?"

"You know, John Nobile, the record holder," I said.

"Um," he said slowly, looking at me suspiciously like I was asking him a trick question. "I'm the record holder."

Sudden recognition shot through my blood and my face flushed deep red. "Oh, you're John!" I exclaimed. "I'm so, so, sorry. I did not even recognize you without your helmet on. It's just been a long couple of days on the trail and I never expected I'd ever see you again. I really am sorry. You caught me. When you walked up here I had no idea who you were."

"That's okay," he said in a defeated tone. "I'm not feeling much like myself either. What about you? Where are you thinking of going today?"

"Well, it is after 10 a.m., and it's kind of nice in Eureka. There's a big motel next door. I might spend the night here."

John gave me a humorous look of horror that indicated he believed I might be serious. "You're joking."

"Of course," I said, laughing. "I'm feeling pretty good right now. I was going to try to reach Whitefish tonight, but we'll see if I make it. I'm kinda just taking it one mile at a time. Like that singletrack connector trail last night. Damn, what a mile!"

"Was that hard?" he asked with genuine confusion. "I don't even remember much of yesterday before that terrible descent."

I laughed. "Your worst part of Canada was my best. I was just up there two hours ago. It was beautiful."

"Hey," he said. "If you're going to Whitefish tonight, do you mind if I ride with you? It would be good for me to take it easy for a day and see if I can recover my knee. Then I can decide whether or not to ramp it up."

"That would be really fun," I said. "I'd love company. But I have to warn you — I'm slow. Mind-bogglingly slow."

"That's good," he said. "Because alone I'd probably try to catch up to everyone and blow out my knee all over again."

We left Subway and rolled out of town together. I breathed somewhat laboriously at our initial pace, but John was hardly breaking a sweat. Because of our pre-race correspondence, John already knew most of my back story. Instead of working through introductions, he immediately launched into a thorough assessment of my bike, complimenting my bag system and criticizing my choice of front shock. He asked why I chose my particular seat and grips. He labeled my components as "low-end but probably adequate." He questioned my platform pedals and running shoes before I fumbled through my frostbite explanation.

"But good tires," he said. "And looks like a solid frame. Is it steel?"

"It is," I said. "Cheap and strong and full of Juneau rust. To be honest, John, I didn't put a whole lot of thought into my bike. I just have the stuff I have. Geoff picked out a lot of it when we were building up the bike last spring. He wanted me to ride the Divide last year. I didn't even consider it then, when we were still together. It's kinda funny that I'm here now."

"Where is Geoff right now?"

"In Juneau, with his new girlfriend," I said, deliberately spitting out the last word. "But it's been a while since we've spoken. I'm not even entirely sure he knows I started the race. Last time I really talked to him, I told him I wasn't going to do it. But he probably checks out the race updates, so I'm sure he knows I'm here."

"So you and Geoff are really done?"

"It appears that way," I said. "It sucks."

"But you're okay now?"

"I'm up and down and all over the map, really," I said. "But I'm working toward moving on. I even went on a date while I was in Utah."

"A date?"

"Yeah," I said. "It was good. I met him last month on a rafting trip in Southern Utah. His name is Hansel. He's a hunky river guide with blond hair and an unfortunate passion for country music. We went to a baseball game."

"How was it?" John asked.

"The home team lost. To be honest, the whole thing was actually a little weird," I confessed. "It wasn't Hansel. He was really sweet, actually. I just don't know how to act around men these days. Dating was fun when I was a teenager, but now it feels like a contrived sort of pastime. At one point during the game, he put his arm around me and I was like, 'This guy is a basically a stranger.'"

"I find that with the women I go out with, it takes at least three dates to work through that initial awkwardness," he said.

I grinned. John was methodical about everything, absolutely everything, even matters of the heart. He was so unlike me in nearly every way. I wondered how long he'd opt to ride with me. A day? Maybe two? A flash of dread shot through me when I realized he might want to ride with me all the way to New Mexico. It would be an easy jaunt for him and comfortable for me, but the possibility of constant companionship stripped away my ultimate quest in the Tour Divide — a pursuit of that quiet place beyond solitude and suffering where I could see through my experiences and expectations into the heart of who I truly was.

"So, um, how's you're knee feeling?" I asked.

"It definitely hurts," John said. "But not as bad when we're moving at this comfortable pace. I'll gauge it tonight, and maybe continue at this pace tomorrow. But by then I really have to decide whether or not I can go at full power, because after tomorrow, I'll have no shot of catching up to Matt Lee."

"And if it still hurts tomorrow?"

"I might tour the Divide with you for a bit," John said. "It's a lot more fun when you can actually sit up and look around once in a while."

I laughed nervously. It seemed unfair to believe that riding with John might spoil the Tour Divide experience for me, but that was the first thought that ran through my mind. Yes, I had feared the absolute solitude of a solo ride, but constant companionship didn't seem like a solution, either. Self-discovery just wasn't going to happen if John and I were constantly regaling each other with stories about the outside world.

It was a race and I could try to shake him off, but that was not only rude, it was also highly unlikely that I could outrun him in any capacity, even if he was injured. And I had to admit, it was fun to have someone to chat with on the long climbs and chase on the long descents. Maybe we could find a better medium. A few days of riding together might work out well.

We pedaled up Whitefish Divide, hardly even noticing the change in elevation as we motored along and talked about our very different lives. John was an engineer and consultant in Fairfield, Connecticut. He was sixteen years my senior, never married, and owned a house in the town where he grew up. Racing bikes was pretty much his only hobby, although he also dabbled a little in sailing and even owned a boat. He told me he once built a human-powered flying machine, vying for a rather large international prize. Now he worked for an independent think tank that specialized in technology so complex he couldn't begin to describe it to me, although I gathered that it had something to do with bioengineering.

The manipulation of nature — that was John's purpose and his passion. He explained to me how he could use a particular type of wheel to cut eighteen percent off his air drag, thereby adding significantly to his power capabilities without even needing to build a single extra muscle cell. He explained that by upping his power output seven percent across the board during training rides, he could build long-distance endurance in shorter blocks of time. He explained how pushing above his threshold for short bursts of time at the beginning of each hill allowed him to breathe more easily on the long climbs. I nodded enthusiastically and understood little of what he was telling me.

"How about you?" he asked. "How do you structure your training?"

"I go until I'm tired," I said. "And then I do it again the next day."

"That's probably not very effective," John said.

"Perhaps not," I said. "But it has made me who I am. And here I am, strangely, riding with you."

John laughed. "Point taken."

We dropped down Whitefish Divide and started almost immediately up another pass. Snow-capped mountains slowly became snow-covered slopes, until a solid blanket of snow covered the road several feet deep. A fine mist floated over the mostly frozen Red Meadow Lake, coating the alpine landscape in a silky curtain of gray. Light rain fell as I pulled on my rain layer — pure PVC plastic, cheap and effective. John donned decidedly more technical gear, thin layers of vests and jackets made out of coated nylon and Gortex, and little red booties to keep his feet dry.

I looked out over the snow traverse with no end in sight. "Ain't no one coming out of that with dry feet," I said. "I'm just hoping the old frostbite doesn't give me trouble."

We climbed onto the snowfield and commenced pushing our bikes across the icy crust as our shins sunk deep into the porous snowpack. Each step was difficult and progress was painfully slow, with the moist chill gripping my face and hands as I labored in the uncomfortable humidity of my non-breathable jacket. Through the delicate mist, a scene of haunting beauty swirled all around us. Shrouded pine trees clung precipitously to the steep mountainside. The lake ice blended with the pale gray sky, and similarly colorless snow filled the remaining space. I started laughing.

"This is awesome!" I called out. "This is my kind of race — exactly the kind of crap I train for! You are good at speed, John, but I am good at ridiculous."

"You're just crazy and you like snow," John grumbled as we stomped through the slush. "I can't feel my toes."

"The secret to comfort in wet weather is not to stay dry, but to stay warm," I said. "Three years in Juneau taught me that. Sweat yourself out if you need to. The rain will find a way in no matter what you wear, so no point trying to keep yourself dry. Just layer up in synthetics and find a way to block out the wind. Wet and warm. That is the key."

"How are your toes?" John asked.

"They're wet," I said. "But I'm wearing my vapor barrier socks, and that helps trap my body heat, so they feel pretty warm."

We moved about a mile in forty-five minutes. Rotten snow continued to cover the road, which was descending so gradually that I began to wonder if we'd ever drop below snowline. John was starting to shiver noticeably.

"I'm going to have to put on my warm fleecy layer," he complained. "I was really hoping to keep it dry."

"Wet and warm," I said. "Wet and warm. Your fleece isn't doing you any good buried in your trunk."

He stopped to put on the rest of his clothing. As I stood in the misting rain, I took comfort in the thought of a second dry base layer still stuffed in my bags. At worst, I could put on my dry clothing and curl up in my sleeping bag and bivy sack for the night. John, whose strategy was to travel light and fast, carried only an emergency bivy and no sleeping bag. With no extra clothing, his only option was to keep moving until he found shelter. I did not envy his position.

Our conversation tapered as we trudged through what turned out to be another half mile of snow, then shivered down the long descent. We sprinted toward Whitefish, working our body temperatures back to normal on the rolling terrain. It was not yet dark when we pedaled into town and stocked up for the next day, so we opted to continue twelve more miles toward Columbia Falls. From a Whitefish payphone, John called ahead to a Super 8 motel that he had listed on his race chart. The laminated sheet listed every motel in every town where he planned to stay on each leg of his heavily structured Tour Divide schedule. Although he planned to end his third day farther south in Big Fork, he included Columbia Falls as an "emergency" option. The towns where he did not plan to stay had no such listings.

"This is very handy," he said.

"Maybe," I said. "Until a big pile of snow slows you up and you have to restructure the whole thing."

"There is no restructuring," John said. "I just keep moving until I'm there."

I laughed. The rural streets glowed orange beneath the sinking sun.

In the warmth of the Columbia Falls motel room, John took a long shower and I called my dad for Father's Day.

"Father's Day is next Sunday," my dad informed me. "But I'm glad to hear from you. How are things going?"

"Really well," I said. "I partnered up with a racer named John. He's one of the fast guys, so he'll probably only stick with me for a day or two. But he's really knowledgeable about the route and the Divide in general, so it's nice to have him around."

"I'm glad to hear that," my dad said. "We were really hoping you wouldn't end up riding in this race alone."

"I'm still probably going to spend a large chunk of time out here alone," I told my dad, quietly hoping that was true.

John nudged me out of bed at 7 a.m. and we left Columbia Falls together, working our way through a snaking terrace of rural streets as I blinked at the whirring pavement.

"Wow, I am feeling crappy today," I told John. "How are you doing?"

"My knee still hurts," John said. "But it's manageable as long as we keep the pace down."

The pace felt plenty fast to me. "So do you think you'll push ahead?" I asked.

"I better give it one more day," he said. "I don't have the accommodations listed on my sheet, but I looked at the maps and I think Seeley Lake would be a good place for us to stay tonight at the pace we're moving. It's a bit off route, but as I recall they have a couple of nice motels."

"Seeley Lake," I said hoarsely. "How far is that?"

"Only about 120 miles," John said. "But there's three passes in there and a big one, Richmond Pass, which last year had a lot of snow."

"Well at least I have snow to look forward to," I said grumpily. "Helps break up the monotony of pedaling."

"Red Meadow Lake was a cake walk compared to Richmond," John said. "You climb more than 2,500 feet, and just when you think you're done with it all, you veer off onto this road that's covered in solid snow, off-camber snow that's so steep you can't even walk through it without feeling like you're going to slide off the mountain. And it goes on for miles. Last year, during the Great Divide Race, I found a water bottle with a note underneath it left by one of the Tour Divide riders, Felix Wong. It said: 'To whoever finds this note, get yourself out of this Godforsaken race while you still can!'"

I laughed. "Felix Wong was a drama queen. I know. I listened to all of the Tour Divide call-ins last year."

"Yeah, it was a bit overdramatic," John said. "But that's what we have to look forward to at the end of the day."

We flew through the town of Swan River without even taking a break. A few miles beyond town, I demanded that John stop so I could pop a few caffeine pills. "I feel like the energy is draining out of my body faster than I can replace it," I said. "It's only day four and I already feel like a shell of myself."

"There are good mornings and bad mornings on the Divide," John said. "You won't feel this way every morning."

I wheezed. "Want to bet? God, and right now we're just riding flat pavement. How will I ever survive three passes?"

"Maybe that caffeine will kick in," John said. "In Seeley Lake, we'll make sure to get you some coffee."

"Seeley Lake, okay," I said. I felt a rush of annoyance at the second mention of the town. I resented being told where I was going to spend the night. That was supposed to be my decision. If I curled up into a snow hole on Richmond Peak, then that would be my stopping point for the night. If I had a surge of energy and felt like pushing beyond it, I would. Having finite destinations cast a soulless shadow over the Divide, as though we had the ability to control all of the challenges the route threw in our paths. John of course believed we did have this power. But I was more inclined to put my faith in the overarching reign of chaos.

We veered onto a U.S. Forest Service road. John pointed out numbers carved into trees by loggers, landmarks that he remembered with photographic exactness. He told me the road was by far the most concentrated region for bears in the U.S. section of the Great Divide Mountain Bike Route, and sure enough, less than thirty minutes later, a sow grizzly bear and two cubs sauntered across our path. I, in all of my Alaska experience, stopped cold and listened to my heart pound violently beneath my rib cage as the bears regarded us with quiet suspicion. John, in direct contrast to my stunned paralysis, laid into his pedals and charged toward the bears, barking like a dog as he rode within a handful of yards from three large animals with sharp teeth, big claws and a reputation for grumpiness. All three of their ears perked up momentarily before they bolted across the road and disappeared into the thick forest.

"I can't believe you did that," I whispered as I crept up behind John, craning my neck to look toward the trees where the bears disappeared.

"You have to assert your dominance over them," John said with professional certainty. "Just like dogs. If they think you're scared of them, they'll react accordingly."

"You mean like leave us alone?"

"No, they'll act defensively," John said. "They figure if you have reason to fear them, they have reason to fear you."

"They have no reason to fear me!" I called out, hoping my voice was loud enough to scare any eavesdropping bruins away for good. "I'm a soft piece of mush with a candy center."

John laughed. "But they don't know that."

I suspected John didn't really understand bear behavior at all, but I admired his boldness. As with most things in the life of a Great Divide racer, perception is half the battle.

We climbed a seemingly endless series of small hills, dropping near streams and veering onto old Forest Service roads so seldom used that they had become long strips of grass with a sliver of singletrack where occasional cyclists still traveled down the center. John told me this section was perhaps the most remote region of the Divide.

"Remote?" I protested. "Not even. My GPS shows us not more than five miles from the Swan Highway. We've been paralleling it all day; it's right down there. I bet you could even see it if we were above these trees. No, this place is just grizzly bears and grass. To me, remote is the middle of southern New Mexico. Remote is the Great Divide Basin."

"Sounds like places remote to your GPS," John said. "The highway may be right down there, but it's not easy to get to from here. On the Basin, there are roads everywhere."

"Yeah, Oregon Trail roads, which haven't been in regular use since 1869," I said.

"Still," John said. "They're there."

Three rangers in a truck approached us and stopped as we pulled beside them.

"Wow, more bikers!" the driver exclaimed.

"Did you see other cyclists ahead?" John asked in an overanxious tone that made me smile, because he sounded like he was already sizing up the mid-pack competition.

"Three guys," the driver said. "'Bout, I don't know, maybe five miles down the road. I don't think they all spoke English, but they looked like Hell. You guys look sparkling fresh compared to those guys."

"Yeah, you can catch 'em," another said. "Good luck!"

John smiled triumphantly as the rangers drove away. "We can pass them for sure," he said.

I laughed. "Does it matter? There must be at least twenty guys in front of me, and Cricket, too. John, you're in mid-pack now. We only care about ourselves, not the competition."

"Liar," John smiled. "You know you care. Anyway, you do look like you're feeling better than this morning."

"I am feeling better," I said. "Either the caffeine pill or the grizzly bears revived me. I'm guessing it was the bears."

We pedaled up a small pass, coasted down, and then climbed another. My adrenaline surge faded rapidly as we approached the looming dread of Richmond Peak. We rode through swampy muskeg so thick with mosquitoes that we both stopped twice to layer ourselves in every drop of DEET we had on us, and then rode as fast as we could across a muddy field that had once been a road.

"The magic speed is ten miles per hour," John said. "You have to ride at least ten miles per hour if you want the mosquitoes to leave you alone."

"What about tailwind?" I mused. "Or really, really persistent mosquitoes?"

"Ten miles per hour," John said. "They'll never bother you as long as you're going at least that fast."

I looked down at my odometer. We were traveling seven miles per hour. I felt I was going as hard as I could without passing out. "Then you go ten miles per hour," I panted, "and when we reach Seeley Lake, I'll buy more bug spray."

"Whatever works," John said.

The sun was settling low on the horizon when the climb began in earnest.

"This is Richmond Peak?" I asked.

"The one and only," John said. The wide gravel road switch-backed up the aspen-choked mountainside. Across the narrow river valley to the east, pine-studded mountains shimmered gold beneath direct beams of low sunlight. I watched John's silhouette disappear around a bend, but his shadow remained stretched over the lower road. I spat quick, labored breaths and drew in oxygen with waning enthusiasm. The trees began to thin as the alpine line drew closer. I could see John's shadow disappearing around distant bends, but had little ability to press harder to catch up. I marveled at the ability of real racers to surge toward a sprint finish when they too were running on little more than fumes, but my body knew too well that a whole lot of survival still lay in front of me.

After two hours of climbing, the sun had disappeared below the horizon and John was standing at the crest of the road, waiting for me. To the newly revealed west, a spectacular light display shimmered through strips of clouds, draped in strands of red, gold and orange, and even blue and green, all woven together in the startlingly big sky for which Montana was famous. Our mountainside was bathed in a warm shade of peach. Cameras did nothing to capture the colors, so we put them away and stood in serene silence together until I noticed John was shivering.

"Perhaps we should get moving," I said.

"You feeling okay?" John asked me through chattering teeth.

"I'm fine," I said. "I took it slow to save some energy for the top. Let's go get us some snow."

John pointed down the road. "You'll want to go that way, and you'll think you should go that way. That road drops down to the highway in about three miles; then it's a straight shot to Seeley Lake. But we don't get to go that way. We get to go the hard way. You'll see."

The wide road fell away as we veered onto a Forest Service road that hadn't been used by anyone besides cyclists and perhaps the occasional hiker in a number of decades. Six-foot-tall spruce trees grew down the center of the doubletrack, which was bumpy and rock-strewn after years of neglect.

"Give this five more years and it'll be indistinguishable from anywhere else in the forest," I said. "The wheels of forty cyclists aren't enough to maintain a trail."

We beat through the spruce bushes and quickly reached the snowfield. In the fading light, I squinted across the mountain. The route seemed to cut directly into the steep slope, but the snowpack stretched over it in a perfect 45-degree angle before dropping off a near-vertical cliff. The only way through it was a line of deep-set footprints. I could see what John meant about sliding off the mountain. If the temperature was below freezing and the snow surface froze, there would be absolutely no way to safely cross it without crampons and an ice ax. At 9 p.m., the temperature was already in the low forties and dropping.

John plunged into the tracks left by other racers. "Snow's still soft," he said. "And this helps. It's pretty hard to find the way down so I'm hoping those who came before managed to."

"Well, if we don't find their bodies, we'll know they did," I said. I followed John through the tracks, pushing my bike through the rigid slush and occasionally punching through the snow to my thighs. The precipice loomed mere inches to my left, and I prayed I wouldn't lose my balance because I wasn't sure I'd be able to arrest a fall. Beyond that, pushing my bike through thigh-deep snow was hard work, and I started overheating rapidly. John stopped often to call back to me in a jittery voice that told me he was more worried about his own chilled state than he was about my pace.

"Go on ahead if you need to," I called out. "I'll be fine."

"We need to find the route together," John called back. "Once it starts dropping down; it's impossible to see in the snow. You'll see."

Nearly an hour and perhaps a mile later, I could see what he meant. The intuitive direction of the route disappeared into a clump of trees, and below us was a less deadly but still rather steep, declining snowfield.

"I think the road normally switchbacks down that," John said. "We should probably just cut directly down."

"I say we keep following the tracks," I said, even though the majority did seem to veer in the wrong direction, and there were several in different directions. "If we lose them, then we'll know it's time to turn back."

We snaked down the slope just as the last hints of twilight disappeared and engulfed the mountain in pitch darkness. John, in his single-minded forward march, surged away from me. Minutes later, I could only pick out a half dozen footprints through the snow, and I vowed not to lose track of the fading evidence of those who came before. When I finally joined John on what appeared to be a muddy road, I felt a sweep of relief.

"It's not over yet," John said. "This road is still terrible for a ways. Steep drops. Big gullies. And there's still plenty of snow. You have to be careful." His teeth chattered as he spoke.

"Are you okay?" I asked.

"I'm really cold," he said. "It's hard for me to keep up my body heat at this pace."

"Yeah, Geoff used to tell me the same thing," I said. "My heart rate would be 150 and his would be beating less than a hundred at my rate of speed. He could never stay warm."

"I'm just going to keep Seeley Lake on my mind," John said. "We should be there within the hour."

The road was everything John promised it would be, studded with large spruce trees, rocks, hard snow, and sudden drops into deep trenches. John descended quickly and I white-knuckled my handlebars, feathered the brakes and fought back terror in an effort to keep up with him. The phantom world disappeared in front of us, buzzing through the narrow beam of our headlamps like flies in front of a projector. Soon the road smoothed out, becoming wider as we dropped ever faster, with mud flinging in our faces and frigid air burning our lungs. Even I started to feel the chill, and

I pitied John, who I figured must have been a popsicle at that point. But I couldn't help but smile wide. Richmond Peak wasn't so high. The snow slope wasn't so bad. It was a beautiful adventure, and this descent was its sweeping reward.

By the time we dropped into Seeley Lake, it was after midnight. The entire town stood still in darkness and silence.

"Crap," I said. "It looks all closed up."

John's face fell into a wild-eyed look of panic. He sprinted in front of me toward the first motel. By the time I caught up to John, he was practically pressed against the locked door of the front office, hand repeatedly pushing a button beneath a sign that read, "Night Bell."

"Please come downstairs, please come downstairs," he chanted as his teeth chattered audibly.

"John, if we can't get a room, what are you going to do? You don't have a sleeping bag."

"We'll have to keep going to Ovando," he said.

"Ovando!" I cried. "John, it's like thirty more miles from here, and it's after midnight. I don't have that much mileage in me tonight. I've been exhausted all day. I need sleep."

"We won't think about that yet," he said. "They'll come downstairs. They will."

After several teeth-chattering minutes, a woman appeared at the door. John gave her an endearing if pathetic smile, and without even a handful of words, she had a key in her hands and was enthusiastically directing us toward a room. John rushed in the door and collapsed on the bed. "Warm!" he exclaimed. "Shower!"

The woman moved to close the door and I asked her if there was a bar in town where we might be able to buy a meal at that time of night.

"They're all closed," she said. "But give me a sec; I'll see what I can do."

She walked away. I had no idea what she meant, until she returned several minutes later with a big Tupperware bowl in her hands.

"It's the tuna noodle casserole we had for dinner," she said. "There's not a ton left, but you can have all of it."

"Wow! Thanks!" I said, and smiled wide. "You know, this is going to be my first hot meal on the Divide!" She smiled back even though she had no idea what I meant by that statement, nor did she realize just how much that casserole meant to me. I stuck it in the microwave, and by the time John emerged from the shower looking relieved, I presented him with a heaping spoonful of the ultimate prize.

"No way! There's food?"

"Courtesy the night clerk at this amazing establishment," I said. "Not only was she not pissed we woke her up, she gave us her leftovers."

John took a bite and grinned. "This is my favorite place on the entire Divide!"

I grinned. It had been a long, physically taxing day that started on the wrong side of the bed, continued on a roller coaster of remote forest and grizzly bears, climaxed on a treacherous snow-covered peak and ended with hot casserole. Even though I had been so annoyed earlier in the day about John's grand plan, I had to agree with him. "Mine too," I said.

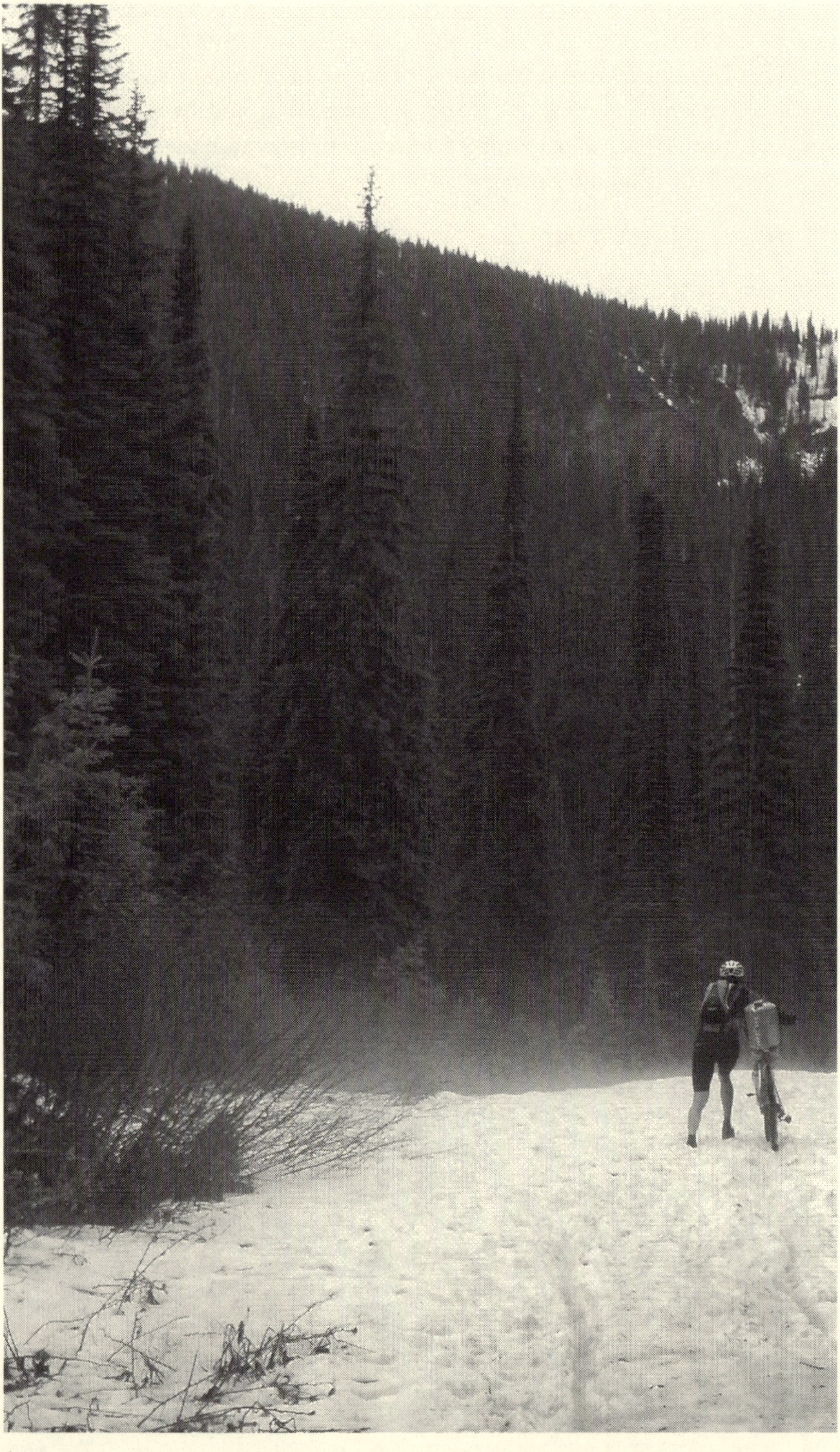

Chapter Eleven
Raising Montana

Page 142 and 143: John Nobile negotiates several miles of snow and avalanche debris on Red Meadow Pass in Montana.
Page 144: Jill Homer rides on a logging road in Montana.

"Maybe we should take an easy day," John said as we rolled away from Seeley Lake, pedaling back up the road we had descended off route late the previous night.

"What were you thinking?" I asked.

"Lincoln is only sixty-five miles from here, with one small pass. Beyond that, there's really only Helena. That's about 120 miles, but there are a lot of big passes between here and there."

"Sixty-five miles," I said, frowning. That was an unconscionably short day this early in a race. I had been tired the day before, but felt strongly refreshed after food and sleep and a relaxed morning. Still, I didn't want to commit to Helena, which was too far away for a 10 a.m. start. John's inability to stay anywhere besides a town irked me, as did his insistence to start a day knowing exactly where it was going to end. But my only other choice was to leave him behind in Lincoln and continue on to some halfway point in the woods. Even though he often took an all-knowing stance toward the rhetorical questions I liked to ask, and even though he had this annoying habit of spinning effortlessly beside me and chatting far too cheerfully as I labored up climbs, I had grown fond of John's company.

"So I guess you surging ahead isn't going to happen at this point?" I asked.

"It's out of the question now," John said. "My knee is still bothering me. It's better than it was in Eureka, but it still hurts. And I'm too far behind the leaders. They're probably south of Butte by now."

"So where do you think you'll drop out?" I asked. "I'm guessing Helena has an airport."

"I could get a flight out in Helena," he agreed. "Butte is good, too. I'll play it by ear. I already have the vacation time, and it has been a lot of fun touring with you."

I felt a renewed surge of anxiety about the possibility of a complete lack of solo time on the Divide. "How long do you want to keep touring?" I said weakly. "Not until the end?"

"No, not until the end," John said. "I don't have that much vacation time."

We rolled through Ovando around lunchtime, but did not stop for a meal despite our shortened schedule. John preferred to eat on the bike, stuffing down energy bars and swigs of florescent orange recovery drink as I munched on almonds and Sour Patch Kids. The convenience store food filled the same caloric deficits as real food, but not the same emotional holes. Eating on the bike was always a joyless chore, a thankless task that required stuffing fistfuls of chewy, processed food between perpetual efforts to steer around rocks and loose patches of gravel. I was beginning to miss plates and forks and actually observing what I was consuming before it went into my mouth.

"We'll eat a good meal in Lincoln," John promised. "You'll like it there. It's nice."

We arrived in Lincoln before 4 p.m., after leaving Seeley Lake at 10 a.m. I felt guilty about our short day, and a little bit restless, but a restaurant sign advertising pasta and fresh salads sounded a siren call that John was all too happy to oblige. We found a hotel that promised hot tubs, and checked in even after the clerk told us the hot tubs were closed. Four o'clock was a bit early for dinner, so we killed some time lounging at a gas station. I wavered for a few minutes at the soda fountain. Back home, I was a voracious Diet Pepsi drinker, absolutely addicted to the crisp texture and lightly sweet flavor of the calorie-free soda. On the Divide, I had begrudgingly switched back to regular soda to help fill an ever-growing calorie deficit. But in Lincoln, with only sixty-five miles and one relatively easy pass behind me, I nudged the plastic cup beneath the Diet Pepsi dispenser. I savored the nutritionally useless soda with surprising revelry, a rush of warmth, and the instant relief of my favorite comfort food.

At the gas station, a large man wearing a cycling jersey and a tiny pair of jogging shorts that did little to hide anything sauntered out of the gas station's adjacent casino. I recognized him as the Italian I had ridden with for a short time on the first day. He introduced himself as Dario, a name I recognized as belonging to a man who had also ridden in the 2008 Iditarod Trail Invitational. During that year's race, he reached McGrath about a day before I did and set out toward to Nome, but ran out of water and ended up begging a ride off a snowmobiler with the Iditarod Dog Sled Race. I didn't need to relay any of these connections to him, however. Dario recognized me instantly. Everyone did. I was the girl.

"Hallo Jill," he said.

"How are you, Dario?" I asked.

"I am good, very good," he said. He pointed to his backside. "Sore, but good."

"Are you staying here tonight?"

"Yes, we stay here for now," he said. "But we leave midnight."

I raised my eyebrows. "Really, midnight? Ambitious."

"Yes." He smiled and nodded, lingered for a few more seconds in a stiff silence and then walked away.

"Damn, midnight," I said. "Eight hours of rest and gone, darkness be damned. I guess we're still up there with the real racers."

"You're really not doing too badly," John said.

"It's weird not to know where anyone is in this race," I said. "And we have no way to find out. Last year, when Geoff was racing the Divide, I knew everything that was going on, almost down to the minute, just based on call-ins and a little bit of tracking. Now I'm actually on the Divide, and for all I know, the winner has already crossed the Mexican border."

"I can promise you they haven't," John said. "Last year, when you were blogging the Great Divide Race, I would call my friends back home and have them tell me what you had written, so I could keep track of where Geoff and David were. After they dropped out, I was far out in front for the rest of the GDR, so there was no real need to check in anymore."

We ate our big meal and fresh salad at the restaurant, took a leisurely walk around town and settled into our beds before it was even dark outside. I started tapping out a blog post on my handheld e-mail device.

"We should get up early," John said as he carefully laid out the articles of clothing he had washed in the shower and dried with some of the six extra towels he always requested from the front desk. "We had a good rest today. I think we should try to make it to Butte tomorrow."

"Whatever you say," I replied lazily.

"It's 130 miles," John said. "And six passes. Lots of difficult logging roads. It's going to be a big day."

"So 6 a.m. wake-up then?"

"I'd say five," John replied. "You'll see. This is likely going to be your longest day of the entire Tour Divide."

Five o'clock was indeed well before dawn, and I was slow to start moving in the early morning. I lingered too long in the aisles at the gas station and insisted on consuming a breakfast burrito, coffee and orange juice before I consented to continuing down the route.

I had already become a connoisseur of Divide sunsets, but the morning's sunrise dawned with more spectacular streaks of light and color washes than any sky I had seen yet. We motored along farm roads beside pink-drenched pastures as an impenetrable fortress of purple mountains loomed in front of us. I whipped out my camera and took a long series of images of John and his far-reaching shadow as I sang out loud the words from a Kodak film commercial that I remembered from my childhood: "These are the moments, don't let them pass you by ... those Kodak moments, don't let them pass you by." John laughed and made his best effort at a funny face, which looked more like a grimacing smile. Still, I could tell the good mood was mutual.

John and I approached the wall of mountains, which revealed their weakness in yet another side-cut road switch-backing up the steep slope. "I'm beginning to notice this pattern about Montana," I said. "It's all climb, drop, climb, drop. Nothing is flat here."

"That's what makes Montana the hardest state," John said. "And the best."

Stemple Pass was every bit as steep as the mountains threatened, gaining 2,000 feet in about seven miles. John waited for me at the top, which I reached long after the chill and color of the morning had faded to warm, direct light. "Well, there's one down," John said as I rubbed my eyes, which were still blurry with sleep, and slathered my arms with sunscreen. "And it's our first Continental Divide crossing. You should take a picture."

"We crossed the Divide back in Canada, remember?" I said. "Elk Pass. On the first day. But, yeah, first U.S. crossing. Which side are we on now?"

"I think we're on the Atlantic side," John said. "Believe me, after a few more of these, you're going to completely lose track."

I looked down at a tiny gurgle of a stream, no wider than a large pencil. "So you're trying to get to the Mississippi," I said to the water as John started pedaling down a nearly level grade. "Good luck with that."

Divide crossing number two came less than twenty miles later, over another broad, rolling pass about 6,500 feet high. The next crest, Priest Pass, elevation 5,994, rolled us back to the Mississippi side of the Divide a mere ten miles later. There was little relief in the continuous grade; even at five or six miles per hour, my legs burned with the searing acid that my muscles usually reserved for a dead sprint. The hard sun hovered in a cloudless sky. I applied another layer of sunscreen over a smear of sweat and dirt, which combined to form a salty, gritty paste across my skin.

We dropped into Helena at about 2 p.m. Cars streamed beside us at speeds that felt disorienting after a long morning of pedaling through forests where we had been more likely to meet a black bear than a human. John and I rode directly to a large grocery store. I rushed inside, almost squealing with delight as I filled a basket with strawberries, oranges, carrots, yogurt, wheat bread, and tuna for lunch. After I amassed my treats, I begrudgingly picked up the necessary chocolate, almonds, gummy bears and Sour Patch Kids I would need for the rest of the day.

"Why is it that healthy food tastes so delicious on the Divide while junk food tastes so crappy?" I mused as John and I devoured large piles of groceries out in front of the store.

"Obviously, nutrition," John said. "But it's also about indulgence and having things you normally can't have. You need a lot of calories to keep going, and you don't want it to weigh very much, so you have to carry junk food. But, wow, I just bought a sixty-calorie peach that weighs an entire pound, and it is delicious."

We finished our lunch and rode toward Helena's main bike shop. My gloves, which were nearly new when I started the race less than a week earlier, had disintegrated to little more than shreds of fabric held together by sunscreen-dirt paste, and I hoped to replace them. John wanted to buy lube and spare spokes. Inside, covered in a thick layer of dirt and holding tattered gloves, I was met with a surprisingly cool reception from the employees of a mountain town shop that seemed to cater only to high-end road cyclists. Two other Divide racers, Cricket and a man named Jeremy, were also holed up in the cramped store, waiting miserably for badly needed repair service that did not seem to be coming.

"How are things going?" I asked Cricket, who I hadn't seen since she passed me in Canada.

"Oh, you know, my bike's falling apart," she chuckled. "Not really. I'm just having them fix a few things, but they sure are slow here. At this rate, I'll never make it to Butte tonight."

"We're shooting for Butte, too," I said. "Did you stay in Lincoln last night?"

"No," she said, "just beyond there, near Stemple Pass. It was cold last night. Nasty with wind and rain."

"Oh?" I said. "I didn't notice." I acknowledged with some guilt that I had stayed in a warm and dry motel room that I hadn't really earned.

At the counter, I waited for five minutes to pay for bike gloves as two clerks stood five feet away chatting with each other and ignoring me entirely. After I finally acquired my merchandise and walked outside, Jeremy, who also had been standing around for nearly a half hour without much help, announced in disgust that he was just going to try to get his bike work done in Butte. The three of us left together.

"Congratulations," John said to me as we started up yet another pass. "You're now in first place of the women's race."

"Ha!" I laughed. "Don't be surprised if Cricket comes charging past us in an hour. That woman is tough as nails."

The fourth pass of the day was a nondescript lump, with an 1,800-foot climb that took us out of the lowlands of Helena. I was feeling surprisingly energetic even though we had already climbed nearly 10,000 vertical feet that day. John motored ahead and I pedaled beside Jeremy, trying to make conversation. Jeremy was a short, broad man — not heavy, just strong. He was about my age, with short, light brown hair and a face frozen in a grimace. His bike was haphazardly loaded with bulging bags, several of which were simply hanging off his handlebars. He generally replied to my questions with single-word answers, if at all, but rather than take offense as I had with Steve, I felt pity for Jeremy. His eyes were glazed and he was breathing heavily. He appeared to be struggling.

"I was going to ride a singlespeed in the Tour Divide," he unexpectedly blurted out after several minutes of silence. "And at the last minute decided to put a cassette on, so I have nine speeds. It's still not enough. My legs are killing me. I have never needed a low gear as badly as I do right now."

I looked down and for the first time noticed his cadence. He turned a single, plodding stroke for every two of mine. My legs spun easy while his worked considerably for every laborious rotation. And there we were, moving at the same rate of speed, even though I was exerting just a fraction of his effort level. I could only smile sympathetically. The bicycle is such a simple machine, and yet the presence of two extra cogs on my crank and a front derailleur to move the chain around made a world of difference between my bike and Jeremy's. Single-speeders tout purity and simplicity, but I fall squarely in the school of thought that technology is a wonderful thing and should be used to its fullest wherever practical and available. Jeremy did not seem inclined to disagree.

John waited at the top and the two of us shifted into our big rings and soon surged ahead of Jeremy, who was spun out in his too-small top gear. We dropped into a thick-forested canyon that seemed eerily isolated from the civilized world. I zoomed in the scale of my GPS screen, seeking reassurance from the fact that we were now paralleling Interstate 15. But the ridge of some very large mountains hid the interstate from view, and we were descending into a world populated by hillbillies and bears.

We turned off Lava Mountain Road, and labored along the deeply rutted, rock-strewn jeep track. "There is a turn here that's crucial," John said. "Watch your maps really closely, because it's easy to miss. It's a right turn that the maps say nothing about. I missed it last year and was lost for more than five hours. Geoff and David missed it too; that was the night they had to sleep in a bathroom."

"It was a shower stall," I said. "At a campground in Basin. I remember that night. I remember having this strange feeling of dread when I heard Geoff's call-in at seven at night announcing he was leaving Helena, and then watching his SPOT tracker make circle after circle in a random area between Helena and Basin. I don't think they got to camp until after three, at a point when he already wasn't sleeping much during the nights. I think Lava Mountain was the turning point for Geoff. The beginning of the end."

"He still rode halfway through Colorado after that night," John said. "Right on my tail."

"Yes, well, for Geoff, he'll force himself into top performance until he absolutely can't function any more. I really think that's what happened to him. People lose interest in this race and drop out; they tout it as a mental battle. But in Geoff's case, I really think his body stopped working. Total shutdown."

"You think so?"

"I believe it," I said. "And that's my main goal in this race, avoiding that. But I'm not too worried. As long as I can keep myself warm and not too frightened, I'll be fine. I'm as conservative as so-called athletes come."

John and I came to a junction that the maps said nothing about. My GPS track turned distinctly to the right. "This is it," I announced. "This is the bad turn."

John glanced around. "Yeah, I'm pretty sure this is it, but not certain."

I smiled. John had his photographic memory and four full races through this section of the trail. I had poor navigational skills and a $200 GPS unit, but I was willing to hedge all of my bets on that one right turn. "Do you think we should wait for Jeremy?" I asked.

"He'll see our tracks. He'll find it," John said.

"Maybe I should draw an arrow in the mud," I said.

John frowned. "I wouldn't do that," he said. "Helping others with navigation is against the race rules. Something like that could get you disqualified. I'm not even sure what it means for you and me to be traveling together, but that GPS of yours seems to know where it's going, so I don't feel like I'm guiding you anyway."

"Huh," I said. "I hadn't even thought of that before. This race really strives to be brutal, doesn't it? The rules won't even let two racers help each other."

"Well, self-support is exactly that," John said. "Since my race is over, I'm only worried about over-influencing you, but you seem to be self-sufficient with or without me."

"Are you kidding?" I laughed. "You're like a Great Divide coach! But, yeah, it's mostly a moral support thing. I know I'd be fine on my own."

"You would," John said. "And will. I've been thinking about dropping out in Butte. Beyond there, I don't even think there's a real town until Jackson, Wyoming."

"You could always jump on I-15 and ride to Idaho Falls," I said. "I used to live there. They have a nice airport. But do what you gotta do."

We continued up the rocky road and I felt a pang of loneliness. For much of the first two days we spent together, I had only wanted John to leave me alone. But we had talked through our life stories, established our boundaries, and found mutual fondness of the hard miles and of each other. I was no longer sure I wanted to give that all up for self-imposed solitude.

The final pitch of the Lava Mountain Road was so steep and rutted that we both had to walk our bikes. Bike pushing is a brutal discipline — much harder than walking and even more difficult than riding when you're dealing with more than fifty pounds of metal and gear. My shoulders burned and leg muscles strained with every ounce of power I could muster, and still I felt like I was pushing a proverbial rock up a mountain, which I was.

But bike pushing is also a fine art, a chance to slow movement to a crawl and observe the surrounding world through a heavy, almost blissful fatigue. Tree bark took on a compelling texture I would have never noticed had I simply flown past during a gravity-fed descent. Sprigs of grass and tiny purple flowers swayed in the gentle breeze, and chattering squirrels scrambled up and down trees. Everything moved as though suspended under water. When eyes are tired and muscles are sore, life seems to fall away in slow motion, like a beautiful dream on the edge between consciousness and sleep.

Lava Mountain topped out at more than 7,000 feet, our highest pass yet. The terrain continued to roll noncommittally through a thick forest of dwarf spruce until, from a clearing far above a narrow valley, I-15 came into view. We coasted into the town of Basin just before sunset, having already ridden twelve hard hours. The slow-motion movement of Lava Mountain was still swimming in my mind. I was ready to stop for the day. But there was no motel in Basin, only a campground, and goals cannot be given up without good reason. I leaned into my handlebars as John fished energy bars out of the compartment on the front of his bike.

"It's only thirty more miles to Butte," he said. "Just one more pass, and it's a small one. We can do it in three or four hours."

"If you say so," I said apathetically.

We turned onto a gravel route paralleling the interstate that the map called a "Non-maintained Cattle Access Trail." The old railroad bed was strewn with large, loose stones, which seemed to grab our wheels and force them backward like a line of rollers in a sadistic fun house. John's bike kicked up a cloud of dust as he fought the rough surface. I bowed my head like a child who, being mercilessly shaken by an enraged caregiver, goes limp in response. Only a few hundred yards to our right, trucks and cars streamed by on the smooth pavement of I-15. I knew the interstate would take us precisely where we wanted to go. It would likely be hours sooner than we would reach Butte at the rate we were traveling.

"You know, all this effort to avoid pavement has got to be the best part of the Divide," I deadpanned.

"Believe me, when the route starts dumping you onto highways, which it will from time to time, you'll change your mind about that," John said. "Do you really want to be riding with trucks on an interstate? Trust me, this is much better."

I looked out toward the traffic stream on I-15, now separated from us by the meandering blue ribbon of the Boulder River. As the sun slipped behind the mountains, its golden light dyed the grass-lined banks in warm tones of sienna and orange. I narrowed my vision until the freeway and deep canyon walls faded into the background, and imagined a stream flowing through a Midwestern prairie — rich, open and quiet.

"I don't know," I said. "It is pretty here. It's just getting dark. And suddenly I feel like it's really late. My body doesn't want to move anymore. I really want to be asleep right now."

"It won't be much longer," John said.

The railroad bed cut steeply up the mountain, away from the hypnotic parade of red taillights on I-15. In the monotone dusk, we hadn't noticed all the clouds building overhead. But just as darkness fell, it started to rain. And as quickly as the first droplets fell, the storm exploded into a drenching shower. Within seconds we were soaked, but stopped to pull on our rain gear just the same. As I stripped off my shoes to pull on my vapor barrier socks, John paced around with the same nervousness he had displayed before Seeley Lake.

"It was like this last year," he said. "I think storms just get caught on the Continental Divide before Butte, and just sit there and get really bad."

We continued climbing through the downpour. The rain came down so hard and thick that it seemed to cut out the light from my headlamp, and I could hardly see John's light as he pedaled faster in the distance. Before I even noticed its brick entrance, the rail trail disappeared into the yawning hole of an abandoned tunnel. Suddenly engulfed in complete darkness, I began to shiver — not from the chill, but from a primal sort of fear. A low continuous moan echoed through the corridor. I glanced around nervously and listened for hints of a train whistle, even though the tracks had long since been ripped from the ground. Since there were no longer trains to fear, I feared the ghost train, with its shrill moan calling out from the eerie depths. Without even noticing, I started pedaling faster, anxious to escape the black and chilling tomb.

I was relieved to see John's light again as he waited for me near the exit. As I shined my own light in his face, a look of distress washed over his pale skin.

"Do you think we should stop here for the night?" he asked.

"What? Here? In a train tunnel?"

"At least it's dry in here," John said. His chin was quivering and his bottom lip looked blue.

"What about your complete lack of camping gear?" I asked.

"I have my bivy sack," he said. "I just need to put on my dry clothes and get warm."

"Trust me, you're not going to get any warmer if we stop," I said. "It's like the underworld of the dead in here. It's claustrophobic and creepy. I would rather walk to Butte in a snowstorm than stay here. But you can stay if you want. I'll even give you my sleeping bag."

"You sure you don't want to stay here?"

"John, I'm sorry. There's no way I can sleep in here. It's like a spooky haunted house."

John grumpily followed me back out into the downpour while I breathed big gulps of relief in the fresh air. "You should just sprint ahead," I told him. "You'll warm up if you start moving faster. You can't stay warm if you stay with me. I'll just meet you in Butte. You're stopping at that bike shop hotel, right?"

"I'll be fine," John grumbled.

"Well, if that's the way you're going to be, I'll just step up my pace," I said. "I want to be done with this freaking day. Do you mind if I listen to my iPod?"

"No, go ahead," he said. "I've got one too."

Together but separate, we tuned in to a soothing cloak of electronic sound, blocking out the pattering rain and brightening the cold darkness. John listened to jam bands like the Grateful Dead and Donna the Buffalo. I tuned in to modern alternative, the Arcade Fire and the Yeah Yeah Yeahs. We both laid into the pedals and nudged our speed back into the double digits. We crossed onto a paved frontage road, with the yellow and red car lights of I-15 flickering through sheets of rain. We ramped up the speed to thirteen miles per hour, and then fifteen, still climbing. I couldn't fathom where I was finding the energy. The day already fell solidly into the top ten most physically taxing cycling days of my life, right up there with my twenty-four-hour-races and individual days on the Iditarod Trail. But John was cold and I was motivated. We were a blur of gummy-bear-powered speed.

We crested our sixth and final pass for the day, Elk Park Pass, elevation 6,368, just before midnight. The gradual climb suddenly dropped steeply in front of us. The wide valley below revealed a sprawl of sparkling city lights, a continent of warmth in a cold and black universe. I gasped in astonishment at the glittering beauty, so novel and complex after eighteen hours mostly spent crawling through 130 miles of open meadows and woods. We rocketed down the shoulder of I-15, hunched deep into our aero bars like road racers in the Tour de France, blinking rapidly against a fire-hose spray of rainwater.

"This is the greatest city in the world!" I screamed into the wind, knowing with smug satisfaction that neither John nor Butte — population 34,000 — could hear me. The golden continent rapidly grew larger until it engulfed us like an oversized blanket. Towering over us now were streamlined overpasses, neon-lit restaurants and ten-story hotels, marvels of modern architecture as great as the Manhattan skyline. I grinned, because I knew that day, I had earned the privilege to rest well.

Chapter Twelve
Savage Side

Page 157: John Nobile watches a storm approach outside Butte.
Page 158: John Nobile rides through a valley in Montana.

I woke up draped in the silky sheets of a luxury king-sized bed, deeply sore.

General muscle and joint soreness is always accompanied by wide-ranging emotions. There is comforting soreness, the kind that comes in the midst of hard training, because it signals sought-after muscle growth. There is satisfying soreness, that post-race glow when a person knows they have met their goals and can finally rest. There is debilitating soreness, the kind that follows injuries, lapses in judgment or an insistence on pushing oneself too hard.

And then there is Divide soreness. Divide soreness is not so easily pinpointed, because it descends in waves over days and weeks. It starts as a sharp tinge in the larger muscles on day two or three. Then it slowly cuts into smaller fibers. Then it seeps into the blood, working its way into the recesses of long-forgotten and little-used regions of the body, such as pinky toes. Just when you find yourself wondering why your pinky toe hurts, soreness has found its way into your brain, casting a pain-soaked pall over even the simplest thoughts and decisions. Finally, Divide soreness needles through to the soul, full of bile and perpetual fatigue, convincing the unfortunate individual that Hell is not death's purgatory but a state of being on Earth, and nothing will ever look or feel good ever again.

Of course, the mercy of Divide soreness is that it doesn't in fact last forever, and comes and goes frequently during the course of the same race, and even the same day. But, leaving Butte, I felt none of the euphoria I had experienced while descending into town. The city looked gray and bland in the light of day, a scattershot of concrete in a wide, barren basin.

"I checked the SPOT standings before we left town," I said to John as we pedaled toward yet another wall of mountains. "I was actually surprised. We really are right in the middle of the pack, right in the thick of it. In fact, the leaders haven't even left Montana yet, but I think Matt Lee will cross into Idaho today."

"See, and you're not even trying yet," John said.

"Oh believe me, I'm trying," I said. "It just doesn't seem like it to you because you're on a joy ride. You only notice how slow we're going when you get cold."

John had taken me up on my recommendation of Idaho Falls as a good place to leave the Divide, and decided to follow me to southern Montana, which meant we would be riding together for at least two more days. I was glad he hadn't decided to abandon the race in Butte, but grumpy enough that morning that I really felt like asking him to press ahead so I could indulge in a few hours of tuned-out solitude. John, on the other hand, had slept great the night before and was able to slam down a huge breakfast even though he insisted on going to the grocery store rather than Denny's, which had been my preference. I had only managed to consume a yogurt and a pound of strawberries before I started to feel ill, and the only thing competing with muscle soreness for my attention was a discouragingly low energy level.

John chatted amicably while I nodded and grunted, wishing he would ride ahead so I could nurse my malaise. Near the top of the first pass of the day, I was rescued by a swift thunderstorm that sent John sprinting away. By the time the rain let up and I caught up to John on the other side of the pass, my sore muscles were finally starting to warm up and the Sour Patch Kids I had forced down my throat were kicking in. John pointed across a large valley bathed in sunlight but ringed by dark clouds.

"That mountain over there, the pointy one, that's Fleecer Ridge," he said. "Hard to believe, huh? That's still nearly thirty miles from here."

"So that's Fleecer, eh?" I said. Fleecer was yet another notorious section of the Divide, a difficult-to-locate intersection with a treacherous, technical descent on the downside. The reputation of these places tended to fill me with a dread that was quickly replaced with glee upon arriving there. I found I preferred the somewhat ridiculous challenges presented by unrideable obstacle courses to the usual physical strain of simply riding long and hard. In fact, all of the places I had been warned about — Red Meadow Lake, Richmond Pass and Lava Mountain — were all the places I already regarded most fondly. At that point, I expected nothing less from Fleecer.

As John put on his warm jacket and leg warmers for the descent, I pulled a little wax-coated cheese wheel from my feedbag, unwrapped it, and popped it in my mouth. As I chewed, the creamy cheese oozed down my throat and lined my stomach with the most incredible sense of health and well-being.

"Oh my God, John, you have to try these things," I said as I fished another cheese wheel out of my bag and handed it to him. "I bought them at the store in Butte. They're like pure happiness wrapped in a ball of wax."

John laughed and popped it in his mouth. "Pretty good," he said. "You need to remember these things. I'm serious. Make a mental note. When you find something that works for you, you don't want to forget it."

We dropped into the valley and crossed beneath the interstate. As we started climbing anew, I looked wistfully down the pavement as it snaked along the basin in a comforting, familiar way. "There's the road of my childhood," I said to John. "Growing up in Salt Lake City, that was the road we used to get anywhere. When I was a surly teenager, I dreamed of moving to California and I-15 was my escape route. It feels so close. Now, if I headed south on I-15, it would take me home."

"How far do you think it is to Salt Lake City?" John asked.

"I don't know," I said. "That's the weirdest thing about paying so much attention to these Divide maps. I could tell you the name of every stream we cross, every valley we pass through, exactly how far it is to the next notable cattle guard, but I have no idea where we are in relation to the rest of the world."

"The Divide is an all-encompassing existence," John agreed.

We climbed Fleecer Ridge on the grass-lined tracks left by trucks, essentially four singletrack trails cut deep into the slope. We neared 8,000 feet, skimming the alpine tundra regions of the higher mountains. The trees thinned and steep meadows opened in front of us. As promised, my GPS track directed me hard right over a route that wasn't a trail at all. There weren't even tracks, just an open meadow stretching toward a dilapidated wire fence. Beyond the fence, the jeep tracks returned. They seemed to fall right off the face of the Earth in a descent so steep and rocky that I wondered if I'd be able to walk my bicycle down it. John was already inching his bike down the slope, looking comically tiny amid the expansive mountainside. I stepped off my saddle, throttled both brakes, and dragged my bike in lurching lunges, stepping sideways on both feet to brace against a freefall. I stepped gingerly around each large boulder, looking up frequently to drink in the vivid greens and tiny yellow flowers splashed across a near-vertical meadow.

The far-rippling landscape in front of me was both familiar in a primeval way and thrillingly new — a region thrust up like broken splinters from the bowels of the Earth. And the only way we could traverse it was a ladder of loose gravel and stones, cascading down the sharp spine of the mountain. Altitude brought us an ability to see worlds that were completely new, and also remember the worlds we had nearly forgotten. As I dropped down Fleecer Ridge, I remembered being a small child and curling my toes around the summer grass. I remembered being a teenager in hiking boots, following my dad along a ridge of the Wasatch Mountains. I remembered being barefoot and in love and clasping hands beneath the cliffs of the Oregon Coast.

"I'm telling you," I called out to John, "I-15 would get us to Lima a lot faster and easier." But, unlike my statement when I left Basin, this time, I really was joking. The trucks and cars trapped on the interstate would never see these mountains, never experience this intense downhill push, never feel the rush of thin air and hard wind and gaping gravity that threatened to tear the skin from my body. It was these difficult-to-reach places that made the riding the Divide worth all of the soreness and fatigue and pain — Red Meadow Lake, Richmond Peak and Fleecer Ridge.

"Woo!" I called out joyfully as I met John at the bottom. "I didn't fall! I'm alive!"

"That is a hell of a hike-a-bike," John said.

"Tough to fathom even jeeps rolling down that," I said. "You know Mary, the woman who finished the Tour Divide last year? She claimed to have ridden down that stretch of trail. Just stuck her butt out and went."

"The whole thing?"

"I think so."

"I don't believe that," John said. "She was either mistaken or she was lying. Maybe if you had a huge downhill bike and full body armor, maybe. But a loaded cross-country bike? It's impossible."

"I don't know," I said. "She had a good story about it. I think it involved some thrashers on downhill bikes calling her a wee little girl."

"What time did Mary finish in, anyway?" John asked. "She has the women's record from Banff, doesn't she?"

"Actually, Jenn Hopkins from the Great Divide Race has that because she started in Banff and time-trialed to the border. I think her time was twenty-eight days. Mary took twenty-nine or thirty. She was going really fast at first, but then she got injured near Lima. Something weird with her leg muscles, too much salt or something. Kind of amazing she finished, actually."

"Twenty-eight days?" John said. "You'll beat that easily. Right now, I think you're on pace for twenty-two or twenty-four days, tops. And if you increase your pace, you even still have a good shot at the border-to-border record."

"Maybe," I said. "But I don't think it would be recognized because I'm breaking that GDR cell phone rule." I smiled, because with John around, I hadn't had an urge to break the cell phone out once beyond a couple of calls from inside motel rooms. My mother was probably wondering why I hadn't called.

John and I descended into Wise River. At the single-room store in town, we caught up with Dario, who was traveling with one other Tour Divide racer whom I didn't know, and Jeremy, who must have passed John and me while we slept the morning away in Butte. Dario and his companion left just as we were settling down with a lunch of Hot Pockets and Pepsi. Jeremy left soon after that, still looking miserable as he limped down the street out of town. After the morning's cheese-wheel-fueled riding, my appetite had waned again and I struggled to force down the relatively small portion of food.

As we pedaled into the Wise River valley, John announced that he wanted to relive his glory days on the Great Divide one last time by sprinting as hard as he could up the final pass of the day.

"I just want to see how fast I can still go. I'll wait for you at the top," he said. "And if I get too cold waiting, I'll go ahead and ride into Elkhorn Hot Springs. It's a nice place. I stayed there last year. You should be able to find it easily enough; just watch for the signs."

Finally alone for the longest period of time I had to myself since leaving Canada, I pedaled south below the waning afternoon sunlight and hummed along to my iPod, sometimes singing loudly as the canyon narrowed and the road began snaking up the mountain. The sun settled directly behind me as the road turned east toward the alpine, casting my long shadow over the gold-tinted tundra.

I pedaled toward the shadow, watching it lumber in front of me like an aloof companion. It wavered as though it wanted to pull away, so I began speaking to it. I remarked how beautiful the meadow was. I asked it to observe the little red flowers lining the road. The shadow maintained a peaceful silence, quietly accepting everything I said.

John, going as hard as he could, reached the pass more than an hour before I did. When I found him at the top, he was shivering wildly.

"Why didn't you keep going to Elkhorn?" I asked.

"I wanted to make sure you could find it," he stammered through chattering teeth.

"Oh good grief," I said. "I'm a big girl, John."

"I'll be fine," he said gruffly. "Let's just get going."

We rode the descent together, gulping down gravity and the unhindered freedom a massive downhill always provides. I gazed up at the warm hues of sunset stretched across the horizon as John looked directly ahead, fixated on the promise of warm beds and showers. I felt the best I had all day and I really wanted to keep going, beyond Elkhorn, beyond the road south, beyond Montana. My shadow faded with dusk, and I decided it was time for John to set me free. But despite his falling core temperature and impatient demeanor, he rode his brakes and stayed parked beside me, as though he suspected I might just shoot past the Elkhorn cutoff and leave him behind.

We turned together into Elkhorn Hot Springs. Twilight still clung to the sky at 9:30 p.m., but the lodge itself was abandoned. When we called earlier, the proprietor had promised there'd be a room for us, so we let ourselves in and placed our stuff in one of six bedrooms upstairs, all empty. We made our way downstairs to the quiet and dark dining room to prepare a meal of convenience store snacks that we carried from Wise River, and soda that we found in a nearby cooler. We left $10 on the counter and a note thanking the unseen proprietor for four cans of soda, and a mention of which room we were sleeping in upstairs.

John nudged me out of bed early the next morning. "We should get going. It might be a long ride into Lima if we get any kind of weather," he said. "That Bannock Road gets some hellish mud after thunderstorms."

As we rolled south, the endless ripple of mountain ranges started to fade into the background and the landscape opened wider into high, arid prairies. The thick pine forests of northern Montana were replaced by sagebrush and grass, already dry and yellow in June. The climbs were more gradual, the descents less thrilling, and it seemed John was finally beginning to tire of my company, often riding twenty or thirty yards in front of me rather than beside me.

Either that, or John expected I was tiring of him, even though that wasn't exactly the case. Initially, I relished in the bouts of solitude. But after several hours of quiet aloneness, spent drifting through the dull hills of the present and the flickering shadows of my memories, I found myself both fascinated and distressed by the landscape inside my head. It was too vivid, too dark, too far from the world around me, and too close for comfort. It left me feeling lost, directionless, locked in a grueling journey that had no discernible end. The outside reality that John provided, with its rational observations, disconnected tangents and long stories about people I did not know and places I had never been, was sometimes irritatingly distracting. But suddenly displaced from it, I realized that John's distractions had been exactly that — a pleasant diversion from my own thoughts, whose company I wasn't sure I enjoyed.

As we climbed into the high, open plain between the Beaverhead and Tendoy mountains, dark clouds started to gather over the rocky peaks in the distance. John slowed to let me catch up.

"You're going to have to kick it up a notch. We can't get caught out here in the rain," he said. "This road is made out of soft clay. It will turn to the worst kind of mud. We'll be stuck out here all night."

The dirt road had a polished, cracked surface like paint on an antique piece of furniture. Flakes of mud crackled beneath our wheels and clung to our rims like cement every time we splashed through a puddle. Under hard rain, the Bannock Road would disintegrate to a swath of mud with the consistency of peanut butter. The sticky, chunky mud would build on our tires and clog up drivetrains until our wheels refused to turn.

"I understand and I believe you," I said. "But we're more than a week into the Tour Divide. We've already ridden 1,000 miles. I am officially One-Gear Jill, and I can tell you, it isn't a high gear."

"Well, you're going to have to try your best," John said. "It's not outside the realm of possibility that you'll have to walk your bike for thirty miles through the mud if you get stuck in a bad storm."

"John, I'm doing the best I can," I said. "Go on ahead if you have to. If you don't see me in Lima tonight, you'll know I'm stuck out here. It's no skin off my back. I'll lay out my bivy and wait for the sun. But if I try to sprint now, I'll really be cooked."

This time, John did not hesitate to leave me behind. Within ten minutes I could no longer see his thin figure ahead on the road, even as the sagebrush-dotted basin opened wider. I took John's advice to heart and tried to increase my pace, but my legs ached with fatigue and pain. Pushing down hard on the tender muscles in my legs felt like a fate worse than mud, and I eased back. The distant clouds darkened and lightning flashed over the mountains. The rumbling thunder carried over the desert plain, but the sky directly overhead stayed mercifully blue.

I started to see deep tracks of bicycle tires followed by footprints that had become fossilized like molds in the clay road. It was obvious that some of the racers who traveled through here before me had become stuck in the mud. Their staggered footprints pressed several inches into the hardened clay. Eventually, the tracks disappeared off the road into the sagebrush, where I suspected my predecessors had sought refuge from the goop.

"Crap, that's going to be us in a few hours," I told my shadow, which was already fading beneath the quickly accumulating clouds overhead. A few sprinkles fell onto my hot skin. I groaned. "Well, this is going to suck."

But the feeling of the first droplets of rain reignited a higher gear that I thought had long since burned out, and my speed did increase as I climbed the last pitch of the broad pass and started dropping into another open valley. Despite the invigorating surge in energy, I gleaned no joy from sprinting. I felt only anxiety as flashes of lightning streaked over the far horizon.

The storm remained on the periphery. As I rode down the valley, the clouds continued to move away, replaced by more blue sky and glaring sun. A hard headwind followed in the storm's wake, blowing out the last fumes of my adrenaline and slowing me once again to a single-gear crawl. I did not grumble because given the choice, I would pick wind over mud without regret.

The valley pinched in and the road turned into a narrow canyon that was lined with sheer rock cliffs. The road surface improved as it meandered into ranch lands, bordered by thin wire fences that created an almost comically weak barrier between clusters of cattle and the bald mountains that towered overhead. I descended along a wide creek as the road wrapped around a ridge and veered directly away from the wind. Flying downhill on smooth gravel with the wind at my back, I clicked up my pace until I suddenly found myself without any higher gears; I had no choice but to coast effortlessly through a blur of speed.

A herd of cattle grazed lazily along the grassy shoreline of the creek. I whipped around a tight curve and surprised a group of four cows and two calves that had been standing in the middle of the road. The animals launched into a full stampede, galloping in front of me as I tore through their cloud of dust, screaming "Yah! Yah! Get off the road!" The small herd split up and veered toward both edges of the gravel. The sound of their hooves echoed like thunder through the canyon. I fearlessly plunged through the center of the stampede, furiously sprinting beside their mud-caked skin and watching their powerful muscles ripple in the sunlight. I continued to scream "Yah!" as one cow looked directly at me, wild-eyed with terror. I pedaled as hard as I physically could and surged forward. I was the cattle driver, the cause of stampedes, a cowgirl without a horse outrunning panicked bovines. Smiling with satisfaction, I shot ahead, leaving the confused cows behind as they slowed to a trot and finally veered off the road.

The canyon opened up and I again found myself dropping into the wide corridor of I-15, with its familiar truck stream roaring southbound. The Great Divide Mountain Bike Route turned south on the frontage road, again facing the strong headwind that had become nearly as impenetrable as a wall. I gasped into the warm air that whipped past my body and threatened to push me all the way back to Canada. It must have been blowing steady at thirty or thirty-five miles per hour — not quite strong enough to stop a fatigued cyclist in her tracks, but close.

I plodded along the flat pavement at six or seven miles per hour, head practically buried between my arms, eyes watching only the slow-moving front wheel and the white line on the road. The wind roared in my ears and I stopped frequently for breaks, turning my back to the blast just so I could stuff down some candy and nuts before the wind tore it out of my hands. For the duration of the seven-mile approach, every time I looked up, I could see the roofs and road signs of Lima beckoning from the edge of the valley. They never seemed to get any closer.

By the time I reached town, John had already gotten a room, taken a shower, and checked the weather and all of the race standings. He had been there for a while, but it was still a couple of hours before dark. I took my own shower and we walked back outside to go to dinner. The wind had only picked up strength. After spending time in the shelter of the room, the gusts felt like a full hurricane blast. My wet hair whipped around wildly and I couldn't hear anything John was saying over the roar, even though he was standing right next to me. He pointed to the mountains south of Lima. Across the sky, a swath of clouds as black as the darkest hours of the night hovered ominously over the ridge. Near-continuous bursts of lightning streaked through the sinister sky. The contrast of darkness and electricity was so stark that the lightning cast discernible shadows on the ground where we stood. Deafening claps of thunder followed too closely behind.

"Holy cow!" I yelled over the roaring wind. "That has got to be the scariest storm I have ever seen!"

"It's coming right for us!" John yelled back.

"Thank God for motels!" I yelled. "I'd probably be crapping my shorts if I were still up on the Bannock Road and I saw that."

As we neared the doors of the restaurant down the street, I noticed a man with a loaded bike walking toward us. Two grocery bags hung from both of his handlebars. They were flapping so loudly in the wind that I could hear them even before I was certain the cyclist was Jeremy, but I assumed it was since no other Tour Divide racer was within fifty miles of John and me.

"Hey!" I yelled when he was in close enough range to hear my voice, about five feet away. "We're going for dinner. Would you like to go with us?"

"No thanks," he yelled back. "I've got dinner right here. I think I'm going to head down the road."

"You're going on tonight?" I said in disbelief. "What about that storm coming in?"

"I checked out the motel but it's pretty expensive," Jeremy said. "And it's early in the day still. I was hoping to get to this campground at Lima Reservoir tonight. The road kinda skirts north anyway and I think that storm is going to bypass it."

I couldn't tell if Jeremy was brave or cheap or completely unreasonable. Hurricane gusts of wind swirled all around us, and we continued shouting over the din even though we were only standing feet apart. I knew that I was willing to give the proprietors of the Lima motel whatever they wanted, even if it was hundreds of dollars, just for the relative comfort of shelter from that storm.

We watched Jeremy's figure disappear down the open road like a rider into the apocalypse. We ducked into the restaurant just before heavy rain started to fall. It pounded the windows as we ate, and fell in wide sheets as we darted back to our warm and dry motel room.

By the next morning, the raging tempest was finally subdued, only to be replaced by an overcast pall and light but steady rain. I had assumed John would continue riding south from Lima toward Idaho Falls, and I would be on my own as soon as we checked out. But as we packed up, John announced that he really preferred to go to Jackson, which was a nice place to rest for a while, so he planned to continue on the Divide for two more days.

"Really?" I asked. "Even though it's raining?"

"Yeah, there's some nice riding past here," John said. I was mildly relieved to hear this. The very real terror of thunderstorms had reignited my reluctance to be alone.

We both overdressed for the weather, and I had to stop a couple of times to strip off clothing. Steady rain pattered on my jacket, and I was already drenched in sweat. I felt warm and relaxed, oddly comfortable in the wet conditions I had become so accustomed to in Juneau. As we pedaled up the road, we began to see more tracks and footprints preserved in the mud. Someone had scrawled the phrase "This effin bites" deep into the clay surface, which was beginning to soften in the rain. "The next 47 miles are very remote," my map warned. "Road can be potentially mucky when wet."

"Crap," I said to John as I observed the sky, thick with storm clouds in every direction. "We're not going to escape the mud today."

Sure enough, within a mile we dipped into a thick, gooey stew that collected on our tires until both wheels on both of our bikes had seized up entirely. I dragged my anchor of a bicycle along the shoulder as John pushed his into the bushes and chipped away at the mud with a stick. After about 300 yards of sweat-soaked struggle, we climbed onto a higher, still muddy, but at least passable bend in the road. I chipped away the cement block of mud still clinging to the wheels and crank and started pedaling.

"Now is the time to find that high gear," John said to me as he shot past. "You're going to need power to get through this."

"Power?" I cried. "You mean like a rocket engine? That stuff is as thick as tar."

"If you crank it really hard, you'll float right through it. Watch."

John plummeted into the next dip and sprinted through the next muddy basin, flinging massive clumps of mud in every direction as he swerved and fishtailed over the wet cement. I could see his legs straining, his neck muscles bulging, and I knew I couldn't match the effort even if I had a vial of methamphetamine at my disposal.

"Whatever," I called out. "I'll see you in Idaho."

But he was already too far away to even hear me. I didn't mind; after all, he had the power to get out of the rain more quickly, so he might as well use it. As I watched him disappear down the next hill, I wondered why I felt so much resentment about it. John certainly didn't have to hang with me as long as he did, and it definitely didn't make sense for him to wallow in this mud, but at the same time, isn't that what he had been doing? Wallowing in the Divide with me? As the days crept forward and John's schedule remained open-ended, his actions confused me more and more. Did he want to stay in the race, or not? Did he want to travel with me, or not? And if he simply wanted to travel with me, but wasn't willing to stay with me when weather conditions got tough, what did that mean?

Fifty miles, six hours of solitude, and many long walks through the mud later, I reached the abandoned ranger station at Red Rock Lake. There, in a low-lying wetland, I encountered the most impassable mud I had yet seen. It seized up my bike within a few steps, and even grabbed my feet and covered my shoes in so much chocolate-colored cement that I could hardly walk. I had no choice but to hoist the heavily loaded bike on my shoulder and trudge through the sagebrush meadow, well off the road. As I was doing this, moving at a rate of about a half a mile per hour, hundreds of wetland mosquitoes honed in on my scent and torpedoed my exposed skin with astonishing accuracy. I threw the bike on the ground and groped for my bug spray, coating myself with all of the DEET I had left. Just a few toxic squirts hit their targets on my arms and neck, and then my bug spray was gone. Since John's mystical ten-mile-per-hour mosquito-free barrier was little more than a silly dream and I still had many open patches of unprotected skin, I had no choice but to pull on all of my plastic rain gear even though I was still sweltering in the humid heat.

"This has got to be the worst place in the world," I said out loud. "Nothing but mud and mosquitoes for fifty miles in every direction."

I spent an hour walking a mile through the thick goop. The army of mosquitoes slammed into my rain layer with such audible frequency that I could no longer tell them apart from droplets of rain. I finally reached the edge of a tiny town called Lakeview — which had no services — but a sight of an old Buick lumbering down the road lifted my heart out of its depths. Surely if a vehicle like that could maneuver from far-away places of civilization into this cluster of buildings, I could maneuver a bike out of it. Sure enough, the road improved considerably on the other side of town, where it had been coated in pebble-infused gravel that was firm enough to lift my wheels away from the mud. I pulled the bike off the road and scraped away pieces of thick mud coating the wheels and frame, breaking three sticks in the process. With the chocolate-colored cement quickly hardening, I finally resorted to removing my gloves and jabbing slimy clumps with my fingers. Soon my hands were as filthy as my bicycle, but at least my drivetrain and wheels had been unlocked. Finally, I was able to ride again.

About five miles past town, the sky grew darker and new streaks of lightning again broke the gray monotony. Without warning, clouds as black as the ones I had seen the night before charged directly over the mountains to the south. A cacophony of electric sound exploded over the open plain and there was nowhere, absolutely nowhere to hide. Before I even had time to assess the situation, a brilliant flash of light erupted less than fifty yards from my bicycle, followed instantaneously by a clap of thunder so deafening that even my vision went black. Terror shot through my body like a jolt of electricity and I pressed into the pedals, sprinting with the adrenaline-surge power of an animal that truly believes it is about to die. There was no room, no time, and no capacity for thought or analysis. The only concept I understood was flight, primal and almost comforting in its absolution.

I charged with blind fury until the thunder decreased once again to a rumble and the sky changed from black to dark gray. When I calmed down enough to look down at my odometer, I was still traveling twenty-five miles per hour on a loaded mountain bike on a flat, muddy road. Later that night, I would check my odometer's maximum speed, which registered at thirty-eight miles per hour. It's possible I forgot to reset my odometer at the beginning of the day, and that was a speed I had achieved the previous day while rocketing down the canyon into Lima. But I can never be sure. And under lightning-charged distress, I wasn't about to discount a dead sprint at thirty-eight miles per hour as beyond the realm of physical possibility.

Much to my relief, the electric climax abated. Unfortunately, the storm symphony's next movement was a sonata of heavy rain. The temperature dropped into the low forties and I couldn't look up without stinging my eyes. I was drenched to the core in both mud and water when I finally crossed the Continental Divide, passing from Montana into Idaho. I arrived at the Sawtell Mountain Resort a couple of hours after John. As he opened the motel room door, he was freshly showered and cheerful, which only added cruel contrast to my bloodshot eyes and solid layer of mud. He asked me how the ride went and I glowered at him, "Pretty much the way it was going when you left. I got stuck in the mud and eaten by mosquitoes. Oh, and I almost got struck by lightning."

He smiled slyly and said in an apologetic tone, "I had to walk some, too, but I missed the thunderstorms. But, hey, they have a hot tub here."

"Great. But I'm going to eat before I shower," I announced. "I don't even care how dirty I am. I'm starving."

I walked to Subway alone and plopped into a booth, smearing mud everywhere I went. Soon after I acquired a foot-long turkey sandwich and a jug of Pepsi, Jeremy wandered into the fast-food restaurant in a similar state of disarray. I was happy to see he survived the night, but confused as to how I had possibly arrived in Sawtell before him.

"When did I pass you?" I asked as he sat down in the booth next to me with an equally large pile of food.

"Hard to say," he said. "It's been a crazy day." He told me a long story about storms and truck-driving ranchers and bike mechanicals that involved other racers whom I also had managed to not see at any point during the single-road route from Lima to Sawtell. I nodded but didn't understand a word of his story, my mind still lost in its own primitive state of flight and survival. We ate our sandwiches mostly in silence after that, occasionally saying things like, "Good bread at this one," and "Weather really sucks right now." I suspected that Jeremy had regressed to a caveman-like intelligence as much as I had.

Back in the hotel room, John was watching some obnoxious sitcom on the television and I consented to finally cleaning myself. After I emerged from the bathroom, I strung my shower-washed clothes around the room and dropped my towel to change into my dry clothes even though John was sitting on the bed just a few feet away. It occurred to me too late that I didn't actually know him all that well, and I should probably be more modest. But just like the mud I carelessly smeared all over a Subway booth for some poor employee to clean up, the intensely self-absorbed focus of the Tour Divide had a way of stripping away social norms and niceties. The more preoccupied I became with my body's comfort and discomfort, the less I was able to view it as a tangible entity in the world I moved through. I descended from not caring to not even understanding how the people around me might interpret that I smelled bad, or think I look like a hobo on wheels, or even possibly find me attractive. But I remembered enough from my old, civilized existence to realize that I was definitely not attractive.

I walked toward the mirror and winced at my reflection, with its charred lips and sunburned skin and swelling mosquito bites. My hair looked liked it had been styled, badly, by a 1980s punk rock beautician. Clumps of hair were permanently matted down in some areas, flying all over the place in others, and tangled against my scalp in the back.

"You know, if I could pack for this trip again, the only thing I would do differently is bring a comb," I said John I plopped down next to him on the bed. "Oh yeah, and only bring one set of clothes. I had no idea I'd be doing my laundry every single night."

John smiled wryly. "Yeah, but what would you wear around the motel then?"

"I don't know. Towel. Who cares? I just coated an entire Subway booth in Montana mud. It's pretty obvious I no longer care about social conventions or personal appearance. But my hair, wow. That's taking lack of vanity to a whole new level of scary."

"I think your hair looks good," John said.

"Are you kidding?" I cried out. "I look like Scarecrow! And not the friendly Scarecrow in 'The Wizard of Oz,' but the really creepy, scary Scarecrow in 'Return to Oz.'"

I grinned at him. I thought I had made a great joke, but John just looked at me quizzically and turned his head away. After several seconds, he said, "So the weather forecast isn't good. We're supposed to get another full day of rain tomorrow. I don't think we're going to run into the kind of mud we hit today, but the next section of trail is this rail bed. It's volcanic soil, always wash-boarded, and it's soft and slow. I think after all this rain, you'll be lucky to do five miles per hour on it. I'm serious. You're going to need a lot of power to get through it, and if you couldn't power through the mud today, I think you're going to have to brace yourself for a slow ride tomorrow."

"Whatever," I said. "I'll turn on my best snow bike slog mentality. I'll be just fine."

"Well, I've been thinking," John said. "If the rail trail goes really slow for you, we could just stop in Ashton. It's a little off route, but it's a good-sized town. It would be a good place to spend one more night together before I head over to Jackson."

"How far is Ashton from here?" I asked.

John drew a breath. "About thirty-five miles."

"Thirty-five miles?" I blurted out, my squeaky voice betraying a sudden flash of anger. "That's all? Why don't you just come out and ask me to quit the race, too? If I do a thirty-five-mile day, I might as well just admit I'm not racing this thing and drop out with you."

John looked hurt. "But what if the rail trail is really as bad as it's probably going to be?"

"Unless I walk the entire thing at two miles per hour and it takes me seventeen hours, I am going beyond Ashton," I said. "Even if it's just five miles beyond Ashton, I'm going beyond Ashton. I am not going to consent to a thirty-five-mile day."

"Okay, okay," John said and sighed. "I guess this might be our last night together, then. I might not ride the rail trail with you tomorrow. I might just take the road because it will be faster. Then it's a direct shot to Jackson from there."

I sat back, calming down. "Oh yeah, I guess you're right. This is going to be our last night together."

John pursed his lips. "Yeah."

I turned and looked into his large, brown eyes. "John, I really need to thank you for sticking with me through Montana," I said. "I had a lot of fun, and I learned a ton. It was fun to get to know you. I'm not sure I would have made it to this point without you. Certainly not in this kind of luxury and with great hair to boot."

John grinned. "I had a great time, too," he said. "I never knew the Great Divide could be so fun."

"Really?" I said. "And yet you come back to the race, year after year."

"Yup," he said. "One course record and three utter failures. But, I have to say, this year was the best failure of all."

"Good," I said. "I'm glad you don't regret your decision."

He shook his head. "Not at all."

I turned to smile at him and he leaned toward me. His eyes were wide and lips tight. I gave him a quizzical look and stood up quickly. "Well, it sounds like I need to get up really early tomorrow to ride — er, walk — the seventeen hours of rail trail," I said. "Better set the alarm, maybe for 5:30? I hope this place has coffee."

"Okay," John said slowly.

I popped a sleeping pill in my mouth and plopped down in the second bed, pulling the covers tight around my shoulders. "Wow, what a day, huh?" I said. "I never thought I'd ride any surface more exhausting than wet slush, but man, Montana mud. What a day."

John let out a weak little laugh. "Yeah," he said. "Yeah."

Chapter Thirteen
Beyond Idaho

Page 175: John Nobile rides toward a rainbow on a country road near Jackson Lake, Wyoming.
Page 176: A farm in eastern Idaho.

The alarm clock blasted static noise at 5:30 a.m. John didn't even stir. I quietly changed from my dry clothes to my still-damp clothes, packed up my bike, and slipped out into the gray, drizzling dawn. The pine trees of Eastern Idaho were the tallest I had seen on the Divide, towering fifty and sixty feet over my head. Even the low branches were draped in satiny curtains of fog.

Just a few miles outside of town, I turned onto the old rail bed. Just as John had promised, the trail was covered in coarse sand. I closed my eyes and tuned into my best recollection of snow-bike slog mentality. I thought of the time I pushed my bike twenty-five miles along the powdered-sugar surface of the frozen Kuskokwim River during the last day of the 2008 Iditarod Trail Invitational. The course grains of wind-drifted snow were so loose that my feet sank deep into the trail, and I struggled to keep my speed above two miles per hour. I recalled the way the frigid wind blew hard at my back, the exhaustion and pain that needled at every part of my body, and the unchanging scenery of the wide river corridor that made me feel like I must have been mad to believe I was actually moving forward. It was all I could do to hold onto my sanity over ten hours of walking across that frozen wasteland. I took comfort in the idea that nothing on the Divide could even come close to that level of slog.

The Idaho rail trail was rippled with washboard bumps and larger waves of whoop-de-dos similar to the moguls made by snowmobiles, but it was hardly soft. In fact, the material that covered the trail was a fine, ashy sand, and rain saturation only seemed to pack it more solidly, like a sandcastle at a beach. If I ignored the jackhammer jolting of the washboard, it was easy to ride ten miles per hour, and not too difficult to increase to twelve or even fourteen miles per hour as the rain streaked down.

The rail bed carved a perfectly straight line across the broad plateau, spanning swamps and cutting visible notches into the pine forest. Lost as I was in memories of the Kuskokwim River, I was struck by how similar the Idaho rail trail was to the Iditarod Trail in Alaska's Susitna Valley, where it followed a straight survey line across frozen swamps and continued, unbending, through pipe-cleaner strands of black spruce trees. The only difference between the Iditarod Trail and this Idaho rail trail was, of course, the absence of snow and the height of the trees.

Soon enough, even the absence of snow failed to register in my mind as the morning faded to a more monotone shade of gray. My memories became so intertwined with my reality that I started to picture myself riding across the frozen muskeg of the Susitna Valley. In my mind, it was still early March, my foot was still unfrozen, Geoff and I were still a couple, and everything still looked and felt very much the same — and yet, irreconcilably different. I shook my head and snapped back to the present, a present drenched in rain and towering trees, a present where John was sleeping back in Sawtell while I faced a broad, uncertain future, all alone.

Sunbeams had started to needle through the clouds as the mountains closed in on both sides of the rail bed. As the canyon narrowed, the trail started dropping toward the Warm River. The landscape was postcard scenic, with soft light shining on broad, bushy trees as the whitewater river roared far below. I imagined a polished locomotive perched on the precipice of that proverbial postcard. One aspect of my personality that makes me a good candidate for long-distance endurance cycling is the fact that I am always impressed by scenery, which translates into motivation to keep pushing toward beautiful new discoveries. The relative ease of the rail trail combined with the surprise emergence of sunlight put me in an incredible mood.

I crossed a campground and climbed out of the river valley, emerging onto another broad plateau striped with bright green rows of potato plants that stretched beyond the horizon. To the far west, the majestic peaks of the Grand Tetons stabbed at silver-lined patches of clouds. I realized with another pang of nostalgia that I was incredibly close to Idaho Falls, a small

Eastern Idaho city where I spent ten months of the rockiest period of my relationship with Geoff, before our final breakup of course. It was 2005, four years since we had struck up a relationship that never seemed to lift out of the "just having fun" phase. I couldn't take our uncertain status and uncommitted life in Utah any more, so I accepted a job 200 miles north of Salt Lake City. While I didn't break up with Geoff, I committed to moving on. My life centered on work and parties and going to the gym. I had few other interests. I stopped riding my bike. I adopted a cat. That was the summer before Geoff convinced me to move with him to Alaska. I had been mostly unhappy, and I had forgotten just how beautiful this region really was.

Eastern Idaho was also as close as the Great Divide Mountain Bike Route was ever going to come to Salt Lake City. It would be a four-hour drive, tops, for my parents to reach this point and whisk me away from my self-imposed sentence of loneliness and fatigue. The thought had crossed my mind several times in the past few days. But when I finally reached my bailout point, I found it to be surrounded in beauty, and it was easy to ignore that option. While my mind was temporarily freed from the struggle and pain, it was easy to make the right choice.

It was just before 10 a.m. when I passed the turnoff for Ashton. I smirked at the idea of stopping to spend the night there, as John had suggested the night before. "That would surely be a grand tour," I said out loud. "Racing three hours a day." It occurred to me after I said it that most people would see three hours a day as a lot of racing. But I had fallen into a rhythm where I felt guilty if my pedaling time came in at anything less than twelve hours, and fourteen or even sixteen hours of constant crank-turning was starting to feel more natural.

As I approached the knife-sharp peaks of the Tetons, John pedaled up beside me. I hadn't heard him over the music on my iPod, and the sight of his red jacket and stoic forward gaze surprised me so much that I jumped.

"Hey John!" I said. "I didn't expect to see you coming this way. Did you get here on the road?"

"No," he said, "I took the rail trail. I was starting to think I was never going to catch up to you."

"Well," I said, "that trail wasn't nearly as bad as you said it was going to be."

"It was well-packed," John said. "Still, you're flying."

"So are you going to take that Ashton-Flagg Road to Jackson?" I asked.

"Even better," John said. "I found a place we can stay tonight. It's called Turpin Meadow Ranch. It's just below Togwotee Pass. It's a little beyond the Jackson cutoff, but they have cabins there and they do big family-style breakfasts. It's normally a horse-riding place, but I told the guy we were on bicycles and he didn't seem to mind."

"Wow," I said, genuinely taken aback. "Really?" I felt a rush of that old resentment about being told where I had to spend the night, especially at a time when I had felt so free and alive about my newfound solitude. At the same time, I was happy to see John, and the prospect of sleeping in a warm bed and eating a hot breakfast was always an appealing one.

As we climbed into the Tetons, John chatted as excitedly and amicably as he had on our first day through Montana. I mostly smiled and nodded, because I felt like I had already told him most of my stories, and I felt a newfound anxiety that he was going to find a way to hang around after the Turpin Meadow Ranch. It had become uncomfortably obvious that John was starting to develop feelings for me, beyond just a mutual liking as good bike-touring buddies. Whether this attraction was a recent development or perhaps had started all the way back at the starting line in Banff, I couldn't be certain. What was even more uncertain was how exactly I felt about this attraction. John was definitely likeable — good looking, athletic, and smart. And he was one of the few men I had ever met who shared a cycling obsession equal to mine. But John was methodical while I was intuitive. John was rational while I was driven by dreams. John lived in Connecticut while I lived in Alaska. John was forty-five years old while I was twenty-nine. Everything about our backgrounds kept us on disparate sides of an unbridgeable divide. John seemed logical enough to recognize this, so I tried not to let my suspicions of romantic intentions worry me too much.

We crossed another state line. The sign was quaintly unceremonious: a rusty brown square that simply read "Wyoming," so riddled with bullet holes that it really looked more like W**m*n*g. John told me to stop so he could take a picture.

"But you don't have a camera," I said.

"With your camera," he replied. "Go stand over there."

I faced him and smiled. "OK," he said, "Lean a little this way."

"What am I, a model?" I protested.

He just laughed and raised the camera. "Be sure to send this one to me after you get to New Mexico," he said. "This is how I'm going to remember you."

I stood stiffly next to the sign. "You should be proud, John," I said as he snapped a series of shots. "I packed my baggy shorts away, so today I'm entirely aerodynamic."

We crested the Ashton-Flagg Road only to see another dark thunderstorm looming over the eastern side of the Tetons. "This is bullshit," I said as we approached the black clouds. "I'm sick of getting rained on."

"We can outrun this storm," John said.

"You can outrun this storm," I shot back. "I'm going to go my own pace. I can't keep your speed no matter how much I'd like to."

"OK. I'll wait for you at the campground," John said. "Unless it's raining. Then I'll wait for you at Flagg Ranch."

"Whatever works," I grumbled. John disappeared into the distance, characteristically into me unless it was raining and the roads were wet, which seemed to be the most common condition of the Divide. Even though I certainly couldn't blame him, I couldn't help but file John away in my growing list of "men who abandon me when the going gets rough."

Jeremy pedaled up beside me as I worked through the series of steep drainages. "Hey Jeremy. How's the nine-speed treating you?" I asked him.

"It still hurts like hell," he said. "But it gets a little better every day."

"I really thought you were beyond here," I said. "You must have left Sawtell after me."

"Yeah, I saw your and John's tracks on the rail trail. I guess you guys are still traveling together?"

"One more day," I said. "He's going to drop in Jackson."

"I'm thinking of dropping in Flagg," Jeremy said. "Stop me if I try to."

"Tell John that," I said. "You're both going to beat me there. I'm fading here."

With that, Jeremy passed, having no low gears to spin slowly up the hill.

But thanks to my low gears and unwavering cadence, I was the only one who got stuck out in the storm. Black clouds rumbled low and dropped quickly with surprisingly violence, light on lightning but extra generous with the rain. The road, maintained by the National Park Service, was mercifully well coated in enough smooth gravel to accommodate two-wheel-drive cars. Even so, my wheels cut a half-inch-deep trench into the mud, but the bridge of gravel at least made forward progress possible. I had been drenched so many times on the Divide that dampness was becoming the new normal, strange for a region that was considerably more arid than my rainforest home. What made the Divide different was that I had to live on the trail; there was no place to hide from the rain, at least for very long.

When I finally reached Flagg Ranch, the storm had cleared but I was dripping with chocolate-colored rainwater. I found John and Jeremy both plopped on a leather couch beside a fireplace. Although decorated with the heads of a dozen dead animals, the resort entry hall was ritzy enough that I felt sheepish about my muddiness, so I perched uncomfortably on the edge of the brick mantle.

"There's a store over there," John said. "You should probably stock up because I don't think we'll make it to Turpin Meadows before the kitchen closes."

I grazed through the novelty gift store, picking up candy and chocolate and looking in vain for some source of protein. There were honey-roasted peanuts and two-ounce containers of tuna salad, but nothing that seemed too nourishing. Hopefully Turpin Meadows had eggs for breakfast, I thought. I walked out with a large cup of steaming black coffee and a chocolate ice cream sandwich that boasted a 560-calorie glut of energy.

"Forget those cheese wheels," I said to John as I returned to the entry hall with the ice cream pressed to my lips. "Coffee and ice cream are my new rocket fuel. Where's Jeremy?"

"He left," John said. I frowned. "I did ask him if he wanted to ride with us," John continued. "He said he had to get moving to make it to this campground up the highway before dark."

"I've never seen a guy work so hard just to sleep outside," I said. "And he's not even gaining any ground by doing it. He's still moving at pretty much the same pace as we are. Maybe we smell bad or something."

"I don't know," John said. "I think Jeremy just prefers to ride alone."

"I'm going to try to catch up to him tomorrow," I said. "He is going about the same pace I am, and it would be nice to have some company after you leave. Maybe I'll just come right out and ask him whether or not he wants to ride with me."

It was John's turn to frown. I thought I detected a slight air of jealousy. "You can go ahead and try," he said. "I really think he's a solo type of guy."

Sunlight returned to the late afternoon sky as we joined the Grand Teton National Park tourist traffic on Highway 89. "I feel incredible right now," I told John. "That was really the most amazing ice cream sandwich I have ever consumed."

"That's good," John said, "Because I see more storm clouds to the east. We still have forty miles to go, but it's all paved. Let's see if we can make it to the ranch by dark."

We sprinted together, and for the first time I felt like I had no problem holding John's more ambitious pace. My odometer shot into the twenties even though there was plenty of rolling uphill to match the descents. The reflection of the snow-capped Tetons sparkled in Jackson Lake, and the patchy thunderstorms did little more than fill the horizon with rainbows. We reached Turpin Meadows at 9 p.m., just a few moments after a neon orange sunset slipped beneath the mountains. The owner of the ranch walked outside to meet John and me, and directed us to a small log cabin at the edge of a horse pasture.

"I'm putting you guys in Osprey; hope that works okay," the ranch owner said, referring to the name of the cabin. They were all named after different animals and they all looked exactly the same.

"I'm sure it will suit our needs fine," John said formally. I wanted to add that we had just finished a 125-mile bike ride at the end of a thousand-mile week and were pretty much so happy for a chance to rest that we'd be willing to pass out in a pile of nails, so our needs were not hard to meet. We propped our muddy bicycles against the porch and walked in the door. John turned on the light of the tiny room and my heart sank.

"Oh," I said. "There's only one bed."

"Is that ... is that a problem?" John asked in a low voice.

"No," I said. "I mean, um, no. Not a problem. It's still a bed. Of course I don't mind sharing with you."

We sat next to each other on the comforter with our respective dinners. John had managed to score a cup of soup and a pre-packaged tuna-and-cracker snack. I had my Flagg Ranch gourmet brownie and the rest of the almonds that I bought all the way back in Butte. As we ate quickly and quietly, John continued to shift his weight on the mattress with a fidgety sort of nervousness that made me feel extremely uneasy. I focused on the mashed brownie I was eating like it was the most interesting thing in the world. The silent tension between us only increased until my already fatigued muscles felt frozen in place. Still, I felt myself flinch as John leaned back to grab an energy bar and brushed his shoulder against mine. Finally, after several uncomfortably drawn-out minutes, John stood up.

"Mind if I take the first shower?" he asked.

"Of course not, not at all," I said. As he disappeared behind the bathroom door, my eyes drifted down to the bed I was sitting on. It wasn't even a queen-sized bed. It was a full-size at best, small and piled with extra pillows. Did John know there was only one bed in this place? Was this intentional? Was John going to try to sleep with me tonight? He seemed more gentlemanly than that, but I couldn't be certain.

How would I react if he did make a move? I thought back to Hansel's truck cab, on the only date I had been on since Geoff and I broke up. It was the day before I left Salt Lake to fly to Denver. Hansel called out of the blue and asked me if I wanted to go to a baseball game. I met him at the stadium. The home team was terrible and lost by nine points. Hansel took me to his house, made two Texas barbecue sandwiches, and drove me back to my car. As we wavered beneath the florescent lights of the stadium, he asked if he could kiss me. I leaned in and planted my lips against his. As thrilling as the initial sensation had been, I felt so awkward and strange that I was truly grateful I was unlikely to ever see Hansel again.

I looked out the window at my bicycle. John would be in the shower for at least another ten minutes. It would be completely feasible to pack up my things, hop on my bicycle and disappear into the night. Of course, John knew exactly where I was headed and was perfectly capable of catching me. Maybe I could hide in the bushes. I laughed out loud. The notion was so silly, and yet to me, the single bed was a real predicament. It wasn't even fair. This wasn't a high school drama; it wasn't a daytime soap opera. This was the Tour Divide, the hardest mountain bike race in the United States. We already had enough to worry about without adding the conundrum of sexual tension. But I had landed myself in this situation. I had welcomed it and coddled it, and now I was going to have to ride it out.

John walked out of the bathroom wearing only a towel and a wide smile. I couldn't help but watch his tan, tightly muscled legs stride across the room and silently acknowledge my equal share of the fault in this chain reaction of chemistry. Still, my stronger urges told me I needed to put a stopper on all of this before my entire Tour Divide experience flared out beneath something I might overwhelmingly regret.

"They have great showers here," John announced.

"Good," I said. "I'll be fast. I'm actually feeling really tired, and I want to get an early start tomorrow, so I'll probably just take a quick shower and hit the sack early."

I carried all of my dry clothing into the bathroom with me, then closed and locked the door. I showered quickly and pulled on all of my clothes, even my arm and leg warmers. "Cold in this room!" I said as I walked back out.

"Do you want me to turn up the heat?" John asked.

"No," I said. "I'm good."

"You said you wanted to start early, but they don't serve breakfast here until 8 a.m. Do you want to wait for that, or do you want to start earlier?"

I sighed. I probably could have dealt with one day without a shower, but I couldn't handle another day without protein. "No," I said. "I'll wait for breakfast."

I crawled into the bed and John settled in beside me. He had at least put on his street clothes since he came out of the shower, but his demeanor was naked with anxiety and expectation. I turned and met his wide-eyed gaze, then sat up quickly. "Almost forgot!" I said as I jumped out of bed. I grabbed my little medicine container. "Ambien," I said as I popped a pill in my mouth and swallowed it without water.

"I didn't take mine tonight," John said. "It's just a short ride into Jackson tomorrow. It won't really matter if I don't sleep all that well."

"If I don't take sleeping pills, my heart will keep me up all night," I said. "I don't think it's dropped below 150 beats a minute since I left Banff."

"I'm sure it has," John said. "You would have had a heart attack by now otherwise."

I climbed back into bed. "Maybe," I said. "I think my heart is just taxed. I feel like I'm both undertrained and overtrained at the same time. Sometimes it's really difficult to cope with the physical strain. There are just so many ups and downs on a ride like this. One minute I feel like I could sprint up Everest, the next I can hardly turn the pedals."

"It's important to keep your energy level in check, and consume some calories before you start feeling down," John said.

"Yeah, well, it's emotional, too," I said. "You spend this much time on a bicycle, and you're bound to hate it once in a while."

"Well, I think you'll find that those moods are directly tied to your physical state," John said. "If you pay attention and avoid becoming too cold, or hungry, or depleted, you'll almost certainly feel happier while riding no matter how long you've been on the bike."

"So all these big emotions can be controlled simply by stuffing a few more candy bars down my throat?" I responded. "Don't you think that sometimes, maybe just sometimes, the things we feel are more powerful and lasting than the things we do?"

John turned to me and smiled. "I think everything has a tangible origin," he said. "But if I really knew how to stay in control all of the time, I wouldn't have scratched from the Divide three times."

"Perhaps," I said. "I guess I'm just one of those people who still likes to believe I'm somehow more than the sum of my parts. But who knows, really?"

"Yeah, who knows," John repeated in my same tone of fatigue-addled resignation. He reached over me and turned off the night stand light. About six inches apart from each other, we laid stiffly in the dark silence. I blinked rapidly with anxiety but the Ambien and the fatigue of the day worked swift and strong, powerful enough to cut through even the tightest tension. Just as I was beginning to drift away, John sidled in closer.

"Jill?" he said with wavering nervousness in his voice.

"Mmm?" I replied, already skirting that paralyzed place between consciousness and dreams.

"If I came to visit you in Alaska, would you show me how to ride a snow bike?"

"Yeah," I mumbled. "Course." I spoke as though standing on the other side of a tunnel, becoming narrower with each ticking second of the mechanical alarm clock next to the bed.

"And you're okay with me leaving tomorrow?" he asked.

"I'll be fine," I said, the words drifting slowly to the surface like bubbles in an ocean.

He moved closer. "You okay?" he asked again.

"Mmm mmm," I mumbled. The last syllable clung to a frozen breath, because I was already gone.

The next morning, we walked to breakfast together. John was as cheerful as ever, doling out advice about bicycle maintenance, good places to stay on the route, and the best places to acquire food. Neither of us said anything about the night before, nor did we ask any questions about it. I ate eggs and fresh fruit with rabid enthusiasm.

"Where are you planning to stay tonight?" John asked me.

"I don't know and I don't care," I said gleefully. "Wherever the wind takes me I guess."

"You should try to make it to Pinedale tonight," John said. "It will be a long day, but there's not really going to be anywhere where you can buy supplies before then."

"I still have plenty of Flagg Ranch brownies," I said. "Full of caloric goodness. I can make it days on those alone."

We finished breakfast and walked into the bright morning.

"You know how to get out of here?" he asked.

"Yes, of course," I said.

"And you know that Brooks Lake is coming up and there's likely to be snow there?"

"Yes, yes," I said. "Don't worry about me, John. I'se all growed up now. You just go home and rest and take care of that knee."

We wrapped our arms around each other in a lingering hug, our first embrace. "Thanks again for everything, John," I said. "The first week of this race could not have gone more smoothly."

"Thanks to you, too," John said. "It didn't turn out like I'd hoped, but I couldn't have had more fun."

We wrapped our arms around each other in one last hug, mounted our bicycles, and turned in opposite directions, riding away from each other for good this time.

Chapter Fourteen
Heart of Wyoming

Page 187: Brooks Lake remains partially frozen in June.
Page 188: A gravel road snakes along the Continental Divide with the Wind River Mountain Range as a backdrop.

The first pass of the day approached 10,000 feet. A stiff blanket of last winter's snow draped down from granite pinnacles and stretched over open alpine meadows. Deciduous tree branches remained bare in late June. Even the air tasted different in Wyoming, with a cold crispness that masked sweet hints of decay, like a walk-in refrigerator in a butcher's shop.

The terrain on Togwotee Pass was similar to Richmond Pass — a calm, gradual climb that took Divide riders to their highest elevations yet, continued down the mountain on a smooth road, and then inexplicably veered off the main route into a nearly impassable mess of snow fields, rocky obstacles, and difficult navigation. But I had enjoyed Richmond Pass, so I didn't feel grumpy when the maps told me I had to turn off the perfectly good, paved surface of Highway 26 and hoist my bicycle up a three-foot-high wall that of snow that covered the alleged Brooks Lake access road, which had been buried since the previous autumn.

I lifted my bike to the top of the snowfield. A single set of footprints and wheel tracks dug a narrow trench down the center of the slushy surface. I wheeled my bike into the tracks and stepped into the footprints. It wasn't much, but I was grateful that a trail had been broken since the previous day's melt stripped away all signs of prior passersby. The tracks allowed me to not only walk more easily, but they helped keep my feet dry.

"Thanks, Jeremy," I said out loud, figuring there was a fair chance he wasn't too far in front of me, although I had started late that morning.

I walked for about a mile when the snowfield started to break up, revealing the dirt below. Saturated with a season's worth of snowmelt, the road was thickly coated in mud the color and consistency of melted chocolate ice cream. I planted one foot on the mud and slid forward. The slimy surface grabbed my feet and pulled me butt-first into the soup. Growling with frustration, I righted the bike and shoe-skied toward the next island of snow.

As the road descended, the snow patches grew shorter, the mud patches longer, and the slimy soup started to solidify and clump up. The consistency took on the properties of wet cornstarch — that goopy substance used by science teachers to entertain children because it looks like liquid and even drips like liquid, but instantly solidifies to a clay-like hardness under any kind of pressure. The Brooks Lake Road was liquid cornstarch, glistening in the sunlight and clinging to my shoes and wheels until both became stuck in place. I took off my bike gloves and used my fingers to scrape away the clumps wedged between the frame and tires. But I couldn't wheel my bike more than a few feet before it locked up with mud again. The adobe clumps were taking on reinforcement from dead pine needles, and the mass was rapidly hardening to the impenetrable density of a solid brick. I felt a sinking sensation of entrapment as I realized that as long as the mud persisted, it wasn't even possible to push my bike.

I zoomed out the screen of my GPS and tried to figure out how long I was going to be stuck like this. The map showed the Brooks Lake loop covering about six miles, and I had traveled just over a mile. I couldn't fathom five miles of carrying my fifty-pound bike on my shoulders, but the map also showed a lodge about halfway around the loop. Maybe the road was plowed beyond the lodge, which would mean it would likely be dry. Still, even three miles was a daunting distance.

I unclipped my frame bag, wedged my arm beneath the top tube, and lifted the bike frame onto my right shoulder. I wrapped my fingers around the stem, trying to keep the front wheel from swinging back and hitting my face. With the leaden weight pressing painfully on my shoulder bone, I took halting steps along the slippery surface. The mud still latched onto my shoes, building an adobe fortress around my feet until they were three times as large as normal, and three times as heavy. I staggered to the next patch of snow, about fifty yards away, and dropped my bike onto the ground, gasping as though I had just sprinted a one-hundred-meter dash.

I walked my bike across the snowfield, still panting but relieved for the relative break. The relief was short lived, because just around the next bend was another long, open stretch of mud. I looked down at the shoes that I had nearly scraped clean. "That's it," I announced to the Brooks Lake road. "I am not walking through that crap again."

I walked to the outer edge of the road. Like Richmond Peak, the road was little more than a notch cut into a steep mountainside. A 60-degree wall of talus plunged into the road, which artificially leveled out to goopy mud for only the width of a narrow two-lane road before plunging into a talus and boulder-strewn abyss below. It was actually impossible to not walk on the road, but I refused to accept that reality. I shouldered the bike and stepped onto the lower slope. With its chunkier boulders, it looked easier to negotiate than the steeper, slippery scree above. But the downside of walking the lower slope was that it forced me to balance and scramble across a minefield of large rocks, and I was carrying an awkward and heavy bicycle in one and sometimes both hands. Another disadvantage of the lower slope was that the price of any mistake was a fairly long fall.

I teetered and panicked, regained my composure and lost my nerve again. By the time I reached the safety of the snowfield nearly one hundred yards later, my heart was beating so rapidly I could feel it pushing out of my chest. That snowfield only lasted ten yards before dipping into another cauldron of mud. What were my other options? I had no other options. I could mire in mud or teeter on boulders, but either way, life for the next unknown number of miles was going to be exhausting, stressful, and hard.

Two miles and two-and-a-half hours passed. The more the road dropped, the drier and less ridiculous the mud became, until the snow was all but gone and the road was almost rideable. I passed the Brooks Lake Lodge and sure enough, the road beyond the resort had been graded and plowed. I hopped on my bike and tore down the hill, gasping at the sudden rush of speed. The crisp air sang out as it rushed past my ears and the patter of mud flinging from my bike joined a symphony of freedom. Within minutes of beginning my effortless, ecstatic descent, I turned back onto Highway 26. Had the race allowed me to stay on the pavement, I would have covered that four-mile downhill section of road in ten minutes.

The six-mile Brooks Lake detour cost me more than three hours of the highest intensity, most frustrating effort I had exerted on the Divide. That knowledge made me smile with satisfaction. After all, if you're going to do something ridiculous like a 2,700-mile mountain bike race, you might as well make it truly ridiculous.

The highway continued to drop along the wide corridor of the Wind River, and despite the obnoxiously slow detour, I was still able to ride forty miles before it was time to start thinking about lunch. At the Union Pass cutoff, I saw a tiny gas station. It didn't look like I could get much there beyond candy bars, but I remembered that somewhere during his long list of advice, John had told me there was some kind of lodge "at the pass." I had so enjoyed my real breakfast that the prospect of real lunch was too much of a temptation. I bypassed the gas station without slowing down.

My maps warned me that it was going to be a "tremendous grunt to get to altitude." But the beautiful thing about starting a day on the Great Divide with a section like the Brooks Lake Road is that it can't really get any worse. The wide, dusty climb to Union Pass was effortless in comparison.

The route gained 2,500 feet in twelve miles — a standard-issue climb on the Divide, only one of many dozens. Spruce trees started to shorten and thin as I rose into the sub-alpine zone until I was surrounded by nothing but snowfields and talus slopes. The Wind River Range carved a majestic horizon in the distant west. The wind itself, above the reach of any kind of obstruction, blew hard and steady at my side.

I stopped to put on a fleece pullover and hat. The wind howled with an eerie sensation of remoteness, like wind driven out of the Arctic. Out in the open alpine, I could see for many dozens of miles in nearly every direction. It was a world ruled by lichens, rock, and distant granite spires, completely devoid of any sign of humanity.

"Is there really a lodge up here?" I said out loud, and the howling wind instantly answered my ridiculous question. What was clear was that I had misunderstood whatever John had said about Union Pass. There was going to be no real lunch up here. I really should have stopped at that gas station 2,500 vertical feet below, because I was a bit low on calories. Surrounded on both sides by hundreds of square miles of designated roadless wilderness, Union Pass was a place humans had largely left alone. I would be alone with it, very much alone, for the next sixty miles.

The road turned directly into the wind and I put my head down, taking the brunt of it through the vents in my helmet while my legs slowed to a familiar headwind plod. Cyclists like to say the wind is a hill you never go down, and in strong wind, with no place to seek shelter, that sense of artificial backward gravity only amplifies. On the gradual, rolling descent, I was slowly losing elevation but fighting a continuous and steep uphill battle.

As I dropped away from the alpine tundra, I found myself no longer in the wooded valleys of western Wyoming, but out on the arid, sagebrush-dotted basins that dominated the rest of the state. The road leveled out in a river valley populated by cows. Thousands of hoof prints had turned the road surface to Swiss cheese, but the mud was dry, so I didn't complain. I crossed a hundred-foot-wide, dirty, emerald-colored canal and realized that trickle of a waterway was the Green River. Where it plunged through the narrow canyon lands of Utah, the Green River was brown, deep, and churning with whitewater rapids that in a not-too-distant past had, on a couple of occasions, frightened me to tears.

"So you're the Green River," I said to the gurgling brook. "You're not so bad up here."

The valley opened wide in front of a cloud-obscured sunset, which cast a peach light across the plains. The thick vapor of my breath clouded the beam of my headlamp as night descended with me, toward an arid landscape that was different than any I had seen yet on the Divide. I had become accustomed to thick forests in my surroundings, and the ragged sagebrush prairie stretching over the horizon brought me a sense of satisfaction, because it was a whole new climate zone, and I had ridden there, on my bicycle, all the way from Canada.

In purple twilight, the scenery faded to a black void with one glittering island of light, which I assumed must be Pinedale even though my map indicated the small town was still twenty miles away. The paved road rolled in and out of drainages but generally sloped downward. I knew I could reach town fairly quickly, but I longed to hold onto the deep silence that surrounded me on the open plateau. In its solitude the landscape kept me company, held me in peace, and showered me with stars. Out of the corner of my eye, I started to pick out nice, hidden areas where I could bed down in the sagebrush.

"I should just camp out here," I thought. "I've ridden my twelve hours for the day; I've done my hundred miles. I can always get an early start tomorrow."

I stopped near a mound to look for a spot out of sight from the road. I opened my feedbag to check my food supply. The bag of Sour Patch Kids I had been munching from had only a handful of gummy snacks left. There was one package of peanut butter crackers, a regular-sized Snickers Bar, and nothing else. I groaned. I had spent the entire day simply grazing and I was so hungry I could have easily eaten five times that amount, standing right there. It was scarcely enough food to fuel me into Pinedale, let alone serve as dinner and breakfast. No, I was going to have to go to town and stock up.

It was after 11 p.m. when I arrived in Pinedale, population 1,412. I was certain everything would be closed, but I found an open gas station with a hotel right next door. The town, a pit stop on Highway 191, had a number of hotels, and the gas station's neighbor looked like the most expensive one. But it had access to food, and that fact mattered more than cash — which has no calories — so I booked a room and walked to the gas station to buy Hot Pockets, root beer, oranges, and a fruit smoothie for dinner.

I checked my e-mail on the computer in the front lobby. John had already sent me a message, telling me he was still in Jackson but was checking up on my SPOT tracker. "Looks like you had some trouble near Brooks Lake," he wrote. "Nice job motivating to ride late into Pinedale tonight."

I smiled because had I slept out in the sagebrush twenty miles west of town, John would have viewed that as a failure, while I viewed the necessity of riding into town as a defeat. "Thanks a lot, John," I thought. "You've made a total comfort tourist out of me."

I checked the race tracker myself. It looked like Jeremy had ridden past Pinedale and was spending the night somewhere east of town. The race leaders were moving through Colorado. A handful of people had dropped out but there were still quite a few orange dots on the route behind me, including Cricket, who had inexplicably fallen an entire day behind my pace and was just leaving Idaho.

"She must have had trouble," I thought. "But she's tough and she out-pedaled me before, so maybe she'll catch me."

I did notice that with John gone and Jeremy little more than a phantom shadow, I was falling into a rather lonely dead zone of the mid-pack. The leaders were surging farther in front, the back-of-pack was dropping farther behind, and I rode alone in my middle bubble, unsure whether I should make a real effort to speed up, slow down, or hold the lonely pace.

But the transition from traveling with John to traveling on my own felt surprisingly comfortable. The sudden lack of distraction was invigorating, opening a floodgate of inner dialogue. I reflected on my simple observations until they took on new dimensions of meaning. When I was too fatigued to reflect, I passed the miles by replaying a limitless reel of memories in my mind. I felt relieved to make all of my own decisions, to ride when I wanted to ride and stop when I wanted to stop. Like a teenager who had recently moved out of her parents' house, I relished in the simple freedoms of adulthood — singing out loud when the mood caught me, eating a bag of gummy worms without enduring an electrolyte lecture, and peeing out in the open.

I didn't motivate early the next day, which I justified because I had arrived late in Pinedale late the night before. I spent the morning doing laundry in my motel, typing e-mails on the guest computer, and making myself waffles in the Continental breakfast room.

"Okay, no more comfort touring," I scolded myself as I walked out of the lobby after 9 a.m. "Tonight we camp in the Great Divide Basin." I walked into the gas station and bought only a day's worth of food because I planned to arrive in Atlantic City early, and I knew I'd move faster if I didn't have a bunch of calories loading me down. John had already told me in his e-mail that Atlantic City was where I should spend the night, so I decided it would be a good place to stock up before setting out into the desert expanse of the Basin.

The route continued to parallel the Wind River Mountains on a dusty desert plateau. As I traveled west, erosion intensified and drainages became steeper, sometimes dropping many hundreds of feet into alkaline creek beds. The landscape was aspen-dotted near the top of the drainages but sandstone red at the bottom. I mopped streams of sweat away from my eyes. Beneath unobstructed sunlight I felt the heat sharply; it was the worst I had experienced on the Divide, although the temperature was still only in the high 80s. I slathered sunscreen on my arms and worked up a breeze by pedaling as quickly as I could muster. I covered the first forty miles of the day without even taking a break.

I crossed the Big Sandy River and climbed back to elevation. The ever-thinning groves of aspen trees had disappeared entirely, replaced by thirst-choked sagebrush. The loose-gravel road was becoming increasingly dustier. I dropped and climbed, dropped and climbed, across an arid landscape rippled by dramatic erosion. The climbs were all steep and short, so I kept my shifter locked in the high downhill gears, standing out of the saddle and mashing the pedals to power quickly to the top.

For a few miles, the road contoured the crest of a broad ridge, the exact boundary of the Continental Divide. Cattle grazed on both sides of the road. I thought with a smile that the cows on the right were peeing into the Pacific, while the urine on the left was headed for the Atlantic. Before the Tour Divide, the idea of the Continental Divide had always been a vague one at best, an arbitrary line across America. But after spending more than a week paralleling its jagged peaks and broad passes, I began to understand the mystique of the Divide and the appeal of following it. This was the backbone of the continent, the beginning of everything.

I mashed up a few more steep drainages before suddenly, about twenty miles from Atlantic City, something in my right knee snapped. I was certain I heard an audible "pop." I cried out in pain and hopped off the bike, staggering to the top before I doubled over and let the pain shudder through. My knee throbbed and I wondered if I had torn a tendon, but after a few minutes I realized I could still bend it slowly. Still, any sudden motion hurt. And the joint was swelling a little and stiffening up. I walked several hundred yards, coasted down the hill, and limped up the next pitch.

The sharp pain began to subside and I started riding uphill again. Spinning the crank lightly helped keep stiffness at bay, but I couldn't put any power into the pedals without considerable pain. I wondered if this was what had happened to John in Canada. He claimed to have put too much pressure on the joint until the whole thing gave out. But I had also had trouble with my right knee in the past, and wondered if this was a return to something my doctor had diagnosed as "angry knee," — commonly called chondromalacia, the injury involves acute swelling of the cartilage beneath the patella.

My pace slowed considerably as I pedaled and walked toward Atlantic City. I wondered if I should take John's advice on staying in town so I could rest my knee and assess the extent of the injury. It was just after 6 p.m. when I arrived. The gravel road dropped into a small valley with weather-beaten houses haphazardly clustered around red dirt roads. There was nothing but open desert beyond. It looked like a set for a Western movie made in the 1950s. A hand-painted sign on the side of the road read "Atlantic City, population 57."

"Oh no!" I cried out. Fifty-seven people? Towns that small rarely have more than one street, let alone services. I had only a couple liters of water and was nearly out of food. I had been depending on that place to stock up for my ride across 140 barren miles of the Great Divide Basin. What did John mean by Atlantic City being a good place to spend the night? How could this place even possibly have a motel? I'd be lucky if it had a cattle trough where I could filter a few liters of water. I decided that from that point on, I was going to assume I had misunderstood everything John told me and would pay much closer attention to the recommendations on my maps.

That is, if I could even ride beyond Atlantic City. My knee still throbbed as I pedaled into town and tried to push down a rising wave of panic. The Great Divide Basin was the most remote, driest section of the entire trip. There was no way I could embark on the crossing with only a few candy bars as my entire food supply. If anything, I needed at least two days worth of food. If something went wrong and I ended up spending a few days out there, it promised to be a dangerous crossing indeed. Plus, I wanted to start the trek with at least nine liters of water. I hoped I wouldn't have to gather it from a cattle trough.

I passed the place that had been listed on the map as the accommodations in town, the Atlantic City Mercantile. A sign on the door of the early-20th-century building read, "Closed Tuesdays." It was, rather conveniently, Tuesday. But a drone of music thumped from the dilapidated looking wooden building next door, and as I approached it, I realized it was a bar.

Inside, at least a dozen people were perched around the counter, and there were even more people in an adjacent dining room.

"Are you guys open?" I asked the woman behind the bar.

"Until seven," the woman told me.

"Do you have food?"

She smiled. "We have a whole menu. Come in! Do you want anything to drink?"

"Pepsi," I said.

"Just Pepsi?" she asked. "Nothing in the Pepsi?"

"Plain Pepsi," I said. "And a glass of water. And maybe an orange juice. Yeah, all three. And do you guys sell any kind of packaged food here, like candy bars and stuff?"

"A little," she said. She pointed to two shelves in the back of the room. "Over there."

The shelves were sparse to begin with, and they held a number of boxes that had already been emptied. They were out of peanut butter cups, M&Ms, Snickers Bars and nuts. I wondered if previous Tour Divide racers were the ones who had cleaned them out. All they left for me were a couple of packages of Oreos, a few trans-fat-laden pastries that looked so stale they were on the verge of crumbling to dust, and individual packets of Spam. Everything was food that I would have regarded with a scrunched nose amid the sweeping selection of a modern gas station, but in Atlantic City, Wyoming, I was thrilled to see it. I cleaned the bar out of their Oreos and pastries and reluctantly grabbed four packets of Spam.

From the restaurant I ordered soup and chicken strips. I guzzled my water and dumped the ice into a baggy to place on my knee, and sat contemplating whether or not I should ride out of town that night. It seemed smart to wait out the injury, but I also knew that pain was more likely to nudge me out of the race if I was surrounded in the convenience of a town. Out on the Basin, I'd have no choice but to pedal somewhere.

As I ate, a petite, older woman with shoulder-length gray hair approached me. "Are you the bicycle girl we saw walking out of South Pass City this afternoon?" she asked me.

"It's highly likely," I said. "I'm Jill. I'm from Alaska, but I'm riding through town with the Tour Divide. It's a race from Canada to Mexico. Maybe you've seen the other bikers come through?"

She shook her head.

"Strange," I said. "There's probably been close to twenty."

A man that had been sitting in the table next to me turned and said. "I saw them. They came through here three days ago! You're way behind."

"And believe it or not, there are people who are three days behind me, some more," I said. "It's a long race. We spread out."

"I think I did see one person in town earlier today," the woman said. "He had a lot of stuff on the front of his bike."

"That was probably Jeremy," I said. "I wonder if he's around."

The woman introduced herself as Marjane and asked me if I wanted to bring my plate over to her table, where her husband, Terry, was polishing off a large pile of ribs. We made our introductions and I explained in more detail what the Tour Divide entailed. It was a race, I told her, but I was really more interested in the tour aspect of it. Marjane told me she had been a

197

wanderer in her own youth, but she married Terry and they settled down in an old gold mill, built of rounded stones, that Terry himself converted into a home.

"We love Atlantic City," she said. "We've been all over but we can't imagine living anywhere else."

As we chatted, she asked me where I was going to stay that night.

"Actually, I should get going soon," I said. "I was going to go a little ways into the Basin to camp, and it would be nice to do the riding before dark."

"Camp out there?" Marjane shook her head. "It's supposed to be a cold one tonight. Why don't you come stay with us? You can take a shower and make breakfast in the morning. It's going to be a cold night for camping out."

I blinked but didn't hesitate long. "Yeah," I said. "That would be great."

A draft carried through Marjane and Terry's old stone house, but it was cozy and reassuring. Terry told me he had built the house himself on top of a mill that had been part of a now-defunct gold mine. Atlantic City had the feel of an old mining town that never progressed past the 1930s. But unlike other historic towns that catered to tourists, that feeling was genuine. Atlantic City was so far off the beaten path that its citizens had little reason to change how they lived over the decades, and the dusty road and creaky whitewashed houses held an air of timelessness.

Marjane showed me pictures of her children and grandchildren and the brochure she wrote for the Atlantic City Historical Society. She pointed me to her computer but admitted she didn't really know how to use it. She gave me a bag of ice cubes for my knee. She opened the cupboards and pointed to the cereal and fruit and filled up the coffee maker with grounds and water so all I had to do in the morning was press "start." She showed me the spare bedroom and shower and gave me a hug goodbye, because I told her I planned to leave by 5 a.m. and there was "no way" she'd be out of bed that early. Her eyes were moist with compassion. My heart was full with gratitude, because although our entire relationship would only span a handful of hours on a Tuesday evening in June, those few hours were filled with all of the warmth and caring of family.

Chapter Fifteen
The Great Divide Basin

Page 199 and 200: The Great Divide Basin in Wyoming.

A layer of frost coated my bicycle as I packed up my stale pastries and Spam and pedaled out of Atlantic City. A chill hung in the pre-dawn air, which was thick with frozen vapor. My right knee was still slightly swollen and stiff, and protested loudly after just a few strokes up the hill out of town.

"Lucky for you, the Basin's pretty flat," I said as I hopped off the saddle and started pushing. The gravel road cut steeply up the bluff, gaining 500 feet in just over a mile. Cold oxygen burned my lungs as I labored around the switchbacks, trying not to think about my knee or the remote miles that lay in front of me.

As I rounded the last switchback onto a plateau, my shoulders relaxed and my jaw dropped. The Great Divide Basin yawned over an unbroken horizon, as vast and open as an ocean. Rolling drainages rippled like waves, clusters of sagebrush appeared as islands, and tall grass shimmered like seawater as it swayed in the breeze. The warm light of sunrise saturated the surface in iridescent colors. Greens took on a florescent glow, browns became bronze, yellow turned to gold. I pulled out my camera to take a few photos, but understood the images would always be a disappointment. Such is the price of great beauty, because while eyes can see and cameras can mimic, only experience and presence can reflect the sublime.

Of all of the regions along the Great Divide Mountain Bike Route, the Great Divide Basin has perhaps the most notorious reputation, at least among racers. Veterans speak of it in dismissive tones and warnings: "There's no trees, there's no water, there's no people, and there's nowhere to get food. There's only wind and heat." It was hard for me to believe that a lack of crowds could be a bad thing on a cold, calm morning, with a pack full of food and water, and the absence of trees to open up a spectacular view. It's on these open plains where the true shape of the world becomes apparent, with its scoured surface and arching horizon. For all of its jagged contours and conventions, from a distance the globe is just that — plain and round.

I felt deeply drawn to the Basin for personal reasons as well. My family on my Dad's side comes from a long line of Mormon pioneers, hearty stock who immigrated to Utah in the 1850s after traveling through this region with a human-powered handcart company. The Great Divide Mountain Bike Route closely parallels the old Mormon Pioneer Trail, crossing historic sites where my ancestors and their families and friends toiled, struggled, and sometimes perished in a harsh, high desert that hasn't changed all that much in 150 years.

Of course I had modern gravel roads to follow, the modern wonder that is a bicycle to propel me forward, and modern knowledge and technology to help guide me. But on some levels, my struggle was not entirely different from the struggles of my pioneer ancestors. Like many of them, I carried my whole life on a contraption that I had to move with my own power. I had to cope with similar isolation and uncertainty. I had to battle a primal sort of pain and fatigue that even 150 years of progress hasn't stripped away. As I gazed out across the prairie, I liked to believe that I was seeing the same things that my great-great-and-so-forth grandparents saw, that I was feeling the same things they felt. Their blood pumped through my veins, their sacrifices inspired me, and their faith drove me forward.

As I pedaled into the rising daylight, a small group of antelope grazing next to the road became startled and sprinted beside me, loping through the brush with enviable grace. I passed the cutoff marker for Willie's Handcart. Marjane had told me this was the site of a Mormon tragedy, where sixty-seven pioneers became trapped in a severe October snowstorm and died. I asked Marjane why they were traveling through Wyoming so late in the year. She told me the pioneers had difficulty with their handcarts. They had built their wheels in the humid east, and when they reached the west, the wooden hubs cracked and broke. The collapsed wheels and required repairs slowed the pioneers considerably until winter caught up to them. It was a quiet reminder of that precipice everybody straddles; that sometimes all it takes is one minor mishap for entire lives to spiral out of control.

The first thirty miles of the day passed in dreams about the distant past, until the present was all but lost to me. Grass shimmered in the sun and breeze, antelope darted beside me, and my imagination didn't have to stretch too far before it was 1854 again. I was still floating through the time machine in my mind when I started up a hill and my crank suddenly stopped working. The bike slowed to a stop. I spun the pedals frantically but the back wheel stayed planted in place until I nearly tipped over. I jumped off the bike. "What the hell?" I said out loud.

I lifted the back end off the ground and spun the crank with my hand. Even as I turned it as fast as I could, the rings did nothing to engage the wheel into motion. I checked to see if the chain was broken somewhere, but it was still intact and the rear cassette still turned with the cranks. I thought with sinking dread that the problem must be my freehub — one bicycle part I definitely did not have the capacity to fix.

A freehub is an internal part of the wheel hub that allows a cyclist to coast. When the cyclist spins the crank forward, the pawls inside the freehub engage and catch the hub, turning the wheel. Then, when a cyclist stops pedaling, the pawls release, which allows the wheel to spin free even if the crank and pedals are not moving. It seemed my freehub was stuck open, which caused the pawls to disengage even when the pedals were being turned. My bike was locked in "coast" mode, a mode that only works if you have gravity working for you. Without a working hub, my bicycle was as useless as a laundry cart.

"Crap! Crap! Crap!" I called out to the still air. I threw my bicycle onto the road and paced around. What were my options? It was a thirty-mile walk back to Atlantic City. Doable in a day, but what exactly could I do when I got there? I needed a new hub — and probably an entirely new wheel. As lucky as I had been in Atlantic City, expecting that town to contain an available 29-inch rear mountain bike wheel was pushing that luck more than a little. There was no way I could walk forward on the route. It was 110 miles to Rawlins with no towns or even houses along the way. I didn't have enough food or water to make such a trek on foot, and hitching a ride forward on the route was a race-ending infraction, although I didn't expect the temptation to arise because I doubted that much vehicular traffic ever ventured out this way.

I remembered from my Iditarod days a trick racers used when their freehubs froze in the extreme cold. They would zip-tie their cassettes to the spokes of the wheel, converting their drivetrain to a fixed gear and bypassing the need for a hub. But I had only heard about this repair in theory. I had never seen it in practice. I carried a few emergency zip-ties, but I only had about five of them. The expectation that five thin strips of plastic could handle all of the thrust and force of 110 miles of gravel-road pedaling seemed dubious at best. If I didn't break the zip ties, I'd break the spokes, I felt certain. And if I broke the spokes, then my wheel would collapse, and I'd really be screwed.

The first thing to do was to make sure the freehub really was stuck beyond return. I walked my bike up the hill and began coasting down it, frantically turning the useless pedals like a rabid hamster. To my amazement, I felt a sudden, hard force on the down stroke, and just like that, I was powering the bike on my own again.

I rode a few hundred yards before stopping. I still needed to assess how much I'd be able to depend on my hub. Sure enough, when I got back on the bike, the hub was stuck open again. I lifted the rear wheel off the ground and spun the crank frantically with my hands until the hub caught. I jumped onto the bike before it had a chance to cool down and pedaled furiously down the road.

What had become clear is that if I wanted the hub to continue engaging, I had to keep the pedals turning. Even during the few seconds I allowed it to rest while coasting down a hill, the pawls would freeze up and I'd have to spin the pedals furiously to release them again. The big question remained in how wise it would be to continue forward on the route, farther into the oblivion of the Great Divide Basin. I could spin the crank to coax the pawls back to life now, but what would I do if and when that technique stopped working? The farther I pedaled from Atlantic City, the farther I was going to have to walk through dusty, open desert should the need arise. The halfway point of the Basin was far away to even think about.

But going back to Atlantic City was a dead end. I couldn't let myself accept it — turning around and potentially ending my race on something as simple as a stuck freehub. I formulated a plan. I wouldn't stop pedaling for the rest of the day. At all. Even on the descents, I would spin the crank wildly to keep up with the speed of gravity, but I would not stop pedaling. There would be times I would need to pee and refill my drinking bladder from my water reserves, and also to change out my maps. Those times would have to be reserved for the only two points on the route that had viable exits within walking distance of an off-route town. The first emergency bailout was at mile 47, about seventeen miles away. From there, I could leave the route and walk fifteen miles north to a town called Sweetwater Station. The second and last emergency bailout was at mile 66, where Jeffrey City lay fourteen miles north. After that, I was pretty much committed to Rawlins. A wave of stress crescendoed through my gut but the plan seemed simple enough. Just don't stop pedaling.

My right knee did not react kindly to the frantic downhill pedaling, but I put the sharp bursts of pain out of my mind. An angry knee was small potatoes compared to a failing bicycle in the Great Divide Basin. To relieve the pain, I stood up in the saddle, which only worked to increase my speed and re-irritate my knee. I arrived at the Sweetwater Station cutoff in what seemed like no time at all. I jumped off the bike, darted into the bushes, ate one of my dust-flavored pastries, refilled my feedbag with Oreo cookies and one of the packets of Spam, and lifted the wheel up to hand-turn the crank. I spun the rear tire for a full thirty seconds, and nothing happened.

"Come on, come on," I coaxed, spinning the crank as fast as I could physically muster. My biceps burned. I thought of the pioneers of Willie's Handcart Company, whose spirits lingered in this desert after broken wheels indirectly led to their deaths. My situation was not nearly as dire as a winter storm in true wilderness, but my heart raced just the same. "Turn, damn it!" I screamed.

I felt a sudden force on the crank and the knobs on the tire lurched forward. I dropped the bike onto the ground and vaulted onto the seat in a single, surprisingly flawless move that didn't even break the cadence of the crank.

Back on my bike, I moved with single-minded purpose toward mile 66. I passed an active oil drill and a handful of ramshackle sheds, but I had yet to see another vehicle or human being. A seemingly endless herd of antelope grazed and trotted beside me. Their grace and ease mocked my awkward dependence on a failing machine, and reminded me that when humans stand alone, our weaknesses outnumber all of the creatures of the wild.

My leg muscles began to burn constantly and my back felt weak and sore. It was day twelve of the Tour Divide, and my body was starting to wear. Many hours of consistent pedaling demanded frequent breaks to cool my overheating muscles and rest my overworked joints, like a rattling old Buick that had to be coaxed along an extended road trip. Without the opportunity for breaks, the fatigue and soreness grew exponentially, until I squirmed and shifted on my bike like a person who can't find comfortable position in bed.

At mile 56, I slurped the last of the water in my drinking bladder. "Crap!" I said. "I knew I should have refilled my bladder at mile 47!" By late morning the heat had built considerably, until I was sure that despite the below-freezing morning, the afternoon temperature was climbing above eighty degrees. But I had to stick to the plan. Every mile I couldn't keep pedaling was a mile I might have to walk, so I had no choice but to keep pedaling.

At mile 62, my throat was dry and my drinking bladder still empty, but my own bladder was completely full. The organ bulged and pressed against my abdomen until I was certain I could feel urine leaking out of my eyes. If it was only a need to pee I might have strongly considered just letting it go — after all, I was already drenched in sweat and wetting my shorts in that manner wouldn't be that much different. But there were other ways I needed to relieve myself, too, ways that I didn't want to end up in my shorts. And that demand had reached a fever pitch of desperation that no amount of fortitude could mute.

"It's only four more miles, just four more miles, be strong, be strong," I chanted to myself. But another, seemingly louder inner voice was screaming, "You can walk four more miles. Just stop! Stop!"

At mile 64, the loud voice won out. The road traveled down a long, gradual slope, and I could even see the junction where I might have to turn, but I could not wait two more miles. I tossed the bike down and darted to a sagebrush bush five feet away. It wasn't very far off the road, but I there seemed little need for privacy. It was in that sensitive position that I saw my first vehicle of the day. The truck rumbled down the Jeffery City road, turned right at the intersection, and drove directly toward me. I ducked lower but I knew that for the most part, I was in full view. I finished my business, pulled my shorts up while still in the squatting position, and slithered away from the brush. I smiled and waved at the driver as he passed and waved back. I was certain he knew exactly what I had been doing, but strangely, I felt no sense of embarrassment. I was too deeply immersed in stress and struggle to care in the least about social propriety and image.

I removed my spare water holder from my backpack and refilled my drinking bladder with lukewarm liquid. After taking a few long gulps, I commenced the hand-turn effort to try to engage the freehub. I spun the crank for a while, more than a minute, with no movement. I stood up, paced around, and then knelt down to try again. Another minute passed. I spun until my biceps burned, but nothing.

"Please," I pleaded. "I need you. Can't you see I need you?"

I decided to try my legs, which had the advantage of more power but also had less balance. I set the bike down and hopped on the saddle, spinning wildly. The bike started to teeter. I put my foot down, then placed it back on the pedal and tried again.

Almost like magic, the bike suddenly lunged forward. "Yeah!" I yelped. "Yeah!" I started pedaling harder, nearly sprinting the rest of the way to the Jeffery City cutoff, where I made a triumphant right turn. I guzzled more water and relished in my renewed comfort. But I couldn't let that complacency last long. I furrowed my brow in deep determination.

"It's Rawlins or bust," I said.

By mile 75, my leg muscles were on fire again, needling my senses like whining children in the back seat of a car. "Are we there yet? Are we there yet? Are we there yet?" I stood and leaned over the handlebars, trying to push out some of the acid that was churning through my veins. As I pedaled in that awkward position, I realized that whatever mutiny was going on in my muscles had blocked out all of the nagging stiffness in my right knee. In fact, the angry knee felt downright chipper as I pedaled unceasingly, traveling in a straight line due south with a hard wind gusting at my side. That feeling didn't seem to transfer to anywhere else in my body.

"We almost didn't get the bike started last time," I finally snapped at my legs. "No way are we stopping now. We'll stop when we hit the pavement. It's not all that terribly far. Like thirty more miles."

I fished my last pastry out of my frame bag and opened the wrapper. I had been saving this one for last; because it was cream cheese flavored, I decided it would be a special treat. I still had my four packets of Spam, which would have to be consumed next, but I was putting off using that calorie source for as long as I could. I bit into another mouthful of disappointment. The cream cheese pastry carried the same taste as its fake-fruit-flavored predecessors — like it had been sitting on a bar shelf for far too long, and had been reduced to syrupy dust. The only difference in this one was a big ball of pasty cheese-flavored substance in the center.

The Great Divide Basin continued, unbroken, uninhabited, unchanging. In the western Basin, drainages rippled through the land. But in the east, a stark flatness emerged. I watched the road stretch ten miles in front of me. An infinity of prairie was only vaguely interrupted by the inevitable curvature of the Earth. But as I rode, tiny contours of hills grabbed my sore legs and then released them. With my battered muscles and ceaseless pedaling, I felt the unrelenting force of every single understated hill — the agony of climbing, the relief of gravity. Even the flat world isn't flat — a reality only cyclists truly understand.

I managed to reach the rough pavement of an all-but-unused Highway 63. The route turned east and the wind shifted comfortably at my back. But the anxiety of the day had worn on me. That same elevated stress level that likely filled my muscles with acid also filled my head with malaise. Before the Basin, I hadn't even noticed any saddle sores on my behind, but by that afternoon I was fully cognizant of every ache and pain. After I stood to relieve the agony in my legs, I had to sit back down on saddle sores that brought tears to my eyes. Even my skin burned in the hot sun, but I couldn't think about stopping to put on sunscreen. It was the ultimate prison of both body and mind — trapped on a bicycle I couldn't bear and couldn't trust, but couldn't abandon.

Even though I carried the burden of nine liters of water on my back, I had been extra conservative with fluid that day, mostly to eliminate that pesky peeing problem. But eight hours of exposure to direct sun and wind had pushed me into a deep dehydration, and suddenly I couldn't drink enough water to relieve a throat so parched that I constantly felt like I was on the verge of gagging. The mechanicals in my bicycle and the injuries on my body felt deeply connected, as though the two weren't even fully separated from each other. I laughed at the idea of becoming "one" with my bicycle, but after twelve days on the Divide, I felt as useless without my bicycle as it would be without me. And as long as my bicycle remained battered and broken, my body wasn't likely to recover.

Just before 5 p.m., with a subdued sort of exaltation, I dropped off the expansive plateau of the Basin and into the gray and sprawling interstate town of Rawlins. Having left Atlantic City after 5 a.m., I had managed to travel the entire 140-mile span of the Basin in less than twelve hours, by far my highest average speed of the entire Divide. For the first time since late morning, I let my anxiety shrink away as I drank in the shot of accomplishment. My athletic feat may have been born of the necessity of not stopping, but it was a feat just the same.

But my victory wasn't just athletic. I had won the race against typical business hours, and there was a good chance that if I could find the bicycle shop in Rawlins, they might be able to help me that night. A mostly deserted Main Street led to a maze of fast food restaurants and strip malls, and despite spending an entire day in the lonely desert, I felt anxious to leave that interstate pit stop of a town. I needed to buy food and a new wheel, and along with the new brakes and other repairs I hoped to have completed, I would likely have to spend the night in Rawlins. But if I could convince the bicycle mechanic in town to repair my wheel that night, I might be able to get an early start, which was my only shot of making it to my next planned destination, Steamboat Springs, 130 miles south, by the following night.

As I rode down a wide frontage road paralleling I-80, I saw Jeremy riding in the opposite direction. I crossed six lanes of traffic to intercept him.

"Hey Jeremy!" I called out. "Awesome to see you! How are you feeling?"

"Better now that I bought this," he said, pointing to the massive bundle on the front of his bike. He still had his usual plastic bags of groceries and his sleeping bag, but he had also added a closed-cell foam mattress. "I started the trip without a pad, but I finally decided to get one and they had one at Wal-mart."

"Wait, you've been camping all these nights without a sleeping pad?" I asked. I just shook my head in disbelief. Between the nine-speed bike and the lonely nights on hard ground, I was beginning to think Jeremy was a masochist. "Hey, do you want to split a room tonight?" I continued. "I have to hurry and find the bike shop before it closes, but I can meet you back around this spot and we can pick a motel. Maybe we can grab dinner."

"No," he said. "I have my sleeping pad and dinner. I think I'm going to try to get in twenty or thirty more miles tonight."

"Okay," I said, disappointed as Jeremy rode away. It would be the last I'd ever see of him. He would stay in front of me for the rest of his race, and eventually drop out in Kremmling, Colorado, with the simple and vague explanation that he would no longer "be Tour Dividing." He was the only competitor to quit the race without providing a long excuse. I would never learn the true nature of his methods or his motives.

I finally found the bike shop at 5:25 p.m. A sign on the door said it closed at 5:30. "I know you're closing soon," I said as I walked in the door. "But I'm in a real bind. Do you happen to have any spare 29-inch wheels here?"

"Twenty-nine-inch wheels?" the white-haired woman behind the counter repeated with a hint of confusion.

"You know, mountain bike wheels. I need a new one with a nine-speed cassette. Or even if you have a fully built bike I could buy one off of, that would work too. I'm willing to pay whatever it costs. Please, I'm desperate."

She pointed to a row of mountain bikes lined next to the window. They all looked like they had been lifted from the Wal-mart inventory lot, and they were all the wrong size, with 26-inch wheels. "That's all we have here," she said.

"OK," I breathed in. "How about hubs? A Shimano XT rear hub? Do you have a mechanic who could rebuild a wheel for me?"

"My mechanic's gone home for the night," she said. "But he'll be in at 10:30 or maybe 11 tomorrow. He doesn't like to get up early. He might be able to help you. I can't really say. We don't have a lot of parts around here, but I bet he'll be able to rig up something. He's great. Only eighteen years old, but he's a mechanical genius."

"Ten thirty," I said. "Is there any way he'd come in earlier? I'm traveling through with the Tour Divide race, maybe you've seen the others in here recently?"

She shook her head. "No, can't say I have."

"Um, anyway, I was really hoping to get out of Rawlins earlier than that."

"I get here at 8:30," she said. "I'll call him in the morning, but I can't promise anything. He's a teenager. He sleeps in. Now, is there anything else I can do to help you?"

I smiled weakly. She really couldn't have been less helpful. I half wished the bike shop had been closed when I arrived in town, because that would have at least allowed me to sleep through the night with a glimmer of hope. If the bike shop didn't have a wheel and likely didn't even have a hub, there wasn't much even a boy genius mechanic could do to help me.

I checked into a hotel room, sat on the neat bed in a too-large room, and stewed in low-boiling frustration. I couldn't decide what to do. I had been having an easier time getting the hub to catch since my initial trouble, but it still gave me difficulty every time. Continuing 130 mountainous miles into Steamboat Springs with a broken hub seemed to be a bad idea, like heading into a long road trip with a slipping clutch. I didn't know when the whole thing would seize up completely, but it seemed likely to happen at a rather inconvenient time.

And there were other problems, too. Both of my brakes had started squealing horribly, meaning I was basically scraping metal on metal with both pads. I had one set of spare pads, but I had already tried to wedge them in my front brakes back in Atlantic City and couldn't get the new ones to catch, so I reinstalled the old ones. I suspected there was something wrong with my front brake caliper, and I didn't want to risk stuffing a new set in knowing they might fall out. Besides, I hadn't been too worried about the lack of good brakes on the mostly flat Great Divide Basin. But once I hit the mountains of Colorado, I would need top-level stopping power.

Beyond these problems, my cables and housings were gummed up with mud and I could no longer shift the chain onto the little ring. I had already tried to lube both derailleurs and the cables to no avail, and suspected they would need to be deeply cleaned or replaced. The prospect of no low gear in the big mountains also was daunting.

I needed outside advice. The rational choice seemed to be phoning John. He would know exactly what I needed to do. If I had the right tools, I thought with a smile, he'd probably be the type of person who could talk me through an entire wheel rebuild. But for some reason, I wasn't quite ready to call him. There was still awkwardness there, a lot of things John and I left unsaid. And then, almost in the same stream of thought that prevented me from dialing John's number, I decided to call Geoff.

"Jill?" Geoff's voice came over the receiver. We had not spoken in several weeks. "What's up?"

"Hey Geoff," I said. "I started the Tour Divide. I'm in Rawlins, Wyoming."

"I know," he said. "I've been watching you. You're doing awesome."

"Well, actually, I'm not doing so awesome right now," I said, and explained my predicament. "What do you think?" I finally asked. "Should I wait here on the unlikely chance that this mechanic can help me, or should I pack up and leave early tomorrow?"

He didn't even hesitate. "I'd leave," he said. "Try to get to Steamboat. They have a great bike shop there."

"But what if I get stuck?" I asked. "And what about my brakes? I didn't have much luck changing the pads in Atlantic City. I don't know if it's me or the brake caliper. Either way, it's not good."

"Just change them out and go to Steamboat to get replacements. You'll be fine," Geoff said as though he was certain of it.

"Okay," I said. "I'm going to think about it."

He paused. "So, how have you been?"

"I've been good," I said. "You know, tired and sore and all that. Well, of course you know how the Divide feels. But I'm having an incredible time. This has been an amazing experience so far."

"I see you've been traveling a lot with John Nobile," Geoff said.

"Yeah, we spent the whole first week together," I said. "It was great. After he injured himself he just wanted to take it easy and tour with someone, and I learned a ton from him."

"But he dropped out?"

"Yeah, in Jackson. I'm alone now, trying to make it work. But suddenly a lot of things are going wrong."

"You're doing great," Geoff said. "You're going to finish this thing, not wimp out like I did."

We chatted for a few more minutes. He told me he was back in Juneau after visiting Misty in Sitka for a week. He told me she was going to stay in Sitka, but he returned to Juneau. He didn't tell me why. He told me he was back at work, and running again, and had some ideas for races in the early fall. But until then, he said, he was just going to run as many mountains as he could find and enjoy summer in Alaska.

"That's great," I said.

"I should probably get going," Geoff said. "But remember that you're halfway done now. You made it through Montana. The hard part's over."

"I sincerely doubt that," I said. "But thanks for your advice. I'll do my best."

I hung up the phone in a wave of emotion — pride, hurt and anger mixed with a hint of nausea. Why did I think it would be so easy to speak to him again? Especially amid the emotional rollercoaster that was the Tour Divide? He was the one person I turned to every time I needed help during the past eight years. But I had forgotten he wasn't there for me anymore, and he couldn't help me, and I needed to accept that. Tears welled up in my eyes. I was safely hidden from the world inside a hotel room in Rawlins, but I wasn't ready to cry about my potential failure in the race and I certainly wasn't ready to cry about Geoff. I had to get out of my head, so I called home.

My youngest sister answered the phone.

"Sara!" I said. "I'm calling from Wyoming!" I tried to sound excited, but I heard my voice crack.

We chatted a little about the race, and then I asked how she was doing. She was engaged to be married in August. My entire month in Utah had been dominated by plans for her wedding. I had been fitted for a bridesmaid dress, made arrangements to fly home from Juneau after returning from the Tour Divide, and spent a fair amount of time hanging out with Sara and her fiancé, getting to know my future brother-in-law. I had struggled with mixed feelings of happiness and jealousy about the idea of my twenty-two-year-old sister getting married after my failure of a relationship. But I was genuinely excited for her, so of course I asked, "How are the wedding plans going?"

"Um, well," she said in almost a whisper. "Well," her voice choked up and I heard her set the phone down. My heart, already racing, already exhausted, developed a clammy chill. Several seconds later, my mom picked up. "Jill?"

"Mom, what's going on with Sara?" I asked.

"She, well, you see," my mom stammered.

"What happened?"

"Oh," my mom said, "Your father is going to kill me for telling you, but Sara called off the wedding. She decided she just wasn't ready to get married."

"Oh no," I said. "That's — that's really hard. I'm really sorry to hear that. But why didn't you tell me before? Why weren't you going to tell me?"

"Well, you're in this race, we know it's hard and it's a lot for you right now," my mom said. "We didn't want to add our problems on top of it."

"Your problems are my problems!" I said. I felt hurt. Since I was a teenager I'd had a difficult time opening my life to my family, but they had been so helpful over the summer and my own awful breakup that I thought I had established a deeper level of trust. I knew my mom was trying to protect me, but she didn't understand that the Tour Divide wasn't about cutting myself off from the world, but connecting with it. "I just asked Sara about her wedding," I continued, knowing my sensitive baby sister was probably somewhere in the background, deeply distraught. "I feel like an idiot."

"I know," my mom said. "I'm sorry." She hesitated. "But Sara is doing much better and she's going to be fine. She made the right decision. But how are you? How are you doing?"

I told her about my comparatively silly bike mechanical drama, leaving out how uncertain I was about fixing the problem. "So I'm going to stay here tonight and wait for the bike mechanic," I said. "I'll lose a half day or so of riding, but I should be fine."

And with that, my mind was made up. I might be stuck in the depressed truck-stop town of Rawlins indefinitely, but I wasn't about to throw caution to the wind.

Chapter Sixteen
Kindness

Page 213: The sun sets over a farmhouse in Slater, Colorado.
Page 214: Kirsten Hendricksen, proprietor of the Brush Mountain Outpost, stands near a handmade sign near Slater, Colorado.

I was pacing in front of the Rawlins bike shop when the white-haired owner strolled up at 8:47 a.m.

"Is your mechanic going to come in early today?" I asked.

"I don't know," she said. "I haven't called him yet."

I sighed. I was hoping she would have at least partially recognized my predicament and rallied the troops the night before. She unlocked the door and let me in. "Would you like to wait for him here?" she asked.

"Actually, do you mind if I start working on my bike myself?" I replied.

"No problem," she said and guided me to the back of the shop. I unclipped all of my bags, balanced the bike on its handlebars and saddle, and set to work. With a garden hose, an old toothbrush, and a can of degreaser, I chipped away at two weeks' worth of ceaseless mud and grime. When the bike reached a state of sparkle, I flipped it over and started lubing the cables and chain, adjusting the stiff derailleurs and tightening the brakes. I removed the front brake pads and tried once again to install my spares, but they wouldn't slide in. I wondered if something was wrong with the pads, but of course the owner didn't have anything resembling a disc brake pad in the shop.

"If worse comes to worst, we might be able to install some rim brakes for you," she said.

The mechanic, a tall, lanky teen with sleep still crusted around his eyes, showed up at 10:45.

First, I showed him my brake caliper.

"Weird," he said. "I don't see many disc brakes in here."

"Really?" I said incredulously.

"Not on the bikes people ride around here."

He grabbed a large screwdriver and started stabbing the center of the caliper. My heart pounded as I listened to the screeching of metal scraping metal inside a very crucial bicycle part that I had no replacement for. He tried several times to wedge the spare pads into the caliper before he finally stuck the screwdriver in and pried a cylindrical piece out of the center. I listened to it ping as he flung it away, and then I watched it bounce on the cement. After that, the brake pads slid right in.

"There," he said as he mounted the caliper back to my bike. "There was that weird piece stuck in there before, but it seems to be working now."

I wondered if he realized that the weird piece he was talking about happened to be inserted inside the brake caliper by the manufacturer itself, and it was probably supposed to be there. But I had been told he was a boy genius and I wasn't in a position to question his judgment.

The mechanic went to work on the rear wheel. He didn't have a single replacement part that would fit on my bicycle, even a freehub body, so he said the most he could do was open the hub, clean out my old freehub, and hope that the removal of a little mud and grime would keep it marginally functional through a couple more days on the trail. I couldn't bear to watch the hack operation so I went to lunch, even though I had already eaten a huge breakfast just three hours earlier while waiting for the shop to open. My race had officially reached a standstill.

When I returned to retrieve my bike, the woman couldn't decide what to charge for the work. She made a few calculations on a receipt tablet and said, "So, is $8.50 okay?"

"Are you serious?" I asked. "Eight fifty?" The mechanic had been working on my bike for more than an hour, and she had let me spend all morning in the shop cleaning my bike and using her tools. I guiltily handed her $20. "I appreciate your help. Here's a tip for the mechanic."

I was back on the road at 12:30. I called in the Tour Divide podcast hotline before I left town. "I lost half a day," I reported. "But I had three huge meals, a good long rest, so in the end it's probably a good thing. But I'm really excited to get back on the road. I'm really excited to be leaving Rawlins."

The afternoon burned white and hot as I pedaled south out of town. Generic storefronts and wind-weathered houses gave way to more sagebrush prairie, as wild and undeveloped as it had been a hundred miles before. I crossed back to the western slope of the Continental Divide on a pass unceremoniously named Middlewood Hill, but the crossing felt satisfying. I always felt more at home on the Pacific side of the Divide. I was back in the West.

But I had also officially left the Great Divide Basin, and the renewed forest, with its sparse aspen trees and stunted spruce, seemed as lush as a jungle. The canyon closed in, the trees grew taller and thicker, and the road snaked higher into the mountains until there was no visual indication that I had ever left Montana.

Evening had fallen by the time I crossed the state line. I didn't recognize the occasion when it happened. There was no bullet-ridden sign or any sign at all. I simply passed into the first town I had seen since Rawlins and noticed that post office display read "Slater, Colorado."

"Yes," I said out loud. "Two provinces and three states down. Just two to go." The simplification made it sound so triumphant. In truth, I was still only about halfway done.

Because of my late start, I only managed to pedal seventy miles before sunset. I vowed to ride late that night. But like clockwork, fatigue began to needle at my brain with the fading light. Endurance racers sometimes call this phenomenon the "sleep monster," because it is so overpowering that we feel helpless to fight it. Sometimes it's all we can do just to hold up our heads with our own necks, to not tip over sideways into the first comfortable-looking patch of poison ivy, let alone turn pedals with any sort of effectiveness. Smart endurance racers know the sleep monster is a demand from the mind, not a need from the body, and that the twisted power play of "mind over body over mind" is in order. The strategy is simple if brutal. Turn your emotions to anger, to fear, to agony, to anything more powerful than fatigue, and the body will overcome the mind's demand for sleep.

But as I churned up the gravel road into a black expanse of wilderness, the only emotion I found was loneliness. It swept over me like the fading light, soft and melancholy and almost indiscernible, until suddenly the landscape became almost unbearably dark and hollow. I recognized myself as a small speck against this great and gaping emptiness, and this realization filled my gut with unfocused despair.

A moist chill clung to the hairs on the back of my neck. The road climbed steeply atop several inches of loose pebbles. The gravel acted as a backward conveyer belt, leveraging strong downhill force even as I climbed as hard as my still-tender knee and overworked muscles would let me. I passed a farmhouse just off the road. Wood smoke puffed from a chimney, and soft golden light glowed through the draped windows. I felt like Ebenezer Scrooge looking in on his nephew's cozy Christmas party, in a bad dream where I was no longer a person but a ghost moving through the night, with no hope of ever being let inside.

I continued pushing toward the unbroken darkness, each pedal stroke feeling more sluggish and more futile. It occurred to me that clouds must have moved in, because I could see no stars. I looked around for any hints of light on the hillside, something to reassure me that others still existed in this dark and lonely place. There were no lights and no buildings, but as I climbed, my headlamp started to shine on human-made signs.

"Private property next three miles," one read. "No trespassing, stopping, or camping."

I shrugged. "Maybe I'll stop after the private property," I thought, and the admission brought a glimmer of reassurance. I pedaled two and a half miles. Then I passed another sign: "Private property next six miles. No trespassing. Warning: Property under camera surveillance."

I rotated my headlamp around, and sure enough, there were little cameras bolted to the trees. This was absolutely ridiculous. Where was I going to camp? Even the black and empty forest was shutting me out.

The sleep monster swooped heavy and low. I could hear it growling in the back of my mind, perched and all too prepared to make its killing blow.

Just as I hung my head and accepted my fate like a squirrel fallen limp in the jaws of a wolf, I rounded a tight corner in the road. A large log structure suddenly came into view. There were several vehicles parked out front, and warm light streamed through the front window. I squinted to make out the building's rustic interior, decorated with dead animals and weathered wooden picture frames. It looked like some kind of commercial enterprise, possibly a hunting lodge, and somebody was obviously home. Maybe they had a room to rent to me. I looked at my watch. It was 10:35 p.m. Much too late to go around bothering people when I had no real reason.

Still, I lingered in front of the building for more than a minute, drinking in the warm light, inhaling the smoke fumes, and relishing the simple existence of that cozy and beautiful place. I thought I saw shadows flickering in the window. I imagined hunters plopped down in front of roaring fires, cradling mugs of hot coffee and beer, and swapping tales about their triumphs in the woods.

I breathed a long and lonely sigh and turned my headlamp back toward the darkness. I hadn't traveled more than fifty yards down the road when I heard a woman's voice say, "Jill?"

I turned and pushed my bike back toward the building. "Are you Jill?" she asked as I approached.

"Yes," I said, nodding with bewilderment at the idea that not only had this complete stranger noticed me standing outside, but she also knew who I was.

"Are you hungry?" she asked.

"Yes," I said, nodding vigorously.

"I've been watching your SPOT," she said, referring to the satellite tracker I had been carrying to broadcast my location on the Tour Divide Web site. "I checked it a couple of hours ago and you were getting kind of close to here. But I was about to head to bed and, damn, I almost missed you! But come in! I have food for you."

I set down my bike and followed her into the lodge. She told me her name was Kirsten. She ran the Brush Mountain Outpost, which was, as I had guessed, a backcountry lodge for hunters. She said she was a big fan of the Tour Divide race, a good friend of race director Matthew Lee, and she made an effort to cater to the racers every time they passed through Northern Colorado. She directed me into the kitchen and showed me a big bowl of freshly sliced fruit.

"Everyone that comes through here always requests fresh fruit. I cut that for you," she said. "And also for another guy that came through here earlier today, but I didn't see him, and he kept going without stopping. He must have missed my sign."

"Wow," I said. "I, I don't know what to say."

"Would you like some coffee? I have cookies. And, um, I have some cheese. Oh! I can make you a quesadilla. Would you like a turkey quesadilla?"

I nodded weakly, overcome with the sheer, overwhelming sensory overload of getting exactly what I wished for.

Kirsten sat me down in a spacious dining room and placed a huge plate of food, coffee and the fruit in front of me. She sat down next to me and started scrolling through her computer.

"Matt's riding into New Mexico today," she said. "He's leading, and I think Chris Plesko and Kurt aren't far behind."

"Wow," I said. "New Mexico. Pretty amazing."

"And Cricket, she's the next woman, right? She's only left Atlantic City. Even though it sounded from your call-in like you had trouble in Rawlins, she's still a couple days behind you. That other woman, Deanna, I'm not sure where she is. Her SPOT hasn't been working."

I nodded. "That's interesting," I said.

"The other guys that come through here always want to know the race standings," Kirsten said. "What do you want to know?"

I shrugged. "Oh, I don't know. What's going on in the world?"

"What's going on ... Oh!" she yelled loudly. "Did you know Michael Jackson died?"

"He died?" I said disinterestedly. "Really?"

"You didn't know that?"

I shook my head.

"How could you not know that?" Kirsten shouted scandalously. "Seriously, how could you honestly not know that? There's no way to even look up without being blasted by news about Michael Jackson. It happened earlier today. I think drug overdose or something."

"No kidding," I said. "I hadn't heard about it yet. Riding the Great Divide is pretty much the cultural equivalent of living under a rock."

Kirsten laughed. "Ah," she said. "That would be the life."

Kirsten offered to rent me a room and I enthusiastically took her up on her offer. "What time would you like breakfast tomorrow?" she asked.

"You have breakfast here?"

"I actually don't have any guests right now, but I'll get up and make it for you. What time to you want it?"

"Ah, I don't know. Is seven too early?"

"Seven?" she said. "Ha! That group of Brits that came through here a few days ago made me get up at 4:30!"

"Well, back here in Tour Divide mid-pack, we have a lot more fun," I said, and she laughed again.

She showed me to a large bedroom in an adjacent building. I lay on a soft twin bed beside a rustic table, listening to the heater hum softly, surrounded in the kind of luxurious comfort that no amount of money can buy. "Human kindness," I thought as I finally embraced the sleep monster in its waiting repose. "Without it, all would be lost."

Morning broke through a solid cover of gray, with a light drizzle amplifying the high mountain chill. Kirsten made me an enormous omelet and a pot of coffee, and we chatted about more current events and race progress. She filled my gaping news holes with more Michael Jackson gossip and refreshingly dire and therefore real stories about Iran and the economy. We exchanged hugs and phone numbers just like new friends. She stood out in the rain to bid me goodbye.

"That road ahead can get pretty muddy," she warned. "Be careful."

I churned up the loose gravel. The road climbed into a large alpine meadow speckled with white flowers. The route turned off the main road onto a primitive forest road blocked by a gate. The rugged trail was merely intended as equipment access to a watershed divide, and promised to gain nearly 2,000 feet in about four miles. "Note," my map warned. "This pass is closed to all but bicycle and foot traffic May 1 through July 1. If you ride during this time, be prepared for snow drifts and/or very muddy and unmaintained conditions."

I pedaled up the rutted but smooth dirt, a relief after the loose pebbles of the improved gravel road. The trail steepened until I was surrounded by snow. I had to cross a few patches on foot, but it didn't block the route. The path narrowed and jutted up a pitch so steep I had no choice but to walk. The drizzling clouds sank and closed in. Thick fog obscured everything more than a few bike-lengths away, draping every rock and tree in eerie satin gowns.

Rain started to fall hard and fast as I crested the top of the watershed divide. The clay surface of the road began to soften. I hurriedly pulled on all of my rain gear, stressed about the quick advance of impassable mud. I had a lot of downhill in front of me and it would be horrible if I was forced to walk most of it.

On the eastern side of the pass, the face of the trail changed completely. Instead of rutted dirt, the road traversed a narrow boulder field, with streams of terra-cotta-colored runoff cascading down the center. I mounted the saddle and vowed to do everything in my limited technical skills to outrun the onset of wheel-sucking mud. I threw all of my weight directly over the rear tire and launched into the descent. The bike clattered downhill like a nearly-out-of-control go-cart, weaving around boulders, splashing through puddles, and bouncing over ruts so big it was all I could do to straighten the handlebars. I throttled the brakes and released them before clamping down hard again, lunging and stopping, weaving and lunging, jerking through an obstacle course on a slope so steep that my chin was practically hovering over my seat. In the roar of the rain and rushing runoff, I didn't notice how bad the brakes had started to squeal. Through my cold-numbed fingers, I couldn't feel how loose the brake levers had become, until I squeezed down on them, and nothing happened.

I had no brakes.

I let out a high-pitched scream and out of sheer panic threw myself directly onto the ground. My left knee smashed into the sharp edge of a boulder. I heard a dull crunch echoing through my helmet, felt my rag doll body go limp and skid several feet across the slick road, and listened to my bicycle clatter to a halt. And then there was only a sharp silence — a single, stunned moment — followed by an electric shock of pain so intense that its muted screams blocked out the roar of the rain. The screams rushed to my throat and I let them out in a loud, long wail. My knee throbbed with rage, truly an angry knee if ever there was an angry knee, and it was my left knee this time.

I allowed myself to lay in disbelief for several minutes. Then I sat up to assess my injuries. I took off my helmet and saw it had cracked near the bottom, but didn't seem too badly damaged. The nylon fabric of my rain pants had torn open, and my tights were sticky with blood. I rolled them up and saw what I expected: a badly bashed knee, already turning purple, swollen, and smeared in wet blood. But nothing seemed broken.

I stood up and limped toward my twisted bicycle. There were several new gouges in the frame. I had managed to completely loosen the seatpost bag during the crash, but none of the straps were torn. The shifter cables were stretched loose but I could set them back in place. I examined the brakes. The rear brake pads, which were nearly worn out before I left Rawlins, had been rubbed down to just a few fractions of a millimeter of thickness. When I tightened the brake caliper as far as it would go, I could coax them to grab the brake rotor, but just barely.

The front brake rotor, on the other hand, was coated in dark gray goo, thick and sticky like glue. As I wiped the sludge away from the caliper, I found only shiny silver metal where the pads had been. The brand new pads, installed just a hundred miles back, had completely disintegrated. There was nothing left.

With a lot of downhill to ride and virtually no braking power, the prospect of getting stuck in the mud didn't seem so serious any more. I picked up my bike and commenced limping down the hill, wincing in pain every time I put any pressure on my left knee. The days-old injury in my right knee, perhaps in sympathy pain, started to throb as well. I had become soaked to the skin in the cold rain, and the slow walking did little to help me build up body heat. I started to shiver with the onset of hypothermia. I was still thirty miles out of Steamboat Springs, so I was going to have to come up with a better plan.

The road grade leveled out ever so slightly, and I decided it would be a good time to try my brakes. I had no front brake. That was a lost cause; I might as well unhook the brake lever. But my rear brake still grabbed. As the route steepened, I squeezed as hard as I could. The bike lurched downward and the brake screeched horribly where metal grabbed metal. I knew using it in that way was going to destroy the rotor, but that was something I could replace in Steamboat. I only needed the bike to carry me down a few more miles of downhill and then I could pedal into town.

My bashed left knee throbbed horribly as I braced my stiff body on top of the saddle. I squeezed the brake lever and inched down the hill, not daring to let gravity take away even an ounce of its tentative stopping power. If I gained any speed at all, I'd have to bail from my bike into yet more unchecked pain, so I rode as slowly as I would if I had been climbing the hill. Without the heat and distraction of physical effort, I shivered in the cold and winced with the jolting pain of even the smallest bumps.

After an hour of downhill struggle, I managed to make it to the bottom of the valley. My hands were so numb I could no longer feel the brake levers beneath my fingers. My frostbite toes had become dead lumps of meat and even my good toes were tingling with cold. I pedaled into the town of Clark and stopped at the store. I was coated from head to foot in mud, quite literally. I saw a hose dangling from the side of the building so I turned it on and ran the entire thing over my head. The hose water felt warm on my skin, even though I suspected the water was not warm. I carefully removed my rain layer, wrung out my hair, and limped into the building.

The Clark store was mobbed with people, and despite my best efforts to clean up, I felt like a caveman stomping into a formal restaurant. I ordered a burrito and a giant cup of coffee and settled into a table located in a dark corner. As much as I had longed for human company a mere twelve hours earlier, all I wanted in Clark was to be left completely alone to soak up my own cold malaise. The people inside the tourist novelty store and lunch counter seemed perfectly happy to oblige me of my solitude, probably only glancing at my disheveled appearance before looking politely away. I sipped the coffee and held a bag of ice to my knee, an almost idiotic-seeming gesture as I continued convulsing with hypothermic shivers.

My knee stiffened up quickly. I stood a few times to grab the burrito I had ordered at the counter and refill my coffee, and each time I had a difficult time just walking across the room. When I sat back down, the joint refused to bend. I stewed in a cauldron distress and defeat. It was just a bashed knee, but if I couldn't bend it enough to even walk across a room without considerable pain, how in the world was I going to pedal twenty miles into Steamboat Springs, let alone another 1,300 miles of Great Divide?

A half hour passed, and then an hour. I sat in the corner, sipping coffee, staring blankly into the unceasing rotation of tourists and wondering if this was real, if this was it, if I was actually contemplating quitting the Tour Divide in Clark, Colorado. But how could I contemplate not quitting? I sipped my coffee. "Just be strong," I chanted to myself. "Be brave."

The inside of the store was so warm. My body was so cold. My knee was so stiff and my bike was so broken. "It's only twenty miles," I told myself. "It's pavement. It's easy."

I sipped my coffee. A woman approached me holding a mop. Without a word, she slipped behind me and plunged it to the ground. As I looked down, I noticed the large puddle of rainwater that had amassed beneath my chair. I looked up at the woman, but she continued mopping without looking back at me, until the puddle was sufficiently smeared out of sight. She lifted her mop and walked away.

I flushed with deep humiliation. It was bad enough to walk into a rural lunch counter and spend nearly two hours stewing in my own failure and defeat. But it was far worse to have someone make a gesture like that on my behalf. I felt like an animal that had pissed all over the floor, something far less than human. I left my coffee on the table, stood up quickly, and with my head down, walked shamefully out the door.

There was no triumph in climbing back onto my bike and pedaling toward Steamboat. My bashed knee screamed in protest, but after a few dozen strokes, the joint pain finally muffled in defeated submission. I spun softly but with unstopping determination, covering the distance in about eighty minutes. It was a respectable speed after a long break in Clark, but the damage to my progress had been done. It was after 4 p.m. by the time I arrived at Orange Peel Bicycle Shop.

"I need to get some work done on my bike," I told the first mechanic I saw. "Can you squeeze me in?"

The mechanic grabbed a roster hanging from the wall. "Let's see," he said. "We can get you in on Wednesday. Do you want to drop it off around nine?"

"Wednesday?" I squeaked. That was a full five days away. "Listen," I said, "I'm just traveling through town. Is there any way you can do a few emergency repairs, um, like right now?"

"Oh wait," he said. "Are you with the Tour Divide?"

I nodded miserably.

"Oh, well, yeah, we do rush jobs with the Tour Divide." He directed me to the back of the shop, grabbed a bike down from a stand and replaced it with mine. "Okay, what do you want done?"

"Well, um, how much time do you have?"

"We close at six," he said. He looked at his watch. "Just about two hours."

"OK, well, there's a lot," I said. "But in order of importance, I need either a new freehub body or a new rear wheel, two new sets of brake pads, a new front brake caliper and rotor, probably a rotor for the back, too, all new cables and housing, new chain and cassette, and, oh yeah, my odometer's been acting up. Do you have a bike computer I could buy?"

He breathed out. "Um. Okay."

"Do whatever you can and whatever you have to," I concluded. "I don't care what it costs."

He scribbled down my long list of requests and I stumbled off to buy something for dinner, even though my stomach was still full of humiliation and a massive burrito from Clark. Every time I sat down, my knee stiffened up like a rusty hinge until the joint was almost unrecoverable. Slowly, with great pain, I could work it loose, but I limped dramatically as I walked down the street. With my broken gait, torn rain gear, and mud-caked hair, I looked less like a bicycle racer and more like a drunken hobo. I wondered if the bike mechanic at Orange Peel was even inclined to take me seriously, or if he had just been humoring me to get me out of the store.

I was guiltily aware that I had only traveled fifty miles that day. If I stayed in Steamboat, I was essentially conceding the loss of an entire day of my already relaxed race pace. But with my bike on the operating table and my knee potentially not far away, I couldn't face the prospect of pedaling out of town that day. I booked a hotel room and called the Tour Divide hotline to broadcast my latest predicament.

"It's just a bummer, bad luck day, but hopefully it gets better," I reported. "The weather is getting better, at least for now. I won't give it any points for lasting more than a few minutes. That's kind of how it's been this entire trip — the weather."

I limped back to Orange Peel at 6 p.m. Five mechanics, seemingly everybody in the shop, were gathered around my bicycle still placing parts and tightening lugs. One mechanic met me at the register and started ringing me up. Despite my assertion that I didn't care about the cost, I watched with dread as he punched in all the numerous parts I had asked for. But it also occurred to me that he was entering everything I had asked for. That meant they had been able to fix every problem I had! He reached the end of the list and said, "I can give you the ten-percent shop discount. It's really just a bulk discount." He punched it in and hit total. I noticed he didn't charge a cent for labor. I smiled and handed him my credit card. Four hundred and fifty dollars was all it took to buy joy.

I watched as the mechanics stayed a half hour after closing time to finish up the work on my bike. It was almost hard to understand. Five complete strangers, who owed me nothing and charged me far less than the work was worth, dropped everything they were doing to fix my bicycle's myriad problems. And there was Kirsten at the Brush Mountain Lodge, calling me in from the dark night. And Marjane and Terry, who offered me compassion and comfort in a vast region of solitude. With its unrelenting physical demands, wildly fluctuating conditions, and sweeping loneliness, the Tour Divide seemed the kind of challenge that no one should be able to take on alone. But thanks to consistent if random human kindness, we didn't have to.

Chapter Seventeen
Turning Right

Page 227: A high valley above the Colorado River.
Page 228: Jill Homer's face is covered in dew on a foggy morning near Steamboat Springs, Colorado.

As I slept in the Steamboat Springs hotel room, my left knee went completely rigid. I could feel it throbbing even before I emerged from the sleep fog that hovered over my head at 5:30 a.m. I swung my leg onto the ground and leveraged it out of bed, but it showed no indication that it was capable of bending, even as I sat back down and gently coaxed it with my hands. The surface of the skin was black and purple, and solidly swollen, like a fresh grape, with a single pathetic band-aid stretched over a continent of still-moist road rash.

Things did not look good. And yet, I had finally surpassed the two-week mark of the Tour Divide and had become a creature driven by habit more than motivation. I packed up my bike, still mud-caked and scratched but sparkling with new parts, like silver jewelry on a very old woman. Together, we limped into the thick mist of morning.

Fog encased the bagel shop, which was as empty and quiet as the air.

I wheeled my bike to the shuttered door where the hours were posted. I walked by this same shop the day before just to make note of its hours, then synchronized my wakeup call so I could show up right at opening time for badly needed coffee and warm carbohydrates. But as I looked closer, I saw that the shop opened at 6 a.m. every day of the week except Saturday, when it remained closed until 6:30. It was, quite conveniently, Saturday.

I groaned out loud. In my pessimism of the evening before, I had failed to buy many supplies. I still had a few candy bars left over from Rawlins and a few organic fruit-and-nut bars I purchased at the natural foods store next to Orange Peel Bicycle Shop. It was enough calories to get to the next town, but nothing I was really looking forward to eating. Still, I realized that if I waited for a half hour for the bagel shop to open, there was a fair chance I was going to lose my nerve and never leave Steamboat Springs. I gulped down this latest defeat and walked my bike back into the mist.

Although I hadn't been able to persuade my leg to bend while walking, the act of sitting on the saddle and pressing hard on the down stroke with my good leg pushed the other one into action. The joint creaked and snapped like a rusted hinge pried open with a crowbar. I groaned in the nauseating agony of the motion, painfully chipping away every last flake of rust until a dull numbness set in.

The air was thick and gray. I assumed that meant more rain was coming. The route quickly directed me away from town and any prospect of passing another food establishment, but I had already resigned myself to the supplies I had. Since everything in my feedbag seemed disgusting, I decided to start with the health food. I bit into the natural energy bar, which was moist and warm — surprisingly delicious. I ate another and then another as my appetite started to spark. It made sense that I was ravenously hungry. I had managed eat part of a small order of nachos since arriving in Steamboat, but I had no appetite after the Clark burrito and hadn't been able to force down anything else. The energy deficit, unnoticed but significant, had only added to my sense of hopelessness.

The new surge of calories filled my body with warmth and well-being just as the fog began to break up around me. At first the monotone world simply faded to a lighter shade of gray, but then genuine streaks of sunlight started to cut through the clouds. Large patches of blue sky opened up, and soon I could see distant houses, rows of crops, fences, decorated ranch entrances, and horses frolicking through green fields in the bright morning. It was a beautiful day.

I began climbing into the heart of the Colorado Rockies. While my morning spin through the rolling Yampa River Valley had allowed my sore knee some relief, there was no hiding from the mountains. I winced with every rotation necessary to gain altitude. The trail squeezed through a narrow canyon beside the roaring Yampa River, wound around Stagecoach Reservoir on a rippled and fun stretch of singletrack, and started climbing loose gravel roads toward Lynx Pass, elevation 8,937.

A break of any kind instantly caused my knee to stiffen up again. Still, I had to make frequent stops just to relieve the building pressure of pain brought on by climbing. The shallow shot of optimism provided by food and sunlight had already evaporated from my bloodstream. Lynx Pass wasn't even the largest pass I planned to summit that day. There were at least three long climbs ahead before I would reach the town where I'd hoped to spend the night, Silverthorne. The map made it hard to ascertain, but I was convinced this stretch of the route would hold as much climbing as my hardest days in Montana, and I was in Colorado now, where mountains rose into high, thin altitudes. It would be a challenge if I was healthy, and a prison sentence for a knee that had no power and simply did not want to bend.

I downshifted to my little ring and spun the pedals gently and slowly up the pass. Exit strategies churned in my head, and their prospects filled me with loathing. The next town on the map was Kremmling. I knew Kremmling was a good place to quit the Tour Divide, because that was precisely where Geoff quit the Great Divide Race the previous year. During his first day pedaling out of Steamboat Springs, he was overcome with exhaustion while approaching Lynx Pass, so he turned around and spent the rest of the day in Steamboat, trying to calm his racing heart and renew his energy. His second time out, he managed to crest Lynx Pass only to decide that his body was definitely done, burned out, worthless. He headed into Kremmling, knowing full well he was pedaling toward his failure. He booked a hotel room and spent two miserable days in town sorting out his affairs and securing transportation back to Utah. He was almost too exhausted to even board the train. Six weeks later, he was back in Juneau but still deep in the throes of recovery, running again but too sore and depressed to join me on even short bike rides. I looked toward the pass with resigned determination. I could not quit at the top of Lynx Pass. I would not drop out in Kremmling.

The downhill coasting provided my knee some much-needed relief. I lifted my leg off the pedal and let it dangle free beneath my body, trying, even if it was just in my head, to drain out the acid from the climb and the swelling in my knee joint. I crossed the highway and turned up Rock Creek where, just around a small bluff, I approached the smiling, waving figure of another cyclist.

The cyclist was a good friend of mine, Dave Nice. Dave was a big guy with a goofy grin, cropped blond hair, and round glasses, given to wearing cotton T-shirts, baggy shorts, and skate shoes on his long mountain bike rides. We had gotten to know each other well through the small world of the ultra-endurance mountain bike racing circuit, held together by the wide world of the Web. The month prior, I had spent a few days visiting him at his home in Hurricane, Utah, where he worked at a bike shop and rode a fixed-gear mountain bike along the cactus-studded desert singletrack in the shadow of Zion National Park.

Dave was crazier about multiday endurance racing than I was. He had attempted to race the Divide during all of the three years prior. In 2006, his bike was stolen right out from behind him as he napped next to the road. In 2007 and 2008, fatigue and injury forced him to quit in Montana. This year, he decided to try something different than the established race, and ride the route from south to north. He started at the Mexican border a week prior to the Tour Divide race and rode north into New Mexico. I had hoped I would meet him along the way.

"Dave!" I shouted. "Dave Nice! It is so awesome to see you here!"

"Yeah," he said with his signature sniff. "I've been watching your SPOTs from my parents' place. I've been meeting a lot of y'all here."

"From your parents' house?" I asked. "Does that mean you're not riding the Divide anymore?"

"I got as far as their house," he said. "It's right on route a few miles from here. I got there, and I knew I was done. By then, it was too easy to stop at the house and go inside. But I'm stoked about getting that far. It's the farthest and fastest I've gone on the Great Divide yet. And it was fun while it lasted."

"That's awesome," I said. "That means all you have left to see is Wyoming."

He shook his head. "I'm done with the Great Divide," he said. "I'm ready to leave it behind."

"Really?" I asked. "After four years?"

"It's just too much to be going on in my head all the time," he said. "Yeah, I'm done."

"Well," I said, "to be honest, you're not missing much with Wyoming."

"So do you mind if I ride with you for a while?" Dave asked.

"Of course not!" I said. "That would be completely awesome!"

"Oh, I almost forgot," he said. "I have something for you." He reached in his messenger bag and handed me a can of Coke.

"I don't know if I can take that," I said. "You know, outside support and all."

"Did you know I was going to be here?" Dave asked. I shook my head. "Then it's not planned support; it's trail magic. You're good."

"I know all about trail magic," I said. "I've been taking trail magic in liberal doses. It's incredibly generous out here."

"Yeah, people on the Great Divide are great," Dave said. "That's why I keep coming back."

We rode a few hundred yards before coming to a large stream without a bridge. I unhooked my frame bag, lifted the awkward bike on my shoulder, and started wading through the water as Dave removed his shoes. I was waist-deep in the rushing current, struggling not to teeter when I looked to my right and saw Dave skimming an ankle-deep sandbar, wheeling his bicycle to the side and laughing heartily.

"So you can give me a Coke but you can't tell me about that?" I called out.

"Outside navigation," Dave shouted back, still chuckling. "That's against the rules!"

We rode down the dirt road, stopping to walk our bikes through several short patches in aspen-shaded areas where the mud became to thick and deep to ride.

"This stuff is nasty," I said. "And it smells, too, like something rotten."

"You're lucky you didn't come through yesterday," Dave said. "It rained all day. The whole road was like this. I tried to leave my parents' house because I was going to meet Jeremy; he's about, oh, probably about a day ahead of you. But I only made it about two miles before I decided it wasn't worth it."

"Wow," I said as I looked down and noticed a deep set of bike tracks and footprints directly beside mine. "I wonder how Jeremy fared in all that."

As we walked and rode, I told Dave about my bike troubles and my various knee pains. I was still feeling the pain as we rode, I told him, but the warmth of the day was helping and I was determined not to quit in Kremmling. Dave, who had an admirable viewpoint about the race and understood it was a victory just to start and make it as far as you physically could, knew exactly why I didn't want to quit in Kremmling. I did not have to tell him. And the reason didn't come up for several more miles.

"Well, there you go," Dave said as we crossed Highway 134 again, just below Gore Pass. "You have now officially traveled farther on the Divide than Geoff."

"Geoff quit in Kremmling," I said.

"Yeah," Dave said. "But he turned off the route here and took the highway shortcut into Kremmling. Now that we're on 212, you're officially farther."

"I know he took the highway," I said. "He still went to Kremmling."

Dave looked up thoughtfully. "Well," he said. "Well you started in Canada."

I smiled. "You're right. I have been farther. Thanks, Dave."

We walked through more patches of mud and turned up the driveway to his parents' house. Since he had already assured me of the legality of trail magic, I felt no qualms about taking him up on his offer of hot lunch, which sounded infinitely more appealing than candy bars. Inside the rather remote log home was an ultra-modern interior, shining with black and chrome amid the generous sunlight of large windows. Dave's grandma, a petite woman in her eighties, listened to my knee story and rushed to grab a jar of blue goop.

"This stuff cures all," she told me. I peeled off my tights and band-aid and rubbed it across the road rash on my still-swollen knee. It stung horribly, but once the numbness set in, I realized Grandma was right. I did start to feel better.

Dave made Spanish rice and fresh salad and Grandma plied me with brownies. "You look too thin," she chided me. "All you bikers look too thin."

I rubbed more blue goop on my knee before putting on my wet socks and shoes. Dave gave me a big bear hug goodbye. "You're going to make it to Mexico," he said. "You're already there."

"Hardly," I said. "But I'm still hoping."

As I had predicted, the route rippled in a long, undulating grunt, climbing hundreds of feet in less than a half mile before dropping again. I crested the saddle of a ridge and observed an expansive redrock canyon cutting deep into the valley below. I was grateful for brand new brakes as I rocketed around tight corners through the pinion and juniper stands, plummeting more than 1,500 feet in a matter of miles.

At the ghost town of Radium, I crossed the Colorado River. Groups of boaters were gathered at the bridge, and down the cliff-lined canyon I could see colorful rafts floating peacefully along the brick-colored water. Their movement looked so graceful, so painless, just floating on a river that, if they stuck with it, could carry them all the way to Mexico. Like the Pacific-bound droplets farther up the Continental Divide, water always finds the path of least resistance. Humans are not nearly so smart.

As promised by my maps, the climb out of the Colorado River gorge was dusty and extreme, and it was only the beginning. The sheer canyon gradually changed from a fortress to a crevice as I rose higher. The view was spectacular, Southwestern with a hint of Rocky Mountain high.

I crested the plateau far above the river and marveled at how normal my knee felt. It was still sore and a little numb from the blue goop, but for the first time I felt like the swelling was seeping out of the joint and being replaced by strength. I continued climbing a gradual incline when a swarm of mosquitoes found me. I had been traveling about six miles per hour when they grabbed onto the light tailwind and hovered beside me, occasionally dive-bombing in for the kill. I ramped up my speed, seven and then eight miles per hour, feeling a heavy throb move through my injured knee before fading in a burst of exhilaration. The mosquitoes surrounded me again and I accelerated to nine miles per hour, and then ten. The hill leveled out. I pedaled harder and faster, the wind streaming in my ears, the mosquitoes falling behind, until I looked back to see a spotty black cloud that had clearly given up.

"Ha ha ha!" I called out. "Ha!" Ten miles per hour was fast enough to outrun mosquitoes. John was right.

I coasted down the long hill with iPod music pulsing in my ears, singing out to the desert plain that was spreading out in front of me. Beneath the afternoon sunlight, I could see glimmers of white light sparkling off metal roofs in Kremmling, far below. "Wake Up" by The Arcade Fire started playing on my iPod, filling the slipstream with triumphant noise: "Children, wake up; Hold your mistakes up; Before the summer turns to dust."

I turned left on the pavement of Highway 9, flying toward Kremmling, a town that was actually off-route by a couple of miles. The Arcade Fire continued to sing: "Children, don't grow up; Our bodies get bigger but our hearts get torn up …"

After just a couple hundred yards of pavement, I followed my maps and GPS into a hard right turn that veered away from Kremmling and rejoined the Colorado River floodplain, traveling upstream. The Arcade Fire launched into a crescendo of renewed victory and triumph: "We're just a million little gods causing rainstorms, turning every good thing to rust. I guess we'll just have to adjust."

My heart swelled to new heights, soaring above the brown river as entire southern half of the Divide opening up before me. I had officially ridden farther on the Great Divide than Geoff did, and it hit me as an enormous victory. I thought that actually arriving at the finish line of the race might feel more satisfying than that moment, but I somehow doubted it. It was perhaps the most satisfying moment of my entire endurance racing career.

Evening fell as I continued the rolling climb, winding around the open plain of Williams Fork Reservoir before rising back into the forest among the red-tinted spruce trees of Ute Pass. As night descended, I fell steeply back to Highway 9 and motored up the gradual climb along the Blue River with the streams of white and red vehicle lights. The former mining town of Silverthorne sat at 9,000 feet. Higher than Lynx Pass and just 500 feet lower than Ute Pass, it was nearly my highest elevation of the entire long day.

It was after 11 p.m. when I reached the center of town. I had taken a generous lunch break at Dave's house, but I still had cranked out a seventeen-hour day during which I recovered an entire knee injury, climbed more than 10,000 feet, and traveled 130 miles, essentially fueled by Spanish rice and energy bars. And of course, every gas station and restaurant in town was closed, but as I neared Interstate 70, I could see lights on in the Wendy's. The door was locked so I pulled up to the drive-through menu board and waited. After several minutes, a crackling teenage voice came over the intercom.

"Um, can I help you?"

"Are you guys still open?" I asked.

"Yeah," he said slowly.

"Can I order something?" I asked.

"Um, only the drive-through is open," he said. "We only serve vehicles at the drive-through."

"But I don't have a vehicle," I said miserably. "I only have a bicycle."

"Uh, sorry," he said. "It's against our rules."

"Please," I pleaded. My high-pitched voice sounded so pathetic it startled me. "I'm really hungry."

"Just a sec," he said. After a minute, the voice came back on. "OK," he said. "Go ahead."

Riding with my elbows on my handlebars and a huge smile on my face, I cradled my bulging paper bag and forty-four-ounce root beer a half mile back to a cheap motel I had seen. Warm in the fleabag room, I ate cold fries and a rubbery chicken sandwich, by far the best victory meal I could imagine.

Sunday morning arrived bright and perfect. I returned to the Wendy's for breakfast, only to be greeted by a group of road cyclists who told me they followed the Tour Divide and knew exactly who I was. They said they were from Denver but drove out to Silverthorne to enjoy a Sunday road ride in the high country. As I pedaled beneath the interstate and connected with a series of bike paths, I realized I had returned to a world of tourists.

Joggers and rollerblades and recreational cyclists wove around me as I made my way toward Frisco along a confusing maze of narrow bike paths. The steady stream of people became thicker as I passed through that town. I started to see large groups of women wearing pink T-shirts, pink socks and pink shorts. Some wore two balloons around their chests like an extra set of breasts. Others wore signs with hand-scrawled phrases such as, "For my mother, Sharon Hutchings" or that listed a few dozen women's names. I had joined the tail end of a breast cancer awareness fundraising walk.

The bike path crowd had become a full clog, but I tried not to be grumpy about it. After all, these women were raising money to fight breast cancer, a cause I enthusiastically supported. I even happened to be wearing my own breast cancer jersey — one of the two bike shirts I had brought with me was a pink Fat Cyclist jersey, an edition created to raise money for the Lance Armstrong Foundation. I slowed to a crawl and wove around the groups, saying "Nice work!" and "Good job!" as I passed. But as the miles wore on, the groups only became larger. The women wore earphones and chatted loudly and completely ignored me as I said, "On your left" or "Excuse me, do you mind if I pass?" When they didn't move to the side of the path, I finally resorted to veering into the field, bouncing over brush and rocks as I passed. I unintentionally startled several women, who jumped and screamed so dramatically that others looked back and regarded me with glowering disdain. Did they really not hear me? Were they really that self-absorbed?

But I tried not to be grumpy. They were doing good. I was the selfish one. I just wanted to be away from the tourist towns, away from the crowds, where I could climb back into the sweeping, lonely mountains that had drawn all of us there in the first place. But the breast cancer walk stretched all the way from Frisco to Breckenridge, an eight-mile span clogged the entire way with more than a thousand pedestrians. It took me nearly ninety minutes to cover a span of the route that should have only consumed about a half hour, for no other reason than the presence of too many people. Even through my frustration, I had to chuckle. You get anything and everything on the Divide.

Freed back to the road, I sprinted past the expensive bistros and luxury boutiques of Breckenridge without even stopping. Several groups of cyclists flanked me as I started up the road to Boreas Pass, but the heavy crowding thinned as the road surface turned to gravel, then narrowed, reaching ever higher. Clean, bronzed, and chiseled athletes flew by on their mountain bikes, slowing only long enough to say, "Damn, that's a lot of gear isn't it?" as they passed. Then it would be my turn to pass an L.L. Bean-attired couple out for a Sunday morning biking date. "What are you carrying in all those bags?" they asked as I churned by.

Above timberline, the open country revealed long pace lines of mountain bike racers in training. Amid 13,000-foot-high, talus-coated slopes, they looked like ants marching up a sandy hill. The elevation was gratifying. Before that day I had yet to climb above 10,000 feet on the Divide, and suddenly I was lifted beyond 11,000 feet. Having grown up a fair distance from the Colorado high country, I could still count all the places I had ever visited above 11,000 feet — the high peaks of the Wasatch Range, Mount Whitney, Deseret Peak, King's Peak, the Tushars, the southwestern San Juan Mountains, and Mount Borah. All of these had been mountain summits sought through the grunt of long hikes and hard scrambles. But Boreas

Pass rolled gentle and wide, and suddenly I was at its summit, elevation 11,400, drinking in the satisfaction of thin air.

Groups of cyclists scattered over the wide saddle. There was an old train station that looked like it had been converted to some kind of tourist trap, mercifully closed on Sunday. The cyclists ate big lunches and chatted loudly and made more comments about my strangely loaded bicycle as I passed. They would spend a little more time up there, drinking in the success of a cresting a hard day's ride or finishing up another great training session before turning around to coast back to Breckenridge. I continued forward down the deserted side of the mountain, on a much rougher but emptier road that allowed me to truly fly.

The first big pass of the day had been conquered and physically, it had hardly even touched me. The swelling had abated in my left knee and left behind a relatively benign bruise. My angry knee finally felt pacified. The soreness in my legs had melted away, and my back finally steeled against its continuously bent-over position. It had only taken me 1,700 miles, but I seemed to have found the "cruise control" button on my bike. I stuffed down Sour Patch Kids and smiled. I had become a Great Divide machine.

As I crossed the high plain below the pass, thunderstorms moved in. With the road stretching in a straight line for miles in front of me, I spent long minutes observing the sky. I watched the black clouds rumble past. I could see their path and speed, and guessed, often correctly, where I was going to get hit and for how long. I mechanically applied my rain gear and continued nonplussed through the driving rain, knowing it wouldn't last long enough to ruin the road.

Then I was hit by hail. It fell heavy and hard, pelting my rain jacket with loud thumps until a marble-sized hailstone hammered my helmet. Still nonplussed, I calmly dismounted my bicycle and squatted in the ditch next to the road, burying my head between my knees until the hailstorm moved along.

I crossed the Arkansas River, having returned to the east side of the Continental Divide on Boreas Pass. In the riverside town of Hartsel, I met several different groups of bicycle tourists. I ate my lunch with a vehicle-supported group that was riding across the country to raise money for affordable housing. There were more than twenty riders, all on sleek road bikes with minimal gear. They had vans to carry all their camping gear and ate three square meals a day. Their lunch was a gourmet spread of cold cuts, fruit, vegetables, and bread, which they didn't offer to share with me as I munched on a package of peanut butter crackers. They weren't so confused by the amount of gear I had on my bike, but they couldn't understand why I would ride a cross-country tour on a mountain bike. I tried to explain to them that I needed a bike that could handle boulders, ruts, and non-maintained trails. I needed shocks to absorb the harsh battering from backwoods gravel roads, and big tires to float on top of mud and sand. The touring cyclists nodded, but I suspected my descriptions were mostly lost on them.

"That thing just looks heavy," one young man said as he took another bite of a thick turkey sandwich loaded with fresh vegetables. I ate another cracker and nodded. "It is."

Even though I had already eaten a decent lunch, I couldn't bypass the general store in town, with its whimsical out-of-commission phone booth and promise of ice cream. I ate my dessert out front beneath a light drizzle with a couple of independent touring cyclists.

"How far do you travel each day?" one asked.

"Oh, I average about a hundred miles," I said. "As few as fifty, as many as 140. But mileage isn't what kills you in this race, it's the climbing. In fact, you get to the point where you hardly notice the miles. And then, of course, there are the conditions. Once you've done a couple of miles in wheel-sucking mud, only then will you understand that a 4,000-foot climb is nothing."

The independent tourists, who rode beefy slick-tire hybrid bikes with bulging saddle bags, seemed a little more inclined to understand the point I was trying to make. I was basically doing the same thing they were, but on a scale that only when I actually set out on the Divide could I even begin to understand. I had once crossed the country during a fairly casual road tour, riding 3,200 miles in sixty-five days. That tour from Salt Lake City to Syracuse, New York, which I rode with Geoff in 2003, was difficult, strenuous and daunting. I suffered my fair share, but it was nothing like the Tour Divide. The Tour Divide takes cyclists to the extreme edges of bicycle touring, the edges where life becomes agonizing, unrelenting, and impossible, and then spins them around 180 degrees into a world of absolute bliss, ease, and joy. I had skirted one edge. I was about to enter the other.

I left the world of humans in Hartsel and started up an unnamed pass in a nondescript part of central Colorado. The high mountain plain pulled me effortlessly forward like a trickle of water, even though I was gaining elevation. A gentle breeze blew, so light I couldn't discern its direction. I crested a small saddle and dropped into another plain. The thunderheads thinned and broke apart, revealing the cerulean sky beyond. Sunbeams illuminated the horizon like distant spotlights, heralding the beginning of a great show.

Life on a bicycle is so simple. You eat, sleep, and ride, then rinse and repeat. On the high mountain plain, it was so easy to slough away all of the rest of it; the little things that add up, the injuries and the heat, the logistics and the repairs, the hunger and the fatigue, the distress about not having enough companionship and then having too much. These problems were all human failings, the outside world creeping in. Firmly locked in cruise control, I only needed to understand the fine mechanics of pedaling my bike. I pedaled my bike, and everything else fell into place, had purpose, and made sense. It was so simple. This was the end point of all of life's struggles, serenity in motion. I eat, sleep, and ride — therefore, I live.

I crested the last saddle of the day and for the first time in quite a while, hit the brakes. For a minute or so I stared directly ahead, genuinely trying to ascertain whether the landscape in front of me was real or whether I had perhaps spent a bit too long inside of my own head. The road plummeted down a red-cliff canyon lined with sapphire blue juniper trees and delicate pinions. Beyond its walls, I saw a great valley more than 7,000 feet below the towering spires of 14,000-foot monsters. Sunbeams escaped from breaks in the dark clouds and cast the amber valley in stark shadows, like burns in a slab of wood.

Beautiful would be the typical word to describe the scene, but it would never suffice. Stunning and spectacular, those were words to describe how the landscape affected me, but I was only a speck amid a universe of rock and river and sky. I finally settled on the word I was looking for as "grace," because only by leaps of hope and faith can a person cross the threshold of the comfortable and the mundane to places so intense that they pierce the soul.

I pushed off the ground and launched down the saddle, falling, falling, falling into a paradise of sandstone and granite, blurred to soft perfection by the wind-driven tears in my eyes. Within thirty minutes I had reached the valley, coasting easily into the town of Salida. I had crossed three passes and ridden 115 miles that day, and I wasn't sure I had felt a single one. I felt as fresh and alive as I would after a full night of sleep. I rolled up to a Mexican food restaurant splashed with bright colors that shimmered in the light of sunset, finally willing to allow that maybe, just maybe, the hard part really was behind me.

Chapter Eighteen
Untouchable

Page 241: A mountain biker charges up Boreas Pass in Colorado.
Page 242: A lone spruce tree grows atop a rock outcropping near Hartsel, Colorado.

I had become an expert on small-town convenience stores. Even independently owned service stations, buried in the most remote regions of the west, all had a near-identical selection of products laid out in a nearly identical way. Their organization was both simple and highly effective, designed for the maximum obtainment of junk food.

I walked into the Salida 7-Eleven with single-minded purpose, knowing I would not pass another significantly populated town on the route for more than 150 miles. I walked down the first aisle, also known as the candy bar aisle, and selected four king-sized Snickers bars — which not only boasted 500 calories each, but were also usually the most popular and therefore freshest items on the shelf. I then grabbed four pairs of Reese's Peanut Butter Cups, prone to melting but probably okay in the high mountain air. The next aisle, the salty snack aisle, held my Corn Nuts, regular nuts, and packages of crackers. The next aisle, the specialty candy aisle, was my favorite. It was here that I was treated to the widest and most thrilling range of selection that can only be found in gummy snacks. I was partial to Sour Patch Kids, but I liked to mix it up with gummy bears and sour worms and sometimes something florescent and obnoxious and full of artificially flavored and chemically colored high-fructose corn syrup. 7-Eleven also carried chocolate-covered espresso beans, a special treat for the mornings I anticipated waking up in a sleeping bag. In the "regular food" aisle, I usually picked up tuna packets and the occasional energy bar. The refrigerated shelves along the outer edge of the store held my orange juice and liters of Pepsi and yogurt and never-ending search for wax-coated balls of cheese. I finished with an extra-large cup of coffee and a quick browse of the gourmet cases in front of the store, where I could obtain 600-calorie "homemade" brownies and the cinnamon roll I planned to eat for breakfast before heading out. Then I'd walk to the counter and dump 10,000 calories — about two days' worth of food — in front of the startled clerk.

"Um, did you find everything you needed?" she asked.

"Oh yes," I said.

The clerk in Salida was more bold than most, and she smiled wryly. "Having a little celebration are we?" she asked.

I smiled back. If I was more bold, or a better actress, I would have launched into a long sob story about how my husband just cheated on me and I didn't want to be in the world any more so I was just going to eat my way into a sugar coma. If I had been even bolder than that, I might have just told her the truth, but instead I said, "Ah, I'm just stocking up."

"Okay then," she said as she slid a heart attack's worth of survival food into a plastic bag. "Have a nice day."

I got another late start in Salida, which I had no excuse for, but the amazing energy that powered me to Salida carried into the new day. Five miles outside of town, I remembered that I forgot to pick up a pair of sunglasses, having lost a pair the day before, after losing several other individual pairs in unknown spots scattered across the Great Divide. In all, I would lose seven pairs of sunglasses on the Great Divide, but I never fretted too much about it because sunglasses, like Sour Patch Kids, were only a convenience store away. I stopped in Poncha Springs, where a man wearing a bicycle helmet stood chatting on a pay phone out front. Propped next to him was a mountain bike bulging with panniers. Given the remote location, I knew he had to be riding the Divide, so I waited until he hung up the phone and walked up to say hello.

The man told me he started in Mexico and was riding the Great Divide Mountain Bike Route north, so he had already crossed paths with most of the Tour Divide racers in front of me. He said having ridden across New Mexico, he couldn't even fathom the pace of the leaders, but I seemed to be moving at a more reasonable clip. He handed me a $5 bill and asked me if I would deliver it to a couple in Del Norte. "We went out for tamales and I never paid them back," he said. "But if you call them up, I'm sure they'll give you something to eat, so there's something in it for you."

I folded the bill into my wallet. "I'll try to remember," I said. "But I can't promise I'll be lucid when I get there."

"Yeah," he said. "You have I think three passes before Del Norte, big ones. Are you going to try to get there tonight?"

I shook my head. "Even if I had actually gotten an early start, which as you can see it's none too early, it wasn't all that likely. No, I'll probably camp somewhere before Del Norte and head in tomorrow morning or early afternoon."

"Yeah, I went through Del Norte three days ago," he said. "But it's been a pretty relaxed trip. These passes in Colorado look monstrous, but they're all on fairly smooth railroad grades and they're not too bad. What you gotta watch out for is New Mexico. Those mountains don't look like much on the maps, but I'm telling you, New Mexico will bring you to your knees."

I nodded vigorously but didn't feel the sting of his warning. Sure, New Mexico was full of bumps, but in the grand scope of things it was, as the saying goes, "all downhill."

We shook hands and turned in opposite directions. I pedaled up the canyon toward Marshall Pass. The descent into Salida had dropped me all the way down to 7,000 feet elevation and I had to climb back up to close to 11,000 again, but I tried not to let the scope of the task scare me. The morning was bright and warm and my legs felt inexplicably strong. I had a feedbag full of fresh junk food and a camera clasped in my right hand. The old railroad bed snaked lazily up the mountainside, providing nearly free passage to the pinnacles in the sky. Everything was going my way. I was untouchable.

About a thousand feet below the pass, an oncoming vehicle approached on the narrow road. It slowed as it pulled up beside me and I groaned. I expected questions and I was in too good of a mood to explain my brutal race to another inquisitive local. The window rolled down and a familiar face smiled back at me. I laughed out loud at the surprising recognition. The man and I had met once before, very briefly, but I knew of him quite well. Mike Curiak was an avid mountain biker and wheel builder who live in Grand Junction, Colorado, which was located several hours northwest of Marshall Pass. I had read extensively about Mike's various exploits and successes via the tight-knit ultra-endurance cycling community of the Internet, but the reason I had met him was because we crossed paths in McGrath, Alaska, in March 2008. Mike had been racing and riding the Iditarod Trail since the mid-1990s, and still holds the northern route record to Nome. He had held the McGrath record as well until Pete Basinger surpassed it in 2007. Mike had mostly given up racing, but he still traveled north every year to tour the Iditarod Trail on an expedition-loaded snow bike. When I met Mike in 2008, he had just arrived in McGrath with a broken tent and stove during his latest trek to Nome. We locked eyes just as I was being whisked away to the airport after finishing my own ride the day before.

"Do you think you'll head back out there soon?" were the only words I said to him as he stood in the front room in his long johns.

"The future is uncertain," was all he had said to me before I nodded goodbye and ducked into the minus-twenty-degree morning.

Now the future had arrived, on a warm day in June 2009, and our paths had collided again in the middle of nowhere that was central Colorado. I grinned. "What are you doing in this part of the world?" I asked.

"Actually," he said, "I'm here to surprise Pete."

"Pete? Pete Basinger? Really?"

Mike nodded.

"So he is riding the Great Divide this year?" I asked. "I had heard rumors he was out there, but he's been like a phantom on the trail. I wasn't even sure if they were true."

"He wanted to keep it on the down-low," Mike said. "Wanted to do it without all of the hype and noise."

"Right," I said. I knew Mike was referring directly to the Tour Divide, a race that was essentially the unwanted stepchild of the Great Divide Race, which Mike helped start in 2004. That inaugural year, Mike recruited a handful of mountain bike racers to join him on the epic race from Montana to Mexico. They aimed to break a record established in 1999 by the grandfather of ultra-endurance mountain bike racing, John Stamstad. One of those racers was Matt Lee, who would eventually fracture away from the Great Divide Race and start the Tour Divide in 2008. Another inaugural Great Divide Race participant was Pete Basinger, a young cyclist from Alaska who didn't have much more than the Iditarod Trail on his race resume. Pete and Mike battled for the lead the entire distance, before Mike finally snatched it away from Pete in the far southern miles of New Mexico, finishing a heartbreaking twenty minutes ahead of Pete at the end of a sixteen-day race. Mike held the border-to-border Great Divide Mountain Bike Route record until 2007, when Jay Petervary surpassed it by finishing in fifteen days and change. John Nobile took it from Jay in 2008.

"So Pete didn't start with the Great Divide Race?" I asked.

"No, he started in Banff about two days before the race," Mike said. "I think he crossed the border close to the GDR, but not with it."

Since Mike set the record in 2004, he had slowly distanced himself from the Divide. The entire time, he maintained that he wanted the race to adhere to the traditional border-to-border route. Matt Lee, who had raced and finished the Divide every year since 2004, argued that Adventure Cycling Association, the organization that established the Great Divide Mountain Bike Route, had since moved the route into Canada; therefore, the race should start in Canada. Mike and Matt would never see eye-to-eye. Matt eventually left the Great Divide Race and created the Tour Divide around a Banff start; he also modified several rules and practices that went against Mike's aesthetic viewpoints on what self-supported racing should be.

In 2008, the Great Divide Race and Tour Divide were very much at odds with each other. Because of its historic precedence, its association with Mike and Pete, and because Geoff participated in it, I had remained a vocal Great Divide Race trumpeter right up until it came time to actually choose an event myself. I knew I had become a defector by starting with the Tour Divide. But I had my reasons and I felt they were good ones, and I didn't feel shame about my choice, even as I looked Mike Curiak directly in the eyes.

"And Pete's going to pass through here, pretty soon?" I asked.

"I expect him too," Mike said. "I saw on his tracking page he was getting into Salida this morning."

"Really?" I said. "Pete's carrying a SPOT?"

"Just to map his own progress," Mike said. "Only a few people have the information to get into the Web site. Geoff Roes is actually one of them."

"Really? Why Geoff?"

"He asked for it."

It hadn't occurred to me before, but Geoff was probably closely tracking everything going on in the Divide, just for the gratification his own interest in the race. This meant there was a good chance he was watching my every move. Or maybe he was purposefully ignoring that information. I wondered, given Geoff's and my role reversal as Divide traveler and watcher, what I would do. Our relationship may be fractured, but we were still sports fans.

"Do you mind if I ride with you for a bit?" Mike asked.

"Not at all," I said. "That would be fun."

Mike pulled his car over and grabbed a bicycle from the back. He had a frame bag just like mine, made by the same one-man company in Anchorage. He showed me its various pouches, one of which he said was specifically custom-made to hold candy. He opened it up and fished out a handful of Mike and Ikes.

"I also have a Pepsi if you want one," he said. "It's Pete's favorite."

"I'm not going to drink Pete's Pepsi!" I cried.

"Don't worry, I have extras." He handed me a liter bottle.

"Four hundred calories of sugar goodness," I said as I raised the bottle in a mock toast and guzzled most of it right in front of Mike.

We pedaled up the mellow grade, spinning easily enough to chat amicably. I did most of the talking, telling Mike about my impressions of the Divide, asking him questions about his Iditarod rides, and plying for information about Pete.

Pete, my Iditarod hero, had a long history with the Great Divide. After just missing out on the record and finishing second in 2004, he returned in 2005 only to experience a Geoff-like "total body shutdown" in central New Mexico. In 2007, he got sick and dropped out in Colorado. But each time, he pushed hard with single-minded drive to set the record, enough so that all the way back in Montana, John expressed anxiety about the rumors that Pete might be riding the Divide. John didn't want to lose the Great Divide record, and he was pretty sure Pete was the only one who was likely to take it from him.

"So how's Pete doing?" I asked Mike.

"Really well," Mike said. "He's hit some weather like all of you have, and he's had some mechanical issues. He had a wheel taco on him on the bike path out of Silverthorne. He had to hitch back to town to buy a new one. He called me to ask about whether or not he should buy the wheels the Silverthorne shop had in stock. I said, 'Do you have a choice?'"

"Man, Pete can not catch a break," I said.

Near the top of Marshall Pass, Mike announced he was going to stop to take pictures of a field of yellow wildflowers that spanned the road. I stopped as well. Never one for close-up shots, I took photos of the stark mountains and gray-tinted clouds in a dark blue sky. "You know," Mike said as we joined up again, "You're one of the few people I've seen out where who really seems to be enjoying themselves."

"That's my whole goal," I said. "Take my hits but take them slow and have a good time."

Mike nodded. "I think you have the right idea."

We stopped together at the pass, looking out over the rippled expanse of the San Juan Mountains. "Be sure to say hi to Pete for me when you see him," I told Mike. "Actually, I guess he's going to pass me today, so I'll just tell him myself."

Mike and I shook hands. For the forty-five minutes we spent together, he never said more than what needed to be said, so he simply advised, "Have fun."

I rocketed down Marshall Pass in a fever pitch of excitement. Ever since I learned Jeremy had dropped out of the race, I knew that I had landed in a dead spot of solitude in the Tour Divide. The next racer in front of me was a day and half ahead, and the next person behind me was a full day back. I had already resigned myself to the fact I was not going to see another Divide racer for the rest of the trip. But this wasn't just another Divide racer, it was Pete! A fellow Alaskan, a friend, and my ultra-endurance racing role model. I expected him to simply pass me, probably saying hello and grunting terse but genuine words of encouragement like "Nice job" or "Good work" before surging ahead toward his record-breaking individual effort. I knew it would only be a few seconds and it would be over, but I looked forward to seeing Pete with buzzing anticipation, just like a shy girl waiting for the most popular guy in school to walk down the hall.

Outside the only store in the town of Sergeants, I met a large group of cyclists that turned out to be the same affordable housing group I had intersected with the day before in Hartsel. The same tall youth who had criticized my choice of bicycle earlier was incredulous about the mystery of how I managed to meet up with them again without taking their route.

"There are no other roads around here," he said.

"Exactly," I said. "That's what I was telling you yesterday. I'm not on the roads. I'm traveling on trails. There are some highways, but mostly it's mud and dirt. This route does everything it can to avoid pavement."

"So where are you headed now?" he asked.

I looked at my map. "Well, let's see ... I guess, well, yeah, I guess I'm on

Highway 50 for the next twelve miles."

"Imagine that, we're going to same way," he said. "Do you want to ride with us?"

I followed the group out of Sergeants. Nearly thirty cyclists strung out along the shoulder of the highway single file, all wearing identical jerseys and riding nearly identical bikes. With my sagging bike bags and fresh coat of mud, I felt like an ugly duckling drafting a flock of swans.

I joined the tall youth and a short, stocky friend of his at the front of the pack. We quickly put a gap on the next group back as I explained to him in greater detail what the Tour Divide was. He told me his group rode hard every day, covering 70 to 110 miles on their road bikes, and still helped with volunteer home-building projects in every town where they stopped.

"That sounds more exhausting than climbing mountains all day long," I said. I had to practically yell over the roar of trucks flowing steadily beside us. One driver laid on the horn and his rig skimmed within inches of our shoulders. "And, man, touring on the road all day long, that would be really stressful," I added. "I forget how much roads suck."

"You get used to the traffic," he said. "It's been a really fun trip."

He asked more questions about my gear and where I camped at night. I tried to answer but it was becoming harder to reply as I gasped for breath and swallowed gulps of exhaust. I looked down at my odometer. We were riding faster than nineteen miles per hour, sometimes hitting twenty miles per hour on a nearly flat stretch of highway. It was faster than I usually traveled downhill on my loaded bike, and I was feeling the burn, with a racing heart and sweat beading up on my arms and face. It occurred to me that it was idiotic to expend so much energy on flat pavement when I had heaps of climbing in front of me. But this home-building cyclist already thought I was a pansy, and he had criticized my mountain bike. I was determined to keep up with him.

I pumped the pedals and fell behind his rear wheel. He responded with more acceleration. No longer chatting, we were full-out racing. The miles ripped by in a heavy blur, where lactic acid overflowed from the frantic pistons that had once been my legs. It stung my eyes and gurgled into my core. I was in pain, but damn if I wasn't going to prove that my overstuffed mountain bike could hold its own. Even the home-building cyclist's friend eventually fell back, and the rest of his group was nowhere in sight when I caught a glimpse of the merciful redemption that was my route cutoff.

"Oh ... here's ... my turn," I gasped. "It was ... nice ... meeting you."

"You, too," he replied. "Good luck in the Tour de ... what did you call it?"

"Tour ... Divide."

"Yeah, Tour de Vise," he said. "I'll look you up."

"Have fun," I panted, whipping a hard left onto the gravel road and slowing to a jerky crawl as soon as he was safely out of sight. Pretty soon the truck traffic was no longer in earshot. Back out in the high mountain plain, I had a full view of every direction for miles, and I could see I was deeply alone again.

I squinted harder, trying to discern any hint of movement down the valley. I knew Mike's choice of where to wait for Pete meant Pete couldn't be more than a few miles behind me. I had pedaled hard on both the descent from Marshall Pass and the highway, but my best effort would still be too easy for Pete. I expected to see him soon.

I first met Pete almost exactly three years earlier, in 2006, during a summer when he stayed in Alaska rather than travel south to race the Divide. We both entered as soloists the 24 Hours of Kincaid race in Anchorage. As is the nature of lap races, the fast soloists frequently passed me. Pete always had a determined grimace on his face as he shot by, but he was always friendly enough to say hello, every time. In the middle of the night, I lost track of him. His tent was always empty and I thought he had dropped out of the race. I found out later he took an unplanned nap in the woods after dozing on his bike, but still rallied to win the race with twenty-one laps. I finished as the top female and fifth place overall with sixteen laps. It was a proud moment for me, and I decided that Pete was my cycling hero.

He was more interesting to me than Lance Armstrong or even John Stamstad, because to me, Pete was a real person. He ate junk food, drove a crappy van, and stumbled awkwardly through media interviews. And then, without glory or recognition, he went on to accomplish biking feats that were, in my mind, every bit as inspiring as winning the Tour de France.

As for my endurance racing career, 2007 was the tipping point. I returned from the Susitna 100 in February with a nearly useless "angry knee" (it was actually an advanced stage of chondromalacia patella). I couldn't ride my bike, run, or even walk without limping, so I spent long mornings in front of my computer, fixated on the reports from the Iditarod Trail Invitational. That year, Pete shot far off the front, moving so quickly in good conditions that people spoke of him breaking the three-day barrier without trying. About halfway through the race, overflow-covered ice forced everyone to take long bypass that added thirty-five miles to the course, but Pete continued charging ahead of record pace. Then he disappeared off the radar for a while, and there were reports of temperatures dropping to forty below. Pete was missing for more than twenty-four hours, and nobody knew exactly where he was. I hit the "refresh" button on my computer incessantly. I watched and waited. I got up in the middle of the night, I snuck peeks at work, and still there was no word from Pete. And then, in his own unceremonious way, Pete popped back on the radar fifty miles from the finish, a mere five hours before the time he needed to break the current record. He reported that he had battled ninety miles of treacherous conditions across the Farewell Burn, riding through a minefield of frozen tussocks that knocked him off his bike "hundreds" of times. It had slowed him too much, I thought. No one can ride fifty miles of snow-drifted frozen river in five hours. But I continued to cheer from afar. I hit "refresh" on my computer. Five hours passed in a blink, and Pete had done it, he had arrived in McGrath, winning the race and shaving a mere twenty minutes off the Iditarod Trail record — Mike Curiak's record.

I was transfixed, inspired, wholly immersed in the grand, terrifying spectacle of it all. "Next year, I'm going to ride in the Iditarod Trail Invitational," I announced to Geoff. "Yeah right," Geoff had replied.

Two years later, on a lonely high road of the Great Divide, I still credited — and blamed — Pete for being the catalyst who set me on my path, inspiring me to make the amazingly complex leap from single-day races to self-supported multiday and winter events. He even helped with the transition, giving advice every time I asked and offering to fix my bike. And Pete had the added bonus of being a genuinely nice and admittedly good-looking guy, two years younger than I was, with a broad chin, a shy smile, and dark, curly hair that exploded in all directions every time he took off his helmet.

I started looking over my shoulder frequently. When I stopped for food or bathroom breaks, I never ventured far off the road lest Pete shoot by as I was hiding behind a bush. I was anxious about the prospect of missing him. I recognized how silly it was to harbor such strong anticipation, but I felt helpless to fight it. Ravaged by two weeks of unceasing mood swings between the highest highs and the lowest lows, my emotions had bled out into the open, laid bare to the world, where they could be deeply cut by everything that touched them. My feelings of happiness, pain, agony, excitement, and even love, were as naïve and affecting as a child's. And just as I had engaged in childlike competition with the home-building cyclist, I developed a childlike fixation on an inevitable meeting with Pete.

I climbed another 10,000-foot pass and descended amid massive sandstone boulders that appeared to have dropped out of the sky, likely deposited by a long-melted glacier. "These rocks are so incredible," I thought. "This would be a cool place to ride with Pete."

Evening fell as I pedaled up a new canyon, still feeling strong even as I surpassed the hundred-mile mark for the day. Sunset hovered in bright strips of crimson over the violet mountains. "So beautiful," I thought. "I wonder if Pete can see this, wherever he is?"

But only silence and stillness followed. I crested Canaro Pass in the darkness. The sleep monster settled over me with crushing accuracy. I had traveled 125 miles that day. Del Norte was still another thirty in the distance. I thought I could manage a late push into town but I was fading fast. A primitive Forest Service campground named Storm King appeared on my left. I slowed my bike and hesitated.

"If I camp there," I thought, "Pete's going to pass me in the night and I'm never going to see him."

The voice of rationality, so easily repressed by my childlike emotions, finally had to shout to get my attention: "That doesn't matter! It's not a big deal!" But the child in me resisted the demand for sleep even as my eyes drooped and body sagged. My maps indicated a long stretch of private property that meant if I didn't stop at the campground, I'd have no choice but to pedal another thirty miles into Del Norte. There was nowhere to camp before town. With an air of defeat, I coasted down the campground's entryway.

"Oh well," I thought as I laid out my sleeping bag and bivy sack. I perked up after a big meal of tuna, Corn Nuts, and gourmet 7-Eleven brownie, and was heartened by the fact I had gotten through another long but physically strong day. I popped my nightly sleeping pill in my mouth and lay down. I blinked rapidly in an effort to keep my eyes open to the blaze of stars overhead, still straining to hear the rattle of bicycle wheels rolling down the gravel road. But as my eyes drooped to a close, I accepted sleep gracefully, feeling pleasantly sad.

I don't know how much time had passed — an hour, maybe two — when strange noises rustled me awake.

"Bear!" My mind raced as I jolted to a sitting position, jerking my head around for a view through the tiny air opening in my sleeping bag. I swung my entire bivy sack all the way around before I saw the dark, human-shaped figure directly behind me, about twenty feet away. The initial adrenaline rush of my bear scare did almost nothing to cut through the disorienting haze of the sleeping drug. The figure appeared as a shadow, blurry and distorted as though obscured behind a thick plate of glass. A pinprick of light whirled around but never pointed directly at me. It appeared the figure was unpacking something. I couldn't be sure, but it looked like a bike.

"Has to be Pete," I thought, though I was strangely indifferent about the prospect. The silhouette seemed to be moving in slow motion. I tried to push the light button on my watch, but it wouldn't work. I stretched my arm out of the tiny opening in my sack and fumbled around until I found my helmet. I wrestled the opening a little wider and tried to turn on the headlamp mounted on top. That wasn't working either. "Argh, this is just some kind of weird dream," I thought as I lay back down. I lost consciousness within seconds.

Then, in what felt like seconds later, I heard noises again. This time, I was much more alert. My head was no longer swimming. I could actually hear specific details in the muffled sounds, such as zippers zipping and water pouring. I opened my bivy sack and sat up. The sky was still thickly dark, and spattered in stars. Frigid air swirled around my skin, causing me to involuntarily gasp. A light-blue layer of frost shimmered on the picnic table beneath a bright moon; the temperature was either at freezing or only barely above. I turned around to see the same dark figure I had seen in my earlier dream, still packing up a bicycle. I pushed my watch, which worked that time. It was 5:30 a.m.

I lay back down and pulled the warm covers around me. "That's definitely Pete," I thought. "And he's leaving now. I should get up, at least go say hi. If I pack up quickly, maybe I could even ride with him for a while."

The voice of rationality laughed at me. "You couldn't keep up with him for a half mile. It's way before your awake time and anyway, it's freezing. You don't want to get up."

The voice was right. I didn't want to get up. And yet, saying hello to Pete was pretty much everything I had wanted the entire day before. But something held me in stillness on the ground. Maybe it was the cold, or the early hour, or just simple embarrassment about walking up to him with my scarecrow hair and two-day stink and saying something as monumentally inconsequential as "hi." Pete was going on to do great things and the last thing I needed to do was get in his way. I closed my eyes and listened as his bicycle coasted by, with a whir of wind and rattle of bike parts that faded quickly into the cold night, and then it was gone.

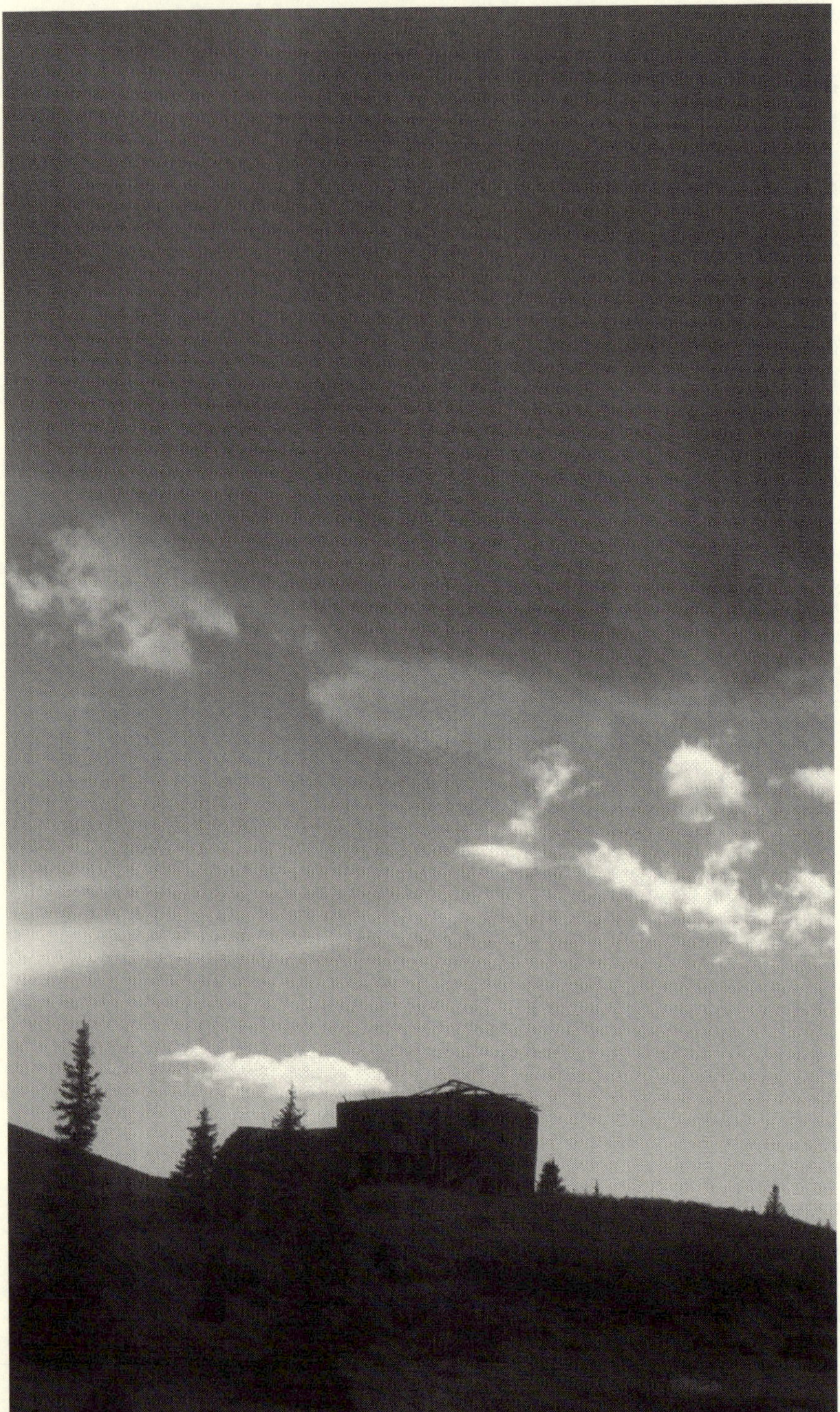

Chapter Nineteen
Stunner Pass

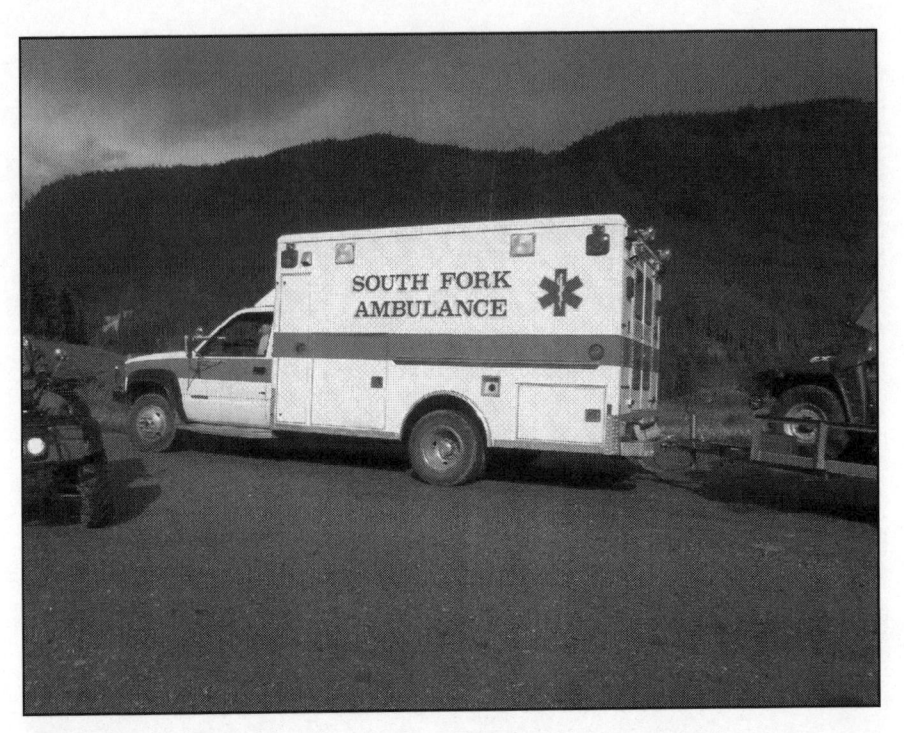

Page 254 and 255: A violent thunderstorm rolls in over mining ruins in the mountain ghost town of Summitville, Colorado.
Page 256: An ambulance carrying Pete Basinger idles near the Stunner Campground.

I woke up to a re-energizing wash of sunlight, but it was too late. I was alone again.

"Would it really have been so bad to get up at 5:30?" I grumbled as I stuffed chocolate-covered espresso beans in my mouth. "I kept the pace with the home-building bikers yesterday; I certainly could have kept up with Pete for an hour or so today."

I sighed. The morning pierced my senses with crisp beauty and I longed to share it with somebody. Pete's company during the ride down the mountain would have been a welcome break from the solitude. Why did I have to be so lazy and slow?

I started down the canyon, which in daylight revealed itself as a place fully entrenched in the Southwestern desert. Smooth, sienna-hued cliffs carved a boxy corridor, and the pink sand was dotted with rabbit brush and yucca plants. The canyon opened into a wide plateau. The route followed a narrow jeep trail that had been dramatically rippled by erosion. I giggled as my bike plummeted into a deep trench and shot back out the other side, sometimes grabbing a few inches of exhilarating air before plunging into the next trench. Where the road wasn't laced in a roller coaster of dirt mounds, it was piled with boulders. But I wasn't about to halt a millimeter of momentum, so instead of finessing my bicycle around the rocks, I bounced directly over them at top speed. It was a reckless way to ride, given my mounting fatigue and loaded bike with all of its awkward extra weight. Only sheer luck kept me from crashing, but I never toppled over. I crossed the narrow headwaters of the Rio Grande and rolled into Del Norte with a huge smile on my face.

It was only 9 a.m. and I wasn't hungry or tired. I felt too good to stop. But remembering the five-dollar bill the bicycle tourist in Poncha Springs had asked me to deliver, I pulled out my maps and looked up the address for Gary and Patti Blakley.

The Blakleys were regular fixtures on the Great Divide Mountain Bike Route, listed on the maps as people willing to providing food and shelter to bicycle tourists. They also were Tour Divide fans, and had a reputation for meticulously tracking racers' progress and catering to all of their needs. Patti found me before I had even arrived at the house and waved me down. I hopped off my bike and followed her down the street. She called in her husband, Gary, to let him know I had arrived in Del Norte. She handed me a giant cup of sweet tea and heated up homemade pizza and peach pie. Gary, a thin man with short, silver hair, paused on the other side of the sliding glass door and took a long look at my bike.

"Interesting set-up you have there," he said as he walked in the door and settled down at the kitchen table. "Frame looks pretty solid, and seems everyone has those frame bags these days. But what's up with the flat pedals?"

"Well," I said, hesitating before I launched into my long frostbite story. "Those are actually my favorite parts on the entire bike." Then I told him why. My toes had bothered me continuously during my summer training, I said, but as soon as I dumped the clipless pretension, the toe pain faded as well. I hadn't had a single foot problem on the Divide.

"I like that you do what you gotta do," he said. "That's one of only a few bikes of any serious Divide racer that I've seen without clipless pedals. But good, solid set-up. A good way to go a long way on a budget."

I handed Gary the five-dollar bill and told him it was from the tourist I had met 150 miles back. Gary flipped open his laptop computer to recite the latest race standings. Matt Lee was going to probably win the race later that day, he told me. Cricket had just called in from Hartsel to drop out of the race. Deanna hadn't been heard from in days, and was still back in Wyoming. There was a good chance I was the only woman left riding in the Tour Divide. I told Gary about Pete and asked if he had seen him. Gary shook his head.

"Matt told me Pete was doing an ITT this year," Gary said. "Pete dropped in to visit us in past years, but maybe he's behind schedule this year."

"I don't think he's behind schedule," I said. "I don't know the time he's making exactly but Mike told me he was flying, and he's probably planning to ramp it up in New Mexico. Pete's just a man on a mission, that's all."

By the time I ate heaping portions of pizza and pie, drank a third glass of tea, finished my grocery shopping, and made a few calls, 9 a.m. turned to 11:30 a.m. I announced I really needed to hit the road, and Patti offered to ride with me the first few miles out of town.

"Where are you headed tonight?" Patti asked.

"I was hoping to get beyond Platoro," I said. "But now I'm not sure. This next pass is monstrous, nearly 12,000 feet. It's probably going to take me most of the day to do it."

"We're about 7,800 feet here," Patti said. "Yeah, it's a healthy climb. It's not gradual like those railroad-grade passes before here, either. Indiana Pass is steep and the surface is pretty loose. And it's so late in the day now. You're likely to hit storms up high. Hard to say right now. The weather looks good, but you can see the thunderheads building over those mountains. Indiana Pass is right on the Divide. It's hard to escape the rain up there."

"I know all about the rain," I said. "I haven't been able to escape it at all, really, this entire trip. I've been rained on nearly every single day."

"Well, I'd be careful if it hits up high," Patti said. "You probably shouldn't plan on going beyond Platoro tonight. There's not much beyond there."

"I'll see how it goes," I said. "If it's raining, I'll definitely stay in Platoro."

Patti turned around near the dead end of the paved road, and I joined the steep, loose gravel to begin the daunting task of gaining 4,000 feet in twenty-five miles, followed by twenty-five more miles of rolling terrain that didn't lose much elevation overall. A cursory glance at my maps warned me that as many as 7,000 feet of climbing waited on the grind into Platoro. But I had done at least that much the day before without daytime fatigue, so I felt confident that section of the route wouldn't be so bad.

As Patti promised, the road took the direct route up the mountain, cutting up fifteen-percent grades on gravel so loose that my rear wheel often just slipped and stopped. I hopped off the bike, walked to a less steep section, and rode until the wheel slipped out again. Keeping my butt planted in the saddle added traction to the wheel, but too much climbing in the saddle made my Achilles tendons scream. It was a brand new source of pain.

Before my GPS even registered 11,000 feet, my energy level had plummeted. My back ached and my legs pumped acid. The sensation was very similar to the discomfort I had felt in the Great Divide Basin but hadn't really noticed since. I couldn't pedal hard without aggravating my heels, so I spun low-gear circles until my rear tire lost traction. I wavered and wheezed. I could almost feel my fuel gauge hovering over "E" as my eyes blinked heavily and the sleep monster sang lullabies in the early afternoon. I forced Sour Patch Kids down my throat, but they did nothing. This wasn't a fuel problem; it was a power problem. I had a full tank and a failing engine.

I rolled over the 11,957-foot summit in a daze. Despite promises from both my maps and GPS that I was at the top, Indiana Pass hardly registered as a summit. It snaked along a talus-coated saddle, dropping ever so slightly into a small bowl before climbing to a new saddle nearly as high. I had become accustomed to sweeping views of valleys on the other side of large passes, but Indiana Pass was simply a doorway into a massive, tightly clustered mountain range. This high point on the Great Divide Mountain Bike Route was merely the base of 13,000- and 14,000-foot giants.

I continued along the rolling pass, feeling a little more energetic as the climbing became less sustained. I dropped and climbed a series of steep drainages, battling up another big pitch toward a place called Summitville. The ghost town, once the highest incorporated community in the state of Colorado, was now nothing more than an abandoned Superfund site. The toxic remnants of the old mine manifested in gravel-buried tailings ponds and scarred yellow hillsides — not the kind of place that entices a person to linger. Farther up the mountain, I passed the collapsed and wind-ravaged buildings of the old town site. One sun-bleached log cabin had been snapped clean in two. Rotten lumber and bricks were strewn across the talus, and most of the homes lay in twisted heaps, as though they had been demolished by a tornado rather than the slow decay of time. The only intact building was a large, two-story wooden structure high on the hillside.

It loomed over the rest of the town, cast in an ominous shadow. Behind it, a massive thunderhead rose from the barren horizon. The cloud was just one shade lighter than black, so opaque that it plunged the ghost town into an eerie twilight. The cloud surged over the Continental Divide, quickly consuming the sky.

As fast as the storm arrived, streaks of lightning began to rip through the inky darkness. A few distant booms set off a cacophony of thunder and electricity, so frequent and intense that nearby rocks rattled. I took large gulps of panic. I was well above timberline, and the collapsed buildings around me hardly counted as places to seek shelter from an electric storm. Even the intact building on the hill looked like it could come down at any moment, and was not easily accessible. I was at nearly 12,000 feet, the tallest thing on a broad talus heap with nowhere to hide.

In front of me, far beyond the massive storm, I saw a thin strip of blue sky. I rode toward it, knowing my only real option was to go farther down the road and pray that I dropped off the summit soon. The storm enveloped me in fog, until I could see little more than the dark pebbles under my wheels, and vague flashes of light tearing through the gray curtain. But I could hear the storm with clattering clarity, and metallic thunder drove me into a frenzy. Out of seemingly nothing I found an explosion of power, fueled by adrenaline and blind purpose.

The clouds began to lift but the road continued climbing. Lightning blasted all around me and I wondered out loud how this road could still possibly be below 12,000 feet. The maps must have been wrong, I thought. The road seemed like it was going to keep gaining elevation until I was the only thing left for the lightning to hit. Light sprinkles started to fall from the sky, quickly growing to large droplets and then to hard sheets of rain. The precipitation became so thick and cold I was convinced it was sleet. After fifteen minutes of terror, I finally began dropping with the downpour, down from the talus and into the relative safety of tree cover. The lightning fell back but the rain followed, dredging up an uncomfortable chill that even panic couldn't mask.

I was drenched to the core by the time I finally stopped to put on my rain gear. It didn't seem to matter. The hard falling rain was going to saturate my clothing no matter what I did. But at least the rain layer would help block the brutal wind-chill of the descent. I put on every piece of clothing I had with me save for one dry base layer. Stopping to deal with my clothes left me so chilled that I was shivering violently by the time I remounted by bicycle.

The road continued to plummet downhill, the rain continued to fall hard, and the chill deepened. Even with all of my clothing on, my body produced only a candle flicker of heat. I occasionally jumped off my bike to try to run with it, just to work up some spark of warmth, but my adrenaline rush had long since flared out and I hardly had the energy to even stagger down the road. I drifted into the early throes of hypothermia. My lips, fingers, and toes went numb. My vision blurred and sometimes doubled. I shivered so uncontrollably that I sometimes jerked my bike randomly in awkward directions, or clumsily wended into turns so wide I almost shot clean off the road. Since I only had a down sleeping bag and bivy sack as immediate shelter, I felt a growing concern for my safety. I'd had mild hypothermia enough times before to know that it's self-perpetuating. If I kept doing what I was doing, it only stood to get worse until my body ceased to function. I tried to comfort myself with promises that Platoro couldn't be far, it couldn't be far now.

But even the bottom of the descent never seemed to come. I had been trembling on top of my bike for what felt like an agonizing eternity when I passed a police car. The car's presence confused me. The traffic I had seen since Del Norte amounted to two trucks and a handful of ATVs. It had been the least populated pass I had crossed in Colorado. A few feet down from the patrol car, a police officer stood outside in the rain, talking to two people draped in brown ponchos. "Great," I thought. "This must mean I'm close to town."

"Hey!" the police officer yelled as I rode past. "Are you alone?"

"I'm alone!" I yelled back. "There's no one else behind me."

A few minutes later, I caught up to two ambulances, inching their way down the rough road. With half-frozen fingers I could not feel, I squeezed on the brakes until I slowed to their speed, five miles per hour. "Must have been an ATV accident," I thought. I rode my brakes behind the ambulances as they negotiated the narrow and rutted road at a pace that could only be described as painful. The awkwardly large vehicles filled up both sides of the narrow road; the thin strips of gravel on both sides didn't provide much room to pass, and it didn't seem ethical to try. The worst thing I could do was hit a blind rut and slam into an ambulance, thereby adding to the emergency they were obviously already dealing with.

So I waited. And coasted. And shivered. My frustration boiled up but did nothing to keep me warm. "Can't they tell I'm in my own emergency back here?" I grumbled beneath clenched teeth. "God, I'm going to pass out from hypothermia behind an ambulance."

Finally, the road dipped into a clearing. It forked and the ambulances turned left. I could see from my maps that I needed to turn right, and my heart sang. I was free! The vehicles slowed to a stop and I veered past them, finally pedaling again toward the last small pass of the day when a voice called out, "Hey! Are you with this biker?"

I turned around and walked my bike toward the first ambulance driver's open window. "Wait," I said with an air of alarm, "There's a biker in this ambulance?"

The driver nodded slowly.

"You mean like a cyclist?"

The driver nodded again.

"Who is it?"

He shook his head. "Sorry. I can't tell you."

My shivering immediately ceased, as though gripped by cold hands of dread. All of the blood drained out of my head and I felt a thick lump of bile gurgle up from my stomach. "Is it Pete Basinger?" I said in almost a whisper.

The driver just nodded again.

A chilled shock of fear shot through my newly empty veins. "Oh, oh no, no," I squeaked. "Is he okay?"

"He's responsive," the driver said. "He's talking to us."

"What happened?"

"He was hit by a truck pulling a horse trailer. Head-on."

"A head-on collision?" I stammered. "With a truck? How fast? Is he going to be okay? Do you know what's wrong?"

The ambulance driver shook his head. "We have him stabilized and we're trying to call in to see if we can land a helicopter in here."

"Where are you taking him?" I said. "Can you tell me where you're taking him?"

"Not sure," the driver said. He leaned over to a man who had stepped out of the second vehicle and mumbled a few things I didn't hear. Then he turned back to me. "Do you want to talk to him?"

"Um, I probably should just let you guys go," I said.

"We're not in a hurry right now," the driver said. "Either way we have to wait to see whether we can get him out of here."

The second man directed me toward his ambulance. I passed the trailer being towed by the first ambulance. In the back, wedged behind a four-wheeler, was the twisted wreckage of a red bicycle, pummeled and gouged with sickening violence. Inside the ambulance, two EMTs sitting next to a stretcher smiled weakly as I opened the door. Pete lay on the stretcher, his entire body covered by a sheet and his head mounted inside an elaborate metal cage that prevented him from moving. His long eyelashes pointed directly at the ceiling; his eyes were fixed and dark. He had several small cuts on his face. Beyond that, there were no signs of injury, but based on the complete covering of his body, the use of that head contraption and the singular severity of a head-on-collision with a truck, I knew his injuries must be serious, possibly grave. I took off my hat and held it like a wet rag, wincing as the icy water trickled down my wrists. The shivering that had momentarily stopped as I talked to the driver came back with powerful force, and it was everything I could do to suppress the urge to rattle like a paint can. I took several deep breaths. "Hey Pete," I said, startled by the shakiness in my own voice.

"Um, Jill?" Pete said hoarsely.

"Yeah, Jill," I replied.

Pete smiled. "Heh. This is pretty crazy, isn't it?" he said.

I didn't smile back. "It's intense. How long ago did this happen?"

"It's been about a three-hour process getting here," he said. "But I don't even know ... where are we now?"

"Stunner," I said at the exact same time he did.

"Stunner Campground," he repeated. "That's what I thought. Did you get hit with any rain?"

I managed to crack a smile. Clearly, Pete had no way of seeing my dripping hat or soaked hair or rain jacket streaked in mud. "A huge amount of rain," I said.

"Yeah, that's why I left Del Norte right away," he said. "I wanted to beat the rain."

"Smart man," I said.

Pete laughed. "I'd say your timing was better than mine."

I mustered my own chuckle. It was such a bizarre accident, in such a remote place. I couldn't imagine an instance of worse timing. "How did it happen?"

"I was coming down the road, doing about twenty-five, and these rednecks were coming around a corner on the wrong side of the road, probably thinking no one else was around. I saw them and swerved, but they slammed right into me."

"Are you in much pain?" I asked.

"It's not too bad," he said. "Now. Those rednecks who hit me were walking around me, talking about what they were going to do with me. That was the scariest part."

We paused and the silence echoed. I looked down, muddling for anything to say.

"So did you see me at the campground last night?" Pete asked.

"Storm King? Yeah, I heard you come in. I was going to get up and talk to you. Sorry I didn't."

"That's okay," Pete said. "I didn't want to wake you up."

"I'm still sorry," I said. "I'm really sorry this had to happen."

"Yeah," Pete said. "Shit happens. Just sucks right now, three days from the end."

Three days," I laughed. If he really thought the next 700 miles was only going to take him three days, it would have put him in a fifteen or sixteen-day finish from Banff. Pete would have obliterated John's Divide record. "I was thinking more like seven," I said.

It won't take you seven days," Pete said. "Where are you staying tonight?"

"I think Platoro," I said. "I'm thinking about just going to Platoro."

"Platoro's good," Pete said. "The cabins there are expensive, but they have good food."

Another pause lingered in the thick air. I felt a strange surge of panic that had no origin or direction, and let my shivering return just to gulp it down. "Well, I should let you guys go," I stammered. "You're in an emergency and stuff."

"Yeah," Pete said. "Good luck."

"You too."

Outside the ambulance, the rain had stopped. A shock of sunlight escaped through a crack in the clouds, casting a nearly opaque rainbow over the Stunner Valley. The two ambulances passed directly beneath the rainbow's arch as they rumbled away. It seemed life-flight couldn't land in this remote hole in Colorado after all.

I watched the vehicles to disappear into the woods. My own helpless inertia lingered long after they were gone. I rubbed my eyes with ice-cold fingers, wiping away a well of tears that felt frozen in place. My hands shook wildly as I pressed them against my cheeks, scraping away clumps of wet mud that were plastered to my skin. I struggled to connect the clasps of my helmet strap over a soggy hat and dripping hair. I straddled my motionless bike. The last climb into Platoro loomed like a sleeping dragon. I stood and faced it, making no movement toward it. My childlike emotions lay in wreckage, disemboweled and scattered along the battlefield of the Divide. I could not cry.

What just happened? Pete was immobilized in an ambulance. He had been hit by a truck. A large trailer-dragging truck, and they had both been traveling fast. He had survived; that was a relief. But how could he not be badly injured? Dread pierced my cold-numbed skin. Maybe Pete had been paralyzed. Maybe his legs or back had been irrecoverably broken. Maybe his whole life had just changed in an unspeakably cruel instant, right there on the lonely descent from Summitville.

Where my joy and anticipation and even fear had dissolved, I felt only grief. I lifted my feet and pressed down on the pedals, turning slow circles that promised no reward. Pete and I had both been out there on the Great Divide, riding the same muddy roads, climbing the same sweeping passes, watching the same spectacular sunsets. Despite our mutual solitude, we had both been bound by this one thing, this totally unique thing, this effort to ride across the spine of the continent as fast as we possibly could. And to what end? To what end? What did we possibly stand to gain? Pete rode heroically for two weeks right into a head-on collision. I rode into a place of lasting isolation, where no friends could wrap their arms around me and tell me everything was going to be okay.

The sunlight disappeared and the clouds plunged the tight canyon into more midday twilight. The rain returned and released my grief from the initial shock of discovering Pete's accident. It trickled through my veins and dissolved the intense focus that had sustained my sanity through the Tour Divide. The race may have been hard, but it was all I had. My eight-year relationship lay in ruins. My demanding job simply waited to fill that empty space with workday drudgery. I no longer had a home. I barely had a car. My bicycle had become my closest companion. And I was lost in a fruitless struggle, chasing phantoms toward nowhere.

Hopelessness loomed and I fought it back with thoughts of the things that were important to me. My family was important to me, my mom and dad and sisters. No matter what stupid decisions I made, or crazy adventures I embarked on, they had always been there for me. My old friends were important to me, the people scattered across the country in Utah and Colorado and California, people I had known for years and even decades, who had watched my entire journey and knew exactly where I came from. My new friends were important to me, my friends in Alaska and acquaintances from the Internet, who understood and shared my passions. My career was important to me; even stressful and demanding as the job could be, journalism embodied the very meaning of life, the pursuit of knowledge and recording of experience. And Alaska was important to me, with a yearning for its beauty and scope that even the Great Divide could not quite fill. And all of that, I thought, was nowhere near. In fact, the longer I pedaled south, the farther I distanced myself from my family and friends and the simple fact that I needed to get on with my life. The future was a shapeless mass that contained nothing I loved. Suddenly, following maps in a silly bicycle race seemed monumentally unimportant.

I crested Stunner Pass in a depth of sadness. Pete had been on pace to break the Great Divide record, something that at least on paper looked important. But what was I? A straggler. An imposter. I stopped pedaling and let the coasting bicycle creep down the road. I could not see beyond the next bend; vile forest swallowed the road into darkness. Above the trees, cloud-filtered sunlight mocked my grief with stoic indifference. I wiped more rain from my eyes, or perhaps the moisture came from tears. I tried to summon the energy to move forward.

"You just have to get to Platoro," I told myself. "There's certainly nothing you can do out here."

I coasted a few hundred feet and stopped again. Through the grayness of grief, a single hopeful idea cast a dull light. I could quit the Tour Divide in Platoro. I could board a bus and head back toward Denver, then fly home to Utah, where I could return to the love of my family and friends and start the daunting journey of getting on with the life I so obviously needed to get on with. This new idea pushed energy back into my legs, and I started pedaling harder down the hill.

I leveled out in a wide valley that still stood above 10,000 feet. Trees choked out the view, but through the woods I started to see cabins. My heart soared. I rode a bit farther and saw more cabins, and a sign that said "Sky View Lodge." I flew beyond that, looking for the gas station or bus station or something that could supply a swift exit from a world of purposeless suffering. Beyond the Sky View Lodge, the town abruptly ceased. I rode to the next bend, but the unpopulated forest persisted. There was nothing ahead but more hateful wilderness, mountains, and rivers stretching beyond the horizon. Platoro was nothing more than a small mountain resort community. There was no bus station. There was no store. There was almost certainly no cell phone reception, and I'd be lucky if there was even a public-use phone. Waves of sadness, no longer relegated behind a dam of shock and confusion, suddenly burst out in a gush of tears. There was nothing in Platoro. Nothing, nothing, nothing.

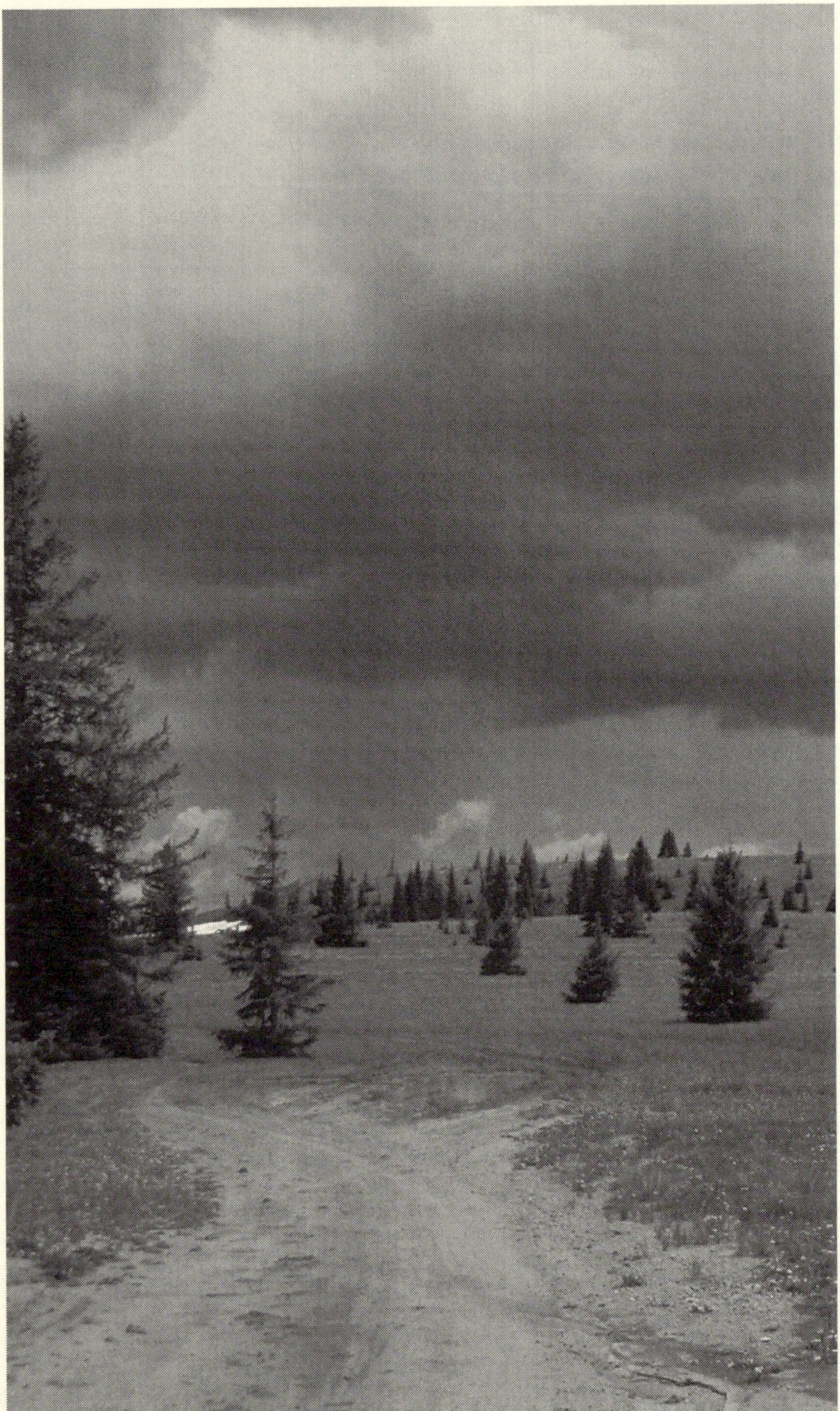

Chapter Twenty
After the Storm

Page 268 and 269: A thunderstorm approaches a high plateau in New Mexico.
Page 270: A meandering gravel road in northern New Mexico.

I approached the Skyline Lodge with trepidation. A dank, deep-set chill lingered in the air and shivering continued to rock my core, but I wasn't sure I was ready to face the strangers inside. It was a private lodge, which meant I might not be welcome there. I was dripping rainwater, convulsing involuntarily, and I was covered in mud. The people inside Skyline Lodge wouldn't see my shattered emotions or pressing doubts. They wouldn't see the struggle of the early afternoon or the fear about my friend. They would only see a dirty, homeless biker. They might even ask me to leave.

A fireplace wider than a wall and taller than my head roared in the front room. Before I could open my blue lips to utter a meager greeting, a woman rushed from behind the front desk and ushered me beside the orange flames. "Oh, you just look like a popsicle," she said. "Here, you can take off your wet clothes and hang them up around the fire."

"Um, thanks," I stammered. I lifted my cold-stiffened fingers to my helmet strap and began the laborious process of peeling off several soaked layers of clothing.

The woman turned and approached a white sheet hanging from a wall about ten feet away. "You must be Jill," she said. "Mmm hmm. And it's 5:30, uh, June thirtieth. OK, I have you marked as "In." Before you leave here, can you mark your time and date out on the line next to your name? We're trying to keep track of everyone that comes through here."

"So you guys are tracking the Tour Divide?" I asked.

"Of course. We see nearly everyone that comes through here, so naturally we started paying attention to the race. It's a lot of fun to watch y'all bike through. I even talked Matt Lee into sleeping a full night here. I'm serious. He was here eight hours. Ate two meals. It's probably one of the few times you'll see him acting like a human."

"That's really great," I said. "Thanks for the, um, fire."

"Oh, and let me grab you a menu," she said. "I assume you'll be wanting dinner. How bout a room? I have cheap rooms upstairs. Fifty dollars and it's yours. Were you planning to stay the night? It's early but I can tell you there's not much beyond here."

"Not much, huh?" I said. I breathed out. "I think I do want that room. Do you guys have a pay phone?"

"No," she shook her head. "We have a courtesy phone outside, but it doesn't seem to work with calling cards. It's really only good for local numbers and some 800 numbers."

"Oh," I said. "Shoot."

"Why?" she asked. "Who you gotta call?"

"Well," I said as my lip quivered. My shivering became more pronounced even as I stood next to a roaring fire. I took a few deep breaths and launched into an explanation of Pete's accident.

"Oh," she said. "We had heard there was an accident up near the pass, but we didn't get much information about it. You say he's a friend of yours? Another biker?"

"I know him," I said. "He's from Alaska. He's riding the Divide, too."

"Pete, let's see," she said slowly, glancing back at the list on the wall.

"Oh, he's not with the Tour Divide," I said. "He's doing his own thing."

"Well, tell you what," she said. "I'll go make some calls around to the regional hospitals, see if I can drum up information. But if you said they were calling a helicopter in, it sounds like they're taking him to Denver. I'm not sure I'll find out much, but I can try."

"Thanks so much," I said.

As she walked away, I first noticed two men sitting on the couches around the fireplace. One wore a trucker's cap and a flannel shirt. The other was a rotund youth with cropped brown hair. Both of them had laptop computers in their laps.

"That's a big bummer about they guy in the truck crash," the guy in the trucker's cap said. "I don't think I've heard his name. Is he on the Web site?"

"Well, he's not in the Tour Divide," I said. "What he's doing is similar to our race, but it's different. It's, uh, I guess it's kind of complicated."

"Oh," the man in a disappointed tone. "Yeah, big bummer. Hope he's okay. But listen to this — Matt Lee's just a few miles from crossing the border. He's going to win the race any minute now!"

"Wow, that's great," I said, feeling a small surge of happiness about Matt's success. "That's about, what, eighteen days? That's really incredible, given how horrible the weather's been and all."

"Yeah," the man said. "Guess that won't quite beat the record. But that's still pretty good; it was already his record. I guess that's seventeen days and a bit."

"From Banff," I added. With the Tour Divide still in its infancy, few people outside the race understood that there were two distances on the Great Divide with two different records.

"But look at you," he continued. "You're way back here in Platoro, and they're still reporting that you're on record pace. They have you pegged for a twenty-five-day race!"

I breathed out. "Maybe."

"Yeah, you should think about moving a little faster," he said. "There's a guy out in front of you less than a day. I bet you could catch him, easy. Overall, you're in fifteenth place right now."

I smiled weakly. All of my fears about the Skyline Lodge, about being treated with cool indifference, had melted away, only to be replaced by something that was almost worse — the friendliness of people who not only had heard of the Tour Divide but were following it closely and judging every move I made as a racer. Meeting a fan was such a rare occasion, and this one just happened to come at a time when I could not care less about the race. I wanted to scream at the guy in the trucker's hat. I wanted to tell him to shut up. My friend had been injured in a terrible accident. He might even be paralyzed. Why in the world would I care that I was in fifteenth place in the stupid Tour Divide?

The woman's calls proved fruitless. I thought about asking the man in the trucker's cap if I could use his computer, but I doubted the Internet would yield much information this soon after the crash. I wondered how many people even knew about Pete's accident. He probably pushed the emergency 9-1-1 button on his SPOT, which meant Mike Curiak would know. And Geoff would know. But the chance that they had any information beyond what I already knew was slim.

For most of the evening, I sat alone in the upstairs room. Every so often I heard peels of laughter from downstairs, where a large crowd of people gathered around the hearth during the after-dinner hours. Their chatter scraped through my ears like a nail on metal. During any other night of the Tour Divide, I would have been thrilled to join them, and relish in the warm company of friendly strangers. But in Platoro, every joyful sound echoed in my mind as hollow screeching, piercing through my thin veneer of stoicism. I just wanted them all go to sleep and leave me in quiet and darkness.

Rain continued to pound the window. My temporary relief brought on by my plan to quit the race dissolved with my conviction to do so. Even if I did quit, I would still have to ride out of Platoro to the nearest real town. I had no idea where that would even be, but the maps promised it wasn't anywhere nearby. And I had a feeling that by the time I arrived at a good exit point, any comfort I would have found in quitting the race would be gone as well. But either way, I was going to have to leave in the morning. I had no choice but to pedal myself out of Platoro. I set my alarm for 5 a.m., but before I even went to sleep, my undulating doubts caused me to re-set it for 7:30.

Homesickness stalked around the empty corners of the room. At ten, I finally took a sleeping pill and laid in the darkness. For the first time on the Divide, the drug did nothing to cut through my pounding doubts and fears. There wasn't anything I wanted more than to slip into unconsciousness and wake up in my own bedroom in Utah, and find out the whole Divide business had been nothing more than a dream. I could hug my mother, and

Pete would still be healthy, and I would be free to go about the business of getting on with my life.

Eventually, I drifted to sleep. I hit snooze on my alarm the following morning. By the time I gathered my stiff, mud-caked clothes from around the fireplace and walked out into a valley drenched in sunlight, it was after 8:30 a.m. — a full fifteen hours after I arrived in Platoro. I could almost feel the disapproving glances of the race spectators where they still sat on couches with their computers.

Outside, a thickly muscled man who introduced himself as a lodge caretaker asked me where I was headed that day.

"Going to the Brazos Ridge today," I said, referring to a high alpine ridge that ringed a large wilderness area in Northern New Mexico.

"The Brazos?" he nearly shouted, then shook his head. "Not a good idea, not with this weather. I fought wildfires in the Brazos for five years. You'll be up to your knees in mud. I'm not exaggerating. Your knees."

"What is the weather supposed to do today?" I asked.

"More of the same," he said. "Nice for a bit, then a lot of afternoon thunderstorms and rain."

"Yeah," I sighed. "More of the same."

"But seriously," he said. "I'd bypass the Brazos. It's a real bitch in the rain."

"I'll do the best I can," I said.

The air was calm and dry, the gravel road was smooth and the grade mostly downhill, but the twenty-three miles into the next town over, Horca, seemed to drag, as though I was towing cement weights behind my bike. I pulled into the Horca store, which was inexplicably shuttered at 10 a.m. on a Wednesday in July. I walked around the entire building and peered in all the windows, but I saw no sign of the store ever being open or planning to open. This meant no supplies for the day. But that seemed a relatively minor concern. The lack of resupply became downright frivolous when I discovered a payphone bolted to the far wall.

With the first shot of energy I felt all day, I sprinted back to my bicycle and grabbed my calling card and six or seven quarters, all I had with me. It turned out to be a pointless gesture because when I picked up the receiver, the line was dead. The pay phone wasn't connected to anything. I blindly punched buttons and even fed it all of my quarters, to no avail.

That, too, was a small defeat, but it made my head spin. Frustration bubbled up from my gut and I lashed out by stomping around the empty parking lot, swearing and screaming, half hoping that some nearby local with a key to the store would see my temper tantrum and let the poor crazy person inside. The Great Divide Mountain Bike Route, in its quest to follow gravel roads and traverse mountains, had landed me in a backwoods so remote that I couldn't even make a simple phone call for more than a hundred miles. It seemed a unique position to be in America, in general, let alone the Colorado Rockies. My inability to communicate amplified my sense of isolation.

I started up the switchbacks to La Manga Pass, no longer impressed by the act of climbing higher than 10,000 feet. In the early afternoon, I dropped down a steep gorge and crossed the New Mexico state line. The only thing to welcome me into my last state before the Mexican border was a cattle guard and a sign informing me I was in Carson National Forest.

A man in a diesel truck approached me from behind and slowed as he passed. "Hey, do you need any water?" he asked me.

"No," I said. I needed food, but water was one thing I did not need. "Thanks, but I have plenty of water in my pack."

"I'm just asking because I've seen other bikers coming through, and they always ask me where they can get water," he said. "There ain't much up here, I can tell you that. Plus, there's a storm coming in and these roads can get pretty sloppy. I'd be careful if I were you. I have a ranch near here. When you get to the next intersection, take a right and it's about two miles down that road. If you need water or a place to wait out the storm, just drop in."

"Wow," I said. "Thanks, really. I guess if a storm chases me off the Brazos, I might just take you up on that."

The climb up the Brazos Ridge was relentless. The snaking railroad grades of Colorado were a distant memory. In New Mexico, roads were cut into the slope like scars, deeply rutted and bleeding with a wash of loose stones the size of tennis balls. I had to pedal with all of my legs' not considerable power just to keep the back wheel rotating. "What are these roads going to be like if they get wet?" I wondered. "Am I even going to be able to walk uphill?"

I passed patches of snow streaked along the hillsides, which amused me because I was in New Mexico and it was July. Thinking back to my frequent brushes with hypothermia and frost on the Divide I thought, "I guess I'm just the kind of person who finds winter wherever I go."

My GPS registered above 11,000 feet. The slope leveled out on a broad plateau, covered in mint green grass and dotted with clusters of small evergreens. Antelope, all taller than the trees, darted across the wide plain. Where the road scarred the plateau, the dirt was dark red, almost crimson, and as smooth as a ceramic bowl. I thought with dread that the road surface actually was dry clay, which tends to become wet clay when it rains.

All day long, the only concern on my mind had been Pete's condition. Even the dire warnings about the weather from the Platoro groundskeeper and the ranch owner did little to rattle through my dark conviction that Pete had sustained life-altering injuries. But as I crested the Brazos Ridge, anxieties about my own wellbeing began to return. To the north, the ridge dropped dramatically into the sandstone canyons of the Cruces Basin Wilderness. To the south, the plateau stretched out as far as I could see. And to the east, the direction I was heading, a billowing thunderhead as tall as a mountain and as dark as midnight churned toward me.

I took deliberate breaths, trying to gulp down the panic that the clouds rumbled and ignited. Thunderstorms were bad enough to see from the safety of valleys. They were terrifying on high, exposed summits. I flirted with thoughts of turning around and descending back to the safety of the ranch house. "Be brave," I chanted to myself. "Be strong." It made me feel slightly better, so I chanted it over and over. "Be brave. Be strong. Be brave. Be strong. Be brave."

As I chanted, a strange, shrill, almost otherworldly sound erupted from my backpack. It rang out into the calm air with such a piercing volume that I jumped off my bike. I calmed my breaths and listened for the source of the ring. My mind shuffled through layers of surprise and confusion, until I remembered that I had turned on my cell phone in the morning, on the unlikely chance that it found a signal. The noise was my cell phone, telling me I had received voice messages.

As far as I could tell, I was nowhere near anywhere. I had a rather large wilderness area on one side of me and an unpopulated expanse of high-altitude desert on the other. There were no towns to the north and as far as I knew, no towns to the south. I felt like I was in the most remote region of the entire Great Divide. But somehow, at 11,000 feet, my cell phone had reached out into a great expanse of open air and found a connection to the larger world. My heart leapt with unexpected joy.

I stood in place lest my phone lose its signal again. I punched in the code for my voice mail. The night before, in Platoro, I had left a message on the Tour Divide answering machine, an 800 number that just happened to work on the Skyline Lodge's courtesy phone. Only able to get through to an answering machine, I left a long, emotional message about what had happened with Pete below Summitville, so the Tour Divide organizers and spectators were aware. As strengthening winds charged up the Brazos Ridge, I listened to messages from six different people, from my parents to my Utah friends to Chris Plesko's wife to Geoff, all reassuring me that Pete was going to be okay. The paramedics flew him to Denver, they told me. It appeared he had a broken collarbone and two broken arms, a lot of cuts and bruises, and a fair amount of pain, but he was expected to make a full recovery.

I called my parents. My dad answered the phone. "Jill!" he said. "Where are you right now?"

"I'm in New Mexico," I said. "I'm actually in the absolute middle of nowhere. But I'm up at 11,000 feet so my cell phone managed to find reception."

"Did you get our messages?" he asked.

"I did," I said. "Everyone told me Pete's going to be okay. That's amazing news. I've been really worried about it, stewing about it, since last night."

"We thought you might be worried," my dad said. "We found the number of his parents and called them ourselves. It sounds like he's disappointed about having to drop out of the race, but he's going to recover."

"That is such a relief to hear right now," I said. "You have no idea."

"And how about you?" my dad asked. "How are you doing?"

"Well," I hesitated. The relief of good news about Pete released a new flood of apprehension that pooled in my throat. I was in the middle of nowhere New Mexico, I was alone, and I was facing a freight train of a thunderstorm headed right for me. I wanted to tell my dad that I was scared, wanted him to be able to wrap his arms around me and tell me that not only was Pete going to be okay, but I was going to be okay, too. Since he couldn't do that, and I couldn't do anything about the storms and the mud, it seemed pointless to draw him into my fears. "I'm doing fine," I said. "I didn't sleep all that well last night, but now that I know Pete's going to recover, I'm sure I'll sleep better tonight."

"That's good to hear," my dad said. "Call us again if you need anything."

I hesitated, trying to think of things I could say to keep him on the phone, but the receiver was already crackling and cutting out. "Not sure I'll have reception much longer here," I said. "But thanks, I'll call again soon."

Released back to my solitude, I charged into the guts of the storm. Lightning exploded on the periphery but didn't venture too close for comfort. My heart pounded but there was nowhere to seek shelter for many miles. I resigned myself to the reality that fate was either going to carry me through, or it wasn't.

The road sloped downhill and rain started to fall. After all of my forays into morasses of mud, rain was starting to scare me nearly as much as lightning. Large, frequent drops stung the exposed skin on my face and arms. I pedaled faster even though speed sharpened the stings. I didn't stop to put on my rain layer. Mud was much more of a threat than hypothermia, and my only defense was to outrun it.

The road became slick and then gooey. I hammered down the hill, but where the terrain leveled out, I had to churn through an inch of mud the consistency of wet glue, and just as sticky. Dry pine needles littered the surface, and the mixture clung to my bike like tiny bricks. Just as it had at Brooks Lake in Wyoming, the adobe stopped me in my tracks. I dragged the bike through a long flat stretch only to be released from wallowing by the merciful slope of a steep hill, where the rain was still running off the surface of the road rather than seeping in. I'd start the process anew, chipping away the mud that froze my drivetrain and wheels and pedaling slowly up the ascent, if I could.

As I climbed the switchbacks of a larger drainage, even gravity didn't stop the road's descent into slop. A thick puddle grabbed my wheel, seizing the bike so quickly that it threw me off balance. I jumped off the saddle and slid backward in the goo, falling to a kneeling position as the bike leaned against my shoulders. I spewed out a torrent of frustration. The tourist in Poncha Springs was right. The groundskeeper in Platoro was right. New Mexico was bringing me to my knees.

After about an hour, the storm began to taper as it rolled west. Blue sky replaced the twilight shade of the clouds, and the sun appeared over the red sand valley. In the mercifully arid air, the puddles on the road began to shrink and dry. The gooey surface hardened and cracked. Clay encased my skin and clothing like a cast, but I was free to ride again. Ahead, both the landscape and the sky opened wide.

But it didn't last. The route turned into another canyon as new clouds gathered overhead. I no longer had the energy to outrun anything, and actually escaping the storm didn't seem very likely. Molded into the road were the tire tracks and footprints of at least three cyclists who had come through before me. It meant that I hadn't been the only one to become stuck in the rain, but it also meant that if it did rain, I would be stuck.

Blurry streaks of precipitation closed in all around me, but didn't drop overhead until I turned off the clay Forest Service road onto the pavement of Highway 64. The rain fell hard for most of the climb, and after five miles and a thousand feet of elevation, it was time to turn off the highway onto yet another clay road. Below the clouds, the day had descended almost imperceptibly into evening. Perched on the bluff above Hopewell Lake, I could see sunset's peach and gold streaks, stripped below the storm to the west. Warm light reflected off the rippled surface of the lake.

There was also a campground at the junction, a well-developed area overcrowded with campers and RVs. It also had a cooking shelter, an outhouse and a water spigot. I pulled my bike into the day-use shelter, which was set apart from the campground and pleasantly quiet. I dug through my feedbag and fished out a half-empty package of beef jerky and a small package of cookies, some of the last of my scarcity of supplies.

"Shoot," I said out loud. "I'm going to have to start rationing."

The rain continued to fall and I knew the road ahead probably contained more clay-like mud that would slow my pace to a crawl. The nearest town that promised any kind of resupply was still thirty miles away, and even if I reached it late that night, those stores would surely be closed. The smart thing to do, I decided, would be to stay at Hopewell Lake and hope the rain stopped by morning, allowing me to descend on what would optimistically be dry roads. I felt a pang of guilt about the shortness of my day — only eighty-seven miles — but it had been a hard day and I'd have to be an idiot to pass up shelter when the evening only promised more rain and wheel-stopping mud.

I rolled out my sleeping bag and bivy sack on the hard concrete next to a sign that said "No Camping." I changed into my dry clothes, strung the wet ones over my bicycle, and crawled into my sleeping bag. I gnawed on beef jerky and perused my maps. Before I even remembered to take my nightly sleeping pill, I dropped out of consciousness with my maps still strewn about me and the beam of my still-lit headlamp pointing directly out the one open wall of shelter, into the night.

Chapter Twenty One
The High Desert

Page 281: The Polvadera Mesa in New Mexico.
Page 282: Cars crowd a narrow road during the Rainbow Family Gathering near Cuba, New Mexico.

Peach sunlight bounced off the wooden beams of the picnic shelter, casting candy stripes of color and shadows on my concrete bed. The morning was warm and bright, and I awoke feeling strangely empty. I couldn't quite pinpoint why. The sun promised dry road conditions and my family had assured me of Pete's health, so I no longer had reason to worry. And still, I felt a dull sense of malaise. It was as though my grief and fear had provided me with renewed purpose that I no longer felt. Grief about Pete's condition drove me forward until I finally discovered the truth. Fear of mud and storms drove me forward until I finally escaped. Now I was back to wondering where I was going and why, and the uncertainty left me feeling hollow.

There were a hundred reasons to give up, but none were convincing reasons. The one thing that had taken over my thoughts and emotions for more than a day — Pete's accident — didn't have the hopeless consequences I had feared. My knees and Achilles tendons still ached, but not enough to keep me from pedaling up hills. I was nearly out of food, but I expected to reach a resupply point before my situation became desperate. As to my need to move on with my life, I only had a little more than 600 miles left to pedal. Surely the rest of my life could wait five more days.

But it's hard to take back a decision to quit once it's promised, no matter how unreasonable that decision becomes. I could still remember the joy I felt when I resolved to drop out of the race just minutes before reaching Platoro, and the ghost of that joy had haunted me every time I felt pain or frustration or fear ever since. I had already quit once in my heart and in my head. How easy it would be to let my battered body give in to the simple relief of defeat.

As I packed up my damp sleeping gear in my mud-caked bike bags, I fumbled for my motivation. I thought about how amazing it would feel to cross the Mexican border and know that I had done it on my own. I thought about the beauty that surely waited me in New Mexico, the redrock and desert sunsets and open mesas. And I visualized the final report I would have to call in to the Tour Divide podcast should I decide to drop out that day: "Hi, this is Jill Homer. I've decided I'm going to bag it. Yeah, I just realized I have an entire life to get on with. Wow, were these past two and a half weeks a waste of time or what?"

The thought made me laugh out loud. And set me to packing faster. It really would be ridiculous to quit the race now. There was no way I'd ever live it down. Just as it had when a store employee mopped up my puddle of rainwater all the way back in Clark, Colorado, the prospect of public humiliation gave me that final boost I needed to keep going.

I crossed the broad summit of Burned Mountain and plunged into a region forgotten by the past two centuries. Hidden in the wilderness-ringed valley of the Rio Vallecitos, the village of Canon Plaza was little more than a cluster of boxy structures, built of cracked adobe and sun-bleached logs. The town and its sister city, Vallecitos, were settled in 1776, and the villages still had the look and feel of a faded oil painting depicting colonial Mexico. Goats bleated behind splintered pinion-branch fences and Native American children ran barefoot down the dusty streets.

I turned right off the main road into downtown Vallecitos, which looked more modern and therefore more rundown than Canon Plaza. Tarps were strung over roofs and every single house had a loose dog or four. The mangy creatures greeted me viciously, barking wildly and snapping at my ankles in gathering numbers. I launched into a wild sprint and grabbed my bear spray out of my backpack's side pocket. As one medium-sized mutt closed in on my shins, I flipped the safety mechanism and pointed the canister directly at its bald, ugly face. I was a finger-flick away from uncorking a cloud of noxious fumes into the mob when I finally passed their imaginary property line, and the pack retreated. I later learned that the main street of Vallecitos is notorious on the Great Divide and even has its own nickname, "Dog Alley."

The road smoothed out over the mesa and joined the corridor of the Rio Chama. I reached the decidedly "real" town of Abiquiu well before lunchtime, feeling the best I had in two days. I found the store and stocked up on everything, because I was pretty close to empty. Beyond my regular assortment of junk food, I even picked up a few local treats, including roasted pinion nuts and chili-flavored chips. The gas station had, much to my astonishment, a hot lunch counter. I ordered a chicken burger and fries, and ate it with an apple, orange, a pound of strawberries, and fresh milk yogurt. I was still hungry when I finished, so I bought a homemade brownie the size of my entire hand to eat for dessert.

Outside the store in Abiquiu, the air was choked with heat. The sun blazed high in the sky and I had to stand in the shade to apply my sunscreen and fill up my two bladders with nine liters of water. I knew I had a long, dry section of trail in front of me, and I did not want to take any chances with fluid.

"Damn, it's hot!" I said out loud as I turned away from town and pedaled up a loose, extremely dusty gravel road. Sweat gathered in large beads on my skin, dripping acidic sunscreen in my eyes and pouring down my arms and legs. I neglected to pull out my thermometer, so I didn't know the real temperature. It was likely in the low nineties, but to my northern blood, it felt like 110.

The massive lunch sat in my stomach like a brick. I filled the rest of my gut with water, every sip I could physically ingest, but I still felt like my stomach was leaching water and somehow not absorbing the food. The climb out of Abiquiu offered no relief. The town sat on the shoreline of a large regional river at 6,000 feet elevation. Within thirty miles, my map promised, I'd be above 10,400 feet. And there was no real relief beyond the pass, no real descent, just climbing and dropping in steep spurts all the way to the next town, Cuba, fifty miles farther. My maps essentially promised me nearly endless climbing and no food services or reliable water sources for the next eighty miles. I braced for suffering as I spun slow rotations out of Abiquiu.

The heat was relentless. It hovered around me in the calm air, and I was moving slowly enough to feel its suffocating embrace. Still, I kept a steady pace, and forced water down my throat because I had a lot of it and knew I needed it. I crossed onto the Polvadera Mesa, where the road conditions deteriorated substantially. The official path was scarcely discernible from the surrounding terrain as it climbed a staircase of slate slabs, dusted generously by unconsolidated, slippery granules of sand and rutted by violent erosion. Even with the error margin provided by the doubletrack road, I struggled to find a line clear enough to allow me to stay on my bike for more than a hundred yards at a time. I just didn't have the power to hoist my front tire onto the rock slabs or wallow in the sand. Forward motion necessitated an infuriating pattern of walk, ride, wallow, walk, and ride. As I stumbled through another wallow, a wave of nausea washed over me.

I halted in my tracks and drew slow breaths of air, but the sensation was too powerful to ignore. I threw by bike into the sand and darted toward the woods, only making it twenty feet off the road before I doubled over and vomited the entire contents of my massive lunch. The puddle was speckled with different colors of food that had hardly digested. I staggered back to my bike and sat on the road for a while until my head stopped spinning and I could stand again.

"Well, that sucked," I said out loud. "That was a whole lot of calories to just lose like that."

I immediately blamed the heat for my afternoon sickness. Or maybe I just needed more water. I took a few delicate sips and resumed the jerky, difficult climb. I still felt vaguely sick to my stomach, but my plummeting energy level was the larger concern. After a few minutes, I decided I needed new calories. I pulled a king-sized Mounds bar out of my feedbag. It had melted to ninety-eight-percent liquid, so I drank the hot glop out of the package. Not ten minutes later, the powerful nausea hit me again. This time, I didn't even bother to wander very far off the road; I just jumped off my bike, turned my head and coated a small bush with a liquefied Mounds bar that looked very much the same going out as it did coming in.

"Crap," I thought as I waited for the hard shock of regurgitation to settle. "I must be sick."

I started to suspect I had food poisoning, and there wasn't much I could do about that. I let my head stop spinning and resumed pedaling uphill. As the climb dragged on, the sickness started to settle. The once powerful but infrequent waves of nausea became a heavy, constant pit in my gut. I tried to force down a few Sour Patch Kids, but even those didn't stay down long. For a while water seemed to stay with me, but eventually, after more than an hour without solid food, I started spewing clear fluid. I continued to climb. I didn't know why I kept climbing. My ability to reason was slipping.

Above 10,000 feet, I skirted the edge of a wide, barren ridge. I staggered on even the slightest hints of uneven ground, and pedaled like a reluctant child on a training bicycle, but mostly I walked. My head felt light and airy, almost enough to make up for the lead weights in my legs. I hadn't kept a single calorie down since the first time I threw up, thereby negating nearly every calorie I had eaten that day. Near the crest of the ridge, my energy levels had plummeted to new lows. Black spots were starting to appear in my peripheral vision, and I felt only partially conscious.

A herd of cattle grazed along the high grassland, just above timberline. Although I was only about twenty-five miles from Abiquiu, I convinced myself I had just met the loneliest cattle herd in America.

"It must be strange for you, living all the way up here," I said to one dull-eyed heifer. "And you," I said to her calf. "What's it like growing up on the moon?"

I walked beside the herd, speaking to every single animal as I passed. "Do you know where I can find water up here?" I asked a big, black bull that had a murderous look in his eyes. "I'm worried I might be getting low on water."

He didn't answer, so I asked the next one. "Obviously, you guys have found water on this ridge. I just want a little I can pump for the night."

Then I actually lingered beside the cud-chewing bull for several seconds, half expecting an answer, when my muffled voice of reason squeaked, "Are you crazy? You're talking to cows!"

A small smile escaped my lips. I was feeling crazy. Beyond the frustratingly silent cows, the features of the ridge throbbed and undulated like a bad 1960s movie about drug trips. The sky was the deepest blue I had ever seen; the puffs of clouds were whiter than white. Even as my nearly anchored feet trudged along the ridgeline, I felt like I was floating through a bright, cheerful corner of outer space. "Ha! I don't think I can feel my legs," I called out to the cows and the blue emptiness beyond. "I'm flying!"

But I wasn't flying. I was barely crawling. And I was still coherent enough to know I was in a bad way. I stopped at the summit, wondering if I should really continue the fifty miles into Cuba with what I suspected was food poisoning but feared might be something much more serious, such as a giardia parasite. I knew I was having a difficult time even keeping water in my body, and because of this I faced dehydration that could quickly become serious. The descent back into Abiquiu, on the other hand, would be relatively fast, losing 4,000 feet in twenty-five miles. I could grab a room at the luxury hotel I had seen in town and wait until the bug worked its way through my system. But if I turned around, could I really expect to coax myself up that climb again? If I really turned around, wouldn't that effectively be the end?

I never really made a decision one way or the other. I just lingered on the summit for a few minutes, looking at my shoes, wondering if I was about to vomit again, and when I looked up, I was facing the road toward Cuba. So I went that way.

The summit, as the maps had promised me, offered no relief. I had barely descended 200 feet before the climb began anew, then dipped and climbed again, until I realized that all I was doing was skirting a parallel line just below the crest of the ridge, dropping and climbing steeply out of every minor drainage that cut vertically into the mountain. Over the first three short ascents, I made my best effort to pedal. But up the fourth climb, my legs stopped moving about halfway up the hill. I didn't decide to stop; it just happened. It was as though I commanded my muscles to go and they refused. I was completely out of gas.

I slumped off the bike and began to stagger, so drunk with exhaustion that I couldn't even walk directly up the road, but had to weave and dip like an inebriated bar hopper. I pushed the bike to the crest and coasted down a few hundred feet of elevation, only to meet a new pitch climbing up the seemingly endless mountain.

I walked a few steps and dropped to my knees. My vision spun in a dizzy stupor and I felt tears streaming down my cheeks. "Please don't make me climb anymore," I pleaded. My voice vibrated like that of a distraught child. "Please, please. I don't want to climb anymore."

But the mountain did not care, just as the cows had not cared and the dusty road of the Polvadera Mesa did not care. No one cared that I was sick and exhausted and descending into delirium. Part of me, perhaps the voice of rationality, wondered if I even really cared.

The terrain started to descend more than climb. The sun slipped behind a distance horizon. Evening fell. All of these details only vaguely registered in my mind, as my body had switched on the autopilot known as "survival mode." I no longer felt distress or drunkenness, or even much fatigue or sickness. I only knew vaguely that I had no power and definitely did not feel like consuming any food. But I knew I had to keep turning pedals, so that's what I did.

I came to a dirty green sedan parked right in the middle of the road. The sight of the car startled me, because I hadn't seen a single person or vehicle since shortly after I left Abiquiu, seven hours earlier. It didn't seem like the type of road such a vehicle should be driving on, either, strewn as it was with boulders and carved with ruts so deep that I couldn't negotiate my bicycle out of them. And sure enough, the front wheel of the sedan was stuck in one of those ruts, high-centered. There didn't seem to be anyone around. The car had been abandoned. Inside, I saw all the debris of a road trip gone awry. Clothing was strewn about the back seat, maps were torn open, and food wrappers littered the interior. But the only thing that registered in my feeble mind was the cooler in the front seat.

"There might be water in there!" I thought. Never mind that I still had several liters of liquid on my back that I had been carrying since Abiquiu, and never mind that the reason I was so thirsty was not because I was out of water but because I couldn't drink any without vomiting. All I understood was that my body needed water, and coolers held water. I wrenched open the sedan's partially stuck front door, knelt on the driver's seat and opened the lid.

Inside the cooler was a green and black soup of the foulest food rot I had ever encountered. A thick vapor of curdled milk, lettuce slime and moldy lunch meat blasted me in the face with all the horror of death. I slammed the lid shut but the damage had been done. I backed out of the vehicle, retching and dry-heaving until I finally vomited for the seventh time that day. An important lesson had been administered that evening — a universal lesson about the consequences of trespassing, the futility of hope, and the impermanence of every facet of civilization. However, I was too far gone to learn anything beyond regret for the tiny puddle of clear liquid at my feet.

By dark, my body's lowest gear started to sputter. Even survival mode was failing; I had tapped every known and unknown well of energy, and I had nowhere deeper to dig. I had no choice but to stop and sleep. I pulled off the road into a nondescript meadow beneath a tall canopy of ponderosa trees. I shuffled through my bike bags until I found the headlamp, bivy sack, and sleeping bag, not remembering where they were stored even though there were in the same place they had been every other night of the trip. I pulled out a Snickers bar and set it in my helmet next to my bag, hoping that sometime in the night I'd find the courage to eat it. I wriggled into my sleeping bag and immediately fell asleep, having made no decision or effort to do so.

Hours passed in an instant. I awoke to muted dawn and the patter of raindrops on top of my open bivy sack. The most horrible hangover headache I had ever experienced pounded beneath my skull. I groaned and zipped up the bivy sack, listening to the rain hit harder.

The voice of rationality spoke first. "If you let it rain on you for too long, you're going to get all of your gear wet."

"Ugh," I grumbled back. "I feel like I just want to roll over and die."

I turned over on my stomach, which was still heavy with a pit of nausea. My head throbbed. I wondered whether I'd even be able to summon the energy to sit up.

"Crap, I really do have giardia," I thought. "I'm not going to be able to get up and I'm going to die of giardia in the middle of nowhere, New Mexico. They'll find my mummified body in a few years and they'll rule it a suicide."

I turned back over on my back. The rain fell harder. My stomach gurgled. But as more consciousness crept into my brain, I began to suspect that the discomfort I was feeling wasn't the oppression of food poisoning. I was just really thirsty — and really, really hungry.

I sat up in a jolt of discovery and wrestled out of my bivy sack. Inexplicably during the night, I had put on my raincoat but torn off my shorts. Forgetting about the Snickers bar in my bike helmet, I stumbled toward my bike in my underwear and bare feet. I tore open my feedbag and reached for the first thing I found, a Nutrageous bar. It suddenly sounded like the most delicious morsel of food ever invented. I tore open the package and gulped it down. The cold clumps of candy tumbled down my throat and filled me with a renewed sense of health. I found a brownie and devoured it, followed by a package of nuts and moist handfuls of Sour Patch Kids. My hands seemed to involuntarily grab at the junk food, allowing me neither the time to decide what to consume nor the ability to stop it. I ate with blind urgency, shoveling in food like a starving wolverine. The voice of reason just laughed with a mixture of bemusement and embarrassment about the uncivilized way in which I was replenishing my badly depleted body.

Eventually, my mouth became so dry that I could not swallow, so I reached for my water valve and took large, delicious gulps, savoring the water even more than I had the food. As I drank, I moved around my makeshift campsite, picking up the miscellaneous objects that had been strewn like an unkempt yard sale around my bicycle. During my apathetic delirium the night before, I had managed to disgorge most of the contents of my bicycle bags all over the ground, and then left them out all night at the mercy of animals and rain. Luckily, nothing seemed to be missing, and after about fifteen anxious minutes, I managed to put the whole damp mess back in order. With a couple thousand calories in my belly, I felt a blast of exuberance about my miraculous turnaround. In reality, my skull still throbbed beneath a pounding headache and I was still deeply dehydrated, but I felt like I had ricocheted off my own deathbed.

Low fog draped the trees and veiled the grassy hillsides. Steady rain continued to drizzle from the pall. I put on all of my extra layers — hat, fleece jacket, vapor barrier socks and rain gear. I was annoyed that I still needed to dress so heavily in New Mexico. Except for a few warm hours in Wyoming and the day before in Abiquiu, the entirety of my Great Divide experience had been wet and cool, not unlike my year-round existence in Juneau. I hadn't yet decided whether the relative lack of heat was a blessing or a curse.

My renewed energy felt strong but my legs didn't agree; still wobbly and weak, they seemed half detached from my body as I coaxed them up the first climb. I kept my head down, blinking against a steady stream of grit and puddle water. Unlike the wild thunderstorms I had encountered elsewhere on the Divide, the storm over my head was bland and thick, apparently settled for a long deluge. Luckily, I had already conquered the most primitive section of the long road, and the surface under my wheels was muddy but generously coated with gravel that provided a bridge over the goo.

It was still before 7 a.m. when I started to see the cars. At first, there were just a few parked in grassy meadows. But after a mile, they sat bumper to bumper along both sides of the narrow road. There were dozens of cars, and then hundreds.

"What's going on here?" I wondered. "I guess it's the Fourth of July weekend. But there's nothing nearby. Even Santa Fe is a long way from here. How is this random place attracting so many campers?"

The strangest part about the line of cars was that no camping gear accompanied them. I didn't see tents or tarps or even sleeping bags strewn in the fields alongside the road. Another mile went by. The vehicles devolved from four-wheel-drive trucks and boring sedans to ancient Buicks, spray-painted Volkswagen vans, and decommissioned school buses decorated with tie-dye curtains. Some of the vehicles had made grievous parallel parking errors and ended up twenty feet down the steep embankment.

The first people I saw were curled up in cotton quilts right on the grass, unconscious and drenched thoroughly in the rain. Then I saw big tents mostly hidden in the woods below. Signs were hand-painted with advertisements such as "Breakfast Bus," "Raw is Law," and "Policemen are your friends." At seven in the morning, only a sparse scattering of people milled about, but the meadows were littered with pots and toilet paper and Styrofoam containers. White plastic bags were stacked in large piles along the road. Dreadlocked hippies stood near the garbage piles with their thumbs out, their own vehicles no doubt parked several miles down the road. They yelled at me to "Get high on life" as I passed, which I found ironic, since I was the one moving down the road while they stood still.

I slowed next to a stocky young man wearing a brown wool poncho and walking a sickly mutt. "What's going on around here?" I asked, although I had already guessed the answer.

"Dude, don't you know?" he said in a slow, raspy drawl stolen right out of the stoner cliché handbook. "It's the Rainbow Gathering. There are, like, ten thousand people all here together. It's amazing, man."

"How long is it going on for?" I asked.

"I think a few more days," he said. "I just got here yesterday. Maybe it was the day before. But, man, I never want to leave. It's beautiful here. Incredible."

I looked up. Carson National Forest certainly wasn't an unattractive place, with its green, rounded mountains, grassy meadows and tall spruce trees. But it wasn't even close to the most incredible place I had seen so far in New Mexico, let alone the rest of the Rocky Mountains. And the Rainbow Family, with its miles of derelict vehicles, mounds of trash, and passed-out hippies huddled in the rain, definitely wasn't doing the forest any favors. I wondered what they even did here all week long, besides eat organic raw vegan food and smoke copious amounts of marijuana. The idea of a few thousand people descending on this pretty if uninspiring piece of public land to live out delusions of peace and love through thinly veiled consumerism and open self gratification, trashing the forest in the process, made me feel both angry and sad. And in my state, those emotions were impossible to hide.

"Do you want me to show you where it's all going down?" the man in the poncho asked.

"No," I said quickly. "No, I just want to get out of here. How much farther to Cuba?"

He shook his head. "Cuba? Like the country?"

"It's the next town over, oh, never mind," I said, doing nothing to muzzle my disgust. Obviously, this guy drove through Cuba to get to the Rainbow Gathering, but never even bothered to take note of the town. He probably came from some gray industrial city in central California and worked at Burger King when he wasn't downloading Grateful Dead bootlegs. I was ashamed of the way I was judging him, looking down at him from the lofty perch of my bicycle seat, but I couldn't help myself. I had my own hippy background, going to Phish shows in high school, attending tree plantings, and joining in the environmental club in college. I had been a longtime advocate of wilderness and conservationism. But in the Rainbow Gathering, all I could see were the abandoned vehicles in the embankment, the piles of trash, and hitchhiking hippies unwilling to walk just a few miles down a road. I wanted to tell all of them to get a bicycle, and try using it to go somewhere, somewhere real, somewhere true, somewhere they discovered for themselves. Couldn't they see that this place was so contrived? That it was just a strip of public forest that had been effectively condemned by the hippy bureaucracy in a misguided search for some kind of Mecca? But I suspected that most of them didn't care about the ideals; they just wanted to get high.

I took off without saying goodbye, smiling at the thought that poncho guy was probably thinking, "That bicycle chick was a real bitch." But I didn't really care. He had no idea where I had been and where I was going, and I had no business trying to enlighten him. My only prerogative was to flee that awkward place before the rest of the hippies woke up and caused horrible traffic jams.

Several more miles of vehicles passed before I was truly alone again. The road wound around the mountainside over the Rio de las Vacas. Below, lush green hills rippled across a broad valley. Tufts of fog draped the dense forest, whose colors and details softened behind a screen of falling rain. The scene was so startlingly similar to the coastal islands of Southeast Alaska that I felt instantly homesick — for perhaps the first time on the Divide. I wasn't homesick for my friends and family in Utah, but for my faraway home in Juneau. I imagined I was descending down a broad trail on Douglas Island, and felt comforted by the image of my rainforest home. The fact that I was pedaling deep into the desert Southwest, thousands of miles from Douglas Island and continuing to travel farther away, was a harsh truth momentarily lost to dreams.

I reached Cuba at 9 a.m., having pedaled thirty miles in two and a half hours. I was still beyond ravenous. I had snacked on the way into town and raided the nearest 7-Eleven while I waited for Subway to open. The day's calories were already approaching 3,000 and I had yet to eat "second breakfast." But, as of yet, none of that food had threatened to come back up. I couldn't decide whether I had eaten something bad in Abiquiu, drank too much water, or reacted badly to that one spot of heat. But I finally felt comfortable ruling out giardia or a virus or some other race-ending malady. I felt cured.

Even though it was only 10:30 a.m. by the time I rode out of town, I was apprehensive about leaving Cuba that day. The next section of route traversed 125 miles of Navajo Indian reservation. Race veterans had warned me that under no circumstances should I camp on "The Rez." It was not only illegal, they told me, but dangerous as well. Since I was a woman, they continued, I should probably consider not stopping at all, lest I surely be harassed by the poor and unfriendly denizens of The Rez. "They don't like any white people," they warned me, "especially white people on bikes." The first town off the reservation was Grants, and I would have no choice but to reach it that night. The road was all paved and relatively flat, but 125 miles was still a long way to pedal in less than a full day, and I still wasn't a hundred percent certain about my recovery.

Encouragingly, food continued to slide down easily and settle happily in my stomach. Even after a second breakfast of a foot-long turkey sandwich, chips, and a brownie, I was munching on Sour Patch Kids less than an hour later. I had become a calorie-devouring machine, and as the energy accumulated, my legs managed to attach themselves back to my body and commenced eating up the miles.

Highway 197 traversed the expansive Chaco Mesa, an open desert rippled with ochre bluffs and arroyos, and dotted with tiny flowers and bushes, none higher than my hips. It was a new world after the thick forests of northern

New Mexico, but maintained a decidedly old-world feel. Adobe structures scattered over the mesa with no obvious attachment to towns, streets, or property of any sort. Vicious dogs darted out from the seeming middle of the desert to snap at my ankles. The occasional white truck rumbled down the pavement, but traffic was sparse at best.

I had made plans to stop at a store indicated on my map, but when I reached mile 48, I realized the supposed store wasn't a store at all, but a laundromat. It was the only commercial structure in the entire area, and it just happened to be a place that was not likely to have food or supplies. A dozen vehicles were parked out front and I expected it to be full of reportedly unfriendly Navajos. Still, even though I'd had a hankering for an ice cream sandwich, the only thing I truly needed was water. It was worth the risk.

The laundromat buzzed with activity on a Friday afternoon. Children darted around the washing machines as women leaned against dryers, chatting in both English and Navajo while they folded clothes. As I had suspected, mine seemed to be the sole white face in the entire building, a white face attached to embarrassingly pale legs and body-hugging Lycra bicycle clothing. But I hadn't even walked all the way in the door when a tiny old man, nearly a head shorter than me, walked up and beamed with a wide, toothless grin.

"Hello," he said. "You need something?"

"Um, yeah," I said. "Is there a place in here where I can get some water?"

He pointed to a bathroom. "In there," he said. "But we have pop machine over that side. You can get a Coke. It's much better."

"Thanks," I said. "Sounds kinda good."

The old man walked with me over to the machine and pulled out a handful of quarters. He moved to drop some in the coin slot before I held up my hand. "Thanks, um, but I have change."

"It's no problem," he said, moving to drop the quarters in again.

"Really," I said, my face flushed with bemusement and embarrassment. "I'd like to buy my own soda." I rummaged around quickly in my wallet and pulled out a bill.

As I sipped a can of Cherry Coke I had just barely stopped the man from buying, he said, "So you are traveling on a bicycle? Where are you coming from?"

"I started in Cuba," I said, thinking it pointless to mention I had actually started the day thirty miles north of Cuba.

"Oh, very good," he said. "And where are you going?"

"I think to Grants," I said. "I'm going to try to make it to Grants."

"No," the man said and shook his head. "No, it's too far. You go to White Horse. I have son there. You go stay with him."

"Thanks," I said. "But I'd really like to make it to Grants today. I think I can do it."

"Oh ho!" he exclaimed. "So you super bike woman! I see. Okay, that's good."

As he laughed, a few of the women approached me and asked me where I lived and where I started bicycling. I told them I lived in Alaska but started in Canada, and that I would end in Mexico. They smiled vaguely, possibly because all of those places were too distant to comprehend. A little girl walked up and gave me the white sheet of paper she had been coloring. I thanked her, folding up the paper and placing it in my backpack. The unconditional caring I had come to know so well on the Divide surrounded this simple laundromat. I smiled. So much for unfriendliness on The Rez.

As I continued south, five different people stopped to offer me water or ask if I needed directions. One woman offered to let me have a sip of her half-empty bottle of Gatorade, an amusing gesture I was almost reluctant to decline.

The rain had stopped before I left Cuba, but all day long, spotty clouds hung over the desert and the temperature stayed mercifully cool, right around seventy degrees — almost unheard of on the Chaco Mesa in July. One of the women I chatted with at the laundromat had even complained about it being "cold," and I realized I had been spared a full day of typical but oppressive heat. It was a big reward for the small price I paid by riding through two hours of rain in the morning, and I was grateful for it.

Thunderstorms built over the distant mountains as I approached Grants. About thirty miles from town, the wind picked up speed and blew directly in my face — twenty miles per hour of backward force. It was a small hit to take in an unbelievably lucky day, but I took it hard, despairing about the significantly increased difficulty in each pedal stroke. I tried to swallow my anxiety about the lightening that exploded many miles in the distance all around me. Still, the storm never planted itself directly overhead, and by the time I plodded in the dull twilight toward the city lights, the lightning-streaked clouds had were disappearing to the east.

I pedaled through town on Route 66, alongside the dilapidated remnants of the glamorous travel culture that the highway once embodied. Boarded-up diners, darkened service stations, and run-down hotels welcomed me to town, the only place on the Great Divide more depressed and therefore more depressing than Rawlins. These conditions always seemed to happen near Interstates, where shiny new truck stops and Wal-marts lined the freeway and historic downtowns lingered in an open state of decay. I checked into a twenty-eight-dollar hotel room before it was even fully dark outside with 155 miles behind me, my farthest day on the Divide.

Chapter Twenty Two
Independence Day

Page 297: A rainbow touches down amid dark storm clouds on the San Agustin Plains in New Mexico.
Page 298: The Pie-O-Neer Cafe in Pie Town, New Mexico.

Never underestimate the disorienting power of pedaling.

On its surface, human-powered motion seems rather straightforward, slow and steady. Because of its unhurried pace, observations from a bicycle are thorough, sometimes excruciatingly thorough. Tiny contours in geography, subtle details in plant life, and changes in weather are all scrutinized and analyzed. Even as fatigue and malaise begin to soften the edges of intellect, cyclists must still observe their environments. Bicycling demands constant if involuntary attention to detail, even when the mind loses focus. In spite of this, or maybe because of it, a cyclists' line of thought tends to shift between confusion and reassessment. Cyclists find themselves pondering, "Where did this canyon start?" or, "When did the forest become desert?" or, "Why in the world is there a river across this trail?" before accepting their new reality without ever really understanding how or why it changed.

Thus was my state of mind as I flipped through the TV channels inside my hotel room in Grants, New Mexico, searching for the weather report. The smiling visage of my state's governor, Sarah Palin, flickered on the television screen, so I stopped to watch. Through gasps of disbelief, I learned that this ambitious politician had resigned from her position as governor of Alaska to pursue a vague retirement that sounded like doing a lot of nothing. Not only was she inexplicably quitting her job, but the announcement that she would no longer head up a small state of 650,000 people somehow mattered enough to the whole world to land breaking coverage on a major cable news channel. I was already starting to believe I lived in the Twilight Zone, so this small shot of reality from the outside world only bemused my numb sensibilities.

"The whole damn world's going nuts," I laughed. I forgot all about the only news that really mattered to my existence as a cyclist — the weather report — and tuned intently into a stream of useless gossip and commentary. After about twenty minutes of Sarah Palin, my cell phone rang.

"Hey Jill. Congrats on making it to Grants," John said on the other line.

"Thanks," I muttered, a little stunned to hear his voice.

"From watching your SPOT, it looked like you slowed down quite a bit during the second half of yesterday, but you really made up for it today. That was what, 150 miles?

"155," I said.

"That's really awesome," he said. "How are things out there?

"Pretty much exactly the same as when you left," I said. "Cold, wet, and stormy."

"Really? Cold? The last time I was in Grants, it was 106 degrees."

"I'd be surprised if it broke seventy today," I said. "It rained for three hours straight this morning. It was downright Juneau-esque."

"That is strange. So how are you doing?" John asked.

"Good," I said. "Well, I was crazy sick yesterday. Parasite or food poisoning or twenty-four-hour stomach flu, I don't know which. I tried to figure out what bad food I could have possibly eaten in Abiquiu. I think it might have been the yogurt. Anyway, I threw up several times. I had no energy, no ability to climb. I walked up every single hill. It was miserable."

"You mentioned in your call-in you weren't feeling well," John said. "I'm sorry. I know that can be rough out there."

"Yeah, rough doesn't quite cover it," I said.

"I know you have a lot to do and don't have much time to talk on the phone, but I thought I'd call you to talk about the next four days."

"Four?" I said. "I was thinking three. Tops."

"Well, yes," John said. "It's only a bit over 400 miles to the border. Three is definitely doable. I just thought you might want to play it conservative because of the weather and the limited supplies along the way. I just checked the radar and saw that massive storm right over you."

"Massive storm? It's not even cloudy here," I said. "I just looked out my window. I can see stars."

"Maybe it's south of you," John said. "Either way, it's right in your path, and that probably means a really muddy road into Pie Town. It's going to take you a while to get there, probably most of the day. But they have a nice hostel in town. You probably want to plan on staying there tomorrow."

"Really?" I said skeptically. "I was hoping to get south of Pie Town tomorrow."

"To where?" John asked.

"To wherever I can," I said, starting to feel an old frustration bubbling up. "That's half the fun of riding this thing."

"Well, also remember that it's the Fourth of July tomorrow," John said. "Those two Pie Town restaurants keep really strange hours, and the chances that they're open on a Saturday that's also a holiday are almost zero. I wouldn't count on them for any food. Get everything you need in Grants."

"I was already planning to," I said in a tone as reproachful as a scolded child's. I felt that John was being condescending or at the very least thought of me as a clueless novice after all this time, even though I had covered more distance on my own than I did with him. Still, I had to admit that I was really hoping Pie Town would at least have drinking water, so his advice was useful in that regard.

"Well, if you do decide to stop in Pie Town, the next stop is a private ranch near Wall Lake. I'll give you the number. Tell them my name when you get there. They will definitely give you a room."

"Thanks, John, but really, I'll be fine," I said, not hiding my exasperation. I knew he was trying to be helpful. Still, he was making a completely unveiled attempt to wield the reins of my Tour Divide effort from afar, for whatever reason. And for whatever reason of my own, I vowed — even if I had to swim through mud until midnight — that I would pedal past Pie Town on Saturday.

A few seconds of silence pierced the unspoken tension. "I've watched what you've been doing, but I've wondered how you've been feeling," he said after the long pause. "It's really good to hear your voice again."

In a rush of self-consciousness, I thought about my bike and body troubles in the Great Divide Basin, being stranded in Rawlins, my crash outside Steamboat Springs, Pete's accident, and my exhausting battles with New Mexico's weather and mud. A lifetime had passed since John and I last spoke.

"I've felt all right. How have you been?" I asked. "How's your knee?"

"It's fine," John said. "I'm already back into training. My short Divide race did nothing to slow that down. Knee's getting stronger, too. But I miss touring with you. I still come home from training rides and take showers wearing all of my clothes, just to relive the old glory days on the Great Divide."

"Ha!" I said. "I hate the clothing showers. That's one thing I won't miss. I found the guest washer-dryer at this motel and locked myself inside the room naked just so I could wash every piece of clothing I had, even my rain gear."

"Did you really?" John asked.

"Actually," I said, "I snuck out with a towel on. A half hour is a long time to sit naked in a public laundry room."

John laughed weakly. "Well, I don't want to keep you," he said. "But please call me if you need anything at all."

"I will." I hung up the phone wondering what it all meant — John, Sarah Palin, the reasons why these flickers of the real world might be reaching out to me, and the reasons why I just wanted to shut them out. I turned off the TV before I found the Weather Channel, confident John's radar observation was accurate. I felt despondent. I took a sleeping pill and slipped into oblivion, only a single notch deeper than my usual disorientation.

On July Fourth, I woke up to brilliant sunlight and crisp air. It tasted like morning in the early fall, with hints of seltzer and wood smoke. I stocked up at the last gas station in town and checked my maps for the phone number to the Pie-O-Neer café in Pie Town. I had already accepted that clinging to the hope it would be open on a national holiday was a futile at best, but I had heard entire legends formed around the pie in Pie Town. That one stop was likely my only shot at human interaction in the next 300 miles, so even a miniscule chance was certainly worth a try. Plus, I would need to restock my drinking water somehow.

At 8:30 a.m., an answering machine informed me that the café was open Wednesday through Saturday, 11 a.m. to 4 p.m. They said nothing about July Fourth specifically, but at least there was a chance they were open that day. Still, even my best-case scenarios made reaching it seem impossible. Pie Town was eighty miles away. Even if there was no mud on the road, an impossible-sounding prospect in itself, my chances of pedaling that far in just over seven hours were unlikely at best. The answering machine beeped, and without planning to, I suddenly launched into a pleading message:

"Hi, my name is Jill. I'm traveling through town on a bicycle with the Tour Divide. Perhaps you've seen other bikers come through. Anyway, I'm calling from Grants. It's 8:30 a.m. Saturday. I'm going to try to make it there by four, but it's eighty miles and with the mud, well, it's not very likely I'll be there before you close. I was wondering if you could leave out some kind of lunch, maybe a sandwich or something, and a piece of pie, and a gallon of water, along with a check, and I'll leave cash. I don't even care what it is. I pretty much just need calories at this point, calories and water. Please. I'm good for it. I have a lot of cash. My name is Jill Homer."

I set out with determination to make the 4 p.m. deadline, come what may. As the derelict highway buildings of Grants faded behind me, a bubble of emotion expanded inside my gut. I felt a strong mixture of gratitude and love, as well as loneliness, fear, and despair. I couldn't discern where this flood of feelings was coming from. My situation was positive, even pleasant. I was rested, well-fed, and riding on pavement within sight of a town full of people. Despite these comforts, tears started to trickle down my cheeks, which erupted into streams, which erupted into open sobbing, complete with flowing snot and phlegmy gulps of air.

Whenever endurance cyclists embark on long races, people often ask us afterward about the specific moment when we first realized we could actually finish what we had set out to do. I always dismissed this question as unanswerable and misleading. To some, I would say that I knew I would eventually finish the Tour Divide when I was all the way back in Montana. To others, I admitted that I wasn't even sure when I made the final right turn sixty-five miles from the border. But if I am truly honest with myself, those minutes I spent sobbing on my way out of Grants stand apart as a defining moment of clarity.

As my tears began to slow and my gasps became softer, I pleaded an open prayer to entities I also felt were indefinable — to my inner strength, to my resolve, the desert, the open road and the powers that be. "Please be with me. Please stay with me. Please help me get through this." Something about leaving Grants told me that, barring breakdown or disaster, I was going to finish the Tour Divide. Since I had no control over breakdown or disaster, I pleaded for help from anything that might.

The powers that be nodded benevolently and swept me along the smooth corridor of Highway 117. The rugged but sheer cliffs of El Malpais National Monument cast the pavement in cool shadow. After thirty-eight miles, the route joined the washboard ruts of a wide county road. The jittery corduroy soon faded into smooth but soft clay. The area had indeed been pummeled by thunderstorms the night before; blood-colored puddles glistened in the road's many dips and potholes. As I rode, my wheels kicked up large clumps of red mud. Still, beneath the late morning sunlight, the mud had hardened just enough to roll into balls and fling away rather than stick to my bike.

"Think light, be light," I chanted, as though sheer force of will could reduce my weight and keep my wheels floating over the jelly-like layers of mud. Atop a paper-thin veneer of solidified clay, I pedaled apprehensively but quickly, coming close to sinking into the soft mud that undulated beneath my tires, but never quite breaking through the dry layer. I smiled at the knowledge that if I had passed through the same area just a few hours earlier, I would have been mired in wet sludge. Every once in a while, the universe rewards late risers.

Just after 2 p.m., after covering nearly eighty miles in five and a half hours, I strode triumphantly into the open doors of the Pie-O-Neer café. The single-room restaurant was set up modestly with modern tables and old Western art. A guitarist and bassist strummed acoustic country ballads as couples chatted softly over heaping plates of pie. A woman wearing a ruffled apron rushed out from behind the counter and threw her arms around me in an enthusiastic hug. "You made it!" she exclaimed. "I can't believe you made it!"

"I made it," I said, smiling widely.

The guitarist had just finished a cover of Johnny Cash's "Long Black Veil." "So you're Jill?" he asked. I nodded. "We did not think you'd make it here until late tonight," he continued. "It rained all through the night last night, just poured. I knew that road was gone. I sometimes take my horses out there and I know how bad it can get. Even they can't get through the mud sometimes. We thought you'd be stuck in it."

"I thought so, too," I said. "But it hardened up in the sun. I got lucky."

"Well, anyway, congratulations on getting here from Grants in just a few hours. That's some incredible riding."

The woman in the apron nodded. "You should have seen Matt Lee when he came through. It was late but I let him in the door. It had been raining hard and Matt was covered in mud. He had this crazy look in his eyes and he just fell in the door mumbling, 'I need food.' I said, 'I know you need food but you're not coming in here until you clean off that mud.' I practically had to push him back out the door. I thought, 'This can't be healthy.'"

I laughed. I was about to launch into my "Here in mid-pack, we have more fun" speech when she grabbed my shoulders and rushed me to a nearby table. "But you must be starving, riding all the way from Grants," she said. "What do you want to eat?"

"Um, what do you have?" I asked.

"Well, we don't have much. The menu's over there on the wall."

Before I even looked at it, I asked, "Do you have salad?"

"Well, I don't have salad, but I have some spinach and tomatoes and other veggies in the fridge. Tell you what, I'll make you one."

"That would be awesome," I said.

"And our special today is spinach quesadilla with fresh salsa. We also have a tomato vegetable soup."

"Those sound amazing, too," I said. "I'll have them both. And salad."

"Do you want something to drink?"

"Um ..." I wavered. I had already ordered three meals.

"Come on, the other Tour Divide guys were just knocking pops back faster than I could replenish them. What do you want?"

"Do you have Pepsi?" I asked.

"Of course," she said. "And you can't leave here without trying a slice of pie."

"Of course I can't." I took a lingering look at the back wall, lined from end to end with towering desserts. "Um, I'll try the coconut cream."

"Good choice," she said. "That one won an award last month from a national magazine."

As I waited for my mountain of fresh food, the guitarist asked me if I had any requests. I couldn't think of many country tunes I even knew, so I requested more Johnny Cash —"Ring of Fire." I imagined riding south toward the desert regions of the Great Divide as he sang, "I fell in to a burning ring of fire; I fell down, down, down and the flames went higher."

As promised, the woman served up cans of Pepsi faster than I could knock them back, and brought me plate after plate of food, hot and fresh and brimming with all the real nutrition I had scarcely known in three weeks of a diet heavy on junk food from gas stations and greasy spoon diners. The woman asked me how my lunch was. "You have no idea how replenishing it is to eat healthy for a change," I said. "If all Americans could feel this way after eating a spinach salad, McDonalds would go out of business. Which would be awesome, because then people like me could actually find healthy food to eat on the Great Divide."

The woman laughed. She asked me about the trail prior to Grants and I told her about how surprisingly remote New Mexico had been. A man wearing a trucker's cap turned from the next table over and launched into a stern warning about the dangers of New Mexico's backcountry. "There are cougars that hunt people," he said ominously. "I hope you have protection."

I pointed to the can of bear spray I had been carrying since Canada and had never even come close to discharging, unless I counted the time I pointed it at the vicious dogs of Vallecitos. "I'm from Alaska," I said. "So I'm well versed in the defense against predators thing." I wanted to tell him that I was far more afraid of mud and lightning, of fatigue and bad judgment, of loneliness and fear itself, but it seemed pointless to argue about the most pressing dangers of the Divide.

I spent much longer in Pie Town than I had intended, basking in the warmth of small-town friendliness and scraping up the last remnants of whipped cream from my pie plate. I was so full that I had difficulty breathing normally, but couldn't remember ever feeling more satisfied. I sat back in my wooden chair and listened to the country band croon about an unhurried life I had all but forgotten.

In the late afternoon, the woman in the apron and guys in the band walked outside to see me off. "It's just about closing time and we're all headed to the lake," she said. "But you have a great ride, and don't hesitate to come back when you're through these parts again. Happy Independence Day!"

"You too," I said, shaking all of their hands. "Thanks for making the best lunch in the entire span of the Rocky Mountains."

I left Pie Town at 4 p.m. into a brand new day. I felt like I was just waking up from a restful sleep, even though I had already pedaled eighty miles that day. "Someday," I thought, "I'm going to be a veteran of this race and people will ask me the secret to success. I'm going to answer, 'human kindness.'"

The roller-coaster terrain crossed the Continental Divide twice. I pedaled past ranches until the valley narrowed into a canyon. Large, triangle-shaped mountains loomed over me once again. The remote road intersected with an abandoned town site, a centuries-old Spanish mission. I got off my bike and explored the eerie remnants of a slab and mortar church, peering into the cracks of boarded windows and gazing up at a hollow bell tower.

Just beyond the town site, I entered Gila National Forest. My maps informed me: "Camping OK next 14 miles." I pedaled beneath gnarled and grand juniper trees, rose back into the ponderosa forest, and crested the Continental Divide once again at a spectacular overlook of the San Agustin Plains below. I could see thunderstorms building over the distant mountains beyond the valley. It was still early in the evening. "If I don't stop near here," I thought, "I'll have to pedal all the way through that valley before I'm back in a spot where I can camp." But I was feeling too incredible to stop. I launched into a gleeful descent toward the darkening sky.

The Forest Service road bisected a remote state highway and crossed onto a country road sparsely lined with private ranches. An occasional ranch house broke the monotony of the sagebrush plains, but for the most part I was wholly alone in sweepingly open space. The wind blew briskly at my side, whipping around and changing directions intermittently as booms of thunder clattered across the desert.

The thunderstorm I had seen hanging over the horizon began to close in. The bulk of the storm seemed to be moving the same direction I was, but I was approaching the dark clouds faster than they were streaming away. I glanced over my shoulder and noticed another storm approaching from behind. Sheets of rain hung like curtains beneath the black ceiling, and frequent flashes of lightning tore through the darkness.

A primal sense of entrapment gripped my core. My heart pounded. I was pedaling in a tiny window of calm, chasing one violent storm even as another chased me. If I pedaled too quickly, I would catch the first storm. If I pedaled too slowly, I would be caught by the second storm. I shivered at the prospect of both scenarios, and vowed to do everything in my cycling power to hover in the hurricane's eye.

Shortly after I made this decision, I heard a sickeningly loud zipping sound shoot out from the back of my bike. The rear tire became more and more bouncy and sluggish until I had no choice but to stop and deal with the flat.

I had been using "Slime" inner tubes, which were filled with green sealant intended to block any punctures in the tube. They had worked beautifully for the duration of the Divide, and I had yet to spring a leak that wasn't quickly blocked, requiring only a few refresher hits from my air pump. This was the first time a tire had gone completely flat. It was my rear tire, which required the loosening of the brake caliper before I could remove the wheel. A rear flat usually took me at least ten minutes to change when I was fresh, and as many as twenty when I was hurried and frustrated. I knew I did not have twenty minutes to spare before I would be caught directly beneath a barrage of lightning and rain. I did not even have five minutes.

"Be brave," I chanted through gulping breaths as I hopped off the bike. "Be strong."

A thick streak of green slime coated the down tube of the frame. I was sure all the sealant had leaked out and there was nothing left to fill the hole. But it was possible that I had just sprung a larger leak that took a while to clog. It seemed worth a try to pump up the tire rather than change the tube right away. The extra time it would take if it didn't work wasn't going to save me from the storm either way, but if that's all it took, there was still a chance I could outrun the air strike.

I breathed in and out with every stroke of the air pump, continuing to chant, "Be brave. Be strong." As I pumped, the sun slipped beneath the nearest mountains. The sky, already under siege, burst open in an explosion of crimson and gold light. The sudden blast of color reflected off the dark clouds in a contrast so bright that the entire sky shimmered. Where sunset's saturated light met the sheets of rain, broad rainbows swept over the desert. I counted five rainbows at one point, arched in wide spans that framed the phosphorescent clouds. And beneath the rainbow stage, steaks of lightning performed a violent ballet.

The scene did nothing to reduce the panic gurgling in my gut. But from where I sat in my shrinking window of calm, trying my best to breathe to the rhythm of my air pump, I knew that I was witnessing a moment of powerful beauty — beauty that was more even powerful than fear. I briefly closed my eyes and tried to absorb the gaping awe, primal wonder and sheer terror that nature was unleashing before me. I felt like I was clinging to the precipice between heaven and hell, and if I happened to fall, no matter which direction I went, I would be wholly absorbed forever.

I snapped my eyes back open and injected a few last shots of air into the tire. It was still fairly soft, but I didn't hear any more zipping sounds, and I thought there was a decent chance that it would hold the air. I hopped back on the saddle and spun wildly, trying to regain the distance I had lost on the second storm. I briefly thought about veering off on a ranch road and sprinting one or two miles to the nearest structure in search of shelter, but I fought the urge. "Be brave," I chanted. "Be strong."

The spectacular light of the sunset lingered much longer than I even thought possible, as though it, like me, was afraid to fade into the darker regions of eternity. It didn't take long to catch the aftermath of the first storm. The road was coated in wet mud and two-inch-deep puddles, but the sky overhead remained mercifully dry. The second storm slowed its advance and started to veer toward the east. As it changed its course, the front storm followed. My own route turned west and began climbing back into the mountains. When I reached the mouth of a canyon, I stopped one last time to look out over the plains of San Agustin. Sunset's crimson and orange flames were almost snuffed out, except for thin, blood-colored streaks that still bordered the horizon. Lightning continued to pierce the purple twilight, followed closely by booms of thunder. As I watched the storm march east, I noticed tiny blue flashes of light erupting from the northern horizon. They confused me at first — they were too low to be lightning, but too large and sporadic to be light from a ranch house. I squinted and realized they were fireworks, exploding over a ranch at least twenty miles distant.

"Oh yeah," I said out loud. "It's the Fourth of July." I paused to focus on the fireworks as tiny streams of blue light sparkled and then faded, over and over. All the while, flashes of lightning and booms of thunder nearly overwhelmed the tiny celebration. "Why don't they just look up and realize that the most spectacular show is going on in nature?" I wondered. Their efforts seemed so small and pathetic in a world that was so vast and so powerful. Humans were nothing out here, nothing at all.

Darkness encompassed me with the rising canyon. For a while I could still hear the thunder from a growing distance, and then only the wind and stillness. Rainwater coated the road and the air was moist and cool. The last tailing clouds from the storms were starting to break apart. A nearly full moon rose overhead, casting a ghostly glow on an assemblage of sandstone hoodoos that bent like petrified zombies in front of craggy cliffs. I rolled out my sleeping bag on the bare dirt beneath a cluster of ponderosa pines. Moonlight filtered through a canopy of needles. With what felt like a paltry sprinkling of effort and a heavy dose of grace, I had knocked out 140 miles in the fourteen hours behind me, with only 250 more to go.

"Thank you," I said in continuation of my morning prayer. "That was a good day."

Chapter Twenty Three
The Gila

Page 309: Storm clouds close in over the Gila National Forest.
Page 310: Jill Homer's bike bogs down in the mud on a clay road in the Gila National Forest, New Mexico.

I awoke to shrill chirping. A red-breasted robin hopped frantically between a several branches directly over my sleeping bag. Her cries echoed through the narrow canyon, still hidden from the sun in the early morning.

"What's the matter?" I said to the bird. "Did I camp beneath your nest?"

I wriggled out of my bivy sack and squinted through a tangle of pine branches. The sky was the color of broth, clear and golden. The robin dropped closer to me, chirping right over my head. "Okay," I said irritably. "I'm getting up."

As I pulled my sleeping bag away, I noticed a small clump of feathers that hadn't been more than a few inches from my head where I slept. I looked closer until I saw tiny feet, beak, a few droplets of blood and a grotesquely twisted neck. A baby bird. Its blood still glistened; it didn't look like it had been dead more than a few minutes.

The adult bird fluttered from branch to branch. Her high-pitched screeching rang in my ears. I jumped backward quickly, dragging my sleeping bag as I went. "I'm so sorry. I'm so, so sorry," I whispered.

As I backed away, the adult robin zeroed in closer to the baby but didn't land directly beside it. Her mournful cries continued to echo through the calm air. "What happened?" I blubbered. "Did it fall out of the nest? Did I scare it?" A well of sadness for the dead baby bird and its grief-stricken mother gurgled up from my gut. "I'm so sorry," I gulped. A few tears trickled down my cheeks. "I am so, so sorry."

I sat down in the grass next to my bike, sniffling and blinking as I rubbed my face. There was so much cruelty in our lives, so much suffering and pain, and we had no choice but to accept everything the world doled out to us in its indifference and chaos. Sandstone cliffs, carved into twisted and grotesque shapes by millennia of heavy erosion, cut an arching shadow over my camp. The robin's grief rang out in a harsh geography built on decay, and the overwhelming scope of it filled me with despair. I hung my head and let my tears fall in the grass, until the voice of rationality finally prodded me: "Do you realize you're crying over a bird?"

I shook my head a few times and tried to pull myself together. I wanted to put sufficiently numbing distance beyond the robin's haunting chirps, so I quickly packed up my bike and ate a brownie while I pedaled up the canyon. Calming silence returned to the air, but physically my body was as good as sprawled out beneath a cluster of ponderosas. Although I tended to feel sluggish most mornings, the effort of this morning mined a low-grade well of energy that was all but tapped out. Even with 600 calories of sugar in my gut, my legs turned as though held together my fraying threads. There was movement but no power, not even when I willed myself to push harder. Lactic acid coursing through my muscles told me I still had fibers to burn, but they were operating at minimum capacity.

"Ugh, rough go of it today," I said to myself. "I guess I have to pedal easy for a while until I get my legs back."

I crossed the Continental Divide twice on tiny bumps of an open plateau, then dropped into open grassland speckled with ranches. I watched a motorcyclist approach from a long distance. His wheels kicked up enviable clouds of dust, and the mosquito whine of his machine mocked my lack of power. He stopped beside me and killed the engine.

"Where you coming from?" he asked.

"I camped in the forest just a few miles back," I said.

"You headed to the Beaverhead Work Station?" he asked.

"Yeah, that direction," I said. "After that, I'm headed back into the Gila for a while. Eventually I'll get to Silver City."

"Silver City? You traveling south on the 150?"

"Possibly," I said. "I pretty much just go where these maps tell me to go."

He shook his head. "Not a good day for it. All this lightning set off a bunch of wildfires, and there are more storms on the way; probably going to bring a lot of rain. I won't even take my dirt bike down there when it's raining because I'd never get it out."

"So pretty bad mud ahead?" I asked. "Sticky mud?"

"Yeah," he said. "Not even passable with a motorcycle. If all you have is a pedal bike, then, well, good luck."

"I guess I'm going to need it," I said.

"Just remember that all of that is wilderness down there, or at least surrounded by wilderness," he said. "I wouldn't count on anyone being around to bail you out."

"I'll be fine," I said with a defeated sigh. "But thanks for the warning."

A few miles after the motorcyclist and I parted in opposite directions, I reached the Beaverhead Work Station. The ranger station was closed on a Sunday morning, but there was a soda machine outside. The plastic case advertising cold Dr. Pepper sent a rush of electric desire through my lukewarm blood. I rushed the machine, only to discover that it could take only coins, no bills. Half-panicked with disappointment and indecision because I didn't want to make a long stop but didn't want to forgo my only treat of the day, I tore through my backpack and bike bags, finding a nickel here, a dime there. I finally emptied the contents of my seat post bag — the hardest to repack — and came upon the mother lode, a quarter. With all of my possessions erratically strewn across the lawn, I walked triumphantly to the machine and fed it seventy-five cents.

I settled in the grass beneath the shade of a large willow tree, savoring tiny sips of Dr. Pepper and plotting my next move. According to my maps, I had about 200 miles left to travel to the Mexican border. It made the most sense to pedal the seventy-five miles to Silver City that day and knock out the remaining 125 on Monday. But it was still early in the day — about 10 a.m. And with the replenishing fuel of the soda, my legs were finally starting to feel a spark of life. Equations and times floated through my mind, and I felt a buzz of excitement when I realized that I had a shot — a real shot — at the overall Great Divide Race record.

The border-to-border record had been set by Trish Stevenson during the 2005 Great Divide Race, and stood at 21 days, 23 hours and 47 minutes. Stevenson was a pro mountain bike racer, and I never even dreamed of challenging her record. Plus, starting with the Tour Divide in Banff threw a wrench in that goal, anyway, because it gave me a 270-mile disadvantage, and I couldn't start the clock at the Montana border with fresh legs. But Tour Divide racers still clocked their border-to-border times separate from their race times, and I had crossed into the United States at 9:45 a.m. Sunday, June 14 — exactly three weeks before. Which meant if I could travel 200 miles in less than 23 hours and 30 minutes, I had a shot at shaving a few minutes off the overall record, on top of shattering the Banff-to-Antelope Wells record by five days.

My heart raced with the sudden prospect of tangible victory. Riding 200 miles in less than twenty-four hours would be an incredible feat in my physical state, but not outside the realm of possibility. For the most part I had been traveling faster than a ten-mile-per-hour average through central New Mexico, and the route ahead held a fair amount of pavement. I would of course have to pedal all through the night, thereby battling the sleep monster for an exponentially longer period of time than I had dealt with yet. But I would be mere hours from finishing the race; I could fight the sleep monster off with sheer excitement of just being done with the damn thing.

There was the small issue that I wasn't racing the Great Divide Race and had knowingly broken one of its rules — cell phone use. But even if the race organization refused to recognize my border-to-border time, I would know I had done it, and that would be enough.

The warnings of the motorcyclist, however, subdued my excitement. I knew that even if I gave it everything I had, the record was far from in the bag. Any amount of mud and walking would thwart my forward progress irrevocably, and there was nothing I could do about it if it happened. But I vowed to work as hard as I could through Sunday, and if I arrived in Silver City in good time and feeling even remotely energetic, I would keep going without sleep.

The wind kicked up as I climbed out of the Beaverhead Work Station. Amid the swirling clouds of dust, my GPS screen flicked off. I stopped the bike and emptied most of the contents of my frame bag, again, until I located spare batteries. With fresh batteries, it turned on for a few seconds before turning right back off.

"Oh no. Oh no, no, no," I muttered. "You can't be broken."

I removed the lithium batteries I carried solely for GPS use and inserted another pair of regular old alkaline batteries. Again, the screen flicked on for only a few seconds and then disappeared in a blip.

"No," I stammered. "Please, not here. Not now." It wasn't that I was solely dependent on my GPS. I still carried all of my maps, which contained all the directions I needed to guide me to the end. But GPS had been with me since the very beginning, since the Spray River trailhead in Banff, when I pushed the start button and reset the elevation profile while forty-one better-prepared racers took off without me. I left GPS on the entire time I was moving, as I climbed and descended, as I plodded beneath wind and rain, as I powered myself across a large chunk of the continent. We had always been together, and together we had logged 2,500 miles and more than 170,000 feet of climbing. GPS told me whether I was on the right track. It told me how far I had to travel to the nearest town, how many feet of elevation I had left to gain before cresting the next pass, and how many turns I had to ignore on the maze of dirt roads surrounding the actual route. It told me the names of the rivers I pedaled beside and the topography of the mountains I crossed. It was not just a constant companion. GPS was my friend. And there, in the rugged and wild Gila National Forest, GPS was my only friend. I did not want it to be broken.

But electronic devices don't have the same affinities toward affection as humans, and GPS's screen stubbornly stayed dark. I removed the device from its handlebar mount, wrapped it inside my hat, and cradled it in the womb of my frame bag. "OK, you've been jolted around a lot in the rain," I said. "You get a break for now. But please start working again soon. This is rugged country coming up. I don't want to get lost."

A few miles down the trail, a loud zipping sound spat all of the air out of my rear tire, again. I grudgingly pumped it back up to forty pounds per square inch. The sealant seemed to be sticking, but I could see solidified green gobs bubbling out of several sections of the tire. With closer inspection, I noticed a dark web of cracks had appeared throughout the sidewall, and that the tread had been worn to tiny nubbins. It appeared that the only thing holding that paper-thin strip of rubber together was the tube itself. Even the tiniest thorns were creating puncture wounds. I groaned. "Please don't melt down on me, too," I said to the tire.

Right on schedule with the passing of the noon hour, black-bottomed clouds rolled over the distant cliffs. The deeper I pressed into the Gila, the darker the sky became, until I could see a torrent of rain form a solid wall a few miles in front of me, even as I pedaled beneath bright sunlight. I crossed into the initial strike zone before I reached the far edge of the storm. Just a few short minutes of downpour had rendered the once-solid road into a chunky sludge the color and consistency of peanut butter. I could only pedal a few strokes into the goop before my rear wheel seized up like the mouth of a greedy kid who had taken too large a bite of a peanut butter and jelly sandwich.

I stumbled off the saddle and picked up the bike. As I attempted to stagger to the edge of the road, the mud caught my right shoe and tore it clean off my foot. Before I could catch myself, I pressed my sock directly into the mud. I could feel the cold sludge pushing between my nylon-covered toes. "Gaaaa!" I screamed, throwing my useless bicycle down on the road as I grabbed my shoe and inserted my peanut-butter-mud-coated foot back inside it. None of it mattered anymore. I was stuck in my tracks. In front of me, the storm stretched over the farthest horizon — many miles of frustration, maybe dozens.

The intelligent thing to do in a circumstance like that would be to sit by the side of the road and wait for the muddy road to dry. But while the storm was traveling slowly away from me, it only seemed to be growing outward in every direction. There was no escaping the rain and if I waited for it, I'd surely have to wait all day and night. The border-to-border record still beckoned. It hadn't become impossible yet. "Maybe," I whispered to myself. "Maybe the road gets better."

I picked up my bike and dragged it several feet off the road, where I could wheel it through the brush. I veered around junipers and stopped to scrape chunks of dark mud off my wheels and shoes fairly often, but walking along the obstacle-strewn shoulder was infinitely more passable than the road itself. One advantage of moving at so slow a pace was that, while I continued to wallow in the storm's remnants, I had yet to catch up to the storm. But the effort was fierce; my shoulder muscles burned and sweat beaded on my forehead.

After two miles of bicycle dragging that consumed more than an hour,

I arrived at the edge of the plateau. At the very least, I wanted to believe I had traveled two miles. My GPS was still turned off and my odometer only registered speeds above two miles per hour, a limit I had yet to surmount since the mud had set in. My eyes struggled to focus as I gazed over the red buttes and deep juniper-studded gorges in front of me. My head was still spinning and my heart raced under the strain of the brute effort — for two measly miles (if that), it had been one of the more physically difficult hours of my cycling career. During my 350-mile traverse of the Iditarod Trail in 2008, I had grappled with unrideable trail conditions, brutally slow forward movement, temperatures down to thirty-five below zero and a twenty-four-hour period wherein I didn't see another person. But in my memory, each of the hours in that six-day race held at least some glimmer of hope, some reason to keep putting one foot in front of the other. In the rain-drenched Gila desert, with more than 2,500 hard miles behind me, my body was left irrevocably exhausted and seemingly incapable of fighting this sticky mud. Worse than snow, worse than wind, worse than thirty-five below, the mud became as insurmountable as a brick wall. I flicked ochre sludge away from my gloves and rubbed my eyes. Over the vast wilderness hung a dark gray pall that filled the sky. It wasn't just a passing afternoon thunderstorm. It was a full-fledged deluge.

The descent into the gorge was rocky and technical, but the steep gravity allowed me to ride through the mud. I passed into the realm of the storm, where hard rain fell in full sheets. Every time I fooled myself into believing it was letting up, the noise of droplets hitting my helmet amplified until it sounded like a thousand hands smacking a metal roof. Rain stung my face and fingers and slowly seeped in through my meager nylon and plastic defenses. Streams of icy water trickled down my legs and back.

At the bottom of the gorge, the road immediately swung upward, climbing more than a thousand feet in three miles. Despite the rockier surface, mud clung to the frame and I struggled to push the bike up the slope. Every step left me panting and sweating, though I could no longer tell the difference between sweat and the rain.

More hours passed this way — climbs so sticky and steep I could barely walk up them, followed by descents so steep and slathered in wheel-grabbing mud that they were only navigable with intense focus and a Zen-like shutdown of natural fear. The torrent continued to fall with duration and volume I scarcely thought possible in the desert. The sheer amount of rain seemed to match the wettest storms I had encountered while riding through the rainforests of Juneau. It pushed me deep into the hopelessness those gray rides often instill — a certainty that it will never stop raining, ever, throughout the span of the rest of eternity.

As I trudged up another thousand-foot climb, the thick aroma of the forest air started to permeate my consciousness. It was a singularly unique fragrance — a savory and spicy blend of cedar and sage with hints of charcoal and wood smoke — remnants of long-snuffed forest fires, perhaps. Infused with the fresh sweetness of the rain and the pungent oils of pinion nuts, the scent swirled around my nose with overwhelming intensity. As soon as I noticed it, I became wholly immersed in its charred, sugary, juniper-imbibed perfume, until I started to feel physically ill. I knew I would never forget that smell, and that it would always haunt me in sickness and pain, the way I always recalled a vanilla air freshener that once hung in my parents' car whenever I came down with motion sickness. Just as that artificial vanilla had become, the smell of the Gila was permeated in repulsiveness so vile that it evoked a hundred memories of suffering. The smell of the Gila was a hate smell. For as beautiful and wild as the landscape was, I hated the Gila.

The road atop an 8,000-foot plateau amid the Gila Wilderness was still too muddy to ride. I trudged a few steps along the relatively level ground before I dropped to my knees in a sink of frustration. Tears spilled over and I rubbed my face aggressively with cold-numbed fingers. "It's impossible," I moaned. "It's just impossible." My shoulders and abdomen were starting to convulse with the deepening chill. The drain of hopelessness tempted me to just sit there, forever, until hypothermia brought a slow but pleasant end. But my ambition and my will to live were stronger, and I lashed out.

In the throes of a temper tantrum, I started to smack the wet skin on my face. "Get up!" I screamed. "Get up!" I slapped at my cheeks until my fingers balled up into a fist. Without any rational reason or decision to do so, I swung hard and punched myself right between the eyes. The sudden blow startled me so much that I stopped sobbing immediately. My forehead throbbed, and when I held my quaking fingers up to the skin, it felt bruised and tender. "Did you really just punch yourself?" I said out loud. It sounded almost as crazy as it felt.

I stood up again, knocked cold back into reality, where the road was still muddy and impassable, but I was alone and without other options. Breathing the relief that is involuntary resignation, I moved to the side of the road and started bushwhacking through the shoulder. I walked another half mile or so until gravel strewn over the road seemed more likely to add traction. I climbed back onto the saddle. The tires managed to continue rolling on top of the mud, but I found little joy in my ability to ride. The shivering throughout my body had become so pronounced that I had a difficult time rotating my feet on the pedals. My nose and lips were going numb; my fingers and toes were long gone. Even if I kept moving, I had no guarantees that hypothermia wouldn't wrap its icy fingers around me before I could gather enough energy to work up heat.

I thought back to my coldest rides in Juneau, January days when sleet fell and the temperature was thirty-three degrees. All of those wet winter rides had felt similar, perhaps even more comfortable than this summer day on the Great Divide. The difference, really, was that during Juneau winters I was generally equipped with significantly warmer gear than what I carried for a summer race through the Rocky Mountains. Also, in Juneau, I at least had a home where I could retreat. In New Mexico, wearing everything I had with me, I felt deeply chilled. My only option for shelter was a down sleeping bag and a water-resistant — not water-proof — bivy sack. The sink of frustration closed in again.

"It's July fucking fifth!" I raged. "I'm in Southern fucking New Mexico! I should have heatstroke, dehydration; I should be licking the edges of sun-blackened milk jugs dropped by illegal immigrants! Anything but hypothermia. Please, anything."

But, as it never had and never would, the Gila did not care. The road seemed to stretch endlessly over the plateau. Since both my GPS and odometer hadn't been working all day, I wasn't completely sure where I was or how much farther I had to travel. I only knew I had to battle my way through this mud-road purgatory until it released me onto pavement — sweet, hard pavement.

Above the gorge, the sandy shelf of the plateau provided an even faster surface, on a rutted track rippled with whoop-de-dos. Still, I couldn't shake how cold and broken I felt, and I continued to cry intermittently as my spirit lashed out against the increasing waves of hopelessness. The rain never left up, not even for a minute, in the eight hours it took me to travel forty-five miles. I was so tired I could feel my heart sputtering.

When I reached the intersection of State Highway 35, I felt like Moses had stepped out and parted the Red Sea. While rain continued to drizzle, I could see hints of sunlight cracking through the clouds over the valley. Streaks of gold lit up groves of deciduous trees, a Garden of Eden in the mud-soaked desert. Despite my limited energy, I sprinted down the pavement in an expression of my relief and joy. I passed a ranger station and stopped at a water faucet to wash the prodigious mud from my body and bicycle. I felt like a Christian reborn. I had been delivered from the Gila! I had walked through the shadow of death and emerged in the light! I was done! It was all fun and pavement to Silver City!

But I was wrong. In not having my GPS to indicate the route farther ahead, I had to turn over my map to learn that the Great Divide Mountain Bike Route didn't follow the highway into Silver City, but in fact crested another thousand-foot pass on the clay surface of the Georgetown Road. The rain had finally faded, taken over by rainbows and the soft pink light of sunset. But an entire afternoon of precipitation isn't going to dry up all that quickly.

And sure enough, fresh, shin-deep truck tracks greeted me at the entrance. Even if I walked inside the tracks, peanut butter mud clumped on my shoes until they adhered to the ground, tugging away from my feet as I walked. The idea of riding my bicycle was a joke, a distant dream; it was never going to happen on the Georgetown Road. I glanced at my maps. The mud road was five miles long. The longest five miles in the history of distance.

Darkness fell as I walked. Another hour passed. Resignation and hopelessness won the final battle in this drawn-out war of emotions. There was no longer reason to cry. A few stars came out, but for the most part, the unseen clouds remained. There was no longer reason to think or feel. All of my extremities were either numb or plodding through a detached sort of auto-pilot. Except for the occasional manifestation of quivering lips or shivers through my core, even my hypothermia had reached equilibrium. I was a dead woman walking.

When I finally reached the pavement of Highway 152, I felt none of the joy I had expected. In my numbness and resignation, even this positive development failed to inject renewed hope. The surrounding landscape was empty and black. There were flickers of lights from a distant city, most likely Silver City, though they looked so lonely and far away that for all I knew, they could have been Las Vegas or Tokyo. I mounted my bike on the highway. The wheels started to move before I even began pedaling, propelled only by simple gravity. I shook my head in astonishment.

"What an amazing invention, a bicycle," I thought. "It can move on its own without any help from me." I pedaled toward the lights, and then they dropped out of sight.

Later, John would ask me what I thought of the "infuriating hills before

Silver City." Apparently, as John told me, there are actually a lot of steep climbs after the initial drop from the Georgetown Road, as the highway crosses a series of drainages that surround the city. I remember none of these climbs or descents. I only remember lights and pavement, and the numbed sensibilities that made me aware of everything and nothing at the same time.

And then, eventually, I arrived at the Silver City twenty-four-hour Wal-mart. I don't remember walking inside. The first minutes of shopping have also been lost to the haze of inattention. When I "came to," I was standing in the produce section beneath the glaring florescent lights of the store. After a day in the gray, wet, unpopulated wilds of the Gila, the sudden barrage of colors and objects was overwhelming. I blinked rapidly amid genuine and utter confusion.

"Where am I? What am I doing in Wal-mart? What year is this? Am I still living in Idaho Falls?" I wracked my brain for any events that took place after 2004, when I was a copy editor at the Idaho Falls Post Register and did all of my shopping at Wal-mart because that was the only place open after I left work. Like a trickle of rain, details started to come back. It was 2009. I was in Silver City, New Mexico. I was riding the Great Divide. And I was nearly done.

I looked in the basket I was holding. I laughed out loud at the food my autopilot had grabbed while I was lost in a daze. The basket held a twenty-four-ounce package of imitation crab flakes, a cup of strawberry parfait, a Snickers bar, a liter of Pepsi and, inexplicably, a glass bottle of sparkling apple cider. I abandoned the cider on a nearby shelf and grabbed a box of crackers, a pound of strawberries, as well as a few packages of cookies, cheese and Sour Patch Kids for the following day. The pound and a half of fish flakes seemed excessive, but I had been craving protein for most of New Mexico, so I decided to keep the package and see if I how much of it I could force down, with crackers, strawberries, and parfait for my late dinner.

It was 11:30 p.m. when I left the store, five hours after the 6:30 p.m. arrival time I had made my goal when I left the Beaverhead Work Station amid a sunny Sunday morning that seemed a lifetime before. My eyes hung so heavily that I could barely keep them open crossing the parking lot, and my chilled body, brought partially back to life inside the store, ached throughout. My knees burned and my Achilles tendons screamed. Even if I wanted the Great Divide border-to-border record more badly than anything I had wanted in my life, I still had only nine and a half hours to travel 125 miles if I wanted to shave even a minute off Stevenson's 2005 time. In my physical and psychological state of decay, I was doubtful of my ability to pedal even one more mile to the nearest hotel. I was glad the goal had become all but impossible. Even the prospect of pedaling 125 miles after a good night's rest filled me with a dread I was all too willing to embrace. Still, I'd be lying if I didn't admit I felt an urge to keep pedaling as I rolled up to the Silver City Super 8. My body and mind were all but broken, but the guilt of a racer burns deep.

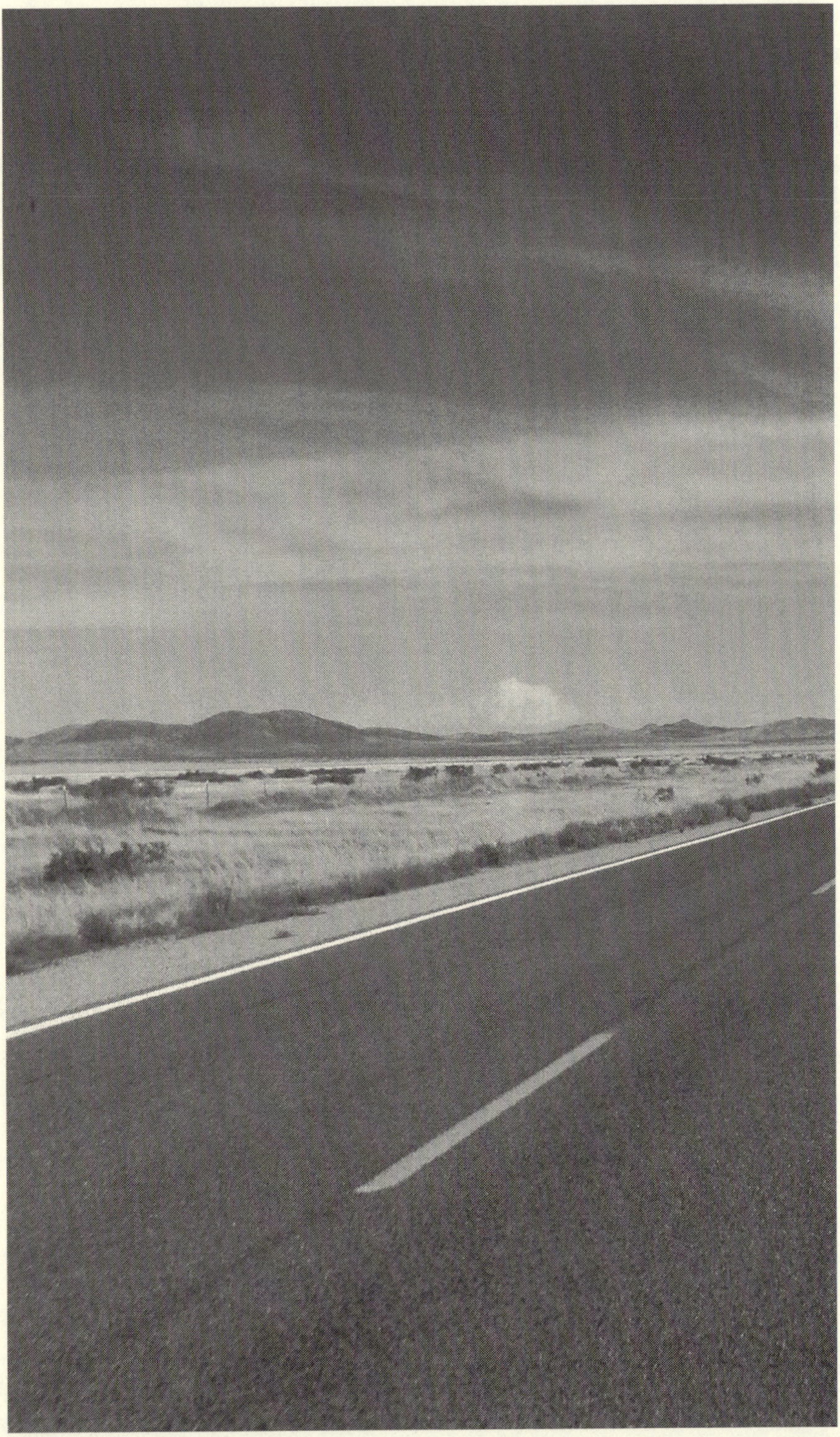

Chapter Twenty Four
The Lonely Highway

Page 322 and 323: "The Lonely Highway" to Mexico.
Page 324: Jill Homer poses at the international border of the U.S. and Mexico in Antelope Wells, New Mexico, after completing the Tour Divide in 24 days, 7 hours and 24 minutes.

A sliver of morning light penetrated the thick brown curtains over the window. They were the same thick brown curtains that blinded the large windows of every room in every small-town motel in America. I opened my eyes to a print of an oil painting, an image of a cowboy riding solo through an open prairie — tranquil, unmemorable, and pressed against glass, just like every piece of art in every room in every small-town motel in America. I threw open the generic beige bedspread and rolled out of the stiff, pressed sheets to greet a morning that was like every morning in my new way of life.

    I hobbled stiffly to the hotel sink, brushed my teeth, applied sunscreen on my wind-chapped face, and peeled off my dry outfit so I could apply the wet clothing I had washed in the shower the night before. I put on my spare pair of clean, dry socks and mud-caked shoes, and limped into the hotel lobby. I filled up a paper plate with stale muffins, bland pastries, and unripe oranges, then limped back to my room and flipped on the Weather Channel. The numbers flashed vaguely along the bottom of the screen. The simple glut of information was difficult to comprehend with my reduced mental capacity. But one report registered: Silver City, high of ninety-four degrees.

"Hot in Silver City today," I said out loud. I munched on the free motel breakfast that was like every free breakfast in every small-town motel in America. The routine had become so entrenched that it took several more minutes for the true uniqueness of my situation to sink in. "Wait a minute. I'm in Silver City right now. I'm 125 miles from the border. Today could be my last day!"

I jolted upright with renewed sense of purpose, threw my stale muffin on the bed, and concentrated harder on the television. The weatherman called for southeast winds — unfortunately a crosswind in the direction I was heading — blowing steady at fifteen miles per hour. "Could be worse," I said. "Ninety-four with a crosswind. Could be worse."

It could be a lot worse. I still had forty miles of sandy clay road to ride, something rain could turn into the same horrifying wheel trap I had slopped through the day before. In fact, humbled as I was in my fear of more rain and storms, the news of heat and wind could not have been more welcome.

I packed up my gear, methodically stuffing my dry clothing back into my seatpost bag. I gathered the rest of my sparse belongings, the toothpaste tube and drug case, and placed them in the exact spot where they had ridden beside me for twenty-four days. I cinched up the straps and closed the zippers. I couldn't believe this might be the last time I'd ever do this during the Tour Divide.

Outside the motel, I found a garden hose and attempted to remove the red clay that had hardened to my bike like cement. I scraped away the brick-hard blocks from the drivetrain, revealing a number of small stones that had become lodged inside the rear derailleur, grinding away at delicate parts and the chain for who knows how long. As I ran the hose around the paper-thin tires, streams of mud revealed webbed cracks in the rubber, threatening to shatter at any moment. A large chunk of foam hung off the saddle. My bike was literally falling apart.

I stood up, turned off the hose, and rubbed my stiff knees and throbbing Achilles tendons. "Just 125 more miles," I said. "Please just hold it together for 125 more miles." I was speaking to my body as much as I was to my bicycle.

On the way out of town, I stopped and bought yet another pair of sunglasses and a large jug of Gatorade. At 7:30 in the morning, the pavement already reflected a barrage of heat. The air was not only warm, but also humid with leftover moisture from the previous day's storm. A stiff crosswind licked at my side.

I followed a ripple of a highway through arroyos and over tiny, dry streams. After my rain-soaked crossing of the Gila, the desert had returned full circle, a desolate panorama of bleached sand, yucca, and cactus.

I turned off the highway onto a sandy washboard called the Separ Road. The sky blazed with a deep and lasting blue, broken only by tiny wisps of white clouds and barren mounds of mountains many dozens of miles distant. The road followed a narrow ridgeline over a sweeping plateau, piled with sand dunes. The mostly flat horizon blurred behind a sparkling heat mirage. Only a twisted barbed-wire fence broke the illusion of perfect inhabitability.

Everyone who had raced the Great Divide before told me that the section between Silver City and the border was the absolute worst 125 miles of the entire route. "It's flat and desert and it's mostly pavement," they told me. "It's hot and the wind is always in your face. And you just want to be done, and it feels never-ending. You just have to put your head down and suffer through it. It's a brutal grind."

Nearly everything I had been warned about was turning out to be true. The flat, hot desert stretched out in front of me and the crosswind grew stronger with the fading morning. But I had no interest in putting my head down and suffering through it. Like the weather, my body had made a one-hundred-and-eighty-degree recovery during the night. Despite my sore knees and heels, I felt like an entirely different person. Rather than feel sore and helpless and plodding, I felt sweeping gratitude for the opportunity to ride my bike in this otherworldly place. By pedal power alone, I'd propelled myself into a stark, colorful desert that so few ever bothered to visit. I had the whole unscheduled day to travel through it, absorbing every delicate color and shape, from silver cactus needles to smooth, red stones. Every scenic vista and mile marker was a simple but finite source of joy, and I consumed them with the exaggerated relish of a child trying to savor a quickly melting ice cream cone. I was struck with understanding that the things I would see and experience that day would be my last on the Tour Divide. For all of the difficulties, the struggle, the pain and grief and occasional hopelessness, my life on the Tour Divide was a very good life. It was a full life, and every pedal stroke I made was a small decision to leave it behind.

I arrived at the intersection of Interstate 10 in an incredible mood, and stopped at what I knew would be my last convenience store on the Divide, a trinket shop simply called "Continental Divide." I purchased a plastic-wrapped sandwich and an ice-cream bar almost out of habit, and sat outside in the direct sunlight, smiling at the gray-faced truckers and frazzled families that shuffled inside. It was a truly hot day; sweat cascaded down my face even as I sat still, sipping a large jug of Cherry Coke. I was seventy miles from the finish and in no more of a hurry than I would have been seventy miles from the start. It was simply too beautiful of a day, and too rich and full of life, to just rush through it.

Beyond the convenience store, the route paralleled the freeway on a rough frontage road, where I approached what would be the final turn of the entire trip, onto a two-lane highway that didn't go anywhere, really, except Mexico. A half-mile distant, I could see the sun-reflecting glow of a vehicle parked at the intersection. As I drew closer, I could see the waving arms of two silhouetted figures. In the relentless glare of the sun, I didn't even realize the figures were my parents until I pulled up beside them and felt my mother's arms clasp my sweat-drenched back.

"You made it!" my mom cried. I looked up and saw flecks of tears in my dad's eyes, which brought a rush of tears to my own eyes.

"You made it, too," I said. "I'm so glad you're here. I thought I wouldn't see you guys until the border."

"We wanted to see you before the finish," my dad said. "We had to call up your sisters to track your SPOT. They told us you were nearly here, and we had to rush from our hotel. You're really flying today!"

"I'm having a good day," I said.

"I just can't believe you made it," my mom blubbered, tears still streaming down her cheeks.

"I'm not there yet," I said. "I still have sixty-five more miles to ride."

"You feeling up to it?" my dad asked.

"I feel good," I said. "But lots can happen in sixty-five miles. At this point, though, I have to get there. If I have to walk the entire rest of the way, I'll get there. If I don't make it to the border, please just run me over with the car."

"So how long do you think it will take?" my dad asked.

I looked at my watch. "Um, maybe six hours. Six or seven o'clock. This crosswind has been slowing me down all day, but at least it's helping keep me cool."

"We'll see you at the border," my dad said. "It's going to be one of the proudest moments of my life."

I smiled. "Me too."

I pulled away from my parents and turned onto the long, unbending arm of pavement dubbed "The Lonely Highway." I knew that, barring a car accident or a catastrophic bike breakdown, my struggle was over. There was no more mud, no more mountains or streams. There wasn't even a gravel road in front of me. I had won the fight. I only had to complete my victory lap, the necessary run around the bases after hitting a home run. I closed my eyes amid the sheer satisfaction of it all, the end. And as can often happen at the threshold of an inevitable end, my entire bike life flashed before my eyes.

I was a seven-year-old with pigtails and Keds shoes, coasting on my banana seat Huffy down East Ridge Road, squealing wildly and holding my feet in the air as the fixed pedals spun in powerful egg-beater circles.

I was a sixteen-year-old in baggy jeans and a Smashing Pumpkins T-shirt, riding with my friends to the mall, that time my friend Casey was hit by a car and talked the driver into giving him two-hundred dollars to keep him from reporting the accident to the cops.

I was a nineteen-year-old borrowing a friend's bike to pedal home late at night, feeling the rush of wind through my hair as the dark world stood still.

I was a twenty-two-year-old in a brand new jersey and bike shorts, standing next to the gaping hole of an old uranium mine outside Moab, Utah, preparing to mount my heavily loaded touring bike for a 600-mile ride across deserts and mountains.

I was a twenty-three-year-old struggling through the tight singletrack along the Yukon River out of Whitehorse, Yukon, living out a dream of riding my mountain bike in the Far North.

It was my twenty-fourth birthday and I was pedaling my loaded touring bike beneath a brutally hot sun toward Park City, Utah, on the first day of a 3,200-mile tour.

It was several weeks later and Geoff was trying to talk me down from a panic as a troupe of several dozen Labrador retrievers blocked the narrow rural road in front of us.

It was October in New York and Geoff and I were pedaling through a snowstorm, gleefully grinding out the last ten miles of our cross-country tour.

I was a twenty-five-year-old, pedaling frantically on a stationary bike in a dark room as neon strobe lights swirled overhead and my spin class instructor barked orders through a microphone.

I was twenty-six and venturing out for the first time after Geoff and I moved to Homer, Alaska, riding along a thin spit of sand that rolled like a tongue into Kachemak Bay.

It was February, dark and raining, and I was pushing my mountain bike through a chilling soup of slush in the Susitna 100.

It was summer and I was cresting the lupine-dotted alpine at the top of Resurrection Pass on the Kenai Peninsula.

It was fall and I was plying my skinny tires through an endless series of deep puddles during one of my first rainy road bike rides after moving to Juneau.

It was spring and I threw my bike down in frustration after attempting to ride with a painfully swollen knee, believing I might never be able to ride a bicycle again.

It was winter and I was pedaling a soft snowmobile trail over a frozen Puntilla Lake, facing at close range for the first time the beautiful and haunting peaks of the Alaska Range, wondering if I had ever before or would thereafter, in all my life, feel so struck by overwhelming awe.

I opened my eyes. A brown mound of a mountain rose out of the desert directly in front of me, much farther away than it seemed. I sighed happily. A vibrant parade of memories filled the empty landscape, reminding me that for everything I had lost, and for everything I had left behind, my past was something that could never be taken away from me. It had happened, it had existed, and it had made me who I was — the kind of person who could ride my bicycle across more than 2,700 miles of rough and rugged terrain in twenty-four days. It was a beautiful past, sparked by adventure and surrounded by the most spectacular colors. My imagination infused it with richness, and it nourished my soul from beyond the arbitrary barriers of time and space.

My mind drifted to the past that Geoff and I shared. It was the better part of a decade — most of my twenties, the best years of my life, and my youth. I had resented him for throwing it all away on a whim, on a notion, on a lark, for a twenty-one-year-old girl. Or, I remembered from our conversation the night we broke up — perhaps it wasn't even her fault. Perhaps she didn't matter. I was never going to be the kind of companion Geoff seemed to desire. What kind of companion that even was, I could only guess. I imagined a spontaneous romantic willing to follow him to the edges of the wilderness. I imagined an untamed stallion galloping into exciting adventures. I could almost see her long, dark hair whipping in the breeze on the edge of a sand cliff high above the sea.

But when she turned to face me, I realized I was looking at an idyllic version of myself. She representing the companion that I longed to be — adventurous, spontaneous, and beautiful. Maybe none of those dreams ever manifested, or maybe they simply didn't work in the practical application of real life. Maybe Geoff's and my entire history had been a failing effort to mash bloated ideals into the unfitting realities of our lives.

As the memories continued to swirl through the desert, I couldn't connect the lines where our beautiful past dropped into this sun-hardened present. Despite our failed efforts to provide each other with happiness, I couldn't accept the notion that we never shared love. But, then again, Geoff had never seemed the type to release the people he loved to the wind. He had always been such a rock. He had been my rock. It was still so difficult to understand.

And yet, at one point, he was there. He had been with me in similar moments of perspective-altering discovery, plying the lonely desert on a bicycle, in that distant past now irretrievably disconnected from this sand basin where I had landed. But our past still lingered in my memories. It had shaped my life, and no one, not even Geoff, could take that away.

A border patrol vehicle passed. The driver turned his head and regarded me with a stony face, his sunglass-shaded eyes betraying no hint of suspicion. But I felt exposed. This was a no-man's land, a true road to nowhere. I suddenly became uncomfortably self-aware.

I turned on my iPod and switched the settings to random shuffle; a selection of 1,387 songs promised to divert my mind from descending too far into the movie reel of my past. Soon Elliot Smith was singing about finding "a beautiful place to get lost." The highway stretched straight and true over the curvature of the Earth. Ever so often, a black cow would look up from a windmill a half-mile from the road, or a roadrunner would leap along the pavement. The wind continued to rustle the spiny brush, but the landscape was otherwise devoid of life.

I had spent so much of my summer fretting and panicking about being alone. Fear of solitude had cast such a thick cloud over my preparation for the Tour Divide that I had entirely forgotten that fear and solitude were precisely what I was seeking in this journey. I needed fear to quiet my ego, focus my mind, and expose my true strengths. I needed solitude to reflect on how those strengths shaped my identity. The object had always been to unearth pieces of myself, new pieces of understanding and strength that I never realized were even out there for discovery. And yet I had let loathing and loneliness nearly blind me to my own presence in the existing moment, until the old and broken pieces threatened to bury me completely. Breaking up with Geoff had been a shuddering jolt to my life's narrative, but it certainly wasn't the end of the story. I felt grateful for the opportunity to open a new chapter after such a dramatic transition — the bottom of 2,740 miles of discovery and introspection.

Still, for all of the solitude I both struggled against and sought, the Divide had provided me with surprising and sometimes heart-rending human companionship. The strangers who were kind to me still filled my heart with gratitude. I reflected on my time with the people in Pie Town, the lodge owner in Platoro, Patti and Gary Blakley, the bike mechanics in Steamboat Springs, and of course Kirsten and Marjane. Their kindness reflected the far-reaching love that all people share, ultimately, and these threads of connection ensure that no one is truly alone.

As a Donna the Buffalo song cycled through my iPod, I wondered what John was doing at that moment. It was hard to believe it had been two weeks since I had seen him last. It was a Monday, so he was probably at work, clicking the refresh button on the Tour Divide tracker displayed on his computer screen. He was probably smiling with the satisfaction of a successful coach, knowing he had played a crucial role in my success. But how crucial was his role? John wasn't with me during the hard times, the rain and mud and chest-convulsing cold. John had been a good companion and a good friend, but ultimately what both he and Geoff taught me was that I only had myself to rely on in the end. I had to truly trust myself when the going got tough. And when the going did get tough, I dug deep inside myself and I persevered. I had been brave on my own. I had been strong on my own.

These warm feelings jolted quickly away as iPod shuffled to a song I had come to associate with that rainy day on Indiana Pass, the day I encountered Pete in the ambulance: "What Sarah Said," by Death Cab for Cutie. The intensity of the emotions I experienced that day continued to haunt me even though the source of those emotions — the conviction that Pete was badly hurt and might die — proved to be untrue. Even in my happy state on The Lonely Highway, tears filled my eyes as the lyrics began: "It came to me then that every plan is a tiny prayer to Father Time."

Indeed, every pedal stroke I made was one of these tiny prayers, a reminder that my only real investment in my future was the steps I took toward it — everything else was just a dream, a plan, or a fear. When I was honest with myself, I had to acknowledge that the lingering grief I felt for Pete's accident was largely built on grief that I felt for the parts of myself I had lost, and that my fear for Pete's future reflected my apprehension that I would never recover my own sense of self. But from the tentative steps I took to board the ferry in Juneau to the excruciatingly heavy steps that carried me into Silver City, I had proved to myself just how powerful unwavering forward motion can be. With every pedal stroke south, I wasn't delaying the life "I needed to get on with" — I was getting on with my life. And in finishing the Tour Divide, I had given myself the most wonderful gift: a preview of the brave and strong person waiting to emerge from my shattered identity.

My leg muscles started to leak lactic acid and I responded by pushing harder. Even with the heat and the strong wind plowing into my face as much as my side, I was keeping my pace steady at fourteen to fifteen miles per hour, an almost unbelievable speed in my state of physical fatigue. The fatigue dulled my intelligence, and my emotions were still those of a child, raw and intense. But now they were tinged with hints of understanding, like a child on the verge of adolescence. Through my earphones, Bright Eyes sang, "Now I am riding ... all over this island ... looking for something ... to open my eyes."

Mile markers ticked down what seemed like ridiculously small numbers. There were thirty-three miles to go. And then, in what seemed like a swift moment later, just twenty-five. My legs ached; my Achilles tendons and knees burned. But I had moved beyond pain, to a place where anticipation trumped almost every other emotion. There were twenty-one miles to go. And then eighteen. I turned up my music louder, letting the miles disappear in my own private chamber of sound.

After mile marker twelve, a car pulled up beside me. I looked over to see my mom rolling down the passenger side window. I pulled one of my earphones out of my ear.

"We thought we might have missed you!" my mom called out. "We were driving down the road, and we weren't passing you, and weren't passing you, and your dad started to drive faster. We thought you might make it to the border before us."

"I feel great!" I yelled back. "Just eleven more miles!"

"You are really cooking!" my dad yelled from the driver's seat. "We'll see you soon!"

"Yeah," I yelled. "Just forty-five more minutes!"

After mile marker 4, the road climbed a miniscule mound of a hill and dropped back into the valley. In the near distance, a tight cluster of trees came into view. From my vantage point, it looked like a tiny island oasis in an ocean of rocks and sand.

"Holy cow, that's Antelope Wells," I thought. "I'm really going to do this thing. I really am." My heart vibrated with a shock of emotions as electric and alive as any of the happiest moments in my life. "I never thought I could ride the Great Divide; I never even believed I could. Really no one believed I could, and I did it. I did it anyway."

As I passed mile marker 1, I purposely hit the "next" button on my iPod to forever cement a finishing song, chosen by serendipity. The song that serendipity picked threw my rhythm off for a second, because it was song I neither knew I downloaded on my iPod nor even owned; in fact, I was only vaguely aware I had ever heard it before. But as the quiet melody filled my ears, the simple lyrics touched my soul. And through the electric echoes of truth, Cat Stevens sang, "Morning has broken, like the first sunlight. Blackbird has spoken, like the first song."

I craned my neck to watch the stark blue sky, strung with ribbons of wispy clouds. The mountains stood in the distance, stoic and unmoving. A grin erupted across my face as the dry wind rushed between my teeth. "Mine is the sunlight, mine is the morning; Born of the one light, Eden saw play; Praise with elation, praise every morning; God's recreation of the new day."

When I looked down again, I could see the arms of my parents, waving wildly like shipwrecked sailors who had just spotted a yacht. They stood in front of a closed gate, blocking the entrance to a border station no larger than a roadside coffee stand. A couple of sun-bleached houses and half-dozen haggard trees were all that distinguished Antelope Wells from the seemingly endless expanse of desert. It was everything I had pursued for twenty-four days — twenty-four days filled with enough joy and discovery and anguish to fill a short lifetime. I raised my left arm in a victorious fist, touched my wheel to the closed border gate, and stepped off my bike for the last time.

My mom rushed up to me and wrapped her arms around me. My dad had a smile as wide as mine. "Just as I thought," he said. "One of the proudest days of my life."

"Oops," I said, "I have to check my time. I looked at my watch. It was 5:24 p.m. "I think that's twenty-four days and um, seven hours. And twenty-four minutes."

"My mom wiped tears from her cheeks. "So is that good?"

"Well, it's the women's record from Banff, by kind of a lot," I said. "I only missed the border-to-border record by about eight hours."

"I can't believe you rode this entire way," my dad said.

"I can't believe I rode the entire Great Divide and the weather never got hot!" I said.

My dad raised his eyebrows. "Actually, the car thermometer said it was 98 degrees when we stopped here. I'd say that's pretty hot."

"Wow," I said. "Really? 98 degrees?" I shook my head in disbelief. "I guess the crosswind helps more than I knew."

My dad turned and opened the trunk. "So what do you want?" he asked as he popped open a cooler. "We brought pineapple and yogurt and cookies and Diet Pepsi."

"Ooo!" I said. "Diet Pepsi. And pineapple."

"Anything you want to do while you're here?"

"I was really hoping to cross the border and get my passport stamped," I said. "But it looks like the border station is closed."

"I think it's only open from eight to four," my mom said. "That's what the sign says. It was closed when we got here."

"Shoot," I said. "I wished I'd known that. I would have gotten up earlier." Which was a lie. As it was, I had ridden the entire 125-mile stretch in less than ten hours, a pace much faster than I'd expected to keep. Ten hours rivaled the time all of the race leaders took to travel that stretch of highway — something my dad had researched so he could guess my arrival time. Since it took the race leaders ten hours to ride from Silver City, my dad later told me, they figured it would take me about fourteen.

"This doesn't look like the kind of place where they'd really mind if you just hopped the gate," my dad said.

"Maybe," I said. "But I'm also guessing they have guns. I feel okay just calling this gate the end. It looks like the end. There's a big stop sign."

"How does it feel to stop?" my dad asked.

"I don't know," I said. "It hasn't begun to sink in. Right now it feels good, and tired, and a little bit anticlimactic."

"I'm sure a few months from now you'll look back on this and be really proud of what you did," my dad said.

"Probably," I said. "Definitely."

"Here, I'm just going to take a few pictures," my dad said, motioning at me to go stand by my bike.

I glanced across the gate to the open expanse of land beyond. "Wow," I said. "I can't believe that's Mexico. It actually is."

I continued glancing south as we removed the bike bags, wheels and seat post, and stuffed the mud-caked, battered bicycle in the trunk of my parents' car. I felt a small sting of guilt as I ducked into the back seat, where my legs instantly cramped up and the desert heat suddenly hit me like a furnace blast. It felt strange to not ride, and to have nowhere left to ride. As there usually is with the accomplishment of any big goal, I felt a little emptiness at no longer having anything to work toward. As memories slipped away to the stark realities of the present, I could only ask myself the inevitable question — how far have I really come? Much more time and distance would have to pass before I could even begin to understand the answer. I closed the car door and took one last, longing look south.

There on the blank slate of desert, where the shadows of barren mountains blackened the sand, I exposed the pieces of myself that would never change — the pieces that drove toward adventure, that ached for truth, that had a limitless capacity to love. I held them open to the sun and wind, for the first time wholly confident that I could strip my body to the barest grains of life, and still these pieces would never leave me, never drift away. Scorched earth shimmered in the low afternoon sunlight, and the wide spine of the continent stretched over the horizon. It just kept going.

2009 Tour Divide

Banff, Alberta, to Antelope Wells, New Mexico
June 12, 2009

42 Starters | 16 finishers | 21 scratched | 5 relegated

Finishing times in days, hours and minutes

1. Matthew Lee, 17:23:45
2. Kurt Refsnider, 18:11:13 (top rookie)
3. Tracey and Jay Petervary, tandem, 18:13:50
4. Chris Plesko, 19:00:21 (single speed course record)
5. Leighton White, 21:05:15
   Blaine Nestor, 21:05:15
7. Steve Wilkinson, 21:10:34
   Joe Meiser, 21:10:34
9. Eric Bruntjen, 21:12:00
10. Alan Goldsmith, 21:12:59
    John Fettis, 21:12:59
    Cannon Shockley, 21:12:59
13. Jill Homer, 24:07:24 (female course record)
14. Trevor Browne, 27:05:42
    Paul Howard, 27:05:42
16. Michael Komp, 31:22:35

Relegated

Dario Valsesia (course deviation), 22:00:30
Jamie Thomson (support violation) 25:06:28
Deanna Adams (course deviation) 31:07:30
Brad Mattingly (course deviation) 31:07:30
Bruce Giroux (course deviation) 36:06:30

Tour Divide Gear Checklist

Frame: 2008 Surly Karate Monkey
Fork: Rockshox Reba Race
Hubs: Shimano XT
Derailleurs: Shimano XT
Crank: Shimano XT
Cassette: Shimano XT 9-speed
Chainrings: Shimano Deore XT
Shifters: Shimano LX
Brakes: Avid BB7
Seatpost: Thomson Elite
Stem and handlebars: Easton
Headset: Cane Creek
Saddle: Terry Butterfly Cromo Gel
Pedals: Bontrager platforms
Wheels: Mavic A 317 Disc
Tires: 29" WTB Nano Raptor
Tubes: 29" Slime Tubes
Grips: Ergon GE1 Enduro
Headlight: Princeton Tec Corona
GPS: Garmin eTrex Vista HCX
Odometer: Cateye Micro Wireless

Backpack: Wingnut Enduro
Water containers: 3-liter Camelback bladder, 6-liter MSR bladder and one 20-ounce bottle.
Also inside pack: Sierra Designs rain jacket and waterproof pants, Katadyn Hiker water filter, toiletries, bear spray, bug spray, sunscreen, Olympus Stylus Tough camera, iPod shuffle, cell phone, Adventure Cycling Association Great Divide Mountain Bike Route maps.

Bike bags: Custom-designed frame bag, seat-post bag and gas tank made by Revelate Designs, **www.revelatedesigns.com**.
Sleeping Bag: Mountain Hardware Phantom rated to 32 degrees
Bivy sack: Black Diamond Winter Bivy
Sleeping pad: Thermarest Pro Lite
Clothing (in seat post bag): Two short-sleeve bicycle jerseys, one pair Fox mountain biking shorts and one pair Nashbar cycling shorts, Pearl Izumi arm and leg warmers, long-sleeve micro fleece pullover, Mountain Hardware beanie hat, ear warmers, two pairs cycling socks, two pairs wool socks, RBH Designs vapor barrier socks, Outdoor Research fleece gloves, Pearl Izumi cycling gloves.

Also in frame bag: Eight AA lithium batteries, two spare 29" tubes, fix kit, bike tool, bike pump, first aid kit, pills, electrolyte tablets, battery chargers, spare headlamp, zip ties, 16-ounce jar of peanut butter as emergency food.

Typical food stash (in gas tank and frame bag): One 5-ounce bag Sour Patch Kids, one 5-ounce bag gummy worms, two king-sized Snickers Bars, two Pearson's Salted Nut Rolls, two 2-ounce bags of almonds, five 1-ounce string cheese sticks or cheese wheels, one 5-ounce bag of Corn Nuts or crackers, two 4-ounce packages of Grandma's Cookies.

Jill Homer runs down a snow-covered slope in the Chugach Mountains near Anchorage, Alaska.
Photo by Dan Bailey, http://danbaileyphoto.com

Jill Homer grew up in Sandy, Utah, and graduated from the University of Utah with a degree in journalism in 2000. She began her career working for weekly and daily newspapers in Utah and Idaho. In 2005, she moved to Homer, Alaska, to pursue adventure in the Last Frontier. She never viewed herself as an athlete, but she was searching for a unique kind of outlet that provided both physical and psychological challenges. Endurance cycling fit that description. Two years of (mainly mis)adventures landed her in one of the most difficult endurance races in North America, a 350-mile winter traverse of Alaska wilderness called the Iditarod Trail Invitational. The unforgettable experience was the genesis of her first book, *Ghost Trails: Journeys Through a Lifetime*. Her second book, *Be Brave, Be Strong: A Journey Across the Great Divide* is a continuation of her ongoing adventures. She currently works as a freelance writer and editor in Los Altos, California.

Printed in Great Britain
by Amazon.co.uk, Ltd.,
Marston Gate.